Tend Your Garden

Frameworks for Writing
Series Editor: Martha C. Pennington, Georgia Southern University

The *Frameworks for Writing* series offers books focused on writing and the teaching and learning of writing in educational and real-life contexts. The hallmark of the series is the application of approaches and techniques to writing and the teaching of writing that go beyond those of English literature to draw on and integrate writing with other disciplines, areas of knowledge, and contexts of everyday life. The series entertains proposals for textbooks as well as books for teachers, teacher educators, parents, and the general public. The list includes teacher reference books and student textbooks focused on innovative pedagogy aiming to prepare teachers and students for the challenges of the 21st century.

Published

The College Writing Toolkit: Tried and Tested Ideas for Teaching College Writing
Edited by Martha C. Pennington and Pauline Burton

The "Backwards" Research Guide for Writers: Using Your Life for Reflection, Connection, and Inspiration
Sonya Huber

Exploring College Writing: Reading, Writing, and Researching across the Curriculum
Dan Melzer

Writing Poetry through the Eyes of Science: A Teacher's Guide to Scientific Literacy and Poetic Response
Nancy S. Gorrell, with Erin Colfax

Forthcoming

Becoming a Teacher Who Writes: Let Teaching be Your Writing Muse
Nancy S. Gorrell

Writing from the Inside: The Power of Reflective Writing in the Classroom
Olivia Archibald and Maureen Hall

Arting, Writing, and Culture: Teaching to the 4th Power
Anna Sumida, Meleanna Meyer, and Miki Maeshiro

Seriously Creative Writing: Stylistic Strategies in Non-Fictional Writing
Sky Marsen

Reflective Writing for English Language Teachers
Thomas S. C. Farrell

Tend Your Garden

Nurturing Motivation in Young Adolescent Writers

Mary Anna Kruch

SHEFFIELD   OAKVILLE

Published by Equinox Publishing Ltd.

UK: Unit S3, Kelham House, 3 Lancaster Street, Sheffield S3 8AF
USA: DBBC, 28 Main Street, Oakville, CT 06779

www.equinoxpub.com

First published 2012

© Mary Anna Kruch 2012

All rights reserved. No part of this publication may be reproduced or transmitted in any form or by any means, electronic or mechanical, including photocopying, recording or any information storage or retrieval system, without prior permission in writing from the publishers.

British Library Cataloguing-in-Publication Data

A catalogue record for this book is available from the British Library.

ISBN   978-1-84553-450-9   (hardback)
         978-1-84553-451-6   (paperback)

Library of Congress Cataloging-in-Publication Data

Kruch, Mary Anna.
  Tend your garden : nurturing motivation in young adolescent writers / Mary Anna Kruch.
    p. cm.
  Includes bibliographical references and index.
  ISBN 978-1-84553-450-9—ISBN 978-1-84553-451-6 (pb)
  1. English language—Composition and exercises. 2. English language—Study and teaching (Secondary) 3. Creative writing (Secondary education) 4. Language arts (Secondary) I. Title.
  PE1404.K687 2011
  808'.0420712—dc23
                                    2011022260

Typeset by S.J.I. Services, New Delhi
Printed and bound in the UK by the MPG Books Group

*This book is dedicated to
Bob, Jennifer, and Emma as well as to the memory of
my parents, Gidio and Betty Jo Scenga –
avid readers, writers, and artists all!*

You are my heart.

Contents

Foreword	xiii
Editor's Preface	xvii
Preface	xxi
Introduction: How I Came to Tend My Garden	1
Introductory Remarks to This Book	2
The Young Adolescent Motivation Model of Writing: An Adaptable Choice	3
Anecdotes, Maxims, and Sample Lessons	4
Rationales for Writing	5
Overview of Chapters	6
How I Came to Tend My Garden	9
Why Middle School Teachers Stay to Tend Their Gardens	17
Concluding Reflections on Introduction	18
1 Nurturing the Whole Learner in an Inquiry-Rich Environment	19
Introductory Remarks to Chapter 1	20
What the Experts Say about Teaching Writing	20
Observing a Progressive Classroom	22
A Learner-Centered Approach	24
Nurturing Positive Self-Image through Literature	32
Enhancing Positive Self-Image through Communication	34
From the Page to the Stage: A Team-Building Unit Featuring Choice	38
The Mismatch between Learner-Centered and Test-Centered Curriculum	44
Practicing vs. Preaching in the Learner-Centered Classroom	45
Concluding Reflections on Chapter 1	49

2 Cultivating a Writing Community — 51

- Introductory Remarks to Chapter 2 — 52
- Planting the Seeds for a Community of Learners — 52
- Learning Models Revisited — 53
- Cultivating the Individual through Constructivist and Sociocultural Learning Approaches — 56
- Learning from the Pros: Sowing the Seeds of Kinship — 57
- Developing a Pattern in Process Writing: One Size Does Not Fit All — 59
- The Human Face of War: A Collaborative Lesson — 62
- The Necessity of Norms — 66
- Monitoring Class Progress in the Writing Workshop — 68
- Managing the Writing Workshop — 69
- The Diamond Poem: A Community-Building Mini-Lesson — 70
- Learning from Experience: Growing by Leaps and Bounds — 79
- Concluding Reflections on Chapter 2 — 80

3 Engaging Young Writers with Relevant, High-Interest Lessons — 83

- Introductory Remarks to Chapter 3 — 84
- Planting the Seeds of Engagement: Conscious Planning — 84
- Learner-Centered Motivation and Behaviorism in Conflict — 87
- Learning from Achievement Motivation Training in Schools — 91
- Classroom Practices that Nurture Motivation — 93
- Six Keys to Nurturing Motivation in Relevant, High-Interest Classrooms — 94
- Arranging for Relevance: Favorite Place Lesson — 127
- Concluding Reflections on Chapter 3 — 132

4 Growing with Process Writing Linked to the Arts — 135

- Introductory Remarks to Chapter 4 — 136
- Inquiry as Motivation to Write in Response to the Arts — 136
- The Power of the Pen: Why We Write — 137
- Art as Invitation to Young Adolescents' Personal Expression — 140
- Individual Purpose and Response to Cultivate Voice — 141
- Process Writing: Cyclical in Nature — 143
- Developing a Unique Process — 145
- Strong Lessons with Flexible Templates — 146

Incorporating Hands-on Art and Other Media into Lessons	173
Responding to Literature and the Global Environment	174
Sowing the Seeds of Aesthetic Writing	175
What is Aesthetic Writing?	177
Growth through Reflective Writing	180
Supporting the Roots of Individual Growth	183
Concluding Reflections on Chapter 4	183

5 Motivating Writing with Choice and Critical Thinking — 185

Introductory Remarks to Chapter 5	186
Criticism and Feedback	186
Response to Writing within Time Constraints	187
The Two Cs: Critical Thinking and Choice	192
Critical Thinking: The First "C"	193
Choice: The Second "C"	210
A Challenge to Teach Our Children Well	233
Concluding Reflections on Chapter 5	234

6 Learner-Centered Writing in an e-Universe — 237

Introductory Remarks to Chapter 6	238
Writing Instruction: Necessarily Progressive	239
Why and How Young Adolescents Write	241
Moving Forward with Study, Planning, and Differentiated Instruction	243
Current Practices and Future Frontiers	247
Accessing Digital Writing Resources	250
Towards a Digital Writing Pedagogy	251
Incorporating Digital Research	266
How the Tech-sperts View Future Instruction	275
Concluding Reflections on Chapter 6	276

7 Sowing the Seeds of Formative, Authentic Assessment — 279

Introductory Remarks to Chapter 7	280
Gauging Growth: An Ongoing, Integrated Approach to Assessment	280
Belief in and Support of Each Young Adolescent Writer	282
Best Practice Pedagogy and Assessment	284

	Reflective Teaching and a Common Paradox	287
	Charting Growth	289
	The Power of Insight and Daily Writing Time	306
	Writing Development through Revision	308
	Considering the Purposes of and Approaches to Assessment	312
	Authentic Assessments Help Make the Garden Grow	319
	Managing Writing on Demand	321
	Concluding Reflections on Chapter 7	323
8	**Maxim-izing Motivation via Teacher Imagination**	**325**
	Introductory Remarks to Chapter 8	326
	Maxims from the Introduction: How I Came to Tend My Garden	328
	Maxims from Chapter 1: Nurturing the Whole Learner in an Inquiry-Rich Environment	329
	Maxims from Chapter 2: Cultivating a Writing Community	333
	Maxims from Chapter 3: Engaging Young Writers with Relevant, High-Interest Lessons	334
	Maxims from Chapter 4: Growing with Process Writing Linked to the Arts	338
	Maxims from Chapter 5: Motivating Writing with Choice and Critical Thinking	342
	Maxims from Chapter 6: Learner-Centered Writing in an e-Universe	345
	Maxims from Chapter 7: Sowing the Seeds of Formative, Authentic Assessment	347
	Concluding Reflections: The Garden Lives and Grows	349
	"Tidal Basin" by Michael Gordon	350
	References	353
	Appendices	
	Appendix A: Books with Strong, Positive, Global Characters	371
	Appendix B: Suggested Resources for "War" Theme	374
	Appendix C: ADVERB (gray) Activity Cards for "You Be the Sentence" Lesson	377
	Appendix D: SUBJECT (pink) Activity Cards for "You Be the Sentence" Lesson	378
	Appendix E: VERB (blue) Activity Cards for "You Be the Sentence" Lesson	379

Appendix F: ADJECTIVE (green) Activity Cards for "You Be the Sentence" Lesson 380
Appendix G. PHRASE (red) Activity Cards for "You Be the Sentence" Lesson 381

Author Index 382
Subject Index 387

Foreword

I met the author of this book, Mary Anna Kruch, almost a decade ago at the National Council of Teachers of English annual convention in Atlanta. There, we bonded quickly because of our similar experiences as middle school Language Arts teachers and because of a shared passion for teaching writing. When I learned that she would be writing a textbook to help illustrate best practices in writing instruction for young adolescents, I was absolutely thrilled. As an Associate Professor of English – Secondary Education at Northern Michigan University, I regularly teach future K–12 educators and have been looking for an innovative textbook in which writing instruction is discussed specifically from a middle school point of view. When I discovered that Kruch's *Tend Your Garden: Nurturing Motivation in Young Adolescent Writers* would provide an effective student-centered approach to motivating young adolescent writers in the face of a standards-driven curriculum, I rejoiced and planned to adopt the book in my English methods courses and to share the text with colleagues in our national professional organization, the Conference on English Education (CEE).

As a former middle school English teacher who directs the English Education program at NMU, I rely upon my own classroom experiences, expert testimony, and current composition theory when introducing best practices for teaching writing in my pre-methods and methods classes. For many years now, I have used one of the most frequently taught English Education texts in preparing future teachers: Nancie Atwell's *In the Middle* (2nd edition, Heinemann, 1998). Although she provides a plethora of bulleted lists mixed with various (somewhat dated) personal anecdotes from teaching in her own non-profit, K–8 demonstration school, Atwell does not present a cohesive argument for inquiry-based learning while addressing such timely issues such as multi-modal responding, connecting writing and the arts/media, technology, and authentic assessment – nor does she address the challenges (and joys) of teaching in public/private schools which do not have the resources of her own Center for Teaching and Learning in Edgecomb, Maine.

What Mary Anna Kruch does in *Tend Your Garden: Nurturing Motivation in Young Adolescent Writers* is to address these topics and many others while presenting specific ways to motivate young adolescents to write in and out of the classroom. Moreover, Kruch's book grounds itself in constructivist and sociocultural theory, as well as holistic education and motivational theory, which helps readers to contextualize appropriate strategies and lesson plans within current theory and best practice.

One connection I see in this book is to the mission of the National Council of Teachers of English (http://www.ncte.org/mission), which seeks to promote "the development of literacy" and "the use of language to construct personal and public worlds." *Kruch views young adolescent writers as active, thoughtful makers of meaning, and invites their teachers to consider themselves as co-learners with their students. Correspondingly, NCTE* encourages English teachers to view writing as "holistic, authentic, and varied" and to:

- Create assignments that ask students to write extensively in a variety of genres;
- Foster a collaborative writing process in which new-media writing is a consistent part;
- Employ both formative and summative assessment to help students grow as writers;

- Engage students in a context-based functional approach to grammar as a part of writing instruction.
  (*Writing Now*, NCTE Research and Policy Brief, 2008; http://www.ncte.org/library/NCTEFiles/Resources/PolicyResearch/WrtgResearchBrief.pdf)

The author of *Tend Your Garden* shares instructional techniques, lesson plan templates, and examples of writing that will help instructors to meet these goals. Kruch's textbook includes personal anecdotes about her thirty-year career as a middle school instructor and well-tested strategies that motivate young adolescents and invite them into the study of writing as a process. Moreover, this book challenges readers to consider their own experiences and writing practices as teachers of writing. Kruch's references to tenets from the National Writing Project as well as those by the National Council of Teachers of English successfully contextualize her arguments about writing instruction and help readers to value their own experiences as writers while considering current academic conversations about how writing should be taught.

For me, Mary Anna Kruch's connection of writing to the arts and media is particularly valuable to those of us in English Education classrooms. I have used Mary Ehrenworth's book, *Looking to Write*: *Students Writing through the Visual Arts,* Heinemann, 2003), in my pre-methods classes for the past seven years or so because it is one of the few texts to discuss in detail how to incorporate art into the teaching of writing. What Kruch's book adds to the mix are specific innovative techniques and structured lessons that teacher educators can employ to help future teachers make curricular decisions that motivate students while nurturing their curiosity, creativity, and love of inquiry. What's more, chapters in this textbook include a multitude of resources for teachers that offer support for teaching writing from a holistic, multidisciplinary, multicultural, multi-modal perspective.

My hope is that through reading this textbook, English educators and future writing teachers will become more invested in creating lessons that reinforce the joy of teaching young adolescent writers as critical thinkers, creative beings, and active citizens of the global community. I thank Mary Anna Kruch for having the courage to share her experiences, insights, and lesson plans for successful classroom teaching focused on understanding and motivating the young adolescent writer. As Thich Nhat Hanh says, "With understanding, those we love [and teach] will certainly flower."

– Kia Jane Richmond, PhD, Associate Professor of English – Secondary Education, Northern Michigan University

Editor's Preface

Dr. Mary Anna Kruch is one of the many unsung heroes of the American school system, a highly creative and passionate teacher who has devoted herself totally – heart, soul, and mind – to the various kinds of work of *being a teacher*. These are extremely important kinds of work influencing the development of the next generation of citizens and so the nature of our society and the course of our history. Yet those who teach, and especially who teach with joy and exceptional skill, often remain unrecognized and unknown as a – and, in the case of some students with whom they spend an entire formative 9-month period, sometimes <u>the</u> – prime enabling and motivating force behind the great effects that others achieve.

Dr. Kruch is one of these prime movers behind what others have achieved, a *model teacher* who, in writing this book, spreads her influence to new and wider audiences of potential achievement. Her work encompasses the field of education, with a particular focus on motivation; the teaching of English, with a particular focus on writing pedagogy; and the teaching of children, with a particular focus on pre-adolescent and young adolescent learners. *Tend Your Garden: Nurturing Motivation in Young Adolescent Writers* demonstrates Kruch's creativity, passion, and wide-ranging experience in these three areas of expertise while also demonstrating her total dedication to teaching in each of these aspects of her work along the entire teaching continuum of *science–craft–profession–art–magic*.

The *science* of teaching is shown in Kruch's review of relevant literature in areas such as motivation and learning theory, the teaching of children and adolescents, reading and writing, diversity and English language learning, and assessment, which form a basis for her discussion, classroom recommendations, and lesson materials. The *craft* of teaching is demonstrated in her strong emphasis on the skill components of both teaching and learning, while teaching *art* is addressed in the emphasis on originality and individuality, and in the inclusion of art itself as a key motivator of writing. Even beyond demonstrating their art, teachers are called to put themselves and their own vision and power into their teaching to make teaching *magic* happen in their classrooms.

The *profession* of teaching is a major emphasis of the entire book, written for teachers on a foundation of knowledge of legislation and initiatives affecting teaching work and reminding teachers to stay abreast of these; drawing on teacher collaboration and the published work of other teachers as well as of professional organizations such as the Michigan Council of Teachers of English, the National Council of Teachers of English, and the National Writing Project; and encouraging teachers to reflect on and to adapt the lesson materials and other teaching ideas provided. A novel feature of the book is its inclusion of teaching *maxims* linked to the discussion as gained through the author's knowledge and career-long experience. Throughout this work, Kruch models a professional outlook on education representing the intersection of the individual and collective aspects of writing pedagogy and teaching more generally.

Tend Your Garden: Nurturing Motivation in Young Adolescent Writers is organized on the model of a flower, with each of the eight chapters forming a petal around the core of the young adolescent learner in an original Young Adolescent Motivation Model, or YAMM. The coverage of the book as this flower unfolds moves from a focus on teaching the whole learner in an environment of inquiry to developing a writing community in the classroom, motivating writing through high-interest lessons that incorporate elements of popular culture and that consider students' specific characteristics, linking process writing to the arts, and using a range of stimuli for adding choice and critical thinking to students' writing. *Tend Your Garden* also includes a chapter on writing in electronic environments and one on ways to handle writing for high-stakes tests within a broader orientation to ongoing, formative assessment. The final chapter pulls together some of the book's maxims into a discussion aimed to celebrate and to stimulate teachers' imagination and vision.

Tend Your Garden: Nurturing Motivation in Young Adolescent Writers is a valuable addition to the literature on the teaching of writing that offers a wealth of insight and practical teaching material for working with young adolescent writers. I hope that all those who read Dr. Kruch's book and try out her teaching ideas will find themselves enlightened as well as enabled and motivated to achieve great things in their own classrooms.

– Martha C. Pennington, Series Editor
Frameworks for Writing

Preface

The concept for *Tend Your Garden* took root several years ago as I observed my then sixth grade students carefully plant the fragile vegetation they had raised from seeds in science class into their own garden in front of the school. Living in the same small town where I taught for thirty years, I had the great fortune and the pleasure to observe students themselves grow and develop from preadolescents into strong, smart, capable young adolescents and, through the years, adults. Equally fortunate, I spent my final twelve years in the classroom with 10- and 11-year-olds, marveling at their enthusiasm, humor, passion, and zest for life, as they grew increasingly confident and independent. I remember the day in the school garden overhearing two young ladies make plans to ride bikes back to school on the weekend to see whether their plants had blossomed. The girls understood that their actions and their attention to each plant mattered – that they had the power to cultivate the vulnerable young plants' growth. In the same way, I accept the notion that teachers' nurturance of learners – offering their support, guidance, and knowledge – results in young adolescents' development into ever more colorful, unique, and bright human beings. After teaching young adolescents for 30 years and moving on to instruct preservice teachers at a four-year university, I found the same to be true in all teaching contexts.

Young adolescents aged 9–13 rarely arrive from elementary school to middle school complete with their identities formed or their self-concepts intact, ready and able to face each and every task and event with confidence, equanimity, and grace. Teachers guide and foster good will and positive outlooks among students by helping them discover that they can expect to receive not just information but also nurturing care and attention when they arrive at school each day. Motivation to learn becomes the driving force in the process of growing into capable, reflective, and independent students and writers. This book was written specifically for readers seeking a clearly demonstrated pedagogical model supported by best practice and research that will enable them to foster excellent writing among their students. My hope is that in applying the principles and practices of this book, teachers will become even more committed to reflective teaching in a learner-centered classroom as they prepare to teach not only content, but, more importantly, children – all the while empowering themselves with the understanding and the joy that comes with a job well done.

This book rests upon the assumption that all young adolescents are worthy of best efforts from teachers, who in turn have the support of parents and the community as a whole.

For, as master gardeners continually observe their gardens and perform the activities of sowing, removing weeds, and determining what methods will best support the plants growing under their watch, so too must teachers keep vigilance over their young charges, providing nurturance, eliminating what prevents development, and continually refining their guidance and instruction in relation to their precious charges. As young plants grow and spread out into ever stronger, ripened vegetation and flora, so too will young writers grow, acquiring the confidence and maturity of knowledge and craft necessary to move towards writing strength and independence. This accomplishment is every parent's hope and every teacher's dream.

These pages represent the sum of not only many years of research and writing about what the above assumption entails, but also the collective, helpful support of family, mentors, colleagues, and friends. First, warm thanks go to my husband and best friend, Bob, for his constant care, humor, patience, and love as the process of writing this book unfolded; thanks to our daughters Jenny and Emma, who are the center of our world and who inspire us with their determined, proactive, fair-minded, and generous approach to life. Particular acknowledgment goes to my editor, Martha Pennington, who invited me to write the book, offering her expertise and nurturance while assisting in accomplishing my life-long goal of becoming the author of a book, as I transitioned from classroom teacher and university professor to writer.

Special thanks to Lois A. Bader, who has served as a strong, supportive role model for me since my early teaching days and who chaired both my Masters program and Doctoral committee. Lois knows how to walk the walk, and she continues to be a source of encouragement and celebration. Thank you, Kia Jane Richmond, Rob Rozema, and Joyce Benvenuto for reading chapters and offering helpful feedback. Thanks to the following educators who have generously allowed me to include their words, spoken and written: Iowa State English Educator, Michelle Tremmel; high school teacher, Dianna Topper; and elementary third grade teacher, Michael Gordon. Additionally, I owe a large debt of gratitude to Louis Romano, an early proponent of middle school education as well as a member of my Doctoral committee.

Finally, an appreciative thank-you to Ginger Schoen, a former middle school colleague, with whom I created many memorable lessons and units, including those motivated by the arts. Ginger showed me that middle school students not only need but also crave parameters as well as choice. Her advice, guidance, and friendship have served me well over many years.

– Mary Anna Kruch, May 2011

Introduction

How I Came to Tend My Garden

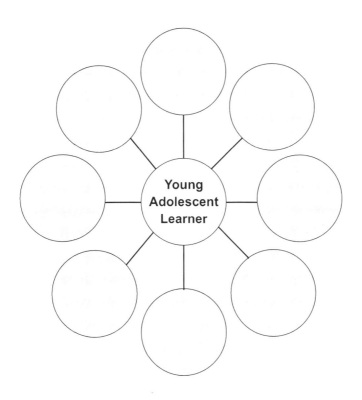

He who plants a tree
Plants a hope.
　　　　　　　– Lucy Larcom, "Plant a Tree" (Larcom, 1879)

Introductory Remarks to This Book

Thirty years of teaching young adolescents have resulted in tremendous growth in me as a teacher, researcher, and writer. In this text, I attempt to channel that growth into suggestions and invitations to teachers who seek varied ways to motivate developing writers in the middle grades (those in the upper elementary and middle school grades 5–8 in the preteen and early adolescent years, generally ages 10–14). Each chapter includes fundamental principles and supportive research on teaching and learning in motivational ways, and personal anecdotes chronicling my progression as a teacher of writing. Many chapters include illustrative classroom lessons – all with the intention of presenting alternatives to traditional, product-based curricula, which continue to be used but *have rarely proven useful* in fostering writing excellence among students in the middle grades.

The primary purpose of the book is to set forth an effective model of writing instruction that is process-based and that motivates young adolescent writers by placing them at the center of planned instruction. The Young Adolescent Motivation Model of Writing (YAMM) has been designed specifically for middle school and upper elementary teachers, particularly those who are largely required to use prescriptive writing materials. The model reflects my long-term growth with respect to research, experience, and knowledge of teaching young adolescent writers as well as preservice and veteran teachers.

A secondary purpose relates to having witnessed firsthand many of the negative effects of recurrent, standardized measures upon students and teachers. Ideally, young adolescents develop and hone writing skills year to year in a forward progression; however, writing is a recursive process, unique to each writer, impossible to adequately measure by a standardized test alone. Middle school teachers know all too well that young adolescents view test-driven, programmed writing as a hoop through which they must learn to jump – but are rarely motivated to do so. The book rests on providing answers to teachers' related questions, which may include:

- How do I motivate students to produce their best writing when the instructional program in use mirrors test preparation rather than authentic writing, and when the summative assessment fails to provide a clear, fair, and manageable picture of the student writers' abilities?
- Are there more formative ways to effectively, fairly, and authentically teach and then measure young adolescents' writing while nurturing their motivation to write?

The Young Adolescent Motivational Model of Writing: An Adaptable Choice

Fortunately, alternative options to test-driven writing instruction exist; such optional paths lead to the same goal of fostering motivated, excellent writers and are open to those willing to reimagine middle-grades learners as the central foundation for whom the writing curriculum exists. Throughout the book, I present, clarify, and discuss the Young Adolescent Motivation Model of Writing (YAMM) and its components in response to the above questions. Developed over time, the model draws upon the stellar work of educators, psychologists, theorists, and writers, such as John Dewey (e.g. Dewey, 1916/1944);[1] Janet Emig (c.g. Emig, 1971); David McClelland (e.g. McClelland, Atkinson, Clark, and Lowell, 1976); Lev Vygotsky (e.g. Vygotsky, 1978); Louise M. Rosenblatt (e.g. Rosenblatt, 1978); Rita and Kenneth Dunn and colleagues (e.g. Carbo, Dunn, and Dunn, 2007; Dunn and Dunn, 1975), and Louis G. Romano (e.g. Romano and Georgiady, 1994), to name a few; and it serves as a resource guide when envisioning learner-centered writing instruction that best nurtures young adolescent writers. The Young Adolescent Motivation Model of Writing visually resembles a flower, placing learners in the center and surrounded by eight "petals," each representing one of the

YAMM's eight components. The components, each of which is presented in a chapter of this book, include:

1. Whole learner in an environment of inquiry;
2. Writing community;
3. Relevant, high-interest lessons;
4. Process writing linked to the arts;
5. Choice and critical thinking;
6. Writing in an e-universe;
7. Formative, authentic assessment; and
8. Teacher imagination and vision.

Each of these components is integral to nurturing motivation in young adolescent writers.

Anecdotes, Maxims, and Sample Lessons

In this and successive chapters I include one or more anecdotes that align with the chapter topic. Here I introduce readers to my early days of teaching and the subsequent discovery of what makes a garden of middle-grades writers grow.

In addition, each chapter presents *maxims*, generalizations in the form of expressions of principle, highlighted in bold font to draw the reader's attention to the statements and suggest their contemplation. These maxims are supported by classroom experience and research spanning almost a century of education.

Mini-lessons and activities included in the chapters represent numerous writing genres, and a set of flexible lesson templates for use by educators in various classroom settings is included in the book. These representative lessons build upon a strong background and application of motivation theory, authentic inquiry, and multi-modal response to the arts and to other experiences. Texts written by experienced writers (sometimes referred to as *mentor texts*) that are illustrative of exceptional craft and content, along with student and teacher writing, are presented as models for teaching and reflective application. Educational resources such as texts, Web sites, and supportive organizations that I have found helpful are also incorporated throughout the book.

Rationales for Writing

Central aims of *Tend Your Garden: Nurturing Motivation in Young Adolescent Writers* are the following:

1. To support the re-establishment of *teachers as experts* and competent planners, dedicated to reflective teaching and learning as well as professional development;
2. To reduce the influence of prescriptive writing programs whose main goal is preparation of students for standardized tests rather than for authentic writing purposes;
3. To assist educators in public, charter, private, and home schools who wish to try a progressive, learner-centered model of teaching supported by best practice research;
4. To demonstrate to teachers that writing and working on authentic writing projects with students can motivate them both – students and teachers – to their highest levels of performance in the classroom as well as on assessed writing and real-world tasks;
5. To provide pathways for teachers to examine some common state writing standards and to see how state and national standards are being met or can be met within their own classrooms;
6. To support reflective, continuously evolving writing pedagogy within a writing process model that can contribute to satisfying, joyous teaching and learning; and
7. To illustrate how in handing over more power and responsibility to the students, teachers may become more empowered to grow and to be part of the classroom community as writers, as facilitator-leaders, and as role models of best practice in the writing process.

Overview of Chapters

As stated earlier, each chapter focuses upon a separate component of the Young Adolescent Motivation Model (YAMM). Chapter 1, "Nurturing the Whole Learner in an Inquiry-Rich Environment," briefly reviews the learner-centered approach, the characteristics of young adolescent learners, and why this approach best meets their needs. In addition, I argue for progressive models of writing using writing workshop pedagogy and then document the theories underpinning process writing. Finally, I review traditional test-driven writing instruction which emphasizes product over process, discuss national government initiatives in support of the traditional model, and restate more appropriate choices for teaching young adolescent writers.

Chapter 2, "Cultivating a Writing Community," presents the rationale for a working relationship of trust in a writing workshop. The idea of investing energy in *supporting and inviting* student participation in learning as opposed to *forcing* learning upon students is a major focus, especially with regard to the continually evolving roles of teachers as guides and active participants in the classroom writing community. Here I present and discuss specific ways to create community within a learner-centered classroom. In an effort to provide a working model for teachers, Chapter 2 addresses the question of how to establish a learner-centered writing workshop within either a traditional 50–60 minute class period or a larger block schedule, which may allow a writing workshop of up to two hours. Here I establish the appropriateness of using the Young Adolescent Model of Writing (YAMM) with regard to community-building and the teacher's roles in implementing this model. YAMM presupposes the establishment of a set of classroom norms to which students contribute their ideas and gives credence to the notion that each class member's academic and personal welfare is at the center of importance, around which all other social and academic matters flow.

Supportive studies accentuating the role that a learner-centered teaching model can play in motivating young adolescent student writers are presented and discussed in Chapter 3, "Engaging Young Writers with Relevant, High-Interest Lessons." Research is presented linking qualities of the middle school writing workshop described earlier to what David McClelland and his associates referred to as *achievement motivation* (McClelland *et al.*, 1976). Motivation theory, which has served as a major influence on my continued research and study, and which has greatly inspired and informed my own teaching of young adolescent writers, is the focus of this chapter.

In Chapter 4, "Motivating Writing with Choice and Critical Thinking," I discuss how the use of teacher and student-posed focus questions, the choice of topic, including controversial issues, and the use of advance organizers in reading and research preparation for non-fiction writing can lead to more critical, deeper understandings, which are then reflected in students' writing. This association and transfer of learning is due in part to students' personal investment in the work, which is a large part of the motivation to write. Because the classroom teacher is an active participant and models all stages of the writing process, I discuss the positive aspects of becoming a reflective teacher and a reflective learner. Finally, research supportive of student choice within a learner-centered model is briefly reviewed.

Inquiry and the role of inquiry-based learning and its applications to motivating adolescent writers are explored in Chapter 5, "Growing with Process Writing Linked to the Arts." Supported by a survey of recent inquiry-based learning theory, Chapter 5 presents three model lesson templates for individual, pair, small-group, and whole-class projects, along with extensive examples of mini-lessons that motivate writers by means of literature, art, music, drama, and real life. The templates are flexible and can be adapted to individual classroom considerations, schedules, and teaching styles, and each of these conditions is explored. Lessons are provided in narrative text, storyboard or visual form, and in traditional outline forms to support varied teacher preferences.

Because we live in a highly technological world in which many students have home as well as school access to technology, Chapter 6, "Learner-Centered Writing in an e-Universe," offers selected resources and illustrative lessons that enlighten and enable student writers to work toward a process of self-regulation and active participation using available technology. Special emphasis is placed on facilitating safe, effective manipulation of Internet research as well as participating in suitable online wikis, blogs, and social networks. Chapter 6 includes discussions of multi-modal responses, use of newer technologies, and a list of helpful professional texts supportive of digital literacies. I argue that, while print-based and digital resources can co-exist in harmony with one another through use of hybrid writing workshops, young adolescent writers benefit the most – academically, emotionally, and socially – when motivated to write with an increasing focus on digital writing forms. Ongoing, professional development for teachers regarding the design and implementation of digital writing workshops must be a priority among parents, school administrators, and the larger educational community.

Sample authentic modes of assessment are given in Chapter 7, "Sowing the Seeds of Formative, Authentic Assessment," for content lessons presented there. The positive aspects of reflective evaluation, peer and teacher response, portfolio assessment and grading, and the role of rubrics in assessment are explored, along with illustrative examples. A discussion of the importance of distinguishing authentic purposes for writing as opposed to writing on demand, and some ways to support students in both types of writing, are included. Because we are living in a standardized age in which writing on demand in multiple genres is required on writing tests, the controversial practice of teaching to the test is explored and alternatives are offered. Finally, the importance of finding and fostering students' levels of self-efficacy, of nurturing self-growth in writing, and of celebrating success in difficult times are discussed.

Chapter 8, "Maxim-izing Motivation via Teacher Imagination," summarizes key information in the book by reviewing selected boldface, attention-worthy statements that appear in each chapter. Following each maxim is a direct classroom connection in the form of specific propositions for classroom teachers that they might reflect upon and perhaps transfer to their unique classrooms contexts.

Next, I share a metaphorical description of the garden, followed by short narratives revealing lessons learned upon introduction to my first garden of middle-grades writers.

How I Came to Tend My Garden

A garden begins as a potentially rich, open field, ready to accept seeds and tiny plants, which gradually grow in substance and beauty. A master gardener carefully and consistently tills the land, sows the seeds, and nurtures plant growth. For many years, I have observed methods of continuous perfecting-and-adjusting, and attention to the weather and to the unique varieties of vegetables and flowers that my mother-in-law, a master gardener, annually takes under her wing. The more they experience the rain and the sunlight, together with Mom's nurturance, the greater the odds that each plant will reach its full potential. When the weather fails to provide what each plant needs, the master gardener steps up. Daily weeding, hoeing, and watering have become satisfying rituals, and she knows the growth patterns, stages, and locations of each onion, tomato, melon, and ear of corn – which need to remain on the stalk or in the soil, and which are ready to harvest.

Our classrooms are also gardens, replete with beauty, possessing untold promise. I chose early on in my career to view my young adolescent charges as intelligent and competent, though often puzzling, living beings – students who could benefit from my knowledge and my nurturing. The challenge of doing so fed my spirit then and continues to do so today. This partly explains how

I first came to tend my garden. The following personal anecdotes substantiate what has become a satisfying, career-long process.

Lesson # 1: Young Adolescents Respond to Authenticity

In 1973, I crossed the threshold of room 31, just 10 years older than my seventh graders. As is the practice of many novice teachers, I found myself trying to please, accommodate, appease, and ingratiate myself to my students – thinking that once I had their freely given attention they would more readily choose to listen and learn. But as I painfully discovered, I would have to establish myself as a presence and as a leader, unafraid of negative response and able to assert my authority as needed, before teaching could occur.

One morning, upon finding that only six of 32 students had completed a homework assignment, I grew too angry and disillusioned to speak: the lesson I had prepared for the day depended directly upon homework completion. Since no classroom management class existed as part of my teacher preparation, I was forced to make a snap decision based on my intuition and meager experience as I attempted to assume the role of teacher. After assigning several pages of book work to those who were not prepared and awarding free reading time to those who were, I sat at my desk, puzzled, working and reworking the seating chart. In an effort to turn the fractured atmosphere into a more productive and positive space, I considered several new room set-ups, like placing my desk at the back of the room with the students' backs to the door or moving the smarty-pants and loud-mouths away from their friends. I felt that the direction of the class somehow depended on my explicit control; however, I came to understand that positive classroom settings may result from students' participation in their own self-control. My job was to bring this about though leadership and guidance.

When I got home that day, I sat for hours at the dining room table, reflecting on how best to begin class the next day as a much more proactive, assertive presence. Couldn't they see that I was the teacher and they were expected to do as I bid them? At that time there were no mentor teachers, no bells to signal the change of classes, and no mission statement. Still, I wanted desperately to prove myself to the principal and my peers.

The following day, I watched several students enter class with eyes downcast, seating themselves at assigned places and taking out their work. I tried not to let the joyful surprise show on my face; but it was too late – they had seen me smile. It occurred to me that this day might turn out worse than the last, but quite the opposite was the case. A few smiles and nervous giggles followed, and the ice had been broken. I no longer felt that I had to become a dictator or wield the yardstick like a sword, as I imagined my seasoned colleagues had done as new teachers.

To my amazement, students listened as I relayed to them why I had felt anger and disappointment at not being able to unfold my carefully planned, hands-on lesson for them the previous day. All but a few seemed genuinely remorseful, and several took part in the discussion, expressing their own surprise at my expectations of high-level, finished work. They thought that because I was young and treated them well, I must be a "pushover." That was the moment I realized that my actions indeed spoke louder than my words, and that was also the moment I first modeled what I considered to be high-quality effort on an assignment.

Lesson #2: Expect to Learn Each Day, Often from Students

In the days before overhead projectors, I copied a paragraph from one of our textbooks onto the blackboard in my neatest cursive handwriting. With utmost care, I replaced dull, run-of-the-mill modifiers with brilliant sensory description. "What else would work here to wake up this sentence?" I remember asking, ignoring the obvious one-word quick responders and calling upon those just beginning to turn their palms upward, thinking carefully before speaking. I made a mental note to myself to expect the unexpected and to provide enough time after asking questions to allow even the most tentative participants a chance to contribute and to feel a part of the classroom community. Also, it was clear to me that once my students discovered the depth and breadth of close reading and thinking which I expected, they would readily throw themselves into not just completing their work, but also trying to please me.

As they exited the classroom, two students told me that they felt closer to me now that I was talking to them from the heart. One young lady with a wry smile said something like, "We are all in the same boat together. We all have to learn something each day." A prime lesson that day for me was that a teacher must be authentic and uncompromising in expectations but also human. The occurrences of the previous two days had sealed the deal for me. I was hooked – not just on teaching, but also on being a teacher of young adolescents. I have often wished I had written each kernel of wisdom from those early days into a journal, to pass along to new teachers in need of a confidence boost. Writing this book is a way, at last, to gather and scatter many of those seeds of wisdom – and also what they have grown into over my many years of teaching.

Lesson # 3: Learning Styles Matter

Because I take an unabashedly humanistic view toward education, the appearance of studies and professional development that stressed the importance of students' learning styles in the 1980s intrigued me. The work of Marie Carbo first caught my eye with a book she and the Dunns wrote, entitled *Teaching Students to Read through Their Individual Learning Styles* (Carbo et al., 1986). It was not long before I recognized the gravity of applying brain research to education; the personal discoveries I experienced in the classroom thereafter still hold many foundational truths that resonate deeply with me. Prompted by my own difficulties as a young adolescent learner, while making continuous application to the classroom, I discovered the absolute importance of observing students; of listening to them with full attention, particularly when they reveal information about how they learn best; and of designing the classroom for optimum learning. Guided by Rita and Kenneth Dunn's *Manual: Learning Style Inventory* (Dunn and Dunn, 1975), I developed experienced "teacher eyes and ears," fine-tuned for opportunities to engage and motivate students. I learned, almost immediately, that young adolescent writing has the best chance for achievement when students know they are valued and provided for, academically and personally.

Effective teachers teach the learner, not just the content.

At about this time, I began to see myself in multiple roles, and I began to view my students as exciting and excitable beings who naturally slid out of their seats and rows quite easily while attempting to find their place of comfort and optimal learning. Larger, movable tables and chairs replaced stationary armchair desks; an old couch, a rocking chair, and beanbag pillows joined the collection of places children could work. Writing centers were stocked with colorful pens, paper, stencils, fountain pens, an old typewriter, and fresh lined paper. Bookshelves became filled with student-authored books and all genres of paperback books, atlases, a discarded globe, a set of encyclopedias, and a shelf where each could mark the day's reading during SSR (Sustained Silent Reading, a daily independent reading time first proposed by Lyman C. Hunt, Jr., in the 1960s; McCrachen, 1971). Students would let the book rest on the designated shelf until the next day's reading time. Free writing time became a gift, and art books joined the colorful paper and pens at the writing center, in hopes of motivating and extending writing.

Excellent, updated reviews of student learning styles and brain-based strategies include Marilee Sprenger's *Differentiation Through Learning Styles and Memory*, Second Edition (Sprenger, 2008), and Rita Dunn's *What If?: Promising Practices For Improving Schools* (Dunn, 2008). Beyond these, I recommend continuous dialog with peers at work and in graduate classes, professional development sessions, and online digital communities such as the NCTE (National Council of Teachers of English) Ning and The English Companion Ning, created by classroom teacher Jim Burke in late 2008 (Burke, 2010).

Lesson #4: Young Adolescents Present a Unique Variety of Needs

It is no mystery that young adolescent and pre-adolescent children between the ages of eleven and thirteen experience their peak of growth during their middle school years. Louis Romano and Nicholas Georgiady refer to the time right before adolescence as *transescence* (Romano and Georgiady, 1994: 17). In their widely cited book, *Building an Effective Middle School* (Romano and Georgiady, 1994), these authors advocate for strong, continuous support of the positive self-concept of the transescent, especially after elementary school has been left behind. Parents, guardians, significant adults, and the greater school community must be involved in nurturing these young learners.

Young adolescent learners have needs and wants that differ substantially from those of students in the elementary and senior high school grades. The term *transescence* includes the prefix *trans-*, which indicates movement across, and the root *essence*, which is the spirit, core, quintessence, or fundamental nature of a living or non-living thing. Donald H. Eichorn described this period of early adolescence as a developmental stage of youngsters preceding the beginning of puberty (Eichorn, 1966). Young adolescents are moving into their own at this age, enduring many physical, social, emotional, intellectual – and, in many cases, spiritual – changes in the quest for their deepest and most authentic selves. Many young adolescents are no longer highly dependent upon the scaffolding (or step-by-step support) once provided by one or two key adults, as in their earlier elementary grades. Nor are they little "junior" high school people who move from class to unrelated class independently, no longer so openly cherished for their individuality, in a setting where the "real" learning of traditional subjects begins.

Far from being self-sufficient learners, they need every bit of our generous nurturing as they live and learn in evolving intellectual, physical, emotional, and social states of development; this development is complicated by the proliferation of adult themes at nearly every turn as they attempt to find the places where they best fit in. Each state of young adolescent development has implications for students, and their development will be discussed in the context of learner-centered writing instruction as well as the curriculum as a whole over the course of this book.

Lesson #5: Young Adolescent Writers Are Not Always Easily Motivated

Naturally, not all students become inspired and motivated to write. Allen Mendler, in his book, *Motivating Students Who Don't Care: Successful Techniques for Educators* (Mendler, 2000: 1–3), says that some youth feel as though teachers are responsible for amusing them, unaware that their accomplishments depend on their attention and continuous practice. Mendler (2000: 3–4) further claims that students' refusal to work may indicate apathy used as an attempt at control, which must be politely confronted. There are myriad ways to stimulate motivation in young adolescents who may have lost interest in learning, given up on themselves, or received many previous signals from adults and peers which prompt them to lose hope.

Students lose less face when they do not understand or are otherwise having trouble if they act as if learning just doesn't matter. Yet teachers and the other significant adults who approach young adolescent writing with an open mind and within a learner-centered model of teaching stand an excellent chance of reaching seemingly apathetic, at-risk students. Since one of my core beliefs as an educator and researcher has always been that *all students are capable,* including at-risk students, I have viewed my efforts toward motivating young adolescents as my personal challenge and also as my reward, when students work at levels beyond compliance and assigned work.

When students work diligently for the satisfaction of learning, teacher and students feel successful; when they compose for the joy of writing, all triumph!

Students' can-do attitude and efforts, even under the most difficult circumstances, have prompted me to find the strategies needed to productively motivate students who have yet to find the satisfaction of a job well done. Most teachers have had similar thoughts and questions, such as:

- How might I encourage, not coerce, less willing students to take part in learning circles, read entire books, contribute to classroom discussion, and create writing of which they can be proud?
- How might writers work with me, exhibiting reasoning abilities and questioning what they don't understand?
- Most importantly, in what ways might I motivate students to begin to understand the nature of learning as a process, particularly within a writing workshop approach?

Too often, young adolescents have been schooled to view writing as a product or a task to finish for the teacher. Having witnessed writing also as a journey of many worthy, satisfying experiences, I set my sights on facilitating students' extended view of writing to include the prospect of taking part in the creation of text for their own purposes. Robert P. Yagelski views the act of writing as having the potential to transform, and he suggests (Yagelski, 2009: 9) that educators concentrate upon the *writer writing* instead of the *writer's writing*, which has long been the status quo. I wholeheartedly concur: think of the freedom and delight of writing for no particular, planned purpose, experiencing a moment, conceptualizing an idea, and letting go of apprehension! Since I am intrinsically motivated to write by the act of taking pen to paper and then crafting bits of passion and life into a tenable whole, Yagelski's ideas hold special meaning for me as a teacher of writing.

Why Middle School Teachers Stay to Tend Their Gardens

As middle school educators, we are aware of young adolescents' constant motion, intrusive at times, charming at other times. The unbridled spirit they exhibit can seep into our hearts. Perhaps only those who have chosen to work with young adolescent students and who understand their worth and what they need in order to thrive in an educational setting can appreciate qualities that others may find irritating or downright maddening. I am speaking of the gamut of highs and lows and even the surprising wisdom possible in this age group, such as the self-conscious laughter that occurs when being asked to stop sending text messages, the times when students leave notes and hand-made cards after a relative of the teacher's has passed away, or show up before class begins to share news about a new boyfriend or girlfriend. Young adolescents share this information because the chosen teacher, a significant adult, has become trustworthy in their eyes. Along with the stress of planning lessons that reflect best practice as well as curriculum standards; answering students' questions; signing passes for them to leave the classroom; and responding to parent, peer, and administration e-mails and phone calls – all while trying to teach a class – those who stay with middle-grades education remain for the long run, for more than a paycheck. What exactly is it that makes us stay?

We have many teaching styles and varied levels of expertise in child development and areas of study, and more often than not, we stay because these young adolescents respond to us. We also stay because we have grown to understand and care about them as individuals and future adults. As Steven Zemelman and Harvey Daniels state in *A Community of Writers: Teaching Writing in the Junior and Senior High School*:

> We believe it is *harder* to implement the process approach to writing at the junior-high and high school level. It calls for more struggle, more work, more upstream swimming by the teacher. But it is also potentially even more valuable at this level, because this is the part

of school we desperately need to reform. (Zemelman and Daniels, 1988: 11; emphasis in original)

To work among young, opinionated, active adolescents is difficult and takes a lot of courage, but young adolescents can also motivate the teacher to find creative ways to assist them as developing writers in safe learning communities. Furthermore, dedicated educators offer students unique opportunities as members of a much larger community – the human race.

Concluding Reflections on Introduction

Underlying everything and anything that I can offer through these pages is a renewed effort to provide for the welfare of our children. If our young adolescents are happy, safe, and actively involved in appropriate activities with peers, and if they are making progress at school, we feel successful as their teachers, parents, and school administrators. This book is an attempt to guide the key adults in the lives of middle school students toward growing into their most proficient selves as learners, and specifically to promote the motivation of these children as developing, successful writers. The belief that young adolescent students will meet or exceed both personal and grade level expectations complements the proposed pedagogical model. Built to empower and enlighten each and every one of them as learners, the Young Adolescent Motivation Model of Writing (YAMM) is my gift to those of you whose major teaching goal is to tend your own gardens of middle-grades writers. Let's begin that process with "Nurturing the Whole Learner in an Inquiry-Rich Environment," Chapter 1.

Note

1. I am using the convention of a slash mark within a reference to indicate the original date of publication of one of my sources followed by the date of publication of the edition I accessed in this work.

1 Nurturing the Whole Learner in an Inquiry-Rich Environment

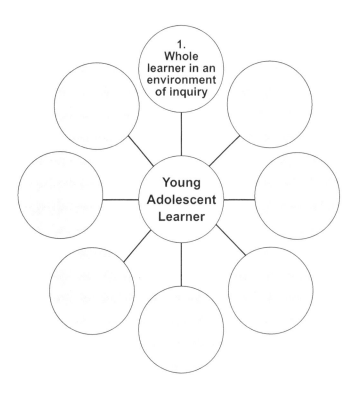

I take it that the fundamental unity of the newer philosophy is found in the idea that there is an intimate and necessary relation between the processes of actual experience and education.
– John Dewey, *Experience and Education* (Dewey, 1938)

Introductory Remarks to Chapter 1

In this chapter, I describe and argue in favor of a learner-centered approach for young adolescent writers. Such an approach considers the whole student, including physical, intellectual, social, and emotional needs – and plans for students' active involvement and future success – all of which are keys to motivating writing. I present a sample unit that directly addresses learners' needs and nurtures their motivation to write, and I argue for teaching young adolescent writers by means of a progressive, learner-centered approach to best nurture their writing growth. Finally, I review national writing initiatives in support of a traditional, more strictly curriculum-centered approach and point out the mismatch in its use with young adolescent writers.

What the Experts Say about Teaching Writing

Many theoretical and pedagogical advances have been proposed and demonstrated by experts in relation to students' composing processes, achievement, and motivation in writings such as those of Lucy McCormick Calkins (e.g. Calkins, 1994), Nancie Atwell (e.g. Atwell, 1998), Patricia L. Stock (e.g. Stock, 1983), Janet Emig (e.g. Emig, 1971), Ralph Fletcher (e.g. Fletcher, 1993; Fletcher and Portalupi, 2001), Donald Graves (e.g. Graves, 1983; 1994), and Katie Wood Ray (e.g. Ray, 2002).

Other experts in the composition field, encountered during my undergraduate university days, include Lee and Allen (1963), in their small red paperback book, *Learning to Read through Experience*. In revisiting this slim volume, which had a huge influence on my teaching from year one, 1973, I notice that the authors published the first edition *twenty years before*. This should not be any more surprising to note than that the quotation at the top of this chapter by Dewey comes from a 1938 publication. Like Dewey, Lee and Allen (1963: v, Preface) link making meaning with experience:

> It is generally recognized that meaning and understanding must have their bases in the experiences of the individual.

The progressive reforms suggested by the educational researchers mentioned above have translated into advances and instructional integration in some, but not enough, classrooms. In *Teachers in Our Nation's School*, John Goodlad revealed what he called "less-than-satisfactory educational practices and the apparent persistence of these year after year" (Goodlad, 1990: xiii). Goodlad was referring to programs representing several types of institutions that prepare teachers based on his work with data from thousands of future educators as well as a broad sample of faculty. *A Place Called School* (Goodlad, 1984) was written – following an earlier field study and other texts written by him and his colleagues, in combination with technical reports and journal articles – just as the United States was in the midst of a wave of school reform. Around the same time, the national bestseller, *Cultural Literacy: What Every American Needs to Know* (Hirsch, 1987), was released after the Exxon Education Foundation funded a grant for the project as a response to the lack of cultural skills among disadvantaged children from poor and illiterate homes and what Hirsch (1987: xiii) called "an unacceptable failure of schools." In that same period, Goodlad (1990: 61–62) reported that most education classes had an almost exclusive focus on the academic subject matter:

> But…teachers, students, and parents in the schools we studied want more than is implied by the words *intellectual development*. They want some reasonably balanced attention to intellectual, social, vocational, and personal emphases….

Goodlad proposed that the teaching profession move beyond the basic three Rs of reading, writing, and 'rithmetic to develop a more holistic approach.

These findings suggested to me as a novice that the teaching profession must take the lead in placing students at the center of learning, while taking into account the *whole child*, meeting students where they are and moving them forward academically.

> *One of the best ways to proceed in the motivation of young adolescents' writing is to discover what key experiences, interests, knowledge, talents, and needs each brings as a whole person to the writing process – and what each can contribute to the community of learners.*

The development of my own expertise and "pearls of wisdom" occurred sporadically, in leaps and bounds; and my passion and eagerness to learn in those early days as a teacher led me to learn from experts, peers, and, most importantly, from my young adolescent students.

Observing a Progressive Classroom

Luckily, I witnessed a version of an open classroom, piloted by one colleague in his mid-1970s classroom, early in my teaching career. This talk of placing more responsibility for learning in the students' hands, terms like *schools without walls,* and the zestful feeling of being on the brink of something new and exciting inspired me to imagine how a progressive approach might take shape in my classroom. However, since the open classroom approach was a new way to look at teaching, not much supportive literature had circulated about such skills as strategic class management, inquiry learning, and student motivation. Since the approach differed substantially from the more common traditional approach that places curriculum at the center of learning rather than *learners*, any move away from the norm proved challenging.

Although there were many conversations and some administrative support, most of my teaching peers simply watched to see how quickly the actual school walls "closed in" on our courageous colleague. While some students were intrinsically motivated to design projects on topics of their own choice and set their own pace as to completing required work, most of his students frittered away each class period until it was almost too late to turn in any work. The novelty of the approach wore off pretty quickly for my risk-taking peer, who, as far as I know, did not attempt to learn more about or reflect upon his evolving role in such a new undertaking. Nor did he reassess and restructure the classroom to try to improve on the experiment the following year.

In my small-town district and many like it, no matter how impressive the information and no matter how moved the mainly novice educators were by the call to reform in such initiatives as *Free Schools* (Kozol, 1972), *Teaching as a Subversive Activity* (Postman and Weingartner, 1969), and *The Open Classroom Reader* (Silberman, 1973), adequate support from administrators, parents, and staff for reforms or new approaches was just not there. Then as now, continuous professional development was needed as a basic support to assure success in any such cutting-edge venture. Buoyed by our brave peer, some of us proceeded to start reforms in our own classrooms, but behind closed doors. Little by little, some of us stepped outside the box to move beyond what David Elkind (2001) called "the obsolete factory model of teaching." Creating a curriculum that honored students as writers and also addressed the school expectations meant moving beyond grammar books and tuning into the worlds of middle-grades learners. I soon learned some important lessons about how to do this.

> ***Teachers tune into young adolescents' worlds by offering choice, facilitating the writing and performance of original compositions, and by taking an interest in inquiry learning.***

As I attended graduate classes for a Master of Arts degree in Reading, I read everything about alternative models of teaching that I could find, including various interpretations of the open classroom approach. From these models, I incorporated components that fit best with students and the flow of planned teaching units, in both the English and the science classes I was teaching at the time. By offering frequent choices for students by means of adjustments in topic or text, by inviting imaginative and different ways to complete an experiment and then write about it, class motivation grew. Moreover, I was relieved that students viewed me less as the font of all knowledge and more as an inquisitive guide in the quest to learn. Best of all, students' interest grew with increasing opportunities to personalize their efforts through more choice and inquiry. The accommodations I made for students at the time assignments were given accounted for some additional work on my part; however, assessment of students' writing became easier because I viewed writing not only as content but also as individual communication. In these ways, my classroom and my viewpoint as a teacher opened up.

A Learner-Centered Approach

Nurturing the Whole Learner

In order to facilitate growth in writing, teachers must find ways to discover the interests, attitudes, experiences, and knowledge that each learner brings to the classroom. I find the whole-learner concept of interacting with the entire student, rather than merely attempting to teach the subject and keep my (psychological) distance, as the most successful way to plan for and guide young adolescents' motivation and achievement in writing. *Whole learner* here refers to the strengths in the craft of writing and to the hobbies, successes, influential life experiences, and wisdom that each young adolescent student brings to the classroom. Here I use the term *craft* because the developing writer attains expertise over time by example and practice, just as a gardeners and carpenters do so in learning their trades. Crafting writing can become an artistic endeavor over time when expertise and creativity grow to surpass the expected and ordinary.

> *Even in each adolescent learner's short life, a great and complex canvas exists.*

Each student's obvious, bright and visible, strengths as well as that young person's less obvious, pale and emerging, strengths are the foundation upon which teachers can plan pedagogical strategies to enhance and nurture each and every one.

Long-time young adolescent classroom teacher and university educator Janet Allen urges teachers to "meet the students where they are" (Allen, 1995: 38), and I enthusiastically agree. It is imperative for students to find their way past awkwardness and self-doubt, and teachers can help by meeting their lack of self-assurance with humor and support. Teachers can also help by believing that each student's ability to speak and write with coherence will eventually be revealed. Perhaps the young woman hesitant to pen her first writing response is a perfectionist with the ability to speak more than one language. Maybe the young man who falls asleep in class stays up late on a regular basis writing sonnets or creating graphic novels, then posting them online for safe, faceless peer feedback. It is only in coming to know each young adolescent for who he or she is that we will be able to build upon their foundation of writing strengths.

The realization for me as a young teacher that those who appear the most belligerent and self-assured and who travel with a pack of similarly behaving youngsters are often those who lack the confidence to walk and act alone. Some young adolescents who fear being called upon in class discussion may indeed produce an embarrassing brand of incoherence, which can be difficult (for the teacher) to see beyond – or (for the student) live down. Rarely do visions of the ugly ducklings in the class blooming into grace and beauty fill young adolescent heads. Consequently, this is one of our continual goals as middle school teachers: *If you build it* (a community of capability and respect) *they* (the learners) *will come*. Once our young adolescents buy into the community of writers, they will have opportunities to grow in self-assurance and skill. As they develop a positive sense of *self* in response to our acceptance of their strengths as well as their struggles, the prospect of involving all students in the building of a classroom community is rife with possibilities for growth in writing as in life.

Process Approach to Writing Instruction

The concept of a student-centered classroom began in reaction to the exploitation of the conventional teacher-centered model, which at its most extreme presupposes that the teacher has a bank of knowledge and the students have little or none. It is difficult to build student self-efficacy and success within such an extreme, reactive model of learning. Still, we learn from educational history that student-centered learning does not mean students learning simply by choice or without guidance. As Parker Palmer reminds us in *The Courage to Teach*:

> When students are put at the center of the circle, teachers may yield too much of their leadership; it is difficult to confront ignorance and bias in individuals or the group when students themselves comprise the plumb line. (Palmer, 1998: 119)

I prefer to use the term *learner-centered* rather than *student-centered*, because the approach and the term focus on the learner in the context of a deep *understanding of the learning process itself* (McCombs and Whisler, 1997). The Young Adolescent Motivation Model of Writing (YAMM) is learner-centered and features a process approach that is most appropriate for 11- to 14-year-old students. Each writing lesson or unit of instruction suggested in the chapters of this book is a development of this model.

The accent on high-interest, motivational lessons inviting students' active involvement within an interdependent writing community, facilitated by an observant, knowledgeable, and supportive teacher places this *process model* in direct contrast to more traditional models of writing instruction. Process writing is an active approach that is conceptualized as a series of steps in which students write for multiple, authentic audiences and for many purposes. Process writing also involves unconscious processes as well as reflective thought, and occurs in *recursive* loops of activity in which the writer's actions within each step from rough idea to finished composition may be repeated until he or she is satisfied with the result, encouraging the attempt of whole manuscripts.

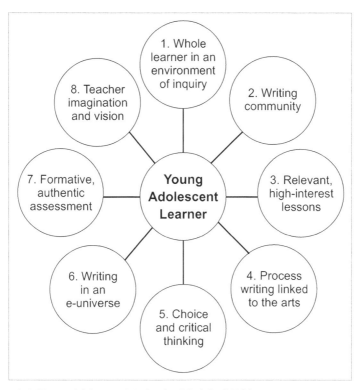

Figure 1.1. Young Adolescent Motivation Model of Writing

Moreover, essays and other genres are not entirely set in their structures, enabling students to develop context, style, and voice (Zemelman and Daniels, 1988: 18).

Active, Multifaceted Teacher Roles

Because the YAMM supports a process model of teaching involving many different types of activities, the roles for teachers are active and multifaceted. The model calls for setting a constructive, positive tone during lessons and one-on-one conferencing, allowing writers the space and silence needed to accomplish their written work as well as students' movement among peers while modeling and reflecting upon their individual processes of writing. Thus, part of the writing process involves oral expression of an individual student's own ideas in conversation with those of others. Jeffrey Wilhelm encourages students' vocal discourse, or "think-alouds" (Ericcson and Simon, 1993); the process of oral reflection, or *meta-cognition*, can be very helpful for students as they contemplate their choices made and the choices yet to be made at each step of developing a piece of writing. The way to serve all children as individual learners is to encourage and celebrate diversity of thought, style, opinion, experiences, and viewpoints. With this in mind, two of the main roles undertaken by a teacher of process writing are those of moderator or facilitator and intellectual leader.

The Young Adolescent Motivation Model of Writing (YAMM), which features a process approach, is most appropriate for 11 to 14-year-old students. Each writing lesson or unit of instruction suggested in the book chapters matches this model. The accent on high-interest, motivational mini-lessons inviting students' active involvement within an interdependent writing community, facilitated by an observant, knowledgeable, supportive teacher, places this *process model* in direct contrast to more traditional models of writing instruction. Process writing is active and is perceived as a series of valued activities in which students write for many purposes and for multiple, authentic audiences.

Any model of writing instruction adopted by a teacher, no matter the point at which it falls on the pedagogical continuum, must include a clearly planned role or set of roles for the teacher. And just as students critically engage in inquiry-based study as part of their writing processes, teachers must also engage critically and reflectively with regard to how best to assume their directive, facilitative, and participatory roles in this process. To enhance their learner-centered approaches, teachers might assume the role of modeling writing process pedagogy in very discrete ways for students. Thus, teachers will be tending their classroom gardens by clearly demonstrating both academic passion and excellence in writing for their young adolescent writers.

Fostering Peer Acceptance and Belief in Self

Young adolescent children can annoy us, raise our spirits, and at times challenge our sanity, but there is nothing like seeing the light go on in these students' eyes! I have often observed these transformations in young adolescents when they are writing. The following two examples highlight a few characteristics that young adolescents exhibit with regard to their literacy and writing, and why the Young Adolescent Motivation Model of Writing offers a real chance for learners' success.

I recall when a student named Maureen worked on composing a descriptive setting for a very personal story about how it feels to be a new student at a school where no one knew she returned home each afternoon to care for younger siblings while her mother was working. Maureen was not only new but also mature, serious, and less vocal than her peers. However, when her response group read the way she chose and manipulated adjectives and prepositional phrases to make each visual feature clear for the reader, she began to feel more included and less the loner who didn't have the luxury of free time outside of class to spend time with the others. I also recall the moment when an energetic special needs child named Donald, who used to boast of never having completed a writing piece on his own, skillfully combined sentences in an expository piece on Nascar racing that created credibility for him with his peers. Donald found a new, more positive and productive way to grab attention.

At the heart of Maureen's and Donald's success lay two necessary young adolescent needs, *belief in self* and *acceptance by peers*, both crucial aspects of their social and self-development.

> **Students sometimes seek self-confidence and peer acceptance in clumsy ways; fulfillment of these needs matters more than an "A" grade or first place in the lunch line.**

In working with and fostering the unique needs of young adolescent writers, we also grow in our significant role as community-builders. And when we teachers provide continuous modeling, reflection, and discourse regarding our own writing processes, we can plant the seeds of writing skill and further nurture the growing seedling of each young adolescent's personal writing as it matures. It takes attentive observation and a deep knowledge and understanding of their diverse needs to make this happen.

Characteristics and Diverse Needs of Young Adolescents

Young adolescents experience their greatest and most rapid physical, intellectual, social, and emotional development between 11 and 14 years of age. It is vital for the school environment to match their needs in engaging and motivating ways. First and foremost is the understanding that no two youngsters are alike with regard to physical, intellectual, or socio-emotional characteristics. Influential, key adults who live and work with young adolescents can observe, study, and nurture each one to his or her full potential. Knowing, accepting, and celebrating the many shades of "normal" which are possible in an adolescent is the key to unlocking potential and nurturing growth in all facets of learning.

Tables 1.1–1.3 show the young adolescent's growth characteristics and match these needs with curricular implications and related suggestions for classroom teachers.[1] Following each table, specific strategies are suggested for roles that can be undertaken by the key adults in the lives of young adolescents as they embark upon their ultimate journey toward motivated, successful young adults.

In Table 1.1, we can see how variance in students' growth is the rule rather than the exception. These precious children want desperately to grow up and out, or become thinner if overweight, and the media have greatly exacerbated their insecurities. Many girls like to read *Teen, Tiger Beat,* and *Cosmo Girl* magazines, but some also still like to do the puzzles in their younger siblings' *Highlights* magazine, and still others enjoy the intellectual gamut of *Girl's Life, Newsweek, National Geographic*, and *The New Yorker*. But the majority of young adolescent females still compare their looks to those of the models in *YM, Seventeen, Elle Girl*, and even

Table 1.1. Young Adolescent Physical Development and Suggestions for School Support

Physical Development Traits and Behaviors	*Suggestions for School Support*
Boys and girls have similar growth patterns, but the timing and degree of changes are variable.	Make use of resources that demonstrate positive body image and tolerance for differences among classmates.
Average height is growth of 2–4 inches per year with a weight gain average of 8–10 pounds per year.	Accentuate understanding of self and others with study of various adults groups who have enhanced society, regardless of weight, height, and age.
Sexual changes vary as to when and how rapidly they occur, with girls generally taller and heavier in proportion to boys.	Provide lessons that illustrate the large range of "normal," including opportunities for discourse, writing, reading, and discussion about characters' physical growth in literature. Allow students easy access to counselors.
Stamina varies among students, likely because of rapid growth spurts. Fatigue may set in, as heart and circulatory systems develop more slowly than bones and muscles.	Formulate school policy regarding appropriateness of homework assignments to ensure adequate play and rest times.
Periods of excessive restlessness, near-hyperactivity, and exhaustion reflect variations in basal metabolic rates.	Provide instruction that makes use of both sedate and vigorous activities, and allow students to bring healthy liquids and snacks to classes lasting more than 90 minutes.

Adapted from information in Table 2.1 and surrounding text in Romano and Georgiady (1994: 27–38).

Bride, and they'd really like to live the life of Mylie Cyrus' TV teen idol Hannah Montana, or of Beyonce or Lady Gaga. Call it a wish, a hope, an impatience to grow up – or, in worse cases, a fear that something is wrong if their bodies do not grow into those of their media idols.

It's not just the girls. The boys compare themselves to one another in the locker rooms, on the playing fields and the basketball courts, and at Boy Scout activities. Boys imagine themselves in another body and in another place and time while reading NASCAR racing and bodybuilding magazines as well as *The Adventures of Spiderman* and the Harry Potter books, or getting lost in Artemis Fowl and Redwall graphic novels. Some will still be reading *Boy's Life* and *Ranger Rick* for some time, along with Calvin and Hobbs cartoons. Others will be content to stay locked in childhood longer than the girls, but eventually the competition and comparison begins. Mom sees her 12-year-old daydreaming at the table, and she urges him to hurry or he'll be late for the school bus; but Mom may be surprised that her youngster is imagining himself in the hopefully near future, finally and triumphantly sporting facial hair! His 11-year-old sister going out the door may be dreading school, sadly wishing she had not blossomed so early to make her the object of teasing among the fifth grade boys – and girls.

Nurturing Positive Self-Image through Literature

Alternative, appropriate literary models in our classrooms showcase and explore the variance in young adolescents' physical growth. Author Chris Crutcher's books – in particular, *Whale Talk* (Crutcher, 2001) and *Staying Fat for Sarah Byrnes* (Crutcher, 1993) – present main characters' struggles with weight and friendships, or the lack thereof. Kate DiCamillo's *Because of Winn Dixie* (DiCamillo, 2001a) and *The Tiger Rising* (DiCamillo, 2001b) provide strong adolescent characters who model integrity, perseverance, ingenuity, and humor in the face of trouble. In *Ironman* (Crutcher, 1995), Crutcher's main character, Bo, struggles with his anger and his hatred of his father, but his rage gives him the energy to be a winning triathlete. Judy Blume's *Double Fudge* (Blume, 2002/2003b), *Tales of a Fourth Grade Nothing* (Blume, 1979/2003c), and *Deenie* (Blume, 1973/2003a) are stories that reinforce the normalcy of annoying siblings, mean peers, self-consciousness, and low self-esteem. No classroom – or home, for that matter – library should be without these books.

Sherman Alexie's *The Absolutely True Diary of a Part-Time Indian* (Alexie, 2007) is an offbeat tale of an adolescent boy, Junior, who chose to leave the Indian reservation to go to a white school in order to make a life for himself beyond the "rez." The humor and raw emotion of the book portray Junior, a misfit in both the Native American and white communities, as a realistic yet successful survivor. Eventually he goes to college and grows up to become the autobiographical young adult writer, Sherman Alexie. These often controversial topics appeal to young adolescent readers. Just like us, today's young adolescent readers are looking to find themselves in the characters they read – and to become inspired by their courage and confidence. For additional, contemporary titles that present strong characters who move beyond stereotypes and who succeed in life – such as Christopher Paul Curtis' *Bud, Not Buddy* (Curtis, 1999), *The Watsons Go to Birmingham* –1963 (Curtis, 1995), and *Bucking the Sarge* (Curtis, 2004); see Appendix A for a complete list. I include these so that you might consider reading them along with the young adolescents in your life, and so that you might spend time in reflection and in discussions that prove meaningful for all.

Teachers can nurture positive physical self-concepts by thoughtful, informed pedagogical planning. Lessons can invite choice of reading both contemporary and classic works in order to provide opportunities to reflect upon and discuss the strengths of the literary characters. Teachers can also arrange small groups of students to study elements of authors' literary craft, such as the use of sensory description, strong dialog, and the element of surprise, and then discuss ways that students can employ these craft elements to establish voice in their own writing. Other lessons may build upon these foundations to include invitations for readers' response by writing a play or short story with a unique main character who finds success in life. The teacher can plan mini-lessons – i.e. short instructional segments focusing upon a particular area in need of attention, in this case, a particular writing skill or literary device – to stimulate peer group discussions within a writing workshop.

For example, focus on developing strong sensory description and adding meaningful, appropriate dialog. Illustrative lessons for such activities are presented in Chapters 4, 5, and 6. Along with the necessary skill lessons, young adolescent writers benefit from lessons that require close reading and thinking about great, published writing (mentor texts) as well as their own work.

> *Lessons that invite opportunities for reflection and discussion about the strengths of literary characters and other literary elements of author's works may serve as instances for student writers to look more closely at the developmental elements of their own writing and their lives.*

The positive self-mirroring provided by reflection on the characters in reading may then reflect into their separate lives – beyond the classroom – building their problem-solving skills along with their developing sense of achievement in writing.

Enhancing Positive Self-Image through Communication

Young adolescents' individual physical growth patterns have many implications for school, and some of these are listed in Table 1.1. Table 1.1 is presented for teachers, parents, and other adults who may spend time with young adolescents and who can model acceptance of their own bodies and encourage students to express their exceptional and unique talents, no matter how ungraceful those may seem at times. We must invite them to participate in activities that are enjoyable and that help them to shine as writers and as human beings. The adults in the adolescents' lives who have "made it" can share an occasional side story about a past struggle when they observe the young adolescent "double-whammy" signatures of despair and impatience. Young adolescents need an occasional reminder that the developmental changes they are experiencing are temporary and that they will indeed survive and even thrive into the future.

Additional implications for writing are presented in Tables 1.1, 1.2, and 1.3. Let's turn our attention now to the intellectual characteristics of young adolescents and the implications these have for the school curriculum, followed by a discussion of ways the YAMM fits their developing cognitive needs.

Table 1.2. Young Adolescent Intellectual Development and Suggestions for School Support

Intellectual Development Traits and Behaviors	*Suggestions for School Support*
Brain growth surges are experienced by 85% of 10–12-year-olds, often leading to new and higher level cognitive processing.	Plan instruction for all intellectual levels relating to immediate as well as long-range academic goals.
An average of 85% of 12–14-year-olds experience a plateau in brain growth. Learners move from concrete to formal operations, relying primarily on concrete operational reasoning.	Focus instruction on reinforcement of existing cognitive and psychomotor skills. Sequence learning objectives to reflect the transition from one set of operations to another; use hands-on activities requiring reasoning about interrelationships.
Students show increased egocentrism and argue to clarify personal thinking as much as to persuade others.	Provide a balanced program of exploratory experiences that support personal development as well as development of values.
Learners are concerned with intellectual, philosophical, biological, sociological, moral, and ethical issues.	Challenge and model thinking abilities via inquiry, study, and debate.
A wide range of skills, interests, and abilities are displayed, and all learners continue to grow toward mental maturity at their own levels.	Provide instruction for each to move successfully at his or her own pace and level without competition, and allow choice and self-selection of reading materials.
Students become more critical of themselves and their appearance; individual differences in creative ability are pronounced.	Provide experiences for individuals to express themselves through art, drama, music, and physical efforts such as sports.

Adapted from information in Table 2.1 and surrounding text in Romano and Georgiady (1994: 27–38).

When it comes to writing instruction, teachers should approach each student as a capable, interesting, and knowledgeable learner, as this attitude positively influences learners' perceptions of themselves as writers. Creating an interdependent community of writers who respect one another and honor one another's diverse contributions to class adds to students' self-efficacy. (A discussion of how to build and sustain an interdependent learning community is presented in Chapter 2.) The classroom needs to be a safe place where students will be offered choice and challenge, and also where they will find success. These are some solid reasons why the Young Adolescent Motivation Model of Writing (YAMM) is appropriate for students. A growing body of research has shown that the more actively involved and the more senses students employ while completing learning tasks, the deeper the learning will be (Chickering and Gamson, 1987; Gage, 1963). Some specific tasks that call upon students to become active learners, using multiple senses, are noted in Figure 1.2.

- ❖ Devise tasks that allow students to link class concepts or readings to their personal experiences or prior knowledge.
- ❖ Ask students to teach difficult concepts to a new learner.
- ❖ Provide controversial topics for debates and ask students to provide reasons and evidence to support or refute a position.
- ❖ Set problems or questions for students to address.
- ❖ Give students raw data (such as lists, graphs, or tables) and ask them to write an argument or analysis based on the data.
- ❖ Provide possible opening prompts or *frame sentences* for the start of a paragraph or short essay; students complete the paragraph by filling out the frame with generalizations and supporting details.
- ❖ Invite students to role-play unfamiliar points of view or "what if" situations.
- ❖ Select engaging readings on current topics, and ask students to write summaries of them.
- ❖ Develop case studies by writing scenarios that place students in realistic situations where they must reach a decision to resolve a conflict.

Figure 1.2. Tasks for Active Thinking and Learning

Active learning takes place when the student is the principal driving force and takes responsibility for gaining his or her needed knowledge and skills. A. W. Chickering and F. Zelda Gamson state that six powerful forces drive active learning: activity, expectations, cooperation, interaction, diversity, and responsibility (Chickering and Gamson, 1987). Although the researchers' findings resulted from the study of university learners, I believe the same findings apply to young adolescents. As Chickering and Gamson (1987: 3) write:

> Learning is not a spectator sport. Students do not learn much just by sitting in class listening to teachers, memorizing prepackaged assignments, and spitting out answers. They must talk about what they are learning, write about it, relate it to past experiences, apply it to their daily lives. They must make what they learn part of themselves.

A more thorough discussion of active learning with respect to critical thinking and choice is presented in Chapter 5. The most important point to stress here is to provide challenging, active work for students that will yield high rates of success.

Young adolescents' fluctuating moods, their friendships and struggles with peers, and their leaps toward independence keep adults guessing. These outward behaviors can be even more disquieting when we realize that the behaviors do not always match students' unspoken thoughts. Below the surface, there may be deep feelings of insecurity, unfairness, inadequacy, and/or low self-esteem. How do key adults in the lives of young adolescents best support their unpredictable, developing social and emotional needs? Suggestions in Figure 1.2 provide insight into students' needs as well as some concrete propositions for understanding their developmental behaviors and what may be going on deep below the surface of those behaviors.

The unit that follows provides for students' developing physical, intellectual, social, and emotional needs and reflects each component of the Young Adolescent Motivation Model (YAMM).

Table 1.3. Young Adolescent Emotional and Social Development and Suggestions for School Support

Emotional and Social Development Traits and Behaviors	*Suggestions for School Support*
Learners struggle to control emotions, express strong criticism of self and others.	Discuss morality, students' values, and consideration in relationships with peers.
Adult criticism is not easily tolerated, and adult attention is sought.	Criticize constructively and in private, plan positive recognition activities, and reinforce positively on a daily basis.
Fear of non-acceptance and possible failure to meet demands of self, school, and home increase.	Plan writing for self-expression and study literary characters and real people with problems that they overcame.
Students waver between their need for direction and their demand for independence.	Provide activities that include independent study and exploration.
Learners require time to reflect upon their development, attitudes, opinions and self-identity.	Provide a quiet corner for independent study, reading, and writing.
Learners develop strong positions on fairness, honesty, and justice.	Allow students to develop a method for creating class norms and demonstrate the need for these in both simple and complex societies.
Family loyalties are less important than those among peers, fueled by a need for social acceptance.	Plan opportunities to reflect upon decision-making within groups.
Collaboration is accepted and observed.	Provide group work inside and outside of school.

Adapted from information in Table 2.1 and surrounding text in Romano and Georgiady (1994: 27–38).

From the Page to the Stage: A Team-Building Unit Featuring Choice

Supervised group activities, such as writing, directing, promoting, or acting in a class play, may allow students to express themselves by choosing tasks that suit interests or enact roles in which they feel strong. The element of choice offers students the opportunity to excel at what each view as a personal strength, rather than being assigned tasks that may cause personal embarrassment. To pique interest and engage student motivation, I suggest "From the Page to the Stage," a unit which I describe here. First, direct a discussion of the American Motion Picture Academy and of the Academy Award for Writing an Adapted Screenplay, along with a selection of the many films that have been developed and adapted from books. Ask students to select a book each would most like to adapt for a film and then prepare to persuade the audience of the benefits of a visual adaptation of the text to a written script, of how best to portray theme and settings, and of which scenes must be included in order to most clearly exhibit the storyline. Students can present their choices, and three most likely adaptations can be selected for groups to work on; then groups can be assigned for writing, promotion, acting, directing, and other tasks, in preparation for eventual performance for school peers, parents, and even the community. In such an undertaking, each young adolescent may find his or her niche. The teacher's roles in these tasks are to facilitate group work, to facilitate the development of students' leadership skills, to encourage professionalism and team-building among learners in the carrying out of tasks, and to assist each group to work toward a common goal.

The steps of "From the Page to the Stage" are described below. Additional lesson and unit plans directed toward utilizing the intellectual attributes of all students in supervised peer groups are presented in subsequent chapters.

The steps of the team-building unit, "From the Page to the Stage," match and illustrate the Young Adolescent Motivational Model of Writing (YAMM) of Figure 1.1, reflecting all eight components: whole learner in an environment of inquiry; writing community; relevant, high-interest lessons; process writing linked to art and other media; choice and critical thinking; writing in an e-universe; formative, authentic assessment; and teacher imagination and vision. Specific unit tasks, processes, and assessments with regard to the "From the Page to the Stage" unit are offered below and matched to the components of the model.

1. Students are asked to search for, discuss, study, and consider a variety of novels or texts that would lend themselves to film and possible theatrical adaptation and then to select one. Students reflect upon the literary and dramatic elements of the chosen text, with the idea of later defending their choices. The activity is one of exploration and inquiry, and it involves the interests, experiences, and knowledge of the student as whole learner, not merely knowledge of the content of a subject. (Reflects Whole learner in an environment of inquiry component of YAMM)
2. Once each student chooses a text or novel, each writes a persuasive essay, making a case for a particular text to be adapted to the screen or stage. A process writing approach is used, involving many peer groups as well as the teacher and any other supervising adults. Students select three texts from among the peer essays that show strong possibility for adaptation, based upon essay writers' arguments and abilities to persuade, as considered individually and in small-group discussions. Next, the teacher asks the class to consider specifically how each of the selected peer essays might be adapted for film or as short plays acted for audiences. Small groups focus upon the necessary tasks of script writing, directing, acting, promotion, and other related activities. Cooperation within and among pre-existing classroom writing communities continues and adds further support. Students lend support, preserving their own identities and contributing leadership, cooperation, enthusiasm, and writing skills, among many other talents and attributes, in the quest for three outstanding scripts and presentations to be performed as school plays. Each brings his or her talents, knowledge, and experience, and builds upon these; the teacher sets up groups in a way that

includes members with a variety of strengths, according to information known about the students. (Reflects Writing community component of YAMM)
3. Prior to each stage of the project, mini-lessons are presented on the relevant topics within the context of student tasks, such as lessons focused on creation of effective dialog, research on period costumes, presentation of theme, selection of music, the traits of an effective director, and the like. These mini-lessons are taught to the entire group of students, and then the teacher readily assists with additional support and application, one-on-one or within groups. When additional students need similar information, the teacher can ask a recently enlightened student to teach peers, which adds to the depth of the student's original learning. (Reflects Relevant, high-interest lessons component of YAMM)
4. Given the general stages in process writing, which are recursive cycles of activities such as prewriting, drafting, self-reading and revision, peer response, editing, publication, and presentation of final draft, students' writing and peer response tasks related to persuasive essay and movie script writing follow all stages, as they unfold in context-specific ways for each writing group and individual writer. (Reflects Process writing linked to the arts component of YAMM)
5. Students employ choice and critical thinking in selection of a text for their persuasive essay on which book could best, in their opinion, be adapted for film or the stage; in determining which persuasive arguments written by their peers are strongest and most influence their votes; in volunteering for and taking on the roles of writers, directors, costume designers, set designers, promoters, actors, and any other roles that arise, within each of the three film adaptation groups. (Reflects Choice and critical thinking component of YAMM)
6. Many stages of the individual and group processes may involve writing resources using computers, such as

digital advance organizers, programs and applications for research on and response to literary criticism, note-taking, composition, and visual, sound, and artistic resources. Final drafts of essays may be composed digitally. If the room is properly equipped and if the teacher is willing, the entire process, including presentation, may be completed by digital means. An excellent resource for this endeavor is *The Digital Writing Workshop* by teacher educator and award-winning author, Troy Hicks (Hicks, 2009). (Reflects Writing in an e-universe component of YAMM)

7. The teacher keeps ongoing notes on progress made by individual students as well as the group; decides upon areas to be taught as mini-lessons to support students' overall work; and directs students to save all drafts of all tasks – particularly writing drafts – along with peer response, writer-chosen revisions based on these responses, and teacher-student conferences. Final versions of scripts are presented as school plays, followed by written reflections by students and teacher. Depending on how the project is set up (i.e. very specifically with task, points, and grades stated in a rubric or more informally stated in a discussion or as a checklist with some flexibility), letter grades can be given, or group and self-assessed grades can be awarded, or both. All are authentic and formative types of assessments that yield insightful information to adolescents as well as document and assess their work. (Reflects Formative, authentic assessment component of YAMM)

8. Prior to the start of the unit, the teacher matches students' major tasks, understandings, and experiences with state and national curriculum standards. The teacher may share the unit with peers for feedback, support, and inclusion of their ideas, incorporating those that may strengthen students' work. During and after the unit, the teacher may also take part in discussions with faculty peers in order to explain the route to interpretation and implementation of standards.

Finally, the teacher invites parents, faculty peers, and other classes to act as audiences for the staged scenes or plays. When the entire unit is complete, the teacher reviews notes conveying students' writing and their ability to cooperate, complete tasks, and perform other activities connected to the project, and then brainstorms future solutions to difficulties that were encountered or that could have occurred. In these ways, the teacher has imagined and invented ways to ensure students' present and future success and use of the unit. (Reflects Teacher imagination and vision component of YAMM)

Planning units such as "From Page to Stage" requires a great amount of teacher energy and much intentional thought and planning to incorporate curriculum standards while instilling lessons with elements that can nurture young adolescent motivation. My experiences, mind, and heart tell me that these efforts reap vast benefits for students. I challenge classroom teachers, administrators, and the larger community outside of the school to muster all of our collective vigor and power as adults who are involved in the education of our youth to nurture, uplift, and support their growth in writing within an inquiry-rich, learner-centered environment. Let us make efforts, individually and together, to spend less time, energy, and money attempting to produce standard, predictable, passive learners. Let us concentrate our efforts instead to meet children's needs as we actively take part in all aspects of their education so that they may grow into active, critically literate, successful writers and prosperous adults.

As in ensuring the growth of a garden, it takes many positive variables working together to assure that learners grow to become empowered, motivated, successful students who can carry this motivation and success forward to flower into adulthood. When I created the graphic for the YAMM model in Figure 1.1, I did not consciously plan its resemblance to a fully opened flower or plant of many petals, but intuition must have, happily (given the theme and title of this book), played a part in this process for me.

The Mismatch between Learner-Centered and Test-Centered Curriculum

It appears that even with a huge store of clearly defined, researched-based reform efforts supportive of facilitating authentic literacy events using students' natural sense of inquiry, these reforms have not had widespread impact on actual practice. Educational trends such as back-to-basics vs. holistic education, phonics vs. whole language, and teaching vs. not teaching grammar have remained topics of continuing debate, reflecting many points along the pedagogical pendulum, reinforcing the traditional versus reformed approaches to learning. Dewey (1916/1944) called the two extremes *Progressive Pedagogies* and *Conservative Pedagogies.* How is it that most initiatives that label themselves as "reforms" continue to concern themselves with raising test scores amidst segmented instruction rather than improvement of students' overall, holistic learning? Experts across many professional fields propose that schools reinvent themselves, just as the mass media and many other fields have done. The reaction to the call for more testing and standardization has consistently set the pendulum back to the traditional, Conservative Pedagogies, which are teacher-centered and subject-heavy, and which support a teach-toward-the-test educational orientation. Reforms geared toward child-centered learning, based upon successful classroom practice and intellectual reasoning, are most often trumped by more standard, traditional approaches. Therefore, the state of education remains stalled, and the debates concerning how to best teach children continue.

These debates are frustrating for most classroom teachers, who understand that teaching reading involves both phonics and whole language, that teaching writing must include grammar, that basics are necessary, and that we do indeed teach whole learners, not merely their brains. The kinds of people who go into teaching realize very well that, in fact, they teach people, not merely school subjects. Teachers are in general well aware that they are not merely teaching the content of the curriculum, nor merely trying to implement a certain method of instruction. Yet, the Balanced Approach, a "judicious mix of content and instructional methods when teaching" (Nettles, 2006), can become overlooked in a teacher's quest for effective teaching approaches that are also efficient in covering curriculum content, especially given that education is by and large a subjective, pragmatic enterprise. While Nettles was referring to the teaching of reading, taking a balanced approach has many educational applications, including teaching and facilitating writing.

Practicing vs. Preaching in the Learner-Centered Classroom

How is it that many preservice teachers, including me, studied and participated in successful field practices within less traditional, more progressive models that differed from grammar school days – only to find that once in the classroom, a disconnect between theory and reality existed? I am sorry to note that the great gulf that exists between what is preached and what is practiced still exists.

Remembering the inspiration of observing one senior professor's use of her own and students' writing to illustrate what have become known in education as "mini-lessons," I wondered why, when I got into the "real world," teachers were mainly using worksheets and grammar books, not only to practice, but to also "teach" complex topics such as writing an appealing introduction. In both university and job experiences, I have witnessed a combination of what Dewey (1938: 8) labeled traditional and progressive education. However, unlike some other fields which have undergone revision and growth at both the theoretical and practical levels, education seems to be stuck in a kind of 1970s theoretical trench in the continuing pursuit of a different, newer model of classroom teaching – while the actual classroom reality remains, in many ways, unchanged from its traditional pedagogies of the past hundred years. With the goal of helping teachers narrow the gap between educational theory and pedagogy, I present some lessons learned, all related to progressive changes taken by novice and veteran teachers in the field.

Lesson #1: Step outside the Classroom Box

Consciously stepping outside the classroom box and into a varied learning garden led some of the more traditionalist colleagues in the schools where I worked to wonder if the more progressive approaches to literacy lacked sufficient rigor. However, challenging learning occurred daily in our classes: current and controversial events such as the war in Vietnam, the Watergate break-in, and a near Presidential impeachment inspired essays, substantive dialog, and energetic debate. We invited our state congresswoman, Debbie Stabenow, to speak of growing reforms in women's rights at an all-school assembly during the first March celebration of Women's History Month, and this led to future discussion and focused writing among students, particularly girls.

While the realism of our larger, global world seeped in I continued to honor the child in each student, who craved humor, logic, and laughter – along with the challenge and engagement of learning. In his landmark book, *The Hurried Child: Growing Up Too Fast Too Soon* (Elkind, 2001), David Elkind bemoans the fact that many of our schools reflect the widespread movement that pushes children to grow up fast. He writes:

> The industrialization of our schools is not surprising.... What is surprising...is that they continue to follow a factory model at a time when factory work, as it was once known, is becoming as obsolete as farming without a tractor. (Elkind, 2001: 49)

In my early teaching days, my school was (and still is) located in a primarily rural, farm-based community reflecting continuous growth and development, while still retaining its identity. However, in many ways, schools in general have not kept their identities but have instead returned, over and over, to more traditional, test-driven curricula – which most often do not reflect what is best for each community's students.

Regardless of the status of a nation's standards, each individual teacher's primary role is to interpret the traditional curricula in progressive, nurturing ways – by virtue of belonging to the teaching profession.

When teachers plan lessons in which they themselves are moved to participate and become engaged, they have discovered that their calling is, indeed, to step outside of the box. Looking at students as developing learners elevates the process of both interpreting standards and then bringing students to life with the teacher's unique expertise.

Lesson #2: Let the Senses Inspire Rich Experiential Writing

Once in middle school, students no longer have the luxury of a morning and afternoon recess as they had in previous years in the elementary grades; their only free time is included in a half-hour lunch break. For that reason, I built in sessions outdoors where we might stretch our legs, soak up some sunshine, and walk along the then empty football field. I might ask students to close their eyes and imagine the contrast between today's brightness and quiet, and the sights, sounds, smells, and feelings they would have during the Friday night football game. I would ask them: What are the sounds and smells now? Listening carefully, they could hear the frogs calling to one another in the swamp near the high school or the low whistle of an oncoming train; they might feel the aches in their growing legs from the five-mile runs in physical education class; or they might smell the new-mown lawn and newly chalked yard lines on the football field. They could see the empty bleachers and imagine them full of noisy, cheering fans; they could see and hear friends calling to one another as they found their places on the benches; they could imagine the smells of popcorn and hot dogs or the feel of holding a cup of hot cocoa, steam swirling drowsily into the dark night sky. Then they would find their clean, dry spots, get comfortable, and open notebooks to try their hand at writing some strong description. I found, at these times, that students were hesitant for class to end, not so much because we had to go back indoors as because we had to stop writing.

Lesson #3: Guide Literacy Learning – Do Not Teach to the Test

Remembering well my own fear of the California Achievement Test in grade school, I planned thoroughly for my students' success. First, I reminded them that they were all capable, that the tests they would take were required, and that they were going to get ready to ace them! I provided examples of short paragraphs with subsequent comprehension questions, similar in form to those they would encounter on the test. I modeled for them ways to analyze each question for key words that would clue them as to whether a literal, inferential, or application answer was called for. In this way, they were preparing for writing appropriate short answers required for their test. The lessons planned were the result of my belief that a fair number of students may comprehend reading but may not be sure of what the test items require. Students' scores would likely be connected to their practice, familiarity with sample items, knowledge, and levels of motivation and confidence to convey reading comprehension.

I took care to make the distinction between writing for tests and writing for authentic purposes, such as our response journals following reading, persuasive essays, editorials, thank-you notes, poetry, and short stories. As I worked on building a can-do attitude among the students, their confidence and pride grew, and they became learners ready for each new challenge. This continues to be one of my greatest rewards.

Whether my students were challenged and were motivated to achieve was revealed in the unlikely form of a standardized test, The Stanford Diagnostic Test, which was given prior to the development of the current state tests to all students to determine their aptitudes in reading, math, spelling, and vocabulary. I found it particularly satisfying that during the years I administered that test, students in my classes, including those reading below grade level, scored higher on the literacy subtests than others in their same grades.

Today's job market calls for adults who possess not only hard knowledge but also the necessary soft people skills of cooperation, problem-solving, organization, leadership, experience, and interest in being part of a team. Standardized tests provide neither information nor any insights about these sorts of critical, soft skills. If society as a whole could be convinced of the weakness of standardized tests, then perhaps education could be elevated to a process-based mode of learning and achievement. An essential understanding of the progressive learning model is one that places learners at the center of a system that has been created for *students*, not for test administrators. It is my intention in this book to make a very large, albeit metaphorical, dent in the aforementioned debates about the place in education of content and process, hard and soft knowledge, especially with regard to motivating young adolescent writers.

Concluding Reflections on Chapter 1

This chapter has presented a view of a learner-centered approach to teaching young adolescent writers which incorporates an inquiry-rich environment, process writing, and varied teacher roles. Having reviewed the physical, intellectual, social, and emotional needs of young adolescents, along with some general and specific curricular implications, the next topic concerns creating an environment where learners' needs are best met. Teachers' interpretation of their classroom roles affects the creation of motivational environments conducive to the development of successful young adolescent writers. Chapter 2 offers pedagogical and theoretical support for a wide variety of teaching roles as the interdependent community of writers is cultivated and nurtured.

Note

1. This information draws upon Table 2.1 and other information on pages 27–38 of Romano and Georgiady (1994); it is substantially revised from that source.

2 Cultivating a Writing Community

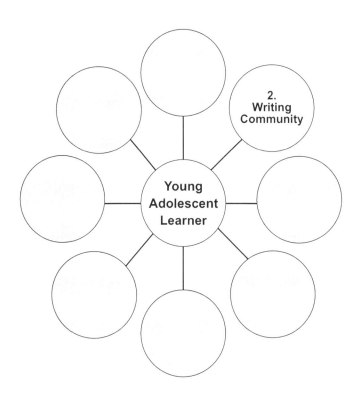

We need a spirit of community, a sense that we are all in this together. If we have no sense of community, the American dream will wither.
 – William Jefferson Clinton, *The Politics Presidents Make: Leadership from John Adams to Bill Clinton* (Soifer, 1995: 3)

Introductory Remarks to Chapter 2

Nurturing young adolescent motivation to achieve quality writing is complex, but the answer lies in humanistic rather than mechanistic responses and solutions. In this chapter, I present an argument for building and nurturing an interdependent writing community of learners who engage in meaningful writing activities within a workshop-based process approach. The idea of investing energy in *supporting and inviting* student participation and relevant learning is one major focus, especially with regard to the evolving roles of teachers as guides and active participants in the classroom writing community. Another major focus is the presentation of specific ways to create respect and trust within a learner-centered classroom that nurtures the well-being and future success of every student.

Planting the Seeds for a Community of Learners

As students continually build skills and confidence in their writing through authentic inquiry experiences on topics and issues of personal relevance, they become increasingly motivated to excel and to go beyond what is asked because they are empowered in a classroom community that will not let them fail. Through careful planning, teachers facilitate young adolescent writers' successful and collaborative communication. The goal for 21st century students has become the ability to collaborate and to convey mutual understandings of diverse and multicultural settings rather than merely to produce efficient and effective workers (Rose, 2009).

As students grow into engaged, critical learners, they are further motivated to express opinions clearly and persuasively, a proficiency that will assist them in interactions with both peers and adults. This process is achievable, but it requires acceptance and appreciation of each child. The primary expectation is that all students will continue to grow as successful writers, with the proper tending and nurturing from teachers in an interdependent community of learners.

One promising approach to developing an interdependent community of writers is to create safety among peer groups and adults in the classroom who are involved in each young adolescent's writing process. Writing that gives an author voice and allows for individual style is often buried deep within a writer's heart and soul, while less interesting writing often springs from a less vulnerable place within the writer. Engaging writing is indeed possible when students work in an environment where trust grows and where their creativity and respect for peers reign supreme. That's no secret; the magic is in the methods. It doesn't take a wizard but rather a patient, persistent, and knowledgeable teacher who views learning as a meaningful calling rather than a race to finish the textbook.

Taking the necessary steps to build an atmosphere of trust, focus, and growing knowledge can nudge a reluctant student to risk using his or her writer's voice to produce work one feels proud of. When such writing is met with respect, authentic feedback, and an appreciative audience, the barriers come down, and a measure of present accomplishment builds toward future success. In a very real way, when a student writer succeeds in writing something that he or she feels proud of, a confident and strong seed has been planted, waiting to push from the ground to reach up towards the air, the sunshine, and further nurturance. Just as seedlings must be carefully planted in fertile ground for a garden to spring forth, so must an interdependent writing community be thoughtfully built and nurtured.

Learning Models Revisited

One of the greatest considerations when planning for process lessons that will lead to student motivation and achievement in writing is the theoretical foundations that support the teaching philosophy. Learning theory should be directly related to the instructional design chosen for the classroom. My development of the Young Adolescent Motivation Model, constructed in response to work with middle-grades writers, is built upon sociocultural learning theory, rooted in constructivism. In what follows, I present a short review of educational theory, along with a discussion of each model's appropriateness for creation of an independent writing community.

During the first fifty years of the twentieth century, the *response-strengthening model of learning*, complete with drill and practice, was the prevalent instructional method of the time (Pantel, 1997: 14). Teachers asked the questions and expected predictable answers from students, and this teacher-student interplay formed the main learning approach based on the psychology of behaviorism (McLeod, 2003). Memorization, repetition, and acceptance of teacher or textbook ideas, rather than independent thinking, resulted in high marks. *Behaviorism*, associated with B. F. Skinner (e.g. Skinner, 2002), incorporates the assumptions that learning is influenced by environmental factors such as external reinforcement and that learning is evidenced by changes in behavior. It does not concern itself with the relationship of the tasks set for learners to their cognitive processes, but rather only with clarifying that which learners need to know (McLeod, 2003: 2). The behaviorist learning model emphasizes reiteration and reinforcement in order to increase preferred behaviors. One of the model's main influences on education was the development and use of instructional objectives signifying that learning is met when a set of expected behaviors has been mastered (Morrison, Ross, and Kemp, 2001). The behaviorist model seems to value recall of precise subject matter over learners' independent thought and is therefore an approach which differs substantially from the Young Adolescent Motivation Model (YAMM), which places the learner at the center of curriculum.

The *information-processing* model (Pantel, 1997: 12) grew out of behaviorism during the rise of the Industrial Age, and it remains the pedagogical and philosophical theory that drives many classrooms today. This theory suggests that knowledge is a concrete unit, which can be transferred from teacher or textbook to students (Pantel, 1997: 12). The information-processing model favors lecturing on of subject information and ideas dispensed to students according to a definite, predictable plan under an assumption that students learn the same way and at the same rate. The model reflects a belief that education, much like an assembly line, must churn out fully developed, complete products of learning containing identical types of knowledge. Grades are awarded competitively, with student scores setting a bell-shaped curve, resulting in few students being able to achieve a real sense of success. It is no wonder that so many young adolescents, exposed to this type of educational model, have very little concept of what it truly means to work as a team, with a group objective, or within a framework of choice and inquiry. And yet, teamwork and inquiry are the very skills that are required in today's service-focused job market.

Constructivism, which more closely approximates the goals and focus of YAMM, suggests that each individual shapes knowledge within his or her own unique social and experiential framework (Sullivan and Glanz, 2006: 15). Lev Vygotsky, considered the father of social constructivism, concentrated his work upon the development of the individual, just as the Young Adolescent Motivation Model revolves around the learner as an individual (Sullivan and Glanz, 2006: 15). Vygotsky, most widely known for his theory of human development (Berryman, Smythe, Lamont, and Joiner, 2002: 117), focused on how humans have advanced so far and in such diverse directions, arguing that not only individuals but also their social groups were key in this human advancement and diversity (Lee and Smagorinsky, 2000: 53). Each person's intellectual framework is composed of that individual's beliefs, experiences, and knowledge. Constructivism holds that, as one encounters new information, it is assimilated into existing cognitive structures to build new knowledge. In a constructivist view, learning is a continuous process of internal negotiation of personal meaning and connection. Under the constructivist theory of learning, instruction occurs within a learning environment that facilitates critical thinking and metacognition; the learners' realization of their understanding is made possible, in turn making way for enhanced analysis and synthesis.

Students are encouraged to engage in social learning activities that have authentic meaning for them as individuals and that promote analysis and synthesis of information in context.

Embedded in constructivism, sociocultural theories of learning focus upon the importance of interaction between people for continued cognitive growth (Lantolf, 2000: 115). Knowledge is located within communities of practitioners and is accessed when learners take an active part in social, cultural, historical, and political discourse and tasks. Sociocultural learning centers upon the collective, growing body of knowledge within the community of collaborative dialog, rather than the development of each individual's unique set of cognitive knowledge (Lantolf, 2000: 113). Sociocultural theories as applied to the classroom support best practices that nurture motivation in young adolescent writers and a respectful, interdependent writing community.

Cultivating the Individual through Constructivist and Sociocultural Learning Approaches

The Young Adolescent Motivation Model of Writing (YAMM) calls for instructional techniques that mirror sociocultural learning theory, which emphasizes the elemental necessity for young people of social interaction with peers as well as adults in order for authentic learning to take place. Pantel (1997: 57–60) notes some appropriate pedagogical practices that support constructivist and sociocultural theories:

- *Scaffolding*: Teachers support young adolescents' unique construction of knowledge through observation and feedback.
- *Fading:* The support such as scaffolding that learners receive becomes less direct as the students take on more responsibility for their decisions about writing, such as which suggested revisions to accept, which topics to explore, and in which genre to write.

- *Cognitive Apprenticeship:* Students learn by taking an active part in tasks about which they want to learn with the guidance and expertise of teachers and others well-informed in the subject.
- *Collaborative Learning:* Students enlarge their understanding of knowledge and concepts by reflecting upon and communicating ideas with others.

While the framework for which the above activities was written for the purpose of comparing various Web-based learning environments, the activities make a perfect pedagogical fit for real, physical classrooms. The facilitation by knowledgeable teachers of scaffolding, fading, cognitive apprenticeship, and collaboration sparks young adolescent writers' engagement and advancement in writing.

Learning from the Pros: Sowing the Seeds of Kinship

Authentic Conversation

One of the first ingredients for a strong community of writers begins with understanding the importance of young adolescents' opportunities for authentic conversation and sharing. Conversation with teachers as well as peers, reinforced positively and modeled appropriately, forms the foundation of a place where trust grows. The classroom thus becomes a *new neighborhood* (Hall and Waxler, 2009) where students can thrive. The importance of teacher-student interactions cannot be underestimated, as these contribute to the strong foundation of an interdependent classroom community. Routman (2000) suggests that teachers circulate and find out what students are thinking as they read, gather information, take notes, and ask questions. Questions to students such as "What are you thinking right now?" "How did you figure that out?" "Why did you do that?" and "What's giving you trouble?" encourage articulation and can be powerful tools for extending thinking when students are researching and inquiring in small groups, as Routman notes. Also, some students want immediate feedback as encouragement to continue with their writing processes, so an allowance for flexibility with regard to movement and talking in the classroom is suggested.

For young adolescents, *writing workshop* implies student investment and ownership. The direct control that a writer has over his or her processes enhances motivation because it builds a sense of responsibility within the young adolescent learner. In addition, being able to consult with peers, sharpen a pencil, or move to the bookcase to retrieve a writing folder contribute to feelings of worth and kinship with others in the classroom community.

A Predictable Process

Presenting and taking part in a process approach every day is also a necessary piece of the community-building foundation. The workshop should include these core components, which contribute to a strong writing community, as suggested by Sipe and Rosewarne (2006: 4):

- Provide opportunities for authentic reading, writing, and peer interactions;
- Explore new genres through full exploration of and engagement in literature;
- Build scaffolding into strategies, development, and organization of ideas within process writing;
- Teach skill and craft lessons focusing upon students' needs; and
- Set up real audiences such as oral and written peer response, conferences with teachers, and Author's Chair.

A further component I would add is to provide time for and to model reflection. The need for privacy in a quiet place where students may collect their thoughts and work individually is necessary for many students at various points in their writing process, so a communication and classroom management system understood between teacher and students must be set up. For example, a teacher may have a set of color cards, each signaling information for students, such as yellow, which could indicate that soon partner and group work will need to end (with the actual ending time perhaps signaled by a red card) in order to transition to quiet work time (perhaps signaled by a blue card). Respect for and an understanding of the learning styles and needs of peers contributes to the interdependent writing community.

Developing a Pattern in Process Writing: One Size Does Not Fit All

It is not possible to create a standard plan that works for all writers. However, while each writer's process differs from that of others, most include certain elements, as described below, or variations of these, though not necessarily in the order shown.

> **Prewriting**: The writer may imagine ideas, take random notes, list details and thoughts, and/or perhaps place them in an outline, diagram, or concept map.
> **Drafting:** The writer puts pen or pencil to paper, types on a keyboard, or continues to float ideas and mesh details into a scheme with an imagined focus within a set period of time ("sacred writing time").
> **Read and Reflect:** The writer reads what has been written and thinks carefully about the tone, voice, required elements of the assignment or genre of writing, and notes other aspects and details to be included in next draft.
> **Revision and Drafting:** While some may write through to "the end" of a piece of other writing, other writers may benefit from intermittent revision while drafting and before completion of an entire work.

Self, Peer, and/or Teacher Response: Outside of the "sacred writing time," the writer may seek feedback from the teacher and/or peers, who then offer suggestions regarding craft and form.

Editing: The writer considers feedback from respondents and makes decisions as to how to respond to word choice, conventions, and craft suggestions.

Publishing*:* The writer produces a draft by hand or computer, including suggestions respondents have made and additional ideas that may have occurred to the writer, and the piece is made part of an individual student writing portfolio or a class anthology, or is submitted to the teacher for reading and possible conferencing. Also, students may want to add a title, create an accompanying piece of art, or a cover page in order to give their written work a more unique, personal quality.

Sharing: Writers share their work in small groups that differ from those of their peer respondents and/or may sign up to share with the whole group in reading aloud in the Author's Chair.

Written Reflection: The writer takes time to read and carefully consider and reflect on the final written product. Some sample questions to which students may respond are: Of what part do I feel most proud? What part was most difficult? What did I learn while writing this piece? Responses may go in the writer's notebook or can be typed up and attached to the piece of writing and placed in individual portfolios.

Many sources that list the stages of the writing process end with either publishing or sharing; however, one of the most valuable aspects of a student's process is taking the time and energy to reflect upon the finalized piece of writing. I always felt I could not give an assignment that I would not like to complete myself, so I took care with the assignments and what I asked of students. Like them, I kept a writing portfolio each year, wrote in response to my own writing, and sometimes shared my writing with students. Accentuating the positive, such as noting one's pleasure in choosing an engaging introduction, along with skills and details learned, goes a very long way towards motivating the young adolescent writer.

> *Written reflection should be modeled, as many students are unaccustomed to giving themselves praise and recognition for their successful attempts at crafting a piece of writing.*

Young adolescent writers will reread and reflect upon those pieces of writing which they deem most worthy – particularly if the topic is engaging and if given adequate classroom time. The final reflective component of the writing process can be an important time for increasing self-understanding, acceptance, and academic growth.

Teachers who work in the most common flexible block schedule may teach language arts and social studies, or science and math, within a 90-minute period. Because teachers can plan projects involving concepts and skills from more than one discipline and because the block can be broken into whatever increments are needed for a given day and lesson plan, they will find it much easier to plan daily time to write. Those working in a more traditional timetable of 50 minutes per class may feel that test preparation and required units or textbook work make it all but impossible to write each day, but it can be done. I have taught in both classroom situations, and I offer considerations for scheduling so that teachers might include mini-lessons within a workshop model such as YAMM for both classroom timetables.

The Young Adolescent Motivation Model of Writing is holistic in that the entire learner and his or her needs are the focus. Regardless of whether the schedule is traditional or flexible, students will appreciate development of a process within the limits of the day, which is predictable and within which they can expect to write often in a variety of genres and for a variety of purposes. If a teacher is working in a traditional one-period, one-class frame, it is suggested to try to form a partnership with a colleague who has the same group of students for a different subject.

The Human Face of War: A Collaborative Lesson

Teamwork models cooperation and motivation on a theme that draws upon students' choice and critical thinking. An example of such collaboration can be found in the lesson "The Human Face of War" (Kruch, 2007), which I created to co-teach with a seventh grade social studies teacher who was planning a unit on globalization and war. An adapted version of this lesson, "The Human Face of War," complete with essential questions, big ideas (themes), and Michigan state curriculum standards, appears in Figure 2.1. This

Grade Level Content Expectations: Michigan	
R.CM.07 *Connect personal knowledge, experiences, and understanding of the world to themes and perspectives in text through oral and written responses.*	
S.DS.07.01 *Engage in interactive, extended discourse to socially construct meaning.*	
W.GN.07.01 *Write a cohesive narrative piece such as a memoir, drama, legend, mystery, poetry, or myth that includes appropriate conventions to the genre employing literary devices (e.g. internal and/or external conflicts, antagonists/protagonists, personification).*	
W.PS.07.01 *Exhibit personal style and voice to enhance the written message in both narrative (e.g. personification, humor, element of surprise) and informational writing (e.g. emotional appeal, strong opinion, credible support).*	
Big Ideas	**Essential Questions**
Reading multiple narrative texts on a theme (e.g. war) can assist in deepening knowledge.	What do students already know about the theme (e.g. war)?
Conversing with peers about a theme influences viewpoints and aids reading between the lines.	What reading processes and group structures lead students to deeper, more critical reading?
Studying a writer's voice and personal style can help students find their own styles and voices.	What discourse and discussion skills will lead to engaged group discussion and analysis on a theme?
	How do writers exhibit crafts in relationship to personal style and voice?
Knowledge and Skills to Be Developed or Reinforced	
Knowledge of reading critically for deeper meaning Knowledge of literary devices such as personification, sarcasm, strong emotion, and element of surprise Working with others to share opinions and deep knowledge Working with others to analyze text for voice and personal style Knowing the conventions of writing genre such as memoir Strategies for infusing voice and personal style into writing	
How will we know that students have learned what we want them to know?	
Task	**Evidence**
Read and respond to narrative texts critically.	Students take notes as they read.
Participate in focused, small-group work about a theme.	Individuals work with peers to analyze theme, author's personal style, and voice.
Write in response to the theme.	Views about the theme are formed, reflected upon, and revised. They are appropriately expressed in conversation.
	Students' memoir compositions reflect deep knowledge of theme, genre, voice, and personal style.

Learning Activities	
1. **Reading for Ideas:** Students read the short story "War Game" by Michael Foreman as well as the lyrics to the song, "Dyin' to Live," by Jonny Lang and jot down notes to these *Focus Questions*: ➢ What do the soldiers on both sides have in common? ➢ What are some new insights about the theme (i.e. war)? ➢ Why might the author have written the song? ➢ What literary devices did both authors use to convey personal style and voice?	1. Building Higher-Order Thinking
2. **Group Discussion:** Working in small groups, students observe group norms (pause and paraphrase each other, monitor air time, etc.) and share insights about the theme and responses to the focus questions.	2. Substantive Conversation
3. **Class Sharing:** Teacher monitors the groups, then asks each group to select and share one response with the whole class.	3. Building Depth of Knowledge
4. **Narrative Analysis:** Again working in small groups, students analyze the narrative texts for author's personal style by the use of literary devices and voice; these elements of craft are shared with the whole class.	4. Higher Order Thinking and Substantive Conversation
5. **Guided Practice:** Teacher asks, "Which lines show strong emotion? Sarcasm? Element of surprise? Internal or external conflict?" Students share examples from their discussion and notes. Teacher records and displays these.	5. Higher Order Thinking
6. **Connecting to Memoir:** Teacher briefly reviews the conventions of memoir and asks, "How would it feel to be in a soldier's shoes?" then asks students to write a sentence expressing a strong opinion about the theme, using one or more literary devices. Some of these are shared with whole class.	6. Depth of Knowledge and Connectedness to the World Beyond the Classroom
7. **Independent Practice and Application:** Students are asked to write a short memoir as a diary entry from the perspective of someone on the front lines. Students infuse their insights with information from the texts, including the literary devices just identified. Sufficient time (about 20 minutes) is set aside for individual work on the draft. Teacher may play the song "Dyin' to Live," if available, for students as they begin to write.	7. Higher Order Thinking, Connectedness to the World Beyond the Classroom, and Depth of Knowledge
8. **Assessment:** Students submit their work, and then are asked: "What did we learn today about reading, conversing, and writing about theme?" and "How have we become more aware of the human side of war?" Students might say: "We learned new information about the theme and formed opinions about it by looking more closely." "We learned what our friends know and believe about the theme." "We discovered the authors' views on the theme." "We will use emotion, sarcasm, element of surprise, and conflict in our writing to express our voices and personal styles." "All soldiers involved in war face similar dangers and emotions, whether they are the enemy or not." (Students continue to work on the memoirs over the next few days in writing workshop.)	8. Depth of Knowledge, Higher Order Thinking, Connectedness to the World Beyond the Classroom, Substantive Conversation

References

Foreman, Michael (1993) *War Game: Village Green to No-Man's-Land*. New York: Arcade Publishing.

Lang, Jonny (2003) "Dyin' to Live" (written by Edgar Winters) from *Long Time Coming*. Santa Monica, California: AM Records.

Michigan Department of Education (2010) *Grade Level Content Expectations*. Lansing, Michigan. Retrieved on 12 December 2010 from http://www.michigan.gov/documents/ELA_Whole_Folder_144868_7.pdf.

Figure 2.1. Sample Lesson: The Human Face of War

lesson involves the reading of a picture book, *War Game: Village Green to No-Man's-Land*, by Michael Foreman, and lyrics to the song, "Dyin' to Live," by blues artist, Jonny Lang. You may find the lyrics to this song at any number of sites, and this text and other resources appropriate to the lesson are located in Appendix B.

Within this lesson are opportunities for students to reflect on what they know and believe about war and international peoples, to discuss with peers their views and the reasons behind these opinions, to read and listen to literacy pieces, one a picture book set during World War I and one the lyrics to a song. These convey conflict from a personal view and echo the global theme that in the end, we are all just brothers and sisters of the human race.

Through this lesson, students may pose questions, clarify thoughts about conflict and war, reflect upon how war impacts family and civilians, and consider what a "normal" day in a war zone looks and feels like. Students look closely at each literary piece for the author's style and voice and for the sensory description used. Thus, standards and goals for both English language arts and social studies are met within a context of student interest. In their final writing, students attempt to apply these crafts to their own writing though a diary entry describing the war zone in terms of its smells, sights, sounds, and feelings of triumph and tragedy. Through their individual and small-group study and discourse, and listening to Jonny Lang's song, "Dyin' to Live," students take part in critical conversations, building their depth of knowledge, connectedness to the real world, and other higher thinking skills. Students also find themselves closer to peers in terms of their similarities, which contributes to the growing, nurturing sense of community. This approach works well in a traditional class period when time is at a premium and you are looking for authentic purposes to write. Students benefit in both subject areas, language arts and social studies, seeing their efforts transcend those subject areas.

In traditional class periods of about 50 minutes, students benefit from teachers' work with another colleague in a team-teaching unit, which gives students opportunities to write and for authentic, purposeful reasons. As a member of a team, teachers can plan their time to be an effective facilitator, especially if classes are combined at planned intervals, so that two teachers work side by side with rotating roles – sometimes taking on more of a leadership role directing the learning or presenting mini-lessons, and at other times giving support to students who may need to be redirected or to have additional assistance. It is not necessary in either a flexible schedule or a traditional class that makes frequent use of team-teaching to meet daily or at the same time every day. When 50 minutes becomes 90 – a double period – the options are many.

When it is not possible to team-teach with a colleague within a traditional teaching schedule, parents and other key adult volunteers in students' lives may be invited to participate and assist in the writing workshop community. Volunteers may be high school students, grandparents, and community volunteers. Some tasks may include assisting students who arrive in the middle of a lesson, giving feedback on student writing, assisting with technology, reteaching of new or difficult concepts, or transcribing for a student who may benefit from assistance in getting down his or her thoughts. Teachers can decide how to best utilize time with volunteers, being keenly aware of the external curriculum requirements and state standards while at the same time planning relevant, high-interest lessons. With a goal of guiding students into and through the development process that writing requires, teachers can plan to have adult volunteers present from the start, so as to get to know both student strengths and teacher planning for each part of the writing process. Volunteers who possess a positive disposition and are familiar with the teacher's procedures merge well into the rhythm of the classroom community as they also provide (sunny) nurturance for young adolescents' writing and sense of self-efficacy.

The Necessity of Norms

Teacher planning often assumes that all members in the classroom community will follow agreed-upon norms. The classroom runs as a steady, predictable unit when all students are consciously aware of expectations for their behavior. I recently visited a seventh grade classroom in a large, urban middle school in Michigan. Classroom norms headed "Creating Excellence in the Classroom through Collaboration" were posted on bright gold cards, located on each set of group tables, and they included:

- Demonstrate respect for one another and for our mutual learning;
- Listen actively to learn and understand;
- Participate actively in learning;
- Set aside judgment; and
- Share "air time."

In that classroom I co-taught the lesson, "The Human Face of War," described earlier in the chapter, written as part of a project for the Michigan Department of Education (Kruch, 2007). Students collaborated in critical discussions about their individual perceptions and viewpoints of globalization and war and about authors' voice in literacy pieces they read, and in their own response to these writings. I mention the necessity of norms now because I believe that an interdependent community of writers is one whose goals and norms are known, posted, internalized, and followed. Also, when norms are internalized, the writing workshop becomes a process with much more clarity, not only for volunteers and collaborating teachers who may be participating in a lesson, but also for the students.

Other less formal norms are also important, and these often become part of an internalized process for the writing community; they too may be displayed for students' easy access. These may include student-created "golden rules," which they have carefully debated and discussed and then have agreed to uphold. For a writing community to be truly interdependent, the golden rules apply to all: students, teachers, volunteers, adult guests, and visiting students. I found that I did not need to apply the consequences of breaking the rules, also created by students, because writers who work within a predictable process will remind one another to stay within the bounds using a simple look or a "shush." Here is a sample list of class golden rules created by one former class:

- Share classroom materials fairly, including clipboards, rocking chairs, and markers;
- Ask for help politely;
- Help others when you are able;
- Keep your work area clean and tidy so class can be dismissed on time;
- Rotate work such as collecting folders and writing the day's agenda on the board;
- Return borrowed pencils and pens; and
- Write your question down and keep working if more than three have their hands up for help.

While the words *norms* and *rules* may connote rigidity, clearly stated boundaries set the tone for a strong sense of community and collaboration. Cooperation requires the participation of all members as well as the understanding that when students meet together in class, they all have work to do. The writing community must be a truly collaborative classroom in order for it to hum along efficiently day to day. Collaborative classrooms, according to Tinzmann, Jones, Fennimore, Bakker, and Pierce (1990), appear to possess four general characteristics: shared knowledge among teachers and students, shared authority, teachers as mediators, and heterogeneous groupings of students. Students take on their roles quite well when continually reinforced through modeling of expected behaviors, in their individual and group work tasks as well as when participating in a writing conference.

Monitoring Class Progress in the Writing Workshop

Throughout the writing workshop stages, the teacher meets with students; in order for conversations to have continuity, record-keeping is essential. Veteran teacher and author Nancie Atwell keeps a running record of each student on a *status-of-the-class* record for a week of writing workshops (Atwell, 1998). Following each student's name, Atwell notes each student's plans for writing, conveyed daily to her at roll call, noting genre and topic of the writing. The writing record also provides information such as whether students are beginning a new piece of writing, continuing a work in progress, or finishing one, and the stage of the writing process at which each currently is working. To this record, I would add a few open lines to record conference notes and reminders for individual writers, such as resources to check and strategies which address conventions, writing craft, organization, and the like. Whether writers are with the teacher for 50-minute or 90-minute periods of time, teachers must remember to continually work at being learner-centered; that is, they must communicate clearly about the nature of the content in their lesson material (why it is important and what is to be learned), and they must be aware of how each writer best learns content and what they care about (Darling-Hammond, 2006).

Following is a narrative explaining a writing workshop on diamond poetry, which may be conducted with classroom volunteers or a team teacher. The lesson may also be done in a flexible block sequence with or without an adult volunteer. The class begins with a mini-lesson related to the writing assignment overall, the prewriting task, and the first draft of writing in response to a writing prompt. Since the process of writing is recursive, student writers would be working at different stages on any given day during the remainder of the assignment.

Managing the Writing Workshop

For maximum engagement of students while keeping with planned curricula, the writing workshop is best set up to coincide with seasonal themes and ongoing units of study. For example, let's say that a teacher wanted to reinforce the use of nouns, adjectives, and action words with students. Since it is March, which in the United States is Poetry Month, the mini-lesson would focus on the form of diamond poems, poetry written in a diamond shape. Diamond poems are made by pairing two opposite nouns along with a group of precise descriptive modifiers. The teacher might select *Winter* and *Summer* as antonyms for a poem written by the teacher entitled, "Out from Under the Snow," to illustrate the gradual change from winter to spring. The poem below serves as the example and can also be the invitation to write.

Out from Under the Snow
Winter 1
Hidden, Dead 2
Slipping, Freezing, Sneezing 3
Colorless, Aching, Bright, Good-as-New 4
Sweating, Whistling 5
Open, Alive 6
Summer 7

The steps of the process through which most students will take their writing, along with suggestions for working through the diamond poem writing invitation, are described below.

The writing process is unique to each individual but usually includes these steps, in roughly this order, though often repeated in recursive looping: prewriting, drafting, reading and reflecting, revision and drafting, peer and teacher response, editing and publication, sharing, and written reflection. This process is natural and fairly predictable, and each stage becomes a signal to students on choices for next steps in writing, along with knowing that an adult is nearby to assist when needed.

The Diamond Poem: A Community-Building Mini-Lesson

Review the terms and concepts of antonym, noun, verb, and adjective. Read the sample poem, asking students to identify each word as to its part of speech; also ask students which pairs are antonyms and to explain how they know this. Ask if they can think of other words with similar meanings (synonyms) that they may have chosen, had they written the poem. Next, ask what shape the words are making (a diamond), and when the change in meaning from one opposite to the other begins (in the middle of line three). Finally, review the directions for each line of the poem and post these for easy student access:

> **Recipe for Diamond Poem**
> ❏ Lines 1 and 7 are antonyms (opposites).
> ❏ Line 2 contains two adjectives describing the noun in line 1.
> ❏ Line 3 contains four verbs specific to the noun in line 1.
> ❏ Line 4 contains three adjectives; the first two describe the noun in line 1 and the second two describe the subject in line 7.
> ❏ Line 5 contains three verbs specific to the noun in line 7.
> ❏ Line 6 contains two adjectives describing the subject of line 7. (Null, 1998)

Ask students to open their writing notebooks to a clean page, place the date at the top, and get ready for a short exercise to get the writing started. The teacher and the volunteer or team teacher do the same. Utilizing the general steps of the writing process, discussed in more depth in Chapter 4, the lesson is presented in full below.

Prewriting

In writing notebooks, ask students to jot down three sets of antonyms that may serve as first and last lines of the diamond poem. A few moments later, ask students for some of their antonym pairs, and list these on the board. (If some are not opposites, help clarify reasonable substitutes for the subjects about which students wish to write.) Going back to notebooks, direct students to choose two from the sets of antonyms written and to create four adjectives for each, keeping in mind that sensory adjectives work very well. Give students about five minutes for this part, and then ask for one or two examples of nouns and specific, sensory descriptive adjectives. If there are volunteer adults in the classroom, they should be "on call" to assist students with disabilities or students who just can't seem to get the word for which they are aiming. Offer the use of dictionaries, thesauruses, and other references. When writing, the teacher and volunteers should access these references as needed to model for students how a writer works.

Drafting

Direct students to return to notebooks, choose an antonym pair, and then, using the "recipe" for diamond poetry, draft a poem. Ask students to imagine what they hear, touch, taste, see, and smell with the chosen adjectives. They should continue working for ten to fifteen minutes. An adult should be available for assistance. If students have laptops, they may use these for their work, saving each page.

In a traditional class period, when time is almost up, let students know they have just a few minutes left and to write down words, details, and notes to refresh their memories for the next writing session. Some may wish to take their notebooks home to finish the poem, but I like students to keep notebooks in class where they will be able to predictably access them during the next writing session. Those who would like to work on the poem at home may make a handwritten copy to take along with them, and they can then leave their notebooks in class. The traditional classes may continue this process the following day. For more flexible schedules that provide a longer chunk of time, students may continue to write for another five minutes. If students have access to computers at school and at home, they may save their drafts and send to themselves as attachments, which they may then open in order to continue writing at home.

Reading and Reflecting

Ask students to pause at this time, inspecting their word choices and searching for possible alternate ideas that may come to mind. Ask each to read the poem thus far silently or aloud for its flow and meaning. If finished with the draft, students can check to make sure the poetry is in the correct form and read each word aloud to "hear" if each suits the message or mood the writer is going for. They can make any needed changes and write questions for peers if they are stuck on a word or need some ideas.

Revision and Redrafting

Ask students to retrieve their writing notebooks and to read over what they wrote yesterday. At this point, they may continue to draft and revise; if finished drafting, writers may join their peer response groups (see next step). Next, ask writers to consider the suggestions for revision from peers, along with any of their own ideas that may have occurred to them since the last writing session. Students should then work on revisions and finish their work in peer groups. Those finishing revisions early may use magazines (I recommend keeping lots of these in the classroom for student use) to make collages illustrating the words and ideas in their diamond poetry; students may also illustrate their poetry using colored pencils.

Peer and Teacher Response

Place students in small groups of two or three students who understand the class norms and work efficiently together. Volunteers may join a small group that may need to be redirected back on topic, or they can individually assist students who have not yet finished a first draft. Hand out a half sheet of paper with the recipe for diamond poems, definitions and examples of the parts of speech used in the assignment, and a short list of questions for peers to discuss with regard to their poetry on a Peer Respondent Form with such questions as:

- ✓ What is the tone or mood of the poem?
- ✓ Do the chosen words fit the tone or mood?
- ✓ Is the poem in its diamond form?
- ✓ What does the writer imagine as the words are read aloud?
- ✓ Does the language flow?
- ✓ Are true antonyms used? If not, suggest some alternatives.

Peers should write their suggestions on the back of the form for the writer to consider. Final decisions on whether to make changes, additions, or substitutions are entirely up to the writer. Writer and peer respondents all sign the form, and the writer places this with the first draft back into the writing notebook.

An alternative to the type of peer response above is a more general PQS (Praise, Question, Suggestion) response, in which each peer takes a half sheet of paper and finds a characteristic in the writing to praise, makes a suggestion for improvement, and then asks a clarifying question. (PQS is explained and demonstrated in more depth in Chapter 7, "Sowing the Seeds of Formative, Authentic Assessment.") Prior to the first writing workshop with peer response, the teacher and two students should "fishbowl," or model, an appropriate and positive peer response session. If class is organized in a flexible block of time, this may be a good point to let students know that there are just a few minutes left to class and that they should write down any details, comments, and ideas to remember for the next writing session.

There will be questions from peer groups such as "Is *squealing* a verb form," Also, you will hear, "May I begin over? I <u>hate</u> what I just wrote!" Some questions and comments, such as the last, will need individual intervention and assistance. I always let students know that every time I look at something I am writing, I make additions, deletions, and changes, and sometimes I just begin over again if I feel that what I've written so far is not salvageable. It is not unusual for a young adolescent not to care for something he or she liked the day before. This may signal a mood swing or just a change of opinion. It is best to provide a quiet place at all times during the writing workshop for writers needing quiet, sustained writing time to work effectively.

Here, teachers may begin with individual student conferences with each student who has gone through the revision process (begin with students with whom you or another adult has yet to meet), and then offer suggestions, encouragement, and praise. Sign the revised drafts after the conferences and ask students to keep all drafts and notes for each piece together, dated, in their writing folder. When I was teaching, I had a file drawer for each of my classes with a different color folder for each class. These were kept in alphabetical order, and finished pieces were clipped together with peer response sheets and other drafts of the same piece of writing.

Editing and Publication

The fortunate teacher or teaching team, such as the one I worked in for my last twelve years in the classroom, has a movable cart with working laptop computers for student use or a computer lab available for student use. After a short conference with students, they are ready to produce their final drafts. This assignment is ideal for a class booklet of diamond poems, so each may type and illustrate the poem, or students may like to write the poem in calligraphy or in fountain pen, or neatly in block letters.

I used to require manuscripts either handwritten in ink or typed in their final drafts, because students take pride in work that is carried through to the last draft and that reflects their voice and style as well as neatness and conformity to conventions. Nowadays perhaps the class types final drafts in a computer lab or at home; maybe a portable cart of laptops can be made available. Those finishing revisions early may use magazines (I recommend keeping lots of these in the classroom for student use) to make collages illustrating the words and ideas in their diamond poetry; students may also illustrate their poetry using colored pencils. For interest and choice, and if there is room to do so, teachers might consider setting up a table in the classroom with art supplies, colored paper, magazines to cut, scissors, glue, fountain pens, ink in various colors for the fountain pens, calligraphy booklets, typing paper, and perhaps an old typewriter. The most important factor for final drafts and publication is giving appropriate time to produce pieces of writing of which each young adolescent writer can be proud.

Sharing

Once the poetry has been written, schedule an Author's Chair time for those who wish to read and share their poem (and art) with the whole class. Making this voluntary at first, and encouraging class members' positive feedback and applause will result in more students sharing writing the next time around. Ask students to store their work in individual writing portfolios, and invite those who wish to hang them up for display to do so.

Written Reflection

This is a step that teachers may also try. They may wish to respond to such prompts as: Were students invited to draw upon their background knowledge of antonyms, synonyms, sensory description, parts of speech, and vocabulary in the prewriting portion of the lesson? Were the directions clear? Were students sufficiently independent so that a short conference was possible with each one? Did students interact respectfully and follow directions during their time in peer response groups? Students might be given some prompts such as these to inspire written reflection:

- What did you like best about the activity?
- What is most pleasing about your writing?
- How did the small-group activity turn out? Was it helpful?
- Were the directions clear?
- Did the activity assist in improving your writing? If so, how so?

The teacher might take time for the class to discuss some of the teacher and student reflections, including class suggestions for appropriate adjustments to one or more aspects of the lesson, such as clarification of directions, a possible advance organizer for prewriting, and the like. Following the discussion, ask writers to make sure their names and the date are noted at the top of their written reflections and then to store response sheets in portfolios.

Ralph Fletcher believes that students learn to write from teachers who design and employ methodology that includes their own expertise and knowledge of themselves as writers (Fletcher, 1993). Fletcher acknowledges that not all writers know how to teach and that it takes expertise to suggest the richness of options and to show how to grapple with a real subject that truly interests a writer. In order for effective teaching of writing to occur in a classroom, students must see processes modeled for them, such as how to handle word choices and select an appropriate order of paragraphs.

> ***When teachers talk with students about their own efforts and struggles as writers, young adolescents can recognize the value of patience and persistence as they struggle to craft their writing into finished products.***

Sheryl Lain, a veteran teacher, literacy coach, and National Writing Project fellow, says that she knew without anyone telling her that students who take part in writing workshop learn how to write (Lain, 2007). Inside many of us lives a combination of our favorite teachers who likely used a more traditional approach, but many of us also know that such an approach does not work for most young adolescents. As a young adolescent, I completed the assigned topic essays and practice exercises out of a grammar book, and I even diagrammed countless sentences with my two-sided red/blue pencil. I did these things for two reasons: (1) I was in a parochial school where those who followed the rules never saw the inside of the principal's office; and (2) I liked my teachers. Apparently, I liked them so much that I chose their field for a career. A considerable amount of my knowledge of how to write for many purposes in effective ways was, however, a result of trial-and-error, accomplished on my own.

Although teachers have good intentions when it comes to preparing students for writing examinations, sometimes called *writing-on-demand*, completing work out of fear and producing predictable, correct essays is no way for students to learn to write. I found this out during my first year at a university where I was one in a class of over a hundred in a lecture hall. I learned to hate writing in that kind of situation. Fortunately, I found comfort and relief in my personal poetry, much of which I have retained in personal journals, while I threw away the papers that received only a grade and such comments as the familiar "awk" or "frag." It seemed easy to fill out the workbook pages on sentence structure back in junior high school, but it was difficult to apply the necessary concepts without direct guidance, even when the only audience was the teacher.

It is essential for young adolescents to become acquainted with their *learning styles*, varied ways of learning such as visual, auditory, and kinesthetic approaches to processing information. Traditionally, students have been expected to learn primarily through the auditory mode by means of teacher talk and lecture. However, young adolescents acquire much more depth and reflective learning via a combination of these styles. Writers can also become acquainted with their writing voices; they must become one with their writing, so to speak. This entails being willing to take risks, choosing which pieces are private, which will be graded, and which will be shared with peers. Essential also is responsive discourse between the student and teacher and between the student and selected classroom peers during all stages of a piece of writing that has been chosen to present, publish, or take to a final draft. Students do want to please the teacher (and other adults), but their main focus should be on their individual understandings of what they are writing and on crafting it in each successive stage, composing and polishing it to its very best version. This focus can be facilitated by a watchful, knowledgeable teacher through conferencing and sometimes through asking questions that help the student look at a line or the organization of his or her piece of writing from a different viewpoint.

Donald M. Murray provides specific, supportive ways to confer with students throughout each of the stages of the writing process in his inspiring book, *Write to Learn* (Murray, 1984/2002). When teachers take on the roles of facilitators and writing coaches and provide helpful feedback rather than merely responding to editing and grading of the final piece of writing, students gain the needed control to see their writing process through from start to finish. For some young adolescents, this is a difficult prospect and may seem overwhelming. That is why it is so vital for teachers to provide time each day for students to write and to reflect upon what has been accomplished. In the writing workshop, the teacher helps students refine their thinking with organizational suggestions and provides thesauruses, dictionaries, and other references in order to help students choose just the right word, thus ensuring that they feel a personal investment and pride in each piece of their own written work. These are ways to create a safe, interdependent writing community. Students learn about writing and about taking part in a vibrant writing community when they witness their teacher working diligently alongside them, when they take time to check a reference, and when a class member is consulted for feedback.

Teachers who model positive writing practices are the sunshine and water that nourish the seedling student roots to form a strong, interdependent network.

Learning from Experience: Growing by Leaps and Bounds

Nancie Atwell reminds us to view young adolescents as individuals and to teach to the needs and intentions of each one (Atwell, 1998). But how do we discover each individual's needs and intentions? Along with keen powers of observation and continuous note-taking, teachers must understand the significance of social relationships – that these take on primary importance and that students want to be involved in all aspects of school work as their self-images lean toward being participants in adult reality. This means that teachers get into the routine of using adult terms in discussions with writers, modeling adult-like interactions with classmates, while at the same time attending to adolescent writers' developmental, emotional, and social issues. These behaviors not only show respect for the young adolescent, they also serve as suitable models for students' interactions with peers. Student communication with adults and peers in the writing workshop is part of a general series of steps in the writer's process; these interactions also serve as occasions to construct theories about writing within the social boundaries of a classroom community. As teachers place more responsibility and decision-making power into the hands of student writers, they must also be aware of students who are not as intrinsically motivated to accept responsibilities. While teachers plan for and look forward to more adult-like behaviors from students, they also need to be cognizant of students' intellectual needs for personal satisfaction, expression, writing community, and school accountability.

Middle-grades educators continue to struggle with ways to motivate their pupils to shine academically while assisting them with the dynamic changes that stem from puberty. Experts suggest that a mix of *rigor, relevance*, and *responsiveness* is critical for directing and supporting student learning, particularly that of high-risk students (Manzo, 2008). To accomplish this mix within a learner-centered writing model such as YAMM calls for keeping the bar high enough to reach standing on one's tiptoes, so-to-speak (*rigor*), while providing assistance for those who need a boost; keeping writing assignments personally meaningful to students through such elements as increased responsibility, engaging small-group projects, and choice (*relevance*); and being willing and able as the teacher to transition back to the role of leader at appropriate intervals (*responsiveness*). We don't do students any favors by offering only a "warm and fuzzy," unstructured free-for-all without the proper infusion of challenge, intervention, and consistent monitoring of academic success as well as withdrawal in young adolescents, as these serve to further the cause of a predictable and supportive classroom community. Once young adolescents truly understand their roles as integral parts of this community, they are apt to grow into first-rate writers.

Concluding Reflections on Chapter 2

To review, planting and nurturing the writing community is dependent upon the efforts teachers make to:

- Plan for and create opportunities for authentic conversation;
- Plan for and create a strong sense of safety, support, and belonging;
- Plan for and create a predictable writing and learning process which includes class norms for student behavior;
- Model their writing processes and talk about these with students; and
- Move easily between teaching roles with respect to rigor and relevance in lessons, and in responsiveness to students' needs as growing writers and adults-in-progress.

In Chapter 3, I turn to specific ways to plan high-interest, context-appropriate lessons and explore practices that support motivation in young adolescent writers. The richness of positive invitation as motivation, relevance in creating lesson plans, and responsiveness in getting to know students' strengths as well as their struggles are highlighted, and several illustrative lesson plans are included to help teachers sow the seeds of and nurture their own classroom writing communities.

3 Engaging Young Writers with Relevant, High-Interest Lessons

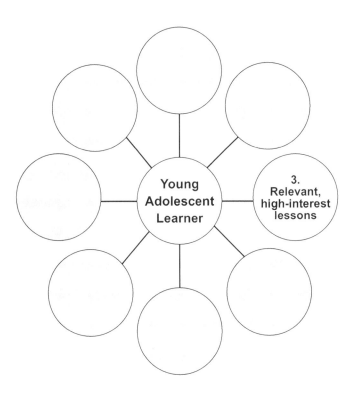

Feelings of worth can only flourish in an atmosphere where individual differences are appreciated, mistakes are tolerated, communication is open, and rules are flexible – the kind of atmosphere that is found in a nurturing family.
— Virginia Satir, *Peoplemaking* (Satir, 1972: 26)

Introductory Remarks to Chapter 3

In this chapter, I present an argument for development of intrinsic motivation, allowing for the realistic time and effort necessary for planting and sowing the concept with students, along with the extrinsic motivation that can be found in schools. Learner-centered teaching sets the stage for nurturing both kinds of motivation by cultivating what David McClelland (e.g. McClelland, 1972) refers to as *achievement motivation.* After a review of the evolving view of motivation theory, I present five keys for teachers to consider as they plan and teach relevant, high-interest lessons to their young adolescent writers.

Planting the Seeds of Engagement: Conscious Planning

Planning for and setting up a nurturing learning environment are best accomplished *in concert* with the writing curriculum. Therefore, becoming familiar with the required school, state, and national standards is a must; even more important is a teacher's willingness to interpret the standards to best fit teaching philosophy, style of teaching, and specific classroom needs. Specific classroom needs embrace the inclusion of planned, differentiated instruction that will likely engage most students with respect to abilities and learning styles. Young adolescent writers become engaged and in a sense blossom when their teachers are knowledgeable of and comfortable with the writing curriculum and then create lessons that bring out the best in each writer. As Satir states in the quotation above, differences are seen not as deficits but as accepted growth opportunities among group members – as in a supportive family. Variables such as students' prior knowledge, comfort levels with peers, and negative self-images can stand in the way of traditionally picture-perfect classroom gardens; however, the unique combinations of students' personalities along with their skill levels and diverse insights can promote exceptional growth in writing. Young adolescent writers' self-efficacy is thus influenced by the teachers' and school's acceptance and expertise in promoting each individual's writing excellence. Writing development therefore depends on a positive learning environment with high interest and high expectations for all. Engaging, rigorous lessons must be planned for young adolescent writers from beginning levels through those identified as gifted.

Norman Vincent Peale aptly linked achievement with one's ability and efforts to visualize the positive (Peale, 1982). Students study and are engaged by adults who exhibit confidence and success through their self-images. Students take note of teachers, parents, and other adults in their lives who not only "talk the talk" but also "walk the walk," that is, whose actions convey the same levels of encouragement and optimism as they espouse.

Teachers who model acceptance and high expectations communicate an understanding that each class member's writing growth holds equal importance and will be fairly nurtured.

The fair, nurturing environment is produced via a learner-centered approach that values students, their learning, and their motivation to grow into proficient writers and that offers continuous, concrete representations of what it means to be a writer. One approach to delivering a successful, relevant writing lesson is to start with the teacher as writer. The teacher can model how one becomes engaged with a topic and share personal struggles, expressing that which young adolescents long to hear: that all writers, even teachers and professional writers, toil. Teaching tales that include directed, positive steps to solve problems further illustrate the value of optimistic, determined effort. For example, one might share the process of research and writing necessary for a paper or project due for a graduate class or a curriculum committee, including working around and through limitations in order to finish work that reflects effort and quality.

In Chapter 1, I presented the Young Adolescent Motivation Model of Writing (YAMM), along with a call for attention to and acceptance of the whole child, including the many diverse characteristics and needs that are integral to each learner. That call itself is a challenge:

Young adolescents become better writers when teachers determine what students already know, what moves and engages them, and what each one can contribute to the classroom community.

In order to determine such information about students, teachers can:

- Listen to and note items of interest, verbal strengths, and areas of concern during class discussion and peer dialog;
- Assign and read (non-graded) journal entries focused on topics of self-efficacy;
- Talk to previous teachers to learn about each student they know;
- Peruse students' cumulative writing portfolios, if available;
- Ask students directly, while interacting one-on-one, about what they feel are their strengths as people and as writers; and
- Resist the impulse to consider only report card grades in learning about and evaluating students as individuals and as writers.

In order to determine the strengths, knowledge, interests, and opinions of developing young writers, it is vital to view the discovery of such information, and student writers themselves, as works in progress.

In addition, teachers and other adults need to keep in mind that the social, emotional, and physical make-up of each learner is in constant flux. This is where *flexibility* enters the planning picture. For example, teachers can model patience in their own writing processes when accessing references for clarification and to strengthen language as well as calling upon peers to give feedback. Making use of these relevant aspects of the writing process encourages flexibility and acceptance of one's own work, and young adolescents take note of these actions, likely replicating them while writing.

Holding individual conferences with students who have prepared questions and comments about their work for teacher response is an essential and also meaningful part of student engagement. A query such as "Jeremy, can you tell me what you felt and what particular character strengths you were going for when you crafted this hero?" is just as important as "Jeremy, the organization of the piece is truly well done! Are you happy with it, too?" In the first question, the student's process is the focus; in the second, praise is given with no specifics. While both will prompt positive feelings for Jeremy about the writing, his response to the process question may result in enlightenment for the teacher – in knowledge of how the student works; what mini-lessons need be planned for the student as well as the class; and what content, craft, and conventions Jeremy uses with facility and flair. If students are to become more proficient writers in their written assignments, on tests, and in their overall approach to writing, we must first lead them to a place where they feel confident and knowledgeable talking about their work.

Learner-Centered Motivation and Behaviorism in Conflict

Based on extensive study of and experience with young adolescents, I view motivation as a cognitive and affective call to action, determined by an intrinsic or extrinsic goal. Jacquelynne S. Eccles and Allan Wigfield note that the word motivation originates from the Latin root *mot*, meaning, "to move," implying action (Eccles and Wigfield, 2002: 110). Since young adolescents' active involvement in learning provides a means of investment in the learning process and some means of control of that process, it follows that students will be more intentionally moved to improve their writing when they actively participate in the process. But how much control do students actually feel they possess when it comes to their own writing?

Jere Brophy notes that students' motivational pursuits are related to their subjective, individual experiences, so that their intended efforts do not always mesh with teachers' more objective or standard, content-based plans (Brophy, 2010: 3). Many teachers must follow a writing curriculum that leaves little room for choice or for sharing control with students – unless those qualities are preplanned and built into instruction. Bernard Weiner, in "An Attributional Theory of Achievement Motivation and Emotion" (1985: 548), posits that the anticipation of success and its accompanying affect guide motivated behavior. With respect to young adolescents, this means that motivation is influenced by a range of social-emotional dynamics, including anger, gratitude, guilt, pride, and shame (Weiner, 1985: 548). It is natural that sharing certain areas of decision-making during the writing process yields some subjective feelings of control for students.

Eric M. Anderman and Martin L. Maehr report that the school environment contributes to several motivational problems experienced by young adolescents (Anderman and Maehr, 1994: 290). Educators' usual inclination, whether consciously or unconsciously, is to judge students' performance by measures of relative aptitude (ability) instead of by the amount or type of progress in learning; this practice tells students that unless they were born with great ability to achieve they are undervalued and the school has lower expectations for their success. Young adolescents in this undervalued position who are also troubled by lack of motivation are often doomed to underachieve; added to this sense of inevitability is a sense of urgency concerning young students who feel devalued. The increased consciousness of budding adulthood becomes a serious matter for teachers, parents, and students alike concerned with assisting undervalued and low-achieving learners toward a future career aspiration and high school graduation. To understand the causes and contexts of motivating young adolescent writers, it is appropriate to first consider views of motivation and how these have evolved.

Past views of motivation are rooted in basic drives and needs such as the requirements for food and human connection (Brophy, 2010: 3). The practice of withholding praise, support, and human connection for growing writers persists today: think time-out corners and detention rooms that become overused or classrooms conducted essentially in silence. Such practices affect young adolescents in especially harsh ways, given students' exceptional needs at this point in their lives for social connection and for building and maintaining confidence in themselves.

The methods of Behavioral psychologists, who introduced environmental stimuli such as an alarm, negative verbal responses, or the withholding of rewards to prompt preferred behavior patterns (Brophy, 2010: 4), also found their way into classrooms, although many might prefer not to view the educational stimuli in a parallel way. While reinforcing positive behavior is a very appropriate response to middle-grades writers, negative or no response resulting from teachers' anger, frustration, or strict focus on content rather than child, especially unaccompanied by helpful explanation and support, is most certainly not appropriate.

Even more unfortunate for young adolescent writers was the application of the information-processing model, which, as presented in Chapter 2, grew out of behaviorism. Students were taught primarily with the end product in mind, as though knowledge was composed of concrete components to be learned independently of, and often without connection to, other knowledge. Rather paradoxically, information was presented and minds were expected to understand and to make the connections – in other words, to independently process the information given.

Beyond the classroom, I have observed a growing trend by governmental officials, parents, and the mass media to direct mainly negative comments toward students' and teachers' academic efforts, particularly as standardized testing is increasingly applied to cure all classroom ills. It's no wonder that some students, particularly the most vulnerable, make conscious decisions to disengage, rather than become motivated to engage, for fear of more negative response from the educational system and from adults whom they view as threats. It's also a wonder that teachers continue to plant inspiration and sow the seeds of excellence and support among their students in the face of the ever louder call and the ever greater push for more instruction that aligns with high-stakes tests. This test-preparation instruction generally includes the unspoken expectation that teachers will respond first and foremost to what is lacking in student writing, a practice that tends to alienate rather than motivate young adult writers.

In many ways, I can identify with the young adolescents today who find themselves in traditional, content-centered rather than learner-centered classrooms. Having attended a middle school that reflected many information-processing model and behaviorist ideas, I was often disconnected and unmotivated to learn for any other reason than it was expected of me. I recall very few occasions of experiencing a connection among class assignments and real world contexts. As I later studied teaching methods and began work in my own classroom, I found that teachers could plan to discuss and show concretely as well as abstractly how sets of information and ideas relate to one another. Perhaps educators at that time and some even now view their teaching roles as largely non-facilitative. Perhaps too, some teachers have not considered motivation, or change in motivation, as part of a process highly dependent on many controllable factors within their reach, beginning with attention to learners' ongoing and complex learning processes. Rather than continue the unsuccessful practice of merely reteaching *information* (not *the whole learner*) to students who do not "get it" the first time, in much the same way as was initially delivered but perhaps with more intensity, why not try another approach? Since learners appear less motivated by efforts to instill a drive to learn *from the outside in*, why not consider motivation as a more *intrinsic* notion, driven by the needs and desires of the student? Eccles and Wigfield (2002: 110) view contemporary theories of motivation as centered on "the relation of beliefs, values, and goals with action," a view that coincides with David C. McClelland's attempt to find answers to the above question, as discussed further below.

Learning from Achievement Motivation Training in Schools

How and what motivates achievement has interested researchers for years and has also been of interest to teachers who are on the lookout for ways to motivate their pupils. Beginning in 1965, theories were developed that involved teaching children directly to reason, talk, and act as successful, achieving persons – referred to in the following studies as the *need achievement motive* or *N-Achievement*. David C. McClelland is among the most notable researchers to conduct studies concerning the subject of achievement motivation (e.g. McClelland, 1972; McClelland, Atkinson, Clark, and Lowell, 1976). Although this research was conducted almost 40 years ago, it has continuing value in the discussion of motivating writing.[1]

McClelland's early studies relate to the growth of achievement motivation in adults; he believed that development of motivation in children as a means of elevating school performance was also worth investigating (McClelland, 1972: 129). In "What is the Effect of Achievement Motivation Training in the Schools?" McClelland (1972) reports on two separate studies involving achievement motivation training in secondary schools and its effect upon students. As reviewed in McClelland (1972), McClelland of Harvard University headed one study funded by the Office of Education in 1965 and one study at George Washington University in St. Louis operated under the direction of Richard deCharms, who had visited Harvard and had assisted with planning of the research.

The studies employed different yet complementary tactics with respect to achievement motivation training. The Harvard group used outside trainers who presented separate motivation courses unrelated to classroom studies to a group of teachers over a period of time, with the thought that the training might indirectly influence their teaching. The Washington group offered motivation training to another group of teachers who incorporated the training strategies directly into topics of study and classroom lessons throughout the school year.

Achievement motivation training consisted of a complete course in thought and action, self-study, goal-setting and planning, and morale-building (McClelland, 1972: 137). Students who received training that involved all or most of the above components and who were taught by classroom teachers over the entire year as part of their regular curriculum (The Washington group) made the biggest strides in their academic achievement (McClelland, 1972: 137). In both site studies, students had a chance to set reasonable goals for themselves rather than the traditional practice of the teacher setting the goals; a level of autonomy thus existed for students in the areas of self-direction and self-reliance. Students who received regular, concrete feedback from teachers were able to approach work in other classroom contexts with more independence and less assistance from teachers. Classroom climate surveys completed following the training or at the end of the school year conveyed students' views of teachers' efforts to restructure their classroom so that they could be motivated to achieve. Analysis of the questionnaire responses showed a relationship between students' perceptions of teachers' efforts and elevated *N*-Achievement scores (McClelland, 1972: 140). In order to disseminate research and training methodology to schools, a training manual, *Teaching Achievement Motivation*, was written by Alfred S. Alschuler, Diane Tabor, and James M. McIntyre (Alschuler, Tabor, and McIntyre, 1970).

McClelland's colleague Richard deCharms examined classes whose teachers had no motivational training as a control group with respect to *origin climate*, a classroom environment where pupils feel more responsibility for learning and are rewarded for their decision-making. DeCharms found that some of the teachers who did not have specific motivational training nonetheless set up classrooms which fostered origin climate through motivation-oriented practices such as goal-setting and choice. These practices resulted in indications from students (via questionnaires) of increased confidence and control of their own learning (McClelland, 1972: 142). In general, McClelland (1972: 143–144) noted the teacher behaviors that are highly correlated with substantial student engagement as the following:

- *Getting attention:* teacher presents lessons with enthusiasm, provoking student thought in an assortment of learning experiences;
- *Insuring participation:* teacher keeps students continuously interested by requiring student responsibility for class discussion in the course of varied learning experiences; and
- *Making individuals feel accountable:* students perceive the teacher as one who knows what's going on at any given minute, is able to address more than one matter at a time, and holds all liable for their actions.

Classroom Practices That Nurture Motivation

While motivation training is effective in the classroom, it may not directly affect the level of achievement. McClelland (1972) concluded that achievement motivation training courses improve school learning by improving classroom atmosphere and teacher management skills. I have found that the above general learning concepts may also apply specifically to writing instruction, when fine-tuned for individual contexts. Additional highly effective techniques, which I have found to specifically affect students' general sense of motivation and engagement, are the following:

- Create a classroom climate that promotes a high degree of interaction with and among students;
- Promote learner responsibility with regard to goal-setting and feeling in control of their means of attaining these goals;
- Provide continuous informal and formal feedback;
- Include student surveys on climate to compare teacher with student perceptions, and adjust approach accordingly;
- Provide opportunities for choice, variety, and interactions with peers;
- Encourage student recognition for their efforts; and
- Plan achievement-oriented activities that invite students to develop and convey original, unique perspectives through writing.

The teacher behaviors and techniques listed by McClelland as well as those I have added above fit logically and easily into the Young Adolescent Motivation Model of Writing because they elevate learners to the central focus of classroom planning, teaching, activities, and assessments. As in the model, the above techniques consider the whole learner, encourage a sense of community, enhance attention, promote relevance in lessons, involve choice and critical thinking, and encourage formative, authentic feedback and assessment. These techniques are also consistent with the Six Keys to Nurturing Motivation in Relevant, High-Interest Lessons as described in the next section. Next, I present each of these keys to nurturing motivation, along with supportive, illustrative lessons, and I point out how easily the motivational teacher behaviors and techniques connect to each key.

Six Keys to Nurturing Motivation in Relevant, High-Interest Lessons

The six keys to nurturing motivation in young adolescent writers through relevant, high-interest lessons reside in the following elements: deep knowledge of students' strengths and struggles; nurturance of the growth of English language learners; flexible teaching roles; relational trust; active promotion of learners' self-efficacy and relevance through teachers' familiarity with popular culture; and application of appropriate, concrete learning strategies, especially with regard to gender.

1. Deep Knowledge of Students' Strengths and Struggles

Getting to Know the Whole Learner

Acceptance and deliberate planning for getting to know the whole learner will give young adolescents the chance for authentic relationships with teacher and peers. This can happen if teachers are aware of their unconscious typecasting of students, are open to the realistic composition of their classes, and seek to get to know each individual well.

Culturally diverse young adolescents are sometimes stereotyped as being either highly capable or probable failures. Gloria Houston points out in *How Writing Works* (Houston, 2004), that teachers as a group may view the world through *middle-class glasses*, perhaps expecting a certain sameness in student backgrounds and abilities, and so must be cognizant of this practice in their writing instruction. When this practice goes unchecked, classroom relationships may be damaged; the practice also results in teachers knowing students only superficially. Students' strengths may go unseen if they are from low-income families; by the same token, students' disabilities can be overlooked if they belong to an Asian culture, when the expectation is that their families promote education and so are often high achievers. It is also not unusual for talented students to go unnoticed when they do not fit the stereotype of a "good student."

Especially in the early days of the school year, teachers might find out which leisure time activities and interests their learners prefer and in which of these they participate. Ways to do so include conducting occasional interest surveys and providing time at the beginning or end of class to ask students if anyone has a special event to celebrate, such as a birthday, arrival of a new baby sister, or a sports game win. Perhaps some achievements have been ignored because we know very little about the particular field or area in which a student has excelled. Also potentially ignored are the student who has recently moved to the school and does not yet feel a sense of belonging; the student who comes to class hungry and cold, even if from an upper class family; and the student who is grieving over a divorce or the loss of a family member. Becoming aware of such significant background knowledge contributes to the depth of a teacher's growing body of information about each individual student, and this information and these experiences will likely spill over and into the young adolescents' writing and their behavior in school. In addition, such knowledge will inform teachers' actions toward and decisions about each young adolescent when planning instruction and assisting students with goal-setting.

Of course, many parents prefer that their children not make family information public, and so teachers are bound to respect their privacy (unless there is a possibility of abuse). If information is not given freely, teachers need not pry. Certainly, if a child appears upset and is tight-lipped about it, or if a young adolescent makes brief mention of an award or other cause for celebration, but does not care to elaborate when asked about this, the teacher must honor the student's wish. At times, students may not display as kind and respectful a temperament as is usual, or they may perhaps overreact to a peer's suggestions on a piece of their writing. It is not likely that all students will be forthcoming about their home, personal, or peer relationships, or about their academic circumstances – that is, not without a sense of acceptance and trust from the teacher. Negative reaction from a teacher in such cases may exacerbate an already negative situation. Teachers can give learners the benefit of the doubt and make light of occasional unexpected, negative behavior; it is better to be fair than "right," and positive, accepting teacher behaviors serve as bridges to understanding students as learners and as people.

Going from the Unknown to the Known by Acceptance and Celebration

How does a teacher go from visceral knowledge about individual students to deep knowledge about what each one brings to the writing community? An appropriate starting point is beginning with what is known. An open-minded educator who is accepting and aware of the rainbow of diversity and home languages is the teacher who celebrates these central features of their students' lives (Gay, 2010). The teacher who plans to get to know second language learners in the classroom invites them to share vocabulary from the home language, provides picture books and young adult novels set in the home countries which convey the true history and authentic representations of the places from which students originate, and asks which holidays are coming up so that the class can learn about the similarities as well as the differences in cultural practices represented in the student body. A bulletin board may be created specifically for celebration of national holidays and customary celebrations as well as those of other countries and cultures which students are connected to or interested in. With these and other behaviors and activities, the teacher shifts from a focus on factual knowledge to an incorporation of culture as an invitation to students to share, to teach, and to learn from each other.

2. Support for English Language Learners

Zoltan Dörnyei, a professor at the University of Nottingham in the United Kingdom whose research and writing focus on motivation of language learners, defines *individual differences* as "anything that marks a person as a distinct and unique human being" (Dörnyei, 2005: 3). Dörnyei (2005) says that because education generally takes place in groups of various kinds and sizes, group dynamics hold an important place in motivating the students who may speak a different language at home and are in the process of learning a new language at school. Therefore, setting up the classroom as an environment conducive to positive social interactions with peers is of particular importance (Dörnyei, 2005: 89). Dörnyei shines a realistic and positive light on individual differences that is relevant to groups of young adolescents, which regularly exhibit a high degree of diversity and whose members grow more confident and motivated when treated as unique, valuable individuals. Group norms are integral to motivation for all individual students, and thus norms must be applied equally in terms of respect for diverse cultures and inclusion of all learners.

In addition to adherence to norms, among the motivational teaching practices Dörnyei provides are the creation of a supportive atmosphere and appropriate teacher behavior (Dörnyei, 2001: 29). For example, while modeling standard English, teachers may also accept some non-standard or other varieties of English (e.g. from other countries), as learners progress toward integration of the standard variety into their language and writing. As English language learners (ELL) come to know English, they experience it as a multifaceted collection of what is spoken at home, regional dialects, idioms, and student slang, in addition to the Standard English they are expected to use in school. It is no wonder that they sometimes feel overwhelmed. Since my teaching district was very close to a large university near an agricultural area, I might welcome a Pakistani, Russian, or Chinese student, along with Hispanic students from migrant families, each new school year. My early days as a reading specialist and literacy coach taught me to provide scaffolding and flexibility to these new students attempting to cope in English by offering the opportunity to use their first language for prewriting and freewrites. Some worked this way at the beginning of the school year or when they entered the class later in the year, and those whose language was written in a different script soon drew the interest of classmates, who asked their new peers how to write and pronounce some words. In addition, teacher-planned, small-group and one-on-one literacy activities serve to clarify contexts and purposes of language for ELL students, further supporting their expanding capabilities as speakers, writers, and thinkers.

While some programs reinforcing grammar and spelling may provide useful practice for language learning, teachers can assist diverse learners by seeking out technology that encourages interactive learning beyond traditional programs of drill-and-practice (Zehr, 2007).

Young adolescents of all abilities and stages of language and writing development can benefit from collaborating with peers to help solve problems requiring the exploration of Web sources.

Peer interactions and students' daily progress in acquiring improved facility in language may be noted on state-of-the-class daily forms and kept nearby on a clipboard for easy access. These reports provide reminders of classroom occurrences and learning, thus adding depth to understanding each young adolescent. The act of pausing to document items of special note shows students a significant purpose for writing, that of recording, which can also be a learning tool. I used to notice my students watching me carrying out this writing function, and some asked for clipboards (which I supplied) so that they too could note their own progress. Others regularly opened their writing notebooks to document points from mini-lessons or ideas recorded on the daily form for the next day's work. Best of all, I observed an increase of concern for the achievement of their ELL peers. In the best-case scenario, the teacher sets the tone and models the behaviors that coincide with learner norms, and the students follow the lead. Culture, language, and customs that help to define an individual learner can become a joyful sense of pride for all.

Figure 3.1 shows a sample page from a state-of-the-class report early in the school year, when teachers are still assessing student needs and getting to know their work habits, engagement level in work, and special abilities that support their writing skills. There are sections on this sample page for noting each student's strengths and struggles, affective state, and possible supportive strategies.

	Aaron	Katie	LaTia	Pedro
Strengths	Fine motor skills Confidence with Spelling Verbal	Organization Descriptive vocabulary	Interacts well socially Uses references as needed	Problem-solver Loves tech and helping others
Struggles	Transitional words Conclusions	Hurries to finish first End punctuation	Helps others to finish and does not complete her work Begins new piece each day	Sequencing plot Sequence words in addition to *and* and *then*
Strategies to Support	Work with magazines: circle *Then, next, finally*, etc. Go to last draft of fable and see where adding one or more improves the meaning	Review exclamation and imperative sentences; find examples in book presently reading: *Hatchet* Ask what feeling or intention is expressed	Model patience; discuss draft of last piece: What does she like best? Why? Genre? What else is needed?	Use laptop and send document with plot of *The Giver*; ask to put plot points in order; bold or underline the words that tell reader what comes next
Affect	Open, willing	Impatient; wanted to talk about new dog and also get to lunch	Low, sad, hungry	Happy, highly engaged

State-of-the-Class Report for Class: 3/4 Date: 4/12/11 Dr. K.

Figure 3.1. Sample Early Page for State-of-the-Class Clipboard

The teacher can have several of the blank state-of-the-class sheets ready for the week, with a separate sheet for the entire class showing the date of the last individual student conference and the progress on a specific writing assignment. If students have a 20–30 minute block of writing time, the teacher can meet shortly with each as well as check back with students who may need additional assistance. If there are adult or high school volunteers helping in the classroom, they may keep their own clipboards with notes and also have access to the teacher's notes.

The practices of providing time to write each day as well as time for face-to-face discourse in ongoing mini-conferences are two of the most significant ways to find out what a child knows in terms of writing content, craft, and conventions.

When written and oral language experiences are built into a predictable schedule, students know that the teacher is interested in their work and that they will not have to sit for several minutes with hands raised, waiting for feedback. I often invited volunteer high school students and adults into the classroom to assist with this process. Teachers need to develop an efficient process that works for their situation, so they may want to consider such options as keeping a rotating list of class members with the goal of reaching four to six students each day, asking students to sign up on the board with the date and their specific question (this facilitates small-group conferences if similar topics are listed), and making the rounds to different students as needed.

3. Flexible Teaching Roles

Teachers' roles extend beyond the classroom, including planning and evaluation of students' work; preparation of materials for classes; and even meeting before or after school, or at a local coffee shop, a parent who cannot meet during regular school hours. As parents also take on new roles in their child's education, a teacher's flexibility in continuous communication can only help young adolescents. It is also part of a teacher's job to take rest and nourishment in order to be ready for the demands of the busy workdays. Lessons stand the best chance of engaging and motivating students when the teacher arrives at the classroom prepared – academically, physically, and emotionally.

Teacher Resiliency

It is clear that teachers lead, facilitate learning, communicate, and instruct; in one day, a classroom teacher will often assume these roles as well as those of curriculum specialist, motivator, guardian, counselor, disciplinarian, technology support person, and collaborator. In addition, a large number of teachers will identify themselves as university night students working on advanced degrees and special certifications, or as having other part-time jobs and occupations, including numerous family responsibilities.

I believe that a teacher's ability to assume flexible teaching roles, particularly with the support of school administration and the community, influences his or her positive attitude and longevity in the field of education. Unfortunately, far too often teachers are not given the support they need nor the recognition they deserve. However, many teachers are motivated by focusing their intellectual and creative efforts on their students, finding great satisfaction in the realization of learner progress. In a study of secondary vocational teachers, M. Craig Edwards and Gary E. Briers concluded that teacher views of self-preparedness and competence with regard to their roles predict work-related stress levels (Edwards and Briers, 2001: 9). Notably, there is a high occurrence of stress related to teacher overwork and the balance of career-family duties, resulting in a national average of nearly 50% of new teachers leaving within the first five years (Bartlett, 2004: 566). Balancing responsibilities within and outside of the classroom is of utmost importance for thriving as a teacher.

Most parents are appreciative of the extra effort their children's teachers put into their work, but some might write e-mails to vent their distress over an issue late at night, rather than make a phone call or set up a conference the following day, or they may present other challenges – partially, I think, because their roles, too, are changing.

As more and more school-related communications are delivered via e-mail or other electronic means, it becomes an important challenge to respond to these. By 2003, my last year in the classroom, I was receiving about ninety e-mails per day relating to school business, necessitating a much earlier arrival each day to address them. Most middle-grades teachers likely experience, on average, over 1,000 personal interactions a day, many face-to-face and many via digital media; therefore, a teacher's problem-solving and organizational skills must become fine-tuned to manage all of these different types of communications. Ultimately, teachers do so by adapting to and reshaping their classroom roles. Becky L. Bobek describes the adaptation as *teacher resiliency*, defining it as "the ability to adjust to varied situations and increase one's competence in the face of adverse conditions" (Bobek, 2002: 202). Bobek (2002: 2002) further states that teacher resiliency is vital to a teacher's decision to remain in the classroom as well as to student success.

Communicators and Collaborators

Since the addition of technologies to learning, many teachers communicate with their students by posting assignments, lesson plans, practice quizzes, and announcements online. Grades are documented in computer grading programs, and weekly progress reports and supplemental instruction for diverse learning styles are written and printed following the end of the school day. Some teachers set up online discussion groups, guidelines for peer response groups, and online journals.

Most times, there are not enough hours in the day to complete all of that is needed and is asked of the teacher. It used to nag at me when I was not able to meet with every student who needed a mini-conference on some problem area. Teachers who are willing to do so may communicate and work with students who seek one-on-one time beyond the class hours. I put this practice to work as a piloted, digital after-school program once the Internet became available to many students. For this informal program, I created an additional screen name for myself and announced in class that I could be reached for assistance by e-mail at home between the hours of 5–6 pm, Monday–Thursday. Through this program, I invited students who had not gotten a chance to talk with me during the day to send me an e-mail question regarding their work, as well as their piece of writing, which they could send as an attachment. Short, follow-up conferences the next class day often encouraged the less confident writer to persist in completion of work. This practice was very helpful in building positive relationships and to me seemed to be an excellent use of time.

If I happened to have extra time on a given day, I would send an Instant Message (IM) to a few students who were online, announcing that conferences were completed, and then exchange IMs briefly with them if they wished to chat with me informally. Today, teachers might conduct face-to-face conferences with students from home on computers via *Skype*, defined by BusinessDictionary.com as "free voice over internet protocol (VOIP) service that allows users to communicate across an Internet connection by combining voice, video, and instant messaging." Although valuable, endeavors like these may lead to overwork and teacher burnout, and so they must be carefully regulated.

In addition to these types of communication, because I worked in a small town and everyone seemed to know me or have had me as their teacher during the thirty years I worked in the middle school, I received many handwritten letters and cherished thank-you notes from families and community members, to which I responded whenever possible with a handwritten note. I enjoyed the chance to get out my fountain pen and attempted to always include an encouraging comment about a student. This took time, but it was time well spent. Even better was my attempt to make one or more phone calls per week passing positive information to parents about their children. One of my team-teaching colleagues had found that the effort had far-reaching, positive effects and had encouraged me to try it. I found that making time for the hand-written notes and phone calls home were both helpful and enjoyable for teacher and students alike, and I heartily recommend these types of communication. The impact of delivering upbeat messages factors strongly into efficient classroom management while generating information essential to planning. Parents are our partners, willing to collaborate if we let them; at the heart of teacher-parent communication and collaboration are the welfare of their young adolescent learners.

Reflective Thinkers

At the end of each day, it is my practice to reflect upon what I have learned, and I have made many useful discoveries over time. I have learned that much can be obtained from face-to-face meetings and conferences via the Internet that can be used for planning and facilitating instruction. I have also learned that developing young adolescent writers always have much to bring to the writing process, whether it is a keen sense of humor, the ability to write with a unique voice, or a unique view of a topic – along with skills and notions for which additional clarification and teaching is needed.

Teachers' reflective thought can take some of the guess work out of planning how to go about assisting students, whether in response to expanding knowledge of conventions such as how to correctly punctuate a compound sentence or how best to state views in persuasive essays. Building upon young adolescents' background knowledge of concepts such as correct use of verb tenses may be reviewed via mini-lessons (short lessons of about 10 minutes each focusing upon a specific teaching point). The lessons can be related to what students already know, assisting with their abilities to assimilate and accommodate knowledge into an overall, comprehensible system.

> ***All developing, writing-related skills become part of the root system for the growing writer as well as a foundation of support and motivation.***

Students of all abilities learn to formulate questions and take notes within the context of teachers' efforts in communicating and working with them. Teacher-student mini-conferences and daily opportunities to write serve as *scaffolds* – temporary, specialized instructional supports – which encourage writers to take additional responsibility for their learning. In these ways, the teacher, who has become a collaborator with students, gains a deeper knowledge of them as writers. Over time and with carefully planned efforts, young adolescent writers feel capable, confident, and motivated enough to push up through the fertile soil and sprout, elegant essays in hand! This is one of the rewards for teachers who tend their gardens well.

4. Relational Trust

Establishing Trust between Teacher and Student

I consider the growth of relational trust, a sense of purpose that we are all connected to one another as human beings, an additional benefit to building a deep knowledge of young adolescent learners. As a full realization and acceptance of each child, relational trust allows the teacher to put his or her ego aside and to convey to each learner that he or she is the significant focus, not the subject being taught.

Relational trust is a soft variable in that it cannot be objectively or concretely measured, but its existence within the classroom is felt all the same. When there is a relationship of trust that exists between teacher and student and a belief that when each puts forth the effort required to fulfill appropriate roles, success can be achieved. Teachers who wish to establish relational trust do not plan surprise quizzes to catch students off-guard, nor do they call on a student to read a literary passage aloud when he or she has yet to preread it or on any student whom the teacher knows or suspects to be unprepared. Teachers do establish relational trust by noting each effort and small success with praise and encouragement and by sticking up for a student who may be cornered by peers in the hall; by preparing students for the demands of standardized exams; by asking students to try again when they have not succeeded on a persuasive essay, and by modeling fair and respectful behavior and helpful responses while in peer groups. These are all ways to nurture relational trust.

As Parker Palmer states, "Good teaching cannot be reduced to technique; good teaching comes from the identity and integrity of the teacher" (Palmer, 1998: 10). Backed by both research and common sense, relational trust is grounded in respect, personal regard, and competence in core role responsibilities. Anthony Byrk and Barbara Schneider conducted an intensive study of Chicago elementary schools and found tremendous benefits of relational trust among teachers, students, parents, and administrators in terms of school reform (Byrk and Schneider, 2003). On a smaller scale, Chandra Muller explored the teacher-student relationship, concluding that teachers' levels of concern and caring positively affect achievement for at-risk adolescents (Muller, 2001). These studies support a strong belief in the importance of relationships and relational trust between teacher and students for enhancing students' academic motivation and success. Students who know they have their teachers' interest and support are indeed more likely to feel a sense of trust, which is likely to affect their motivation and success in learning. Relational trust contributes to the deep knowledge that children are not broken or incomplete machines to be fixed or problems to be solved, but rather budding plants to be nurtured and tended as they grow.

Illustrative Example: The Great Houdini

When our school moved to a newer building about midway through my teaching career, my classroom contained a small stage, perfect for theater and class presentations. My seventh grade students were asked to chose biographies of a famous scientist, author, artist, musician, movie star, or sports figure to research and write about, concentrating on personal characteristics and the steps required in a plan of hard work to achieve their subject's level of success. As a motivational device, the project would culminate in a videotaped presentation of students in costume for an audience of peers and invited adults. I allowed students to talk before and after their reading and work sessions, for the purpose of discussing ways they might impart the personalities of their subjects to their upcoming presentations. Hoping to inspire collaboration of ideas, I taught mini-lessons on research and peer discussions, and I reviewed the characteristics of various writing genres. Students could choose the genre of choice for their report, such as a ballad, a poem, a short play, or a traditional report form.

During three weeks of preparation, students convened in peer groups, writing drafts, revising, editing, typing, and deciding upon appropriate props and costumes. Those who wrote short plays asked classmates to take parts and perform, so there was a great deal of practicing; one student who wrote a ballad asked if she could also write the music and perform her piece via guitar. Predictably, not all of my creative young adolescents had as much poise or courage to go beyond sharing the story and success of their chosen famous person by donning a costume. One young man who reported on *The Great Houdini* asked a good friend from another class to assist him with a magic trick or two, but unfortunately experienced an embarrassing and frightening incident.

After witnessing young, enthusiastic adolescents' work as Marilyn Monroe, Jimmy Connors, Albert Einstein, Mother Theresa, President Reagan, Michael Jordan, Jacques Cousteau, and Kristy Yamaguchi, a student named Michael (Harry Houdini) and his assistant, Boris (James), appeared on stage. Michael and Boris presented their practiced trick that included water glasses and a straightjacket. All seemed to be going well until Harry placed Boris in what looked like real handcuffs. Now, I had not seen this trick as part of Michael's dress rehearsal the previous day, so I hoped he had practiced at home and also that he had a key if he needed one. (This was the early 1990s, prior to the 9–11 terrorist attacks which inspired schools to prohibit any type of weaponry in school, so the handcuffs as a prop may have been all right, had the trick worked.) But the trick did not work; Boris (James) got very agitated and began to scream, first for attention and then in real fear. While Michael frantically searched his pockets for the key, I escorted both students off stage, got the next presenter on stage, and placed my colleague whose class was in attendance in charge for the final presentation and dismissal to lunch. As Michael walked off the stage, it was evident that he had a slight mishap with his bladder – all of course, caught on tape. I told the tech aide to leave the videotape in my bottom drawer, which he did.

To a young adolescent, this is his worst nightmare. Hoping that few people if anyone saw the accident, I hurriedly walked the boys to the office, where the custodian removed the cuffs by using a tool that resembled a wire-cutter. Michael was then driven home and kindly given the rest of the day off.

Given our small town school, the story of Michael's mishap would spread as quickly as wildfire, so upon leaving the school office, I went to the front of the lunchroom to let everyone know that James was good as new. Also, since one of Michael's tricks involved water, I said something to the effect of, "Michael will be returning soon once he changes clothes; the glass of water must have spilled all over him." That may have been the case; I don't know, because when I returned to my classroom, the stage was back in order, chairs returned, and desks were back in their usual order.

Upon his return to school, many students viewed Michael with admiration and interest, along with a confidence I had not, heretofore, observed. Later, I fast-forwarded the videotape to Harry Houdini and stopped it just before the handcuffs incident, while the audience filled Michael's ears with applause for the trick with water. I then erased the next two minutes of confusion onstage, ending the tape with the final performance and a promise to make Friday our "movie day" to view and enjoy the presentations upon which so many had worked, making the event come together as a memorable classroom collaboration.

The happy ending came about when I read Michael's note to me in my yearbook that June, informing me that I was not only his favorite teacher, but also a genius and BEST teacher in the WORLD! Now, I would call that relational trust. Upon reflection on that day, I recognized that many of my middle school colleagues likely provided safety nets and kindnesses to save face and to build trust with their students, viewing it as just part of the job.

5. Self-Efficacy and Relevance through Popular Culture
Helping Students Set Individual Goals

Active involvement of students in their learning takes place in many ways; some a teacher can readily see, and others the teacher cannot. For example, planning exploratory and problem-solving activities with peers in small groups, discussed earlier, are concrete, observable ways to increase student involvement. Students, like us, often have an ongoing dialog in their heads concerning their own abilities, and this is part of what a teacher cannot see. Of course, teachers need to help support and develop students' sense of self-efficacy in all they do. Students unconsciously set negative goals when conscious, planned goal-setting is not part of their regular routine. Naturally, learners who have great support and motivation at home and those who are intrinsically motivated are likely to also unconsciously set high goals for themselves. While these self-set goals are often more helpful than ones set by others, at times students overestimate how much they should have learned or how far they should go within an unrealistic time frame. This differs from learners who are self-motivated to slightly overachieve and from learners who have excellent organizational and study habits. Therefore, we must plan for students' individual goal-setting, which presupposes that learners are aware of their strengths as well as their areas needing further work. In order to have this knowledge, time must be allotted for continual self-reflection and self-evaluation, for celebration and sharing of student-chosen best writing, and for peer feedback – all in addition to what the teacher can share evaluatively with individual students.

> *Young adolescents' goal-setting depends, to a great extent, upon their levels of reasoning as well as how they view themselves as learners.*

No one set of goals is relative to an entire class, so learners must be aware of what they know, document their progress with guidance from teachers, and then set short-term and long-term goals. Taking into account that students also have differing understandings of knowledge and concepts, it is well to talk about sample long-term goals and the short-term goals and steps needed to succeed in reaching these. Goals may be set in students' own words, once the teacher has decided how goals translate from the language of Common Core or other required standards into their writing classroom. (Common Core Standards developed for all public American schools are discussed in more detail in the Introduction.) Given that young adolescents are in the process of learning how to write well, their background knowledge as well as their developmental levels must be considered.

What Piaget Would Say

Piaget viewed children as continuously creating and recreating their own representations of reality and as attaining mental growth or reasoning levels by integrating simpler concepts into higher level concepts at each stage. Piaget (1969/2000) described three processes within this integration: *assimilation,* the process of bringing in new information; *accommodation,* adaptation of one's ways of thinking to new experiences; and *equilibration*, the interaction between bringing in new information and adapting to it. Depending upon what level of reasoning and which of these processes are at work in learners' thinking, goals may be realistic or unrealistic for them. Young adolescent writers can therefore benefit from some modeling within mini-lessons prior to attempting to set their short-term and long-term goals.

In arguing for a timetable established by nature for the development of children's abilities to think, Piaget and Inhelder (1969/2000: 4–12) outlined four stages in that development.

> The first is the *Sensorimotor Stage*, from birth to age 2 years, when children are concerned with mastering their own innate physical reflexes and extending them into pleasurable actions.

The second is the *Preoperational Stage*, from age two to age 6 or 7, when children learn to manipulate their environments symbolically through inner representations about the outside world and to represent objects with words and manipulate them mentally, just as they earlier manipulated the physical objects themselves.

The third stage is the *Concrete Operational Stage*, from ages 7 to 11 or 12, when children begin logical thought processes and classification of objects by their likenesses and differences, and when they begin to understand the concepts of time and number.

The final stage is the *Formal Operations Stage*, from approximately age 12 into adulthood, when young adolescents master logical thought and employ a more orderly process of thinking that allows for more flexible types of mental experimentation, and when they manipulate abstract ideas and understand the implications of their own thinking and that of others.

Through the years, researchers have studied Piagetian theory to find applications to teaching and learning. Patricia Kimberley Webb, one such researcher, states that learner involvement is mandatory if we accept Piaget's concept that each learning experience involves a restructuring of students' cognitive schemas (Webb, 1980). While many implications of Piaget's work have been found to apply to teaching and learning, here I argue strongly for the necessity of active student involvement and for the consideration of young adolescents' levels of reasoning in their goal-setting.

Some students may never reach the formal operations stage due to learning or other types of disabilities. In consideration of special education students in class, teachers can support their growth in writing with fewer verbal directions, more hands-on experiences, and increased response time, and by assisting in their feeling of safety and developing self-efficacy. We must remember that each student has capabilities and that many are diamonds in the rough or still seedlings in the sense of their future blossoming. Also, regardless of strengths and struggles, if students are to truly become more proficient writers, they must take responsibility in helping to set their goals, and these goals must be individually realistic.

Popular Culture as Relevance in Goal-Setting

I have long noted that students are more attentive when the teacher stays current with what is relevant to them. This is the students' culture, generally also referred to as *popular culture*, including popular music, television, and interactive media sites, to note just a few examples. Figure 3.2 below, written as a dialog, is an example in the form of class discussion about short-term goals with respect to their use of IMs and text messages (via cell phones), both relevant components of their popular culture.

The sample dialog would take about ten minutes, and it could continue with several additional short-term goal statements from individuals and pairs written on the board for all to see. Josh, the student who said he usually did not have a plan for research and ended up just surfing the Web, may have found a great system for himself. In listing his short-term goals for going about researching topics on the Web, he may also be generating a set of directions for himself that he could print out and post near his computer as concrete reminders.

> **Getting young adolescents to think about what a next step would be, once the original short-term goal has been reached, is integral to setting up long-term goals.**

An idea for a mini-lesson, perhaps the following day, could include asking students to reread and think about the short-term goals listed, and then reflect on what these short-term goals might add up to as a long-term goal, in a time frame of weeks, months, or even a semester or academic year. It is important to have young, sometimes impatient, young adolescent learners list several

Dr. K: I have been noticing lately, while exchanging IMs and texting with friends and students, that students use more digital slang and, in general, spell out their conversations with far fewer full words than adults.

Marie: Yeah, it's called being able to respond fast, Dr. K! Also, our parents sometimes look at our IMs and texts over our shoulders, so it's good to talk in code.

Dr. K: Oh, you mean like, "PIR!" meaning, "Parent in the room?"

Marie: Exactly! Also, just being able to leave out words and insert others, like "w/" in place of *with* is helpful. You know, my friends aren't going to correct my spelling!

Josh: That's for sure! I also use a few different screen names, and I block people I don't want to talk to when online.

Dr. K: I'll bet a lot of new words have sprung up and have come into use on the Web in the past year that may have been added to the dictionary.

Marie: You mean, like the REAL hardback dictionary, not the online one?

Dr. K: Yes! It would be fun to see if we can not only think of words we have seen or have used online or text messages by phone (that are printable and in good taste) but also look for some new ones that may have been added officially to the English language. Are you guys up for a little research and discussion?

Josh: Yeah, I need to work on my research skills. I usually just log on and start surfing the Web, and it takes me a long time to find what I am looking for, because I don't have a goal – or I forget what it is and just start looking at favorite sites until someone IMs me or texts me!

Dr. K: That's what I'm talking about! Let's think of how we would state a goal for those who want to improve research skills and are looking to get organized. Mickie, do you want to give it a try?

Mickie: How about…. Oh, well, I don't actually have a clear goal yet.

Dr. K: How about if we pair off first, brainstorm with a partner one or more words from IMs and the general use of the Internet that you believe may have recently found their way into our language, and then write down a sentence specifically stating how you may want to begin researching the words. Josh, you could make your goal more specific yet and write a sentence about what you will do first, before you begin surfing the Web.

Josh: OK, I will write a list in order. How's that?

Dr. K: That works!

(Students pair up; note a few words they think may have been added to the dictionary, and jot down a goal statement for beginning research.)

Amy: Dr. K! This is kind of stupid. Most of us will Google Wikipedia.com and see what's there first.

Dr. K: Try another way to go about it. Wikipedia.com is a collection of anyone's ideas of "facts." Like most wikis, all you need is the password to add information to a page. You want the <u>truth</u>! You know, facts that can be documented in several places.

Amy: I see what you mean!

RELEVANT, HIGH-INTEREST LESSONS   115

> (After a few minutes, when most pairs look like they have their task completed, continue the class discussion.)
>
> **Dr. K:** Elliot and Josh, are you ready to share what you came up with?
>
> **Elliot:** OK, here are some terms we think may be in the dictionary: *mouse potato, mashed up,* and *spy ware.* Josh will share his goal.
>
> **Josh:** To begin researching, I will write down what I already know about a subject, and then do a Google search with two or more key words, and check several sites to document.
>
> **Dr. K:** Elliott, you may have some winners! And Josh, you have stated an excellent short-term goal. What would you do next, once you have located some information?
>
> **Josh:** I will write the info when using the Inspiration program to take notes or else in my notebook to support what I already know, and then I will list what I do not know.
>
> **Dr. K:** That's great! You can even use the two goals you have stated as two short-term goals, and like you said, write a few more, numbering them in the order you think would work for you. A long-term goal may be: I will use two or more appropriate Web sites or other references to document answers to a research question. Or: I will use my findings to add meaning, detail, and support to my writing.
>
> **Dr. K:** All right, now let's take a look at some other statements of short-term goals. Susan and Sheila, what did you find?

Figure 3.2. Classroom Discussion about Goal-Setting

short-term, doable goals prior to listing a long-term goal, such as writing an outstanding report which could win an award or a grade of "A." Taking time to assist students with imagining short steps that build toward a larger goal within reach is an excellent way to further their active classroom involvement.

An Invitation to Set Goals: The Stairway

The invitation to set goals for students may take place within a conversation, and it may sound something like this:

> "It is still very early in the semester. Once you have accomplished the two short-term goals, which you may need to practice each day before they actually become part of your research or study habits, what might you like your writing to look like or show by the end of the semester?"

"How about if you place the short-term goals you have listed so far onto a set of stair steps, which you may draw in your writing notebook for future reference. Leave a few blank steps. Now think about a bigger goal that may take until semester's end to reach, and note that at the top of the steps, which we will call the "Stairway to ___ (fill in your name) __'s Heavenly Writing. For example, a bigger goal that would take a series of small steps for me at your age may have been *highly improved spelling.* It may sound small, but while I was great at making lists of spelling words, the correct spellings did not always find their way into my early writing drafts. That might serve as a long-term goal. Another short-term goal I might have added to my set of stair steps could be *more frequent use of references to check words about which I am unsure.*"

"So, for this part, I invite you to select a writing goal for yourself to place at the top of your Stairway to Heavenly Writing. Then take some time to think about what steps are needed in between the ground floor and the top of the stairs, and list a couple more. These are your short-term goals. Let's take some time to reflect and write, and I will do the same, as I have a few ideas in mind for improving my writing. Let me know if you have any questions. Let's begin now."

The sample dialog, which makes use of figurative language, imaging, and the stairway image, illustrates the connection between shorter and longer-term goals. The upbeat tone with which the teacher conducts a short lesson and the examples provided for students demonstrate both an invitation to students as well as the fact that goal-setting is a priority.

Nurturing Response through Relevant Mass Media

Like my school days in the 1960s, students today are affected by and can become engaged with the power of history-making world events. The election and inauguration of Barak Obama marks the first time since the War in Vietnam that a President has taken office while the United States is at war. Election night news broadcasts employed holographic images, three-dimensional pictures and interviews, and an acceptance speech unlike any other in the history of American politics, given the election of an African American President and the digital and media enhancement delivered to massive audiences, both live and distant.

Following the celebration and wonder of a new Presidency, Mr. Obama's work has included the rebuilding of global relations, reform of the health care system, and financial reform. For the future, the President will work to bring the wars in Iraq and Afghanistan to an end while committing aid to other countries in states of conflict or disaster. In addition, the President will work to improve the worst economy since the Great Depression, find common ground within a partisan U. S. Congress, create an equitable system of taxation, and manage sustainability within the global environment. It can all be rather overwhelming for students to know that they live in the most powerful and richest country in the world, which is yet a country beset by what appear to be monumental problems. Many young adolescents are directly affected by one or more of these issues, whether they have a family member or friend in the armed forces, one or more of their parents has taken a pay cut or has lost a job, a home has been foreclosed, a grandparent cannot get necessary medical treatment, or there is less food on the table and less money in the bank than was the case a few years ago. Add these scenarios to the daily grind and challenges of being a middle school student, and youngsters have more than enough genuine subjects about which to write. Some young adolescents may not, as a rule, read, converse, or even view information (i.e. on television or the Internet) about local, state, national, and/or global issues. Some or most of students' information about the world is incomplete, as it may come from the opinions of friends and family or the viewing of headlines on their computer home pages. What can teachers do to open up the world for young adolescent writers? Lessons can be planned to include political or environmental issues, which provide opportunities for students to actively build knowledge and understanding while forming opinions. More fully formed opinions may then take shape during conversation with peers and through thoughtful written response. Such discourse and writing can also serve as stress-relievers for young adolescents struggling to understand issues and problems for which there are no easy solutions.

The Role of Relevance in Motivation

Another note about the importance of popular culture as it relates to motivating student writers is in order. As is sometimes the case, that which appears to have personal relevance is often that which most strongly motivates writers. For example, music has always been important to me, and even as an adult I listen to pop, blues, country, and rock music. Like many others, I view some music as poetry. As is the case with many young adolescents, song lyrics can soothe, help express what sometimes cannot be put into words, or even assist with releasing tension. So when I get the chance, I share my love of music with anyone who will listen to music with me. In conversation with students, some will respond with a song title and why it is significant – that is, what need or purpose the song may serve for them. As quickwrites, teachers can share an opinion of a song and then ask students to do the same with a song or poem of their choice in a short, 5-minute writing task. While many times quickwrites are not shared, students will want to share some of their responses to this one. At times, it is in listening to others that we learn the most about them – their preferred styles of music and verse, what makes them tick, and even a recognition that writing has many worthy purposes. My job has always included learning what is necessary to bring about desired outcomes in my job. Perhaps I'd rather not hear that another sequel to the teen films *Halloween* (www.halloweenmovies.com/) or *High School Musical* (tv.disney.go.com/disneychannel/.../highschoolmusical/) has been released, but these films have meaning for many young adolescents. I can teach patience, goal-setting, the content and craft of writing, and how to make appropriate choices; students and what is important to them as human beings continually inform my teaching.

Besides their social relationships with peers, students find meaning, comfort, and solace in music, literature, and the life stories of others portrayed in film and television.

Familiarity with past, present, and evolving popular culture can therefore be viewed as another flexible role for teachers. Education, like music and film, needs to reflect society and thus learners' experiences that influence such important aspects of their lives as conversations, their relationships with family and friends, and, we hope, their writing.

Young adolescent writers' identification with topics of interest and appeal often become those that they share with peers via spoken conversation and e-mail, feeding their curiosity and fueling extended concentration. Young adolescents who enjoy gaming may collect particular trading cards; those who are keen on the films *Twilight, Eclipse,* and *New Moon*, all based on Stephanie Meyer's books, may be drawn to seek new and extended information about the literary and film characters, future Twilight series titles, or perhaps vampires in general. The practice of "writing about what you know" is especially helpful to students in setting short-term goals because students become motivated when their studies, particularly their research and writing, reflect what they know – and what they know most is how communication in its human forms through discourse, the Internet, and through music, video games, and films influences them and moves them to action. Teachers who desire to motivate young adolescent writers need to take advantage of this knowledge and build it into their roles as educators and as writers.

Additional relevant topics about which students might be motivated to write are:

- How can adults help with teen grief?
- How might I respond to a natural disaster such as a forest fire, tornado, or volcanic eruption if I were a government or other official?

- Divorce and separation of parents: how does this affect my brothers, sisters, and me? Will I have any say? How much is out of my control?
- After-school free time: outside or inside? Active or passive? How does it differ from parents' experience?
- Should students wear uniforms? If so, why? If not, why not?
- Should everyone who wants to be on a team be allowed to play?
- Lowering the voting age to 18: how might one vote make a difference?
- The Internet: what are reasonable limits for students?
- Why I should win *American Idol*, *Dancing with the Stars*, *Survivor*, or some other television contest
- Ten qualities of a friend
- Where I would most like to travel for pleasure and for learning about my genealogy
- The best gift I have ever given
- Best arguments for getting and keeping a pet

6. *Concrete Learning Strategies with Appropriate Regard for Gender*

Creating a Fair Classroom Environment for Girls and Boys

During the past twenty-five years, curriculum innovation has included expanding roles and opportunities for girls and women in literature and within texts and other educational media, especially in the areas of mathematics and the sciences, where males have often dominated. Also, increased knowledge about engaging and assisting adolescent boys socially and academically has become available.

Mary Pipher's New York Times bestseller, *Reviving Ophelia: Saving the Selves of Adolescent Girls* (Pipher, 1995), placed new emphasis on gender bias and girls' rights to a gender-free existence, telling some striking tales of girls whose physical existence has been endangered. Pipher (1995: 12, 267) refers to the "girl-poisoning" culture of drinking, uncomfortable high fashion, and sexist connotations about what it means to be social and have friends; the struggle to stay true to oneself may cause girls to withdraw. Pipher (1995: 158) notes that, regardless of the progress of feminism, adolescent girls continue to suffer abuse and increased depression, and girls resort to self-hurt such as anorexia. Pipher nevertheless offers some suggestions for empowering young women, such as providing strong female role models and mentors for adolescent girls; invitations to take part in traditionally male fields such as engineering, technology, and architecture; and celebrating each intellectual, social, and emotional triumph, small or large, in order to build future successes. Sherrie A. Inness maintains that the portrayal of females in books influences a young adolescent girl's self-image; from these she forms a picture of her worth, pride, and intellectual ability and potential (Inness, 1998: 166). Images in other media such as film and advertisements on television; degrading lyrics in music; and unkind photos, gossip, and lies or criticism that appears on hand-held, digital media such as cell phones also affect a young adolescent girl's view of herself.

The book *Strong, Smart,* and *Bold: Empowering Girls for Lives* (Fine, 2001) begins by asking the reader to imagine a world where a girl is not limited by the fact that she is female. Texts such as these and a plethora of scientific and psychological studies have challenged long-held stereotypes and have underscored the necessity of fair and equal treatment of students inside and outside of the classroom.

Developmental Differences between Boys and Girls

So far, the accent has been on girls and women, but recently, the tables have been turned, with a major curriculum focus on boys' learning gap in reading and writing. Applying brain-based gender research related to academic performance and classroom behavior, researchers have determined that girls put forth more time and effort in studying than boys, and they enroll in more difficult courses in the middle grades, where choice is involved. Boys are more competitive and more physically antagonistic, and they choose behaviors that draw them into the spotlight most often. Differences between the ways girls and boys learn are not indicative of gender superiority or inferiority, and brain differences are best perceived as a spectrum (Gurian and Ballew, 2003: 16).

Because females' brains mature more quickly than those of males, girls tend to attain composite verbal skills a year earlier on average, exhibiting larger vocabularies and more advanced linguistic knowledge of grammar than boys by the time they reach school. The *corpus callosum*, the bundle of nerves connecting the right and left hemispheres of the brain, is about 20 per cent larger in females, and there is more and quicker development in the prefrontal lobes, where emotion is regulated and decision-making occurs (Gurian and Ballew, 2003: 27). These physical and emotional development patterns partially contribute to why girls are about one and a half years ahead of boys in reading and language arts. Since boys trail girls in writing and reading, many educators, myself included, feel that the focus ought to shift from advocacy of science and mathematical skills for girls to support for boys in writing and reading.

In addition, female learners emphasize left-hemisphere, conceptual development and do not have as many attention problems as do male learners. Females also secrete more *serotonin*, a hormone that tends to stabilize emotions, than males, and so are less inclined to act up in class. In general, males compartmentalize knowledge within different areas of the brain rather than making holistic application among the various facts and concepts they have learned and suffer more learning disorders than girls do (Gurian and Ballew, 2003: 60). Two-thirds or more of the cases of learning disabilities in the average classroom are males, many of whom have been misdiagnosed as having Attention Deficit (Hyperactivity) Disorder (ADD/ADHD), a neurological condition that makes it difficult for people to inhibit their spontaneous responses – responses that can involve movement, speech, and attentiveness.

Writing instruction and experiences that require boys to be more mentally, physically, and socially active positively affect their writing skills (Gurian and Ballew, 2003: 113).

In addition, especially during the early teen years, the maturity gap between males and females becomes more obvious, and can contribute to learners' difficulties and so should also be a factor in teacher planning. Girls thrive in an environment which lends itself to their taking control of their own learning, once given boundaries and directions, with little external authority or discipline, whereas many boys, whose hormones are peaking, work best with strong authority and discipline to assist them until they learn to manage themselves. Planning for and interacting with young adolescents is made more difficult because most teacher education programs offer no training in brain development or male-female differences. Thus, in most cases, there exists a cultural gender bias within education.

Directions for Educators

Since boys get called upon more often and command more discussions, the voices of girls can be silenced, particularly when it comes to debates and persuasive arguments. Female students tend to avoid argumentative conversations, having been reinforced in less confrontational behaviors and having learned to be more accommodating. Along with lack of training for educators, the preponderance of male role models in historically patriarchal societies rather than female role models in literature may unconsciously lead males to assume they are inherently privileged. Instead, teachers may focus on planning instruction with texts and other resources reflective of strong women and their growing move into higher paying positions as well as their roles as heads of families.

> ***More attention to treatment of gender in classrooms enlightens teachers and students, motivates reflection, and encourages equal and appropriate treatment of all.***

Provision of activities that lend themselves to all learning styles can assist both genders. Since high-interest, relevant teaching practices influence young adolescents' motivation to write, let's first look at some specific, best practice for boys.

Nurturing the Writing of Young Adolescent Boys

Ralph Fletcher suggests some specific ways for teachers to encourage boys and to support their writing (Fletcher, 2006). He encourages teachers to accept boys' more violent writing, not necessarily inappropriate language or themes, but to allow expression of how they play and what fills their heads. Generally, female teachers do not feel comfortable with boys' war stories, but as Fletcher says, "That's where they live!" (Fletcher, 2006: 49). While most boys who experience a guns and war stage grow out of it, giving them some choice and encouraging writing about topics to which they feel drawn goes a long way toward engaging and motivating young adolescent males.

Fletcher (2006) lists several topics that may interest young adolescent boys; these tend to be heavily action-packed and not especially solicitous. Some of these are: aliens, monsters, military situations, hero stories, tough characters, robots destroying evil characters, video games, driving fast cars, dislike for school, and fantasy worlds. Boys' focus in stories at this age is on action, not conversation, because boys are generally not interested in people's innermost thoughts and secrets.

To illustrate boys' writing, one of the best stories written by an otherwise quiet, uninvolved student emerged when I asked students to write children's stories and illustrate them as final projects at the end of their sixth grade year. We were to read these to second and third grade classes, so we talked a lot about our audience. Reed had terrible handwriting, and the first time I met with him in conference, all I could decipher was that the story seemed to be set in the future in outer space. It was not until a little later, when I typed his first draft for him, that I noticed that nearly the entire text was filled with conflict and destruction, space ships blowing up, and the forces of evil being smashed to bits. What made Reed's story engaging was his attention to details and sensory description. There were several comic-book-like sounds throughout the text like <BOOM! >, <KABOOM! >, and <POW! >. Also, since Reed's drawings were not very clear, I introduced him to a graphic arts program by means of which he could create the illustrations on his computer screen. Needless to say, this was his favorite piece of writing all year, and in a student-led conference in discussion of his portfolio with his parents, he proudly reached for this story he had written and illustrated, and he read each word with amazing emotion and phrasing. He had practiced it over and over in front of the mirror, his mother had said, prior to reading it to a group of third grade boys, who were, by the way, spellbound by the story and the author.

In *Going with the Flow: How to Engage Boys (and Girls) in Their Literary Learning* (Smith and Wilhelm, 2006), authors Michael W. Smith and Jeffrey D. Wilhelm discuss many kinds of supportive pedagogy for young adolescents who attempt to make meaning while reading and in preparation for writing response to textbooks. Given the increasing rate of student dropout and standardized tests requiring students to apply what they have read, a major classroom goal for teachers might be for students to convey their comprehension of texts through written response.

Smith and Wilhelm (2006) write of students' *transference of knowledge*. As educators, we want to plan for our students to transfer what they have read and learned from non-fiction as well as fiction texts in our classes. To make this transference of knowledge requires its connection to their personal experiences and then to their lives. While the transference of knowledge is obviously of great importance, research findings over the past nearly 100 years demonstrate that educators and institutions have not, for the most part, successfully supported students' transference of knowledge (Haskell, 2000). Robert Haskell concludes that the transfer of knowledge cannot be accomplished without specific conditions being met. All of the conditions are within the control of teachers, if only teachers make them a major focus and consciously plan for these (Haskell, 2000: 26):

- Students must have an understanding of both concrete as well as abstract, conceptual knowledge to be transferred;
- Teachers must promote a classroom culture of transfer through practice and modeling of related behaviors.

In providing for abstract, higher-order thinking and knowledge transfer, teachers can build inquiry, exploration, and high-interest lessons that increase students' depth of knowledge. In general, units of study that bridge and transfer information from school to relevant, real-world contexts will assist knowledge transfer. Examples include the planning of lessons requiring substantive conversation and writing about characters in students' reading to whom they can relate; lessons with opportunities to pose questions and search for answers about issues such as the future of the space program, physical fitness, national sports and the use of steroids, alternatives to fossil fuels, and the use of digital, hand-held devices for educational purposes; and lessons that draw upon students' real-life experiences with step-families, car travel mishaps, the loss of a best friend, thoughts about politics, and religious choice.

Empowering Young Adolescent Voices through Concrete Norms

Although the dominant mode of composition in middle school classrooms may be labeled "assign and assess," this method lacks the spirit and engagement that students need to get into what Smith and Wilhelm (2006) refer to as the conditions of "flow experiences," a phrase first coined by Mihaly Csikszentmihalyi (Csikszentmihalyi, 1990). Flow experiences are related to highly engaging behaviors and settings that motivate happiness and self-confidence; students' focused practice following teachers' continual, specific feedback on writing competence might produce flow experiences. Smith and Wilhelm say that students often do not feel competent because they have not mastered the content and subject knowledge about which they are assigned to write. Also, young adolescent writers have not always been made aware of the norms for success on an assignment. I advise specificity on matters like grammatical conventions and the areas of content on which students have excelled, with teacher comments supportive of writers' word choice and individual writing styles. While rubrics are designed to clarify desired conventions and craft, they can also stifle student voice and connection to topic, in the attempt to present standard forms that also may impede the writer's style. Young adolescent writers benefit from writing instruction that reviews and builds upon the qualities of writing within specific genres.

Adolescent learners can become frustrated rather quickly unless they have continuous, informal feedback from peers and the teacher and unless they are sure they are on the right track. Students appreciate the availability of honest, concrete feedback built into their writing process. Once young adolescent learners are sure they have used the correct form of an assigned genre, they can move forward with energy, voice, and style, such as humor or metaphor. In other words, once students know they have correctly applied generic form to a given writing assignment, they can concentrate on crafting the content to reflect their individuality and writing style. Young adolescents revel in the freedom to express themselves when given adequate direction and encouragement, often resulting in their writing growth. In such a case, feedback is nurturing support and assists writers with the development of confidence in their writing abilities and with connections to peers, teacher, audience, and the written work itself.

Arranging for Relevance: Favorite Place Lesson

Young writers, like most of us, build confidence with success. When a special, personal interest is the focus of an assignment, supportive mini-lessons are planned, and boundaries are broadened, young adolescent writers often find success. Success can be further enhanced with adequate time to write, teacher and peer response, and the addition of a treasured object. In Figure 3.3 below, I present a flexible lesson template designed to provide writers with some prewriting considerations and related writing assignment goals.

The general idea for the lesson came from an end-of-year informal evaluation of student writing by the English language arts

I. **Student Goals**
   - Recognize strong leads using *varied sentence structure*, *sensory description*, and *writer's voice in mentor texts*.
   - Create a *strong lead* (Begin with a question, a phrase, a dialog, or another way to engage the reader).
   - *Include sensory description* (Try imagery, or ask yourself: "In this place, what do I hear? Smell? See? Feel? Touch? Taste?").
   - *Convey voice* in descriptions of favorite place (Try reading the writing aloud to see if it sounds like you could be talking; try humor or infuse the words with your emotions in memories of people, places, music, and objects that remind you of or connect you to the place).
   - *Construct or find an illustration* – hand-made, hard copy, or digital text/graphic; song lyrics; or an object that helps connect the writer to his or her favorite place.

II. **Prewriting Questions to Consider**
   - Is there a special spot you like to go to think?
   - How do you feel when you are there? Can you smell or hear anything?
   - Why do you like to spend time in this place?
   - At what times do you go to your special place?
   - What specific feelings are associated with this place?

III. **Suggested Approaches to Consider**
   - Describe a place where you go that helps you work out a problem, gives you comfort, peace, enjoyment, or just time to think.
   - Recall and tell about a time you went to your favorite place and why.
   - Explain why your spot is so special to you. Describe the positive aspects of this place using your senses, including your sense of touch and positive emotions.
   - Use examples in your writing from real life, from what you have read or viewed, or from your imagination, remembering that your audience includes both students and adults.

Adapted from Profiles in Writing 2000 –2003 Student Copy, Williamston (Michigan) Middle School Informal Writing Assessment. Used with permission from 2003 Sixth Grade English Language Arts Teaching Team.

Figure 3.3. Writing Guide for Students – Favorite Place Lesson

teachers in my sixth grade team as a way to provide information about students' writing abilities to the seventh grade teachers, along with sample student texts that could be used as models in the next academic year. My colleagues and I applied state standards in a holistic rubric of our creation, removing names from students' works but identifying them by teacher. While teaching preservice teachers at the university level, I shared the assignment and student writing samples to illustrate the range in writing abilities among students. Here I present a writing workshop experience designed to take place over 2-3 class hours, complete with mini-lessons, writing guide for students, a student writing sample, and an informal assessment focused on crafting strong narrative introductions, addition of effective sensory description, and conveyance of writer's voice.

Students show evidence of learning throughout the lesson, and the final writing serves as an authentic, formative assessment. Through the writing, the teacher should be able to note the students' understanding of the use of sensory description in personal narrative and sense of place. Students taking part in a lesson such as this will likely be highly engaged with the topic and the use of both literature and art.

Within prewriting activities and mini-lessons, I chose to include older, partially illustrated copies of the classic novels *Little Women* (Alcott, 1955) and *Kidnapped* (Stevenson, 1926), along with some children's books with beautiful illustrations to assist writers' visual connections and eventual translation of settings to written language. Because students benefit from additional guidance, for this particular writing activity, I include a writing guide. The Writing Guide for Students: Favorite Place Lesson (Figure 3.3) reviews goals for the lesson, reminding writers of the focus areas upon which their writing will be judged and providing prewriting questions and suggested approaches that writers may take to the assignment. A short, holistic checklist and scoring guide is also presented rather than a rubric in Figure 3.4, as I thought too many limitations might stifle student motivation and expression on this particular assignment. Also, the evidence of student writing development and growth can be clearly evaluated, accommodating student strengths rather than focusing on one standard list of skills for all.

During the stages of the writing workshop, the teacher is available to provide one-on-one feedback. The checklist and

---

CHECKLIST

A. Personal Narrative

___ Apply writing skills and literary craft previously studied and reviewed
___ Show evidence of engaging introductions using varied sentence structure and other means
___ Show evidence of effective descriptions by means of imagery and sensory description
___ Demonstrate writer's voice
    ___ Demonstrate the use of literary devices, when appropriate, such as:
    ___ Personification
    ___ Simile
    ___ Metaphor
    ___ Alliteration
    ___ Hyperbole
    ___ Dialog
___ Apply correct spelling
___ Apply correct conventions in usage, grammar, and punctuation
___ Follow the steps of the writing process
___ Make use of class and digital writing resources
___ Write the final draft in ink or type on computer and print
___ (Other) _____

B. Connecting Object, Art, or Media

___ Construct or find an object or create a hand-made or digital text/graphic that helps ties the writer to his or her favorite place.
___ Convey connection between illustration or object and personal narrative by adding a short explanation at the end of the narrative, as an endnote.
___ (Other) _____

SCORING GUIDE

A	B	C	D	E
All of the qualities above are evident.	Most of the qualities above are evident.	Many of the qualities above are evident; some work is incomplete.	Few of the qualities above are evident; conferencing is required for rewrite.	Work is unacceptable; conferencing is required for rewrite.

Figure 3.4. Checklist and Scoring Guide – Favorite Place Lesson

scoring guide given in Figure 3.4 are based on student goals and can be used to provide teachers information concerning the progress of each writer. It may also reveal writing proficiencies that need to be addressed in future writing instruction.

For some additional motivation as well as a way to inform teaching, students can offer feedback on what they liked best

---

Listen to the Quiet

On a worn, cushy green court normally trampled by bodies and filled with urgent yells and not-so-nice responses, I can listen to the quiet. My favorite spot is a place where I can relax on my feet and do all the thinking I need to do at the same time. There are no coaches yelling in your ear, no one in the crowd yelling and booing if you miss a shot, and no players putting you down if you mess up a play. When no one is there but me, the outdoor basketball court is an oasis from the day's commotion and the oncoming evening of homework and little brothers.

When I am on this court, I smell rubber from the basketball, a gift from my grandfather. I also catch the scent of tennis shoes that have never been worn outside. The little bumplets on the new ball rub against my hand in a friendly way that makes me want to make each basket. The lines of sweat running in lines down my face, arms, and legs are proof of my effort. The light traffic of living in a small town fades off into the background, and I, a stomping giant, make the only sounds as I dribble the ball down the court in swift bounces. The court is all mine to control, faking left and right, running away from imaginary rivals.

The best part of this place has to be what is absent. No large box-type contraption hangs on the dirty beige wall, clock running down and emitting annoying beeps. This outdoor court has no walls, just the old maples and oaks that shade and protect, guarding my temporary alone time. This kid is making the most of his favorite spot, a place I can listen to the quiet and myself.

Figure 3.5. Writing Sample – Favorite Place Lesson

about a particular lesson and what suggestions they have for the next time it is taught.

The combination of imagination, finding comfort in a favorite place, and art encourages students to become involved actively and thoughtfully in discourse and writing response. A writing sample is represented in Figure 3.5.

The Favorite Place writing activity described here not only represents an occasion to informally assess students' writing; it is also a high-interest writing workshop experience in which young adolescents are given time and direction to thoughtfully plan and write about a place of personal significance while connecting the topic of the composition to an object, a piece of art, or other media. I have found that the activity works especially well early in the year because it provides an opportunity for students to reveal some personal interests and background while strengthening relationships with peers – components that add relevance for writers and also build a powerful writing community.

Concluding Reflections on Chapter 3

To summarize, nurturing young adolescents' motivation with relevant, high-interest lessons resides in the following elements: deep knowledge of each student's strengths and struggles through continuous informal assessment; flexible teaching roles; relational trust; active involvement of students in their learning and familiarity with popular culture; and the application of appropriate practices and concrete learning strategies, especially with regard to gender.

Below is a recap of what I consider the most appropriate and concrete learning strategies, all research-supported. As an exercise, you may wish to check the boxes of the practices and strategies that you may already be using, and then seek to include one or more of the others not currently in use each week. You may find lessons grow in relevance as young adolescent writers' motivation takes root.

- Provide time to write each day within a predictable schedule.
- Conduct ongoing writing conferences, and extend these if possible, after school.
- Document student learning and student goals.
- Offer English language learners the choice to use their home language for early drafts.
- Plan a small-group or partner activity each day to clarify contexts, to provide practice in oral and written language, and to build community.
- Know students' levels of learning.
- Invite students' interests into the writing process.
- Enlarge the view of "a good writer."
- Provide advance organizers for literary tasks.
- Assist and model goal-setting for students.
- Provide activities that lend themselves fairly to students of different genders.
- Ask students for feedback on your lessons.
- Allow more response time for questions.
  - Decrease verbal instruction and add experiential activities.
  - Add occasional independent study as a choice.
  - Provide psychological safety.

In Chapter 4, I discuss the role of inquiry-based learning and process writing with respect to young adolescents, and I present a set of flexible lesson templates for teachers in planning their individual, pair, small-group, and whole- class lessons. Finally, I argue for the inclusion of the arts and other media in writing instruction, and I offer several illustrative writing invitations.

Note

1. McClelland's work on achievement motivation inspired my own doctoral research and dissertation in which I analyzed high-interest, low-level fiction in relation to McClelland's need achievement motive.

4 Growing with Process Writing Linked to the Arts

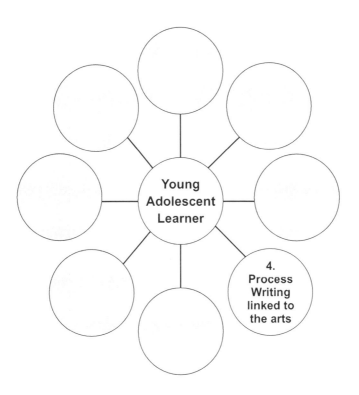

Painting is poetry that is seen rather than felt, and poetry is painting that is felt rather than seen.
 – Leonardo da Vinci, *A Treatise on Painting* (da Vinci, 2002)

Introductory Remarks to Chapter 4

Inquiry-based learning is often linked to study in science, literature, and mathematics within efforts by students to master subject matter content and skills, including writing skills within the content areas (National Council of Teachers of English, 2008). While Chapter 5 concerns itself with choice and critical thinking, including inquiry, here I propose that inquiry-based learning can motivate young adolescent writers when the arts are introduced into classroom lessons. Students take part in inquiry learning when their interests, curiosity, and wonder are fueled by observations (e.g. about a piece of art), which then stimulate questions or link previous experiences to new understandings. Inquiry through the arts is powerful learning because it is open-ended and personal, and because students are actively engaged in their work. In this chapter, I argue that application of the arts, including the media of music, drama, film, literature, and graphic digital media, nurtures motivation in young adolescents to write authentically and critically while growing in self-confidence. For students with diverse needs, the arts and the various media within arts offer alternative pathways for creative expression and empowerment, for young adolescents' perception of their progress is integral to their actual success. Research that underpins this argument is presented, along with several classroom lessons linked to art which are based on a process writing model within a writing workshop approach.

Inquiry as Motivation to Write in Response to the Arts

Although content skills remain the focus in many classrooms, students also need to be able to think critically and problem-solve by asking and then finding the answers to their questions. Driven by active inquisitiveness and creativity, young adolescents' motivation increases through independent and small-group work as they approach higher levels of learning – and their future work places.

Because we communicate by means of both face-to-face and digital discourse, we write more and we write in different ways than in the past (National Council of Teachers of English, 2008). In addition to technological changes, today's students, to an increasing degree, communicate globally, so they are experiencing many cultural changes as well. This said, young adolescents must be more than empty vessels waiting to be filled with subject-area content presented by their teachers; they need to become increasingly independent, curious learners and thinkers who build upon prior knowledge and understanding through inquiry, particularly when it comes to writing tasks. Incorporating one or more of the arts into classroom lessons is one very effective way to motivate deep, critical thought and inquiry – and writing response.

> **Art** *can be considered in a holistic sense to include not only the viewing or making of art per se, but also reading and experiential transactions with literature, poetry, drama, dance, music, film, and sometimes digital and mass media – all of which can be part of a writing class and can serve as stimuli to inquiry learning.*

In a learner-centered classroom in which teachers plan with student motivation in mind, young adolescents can thrive as they move toward thinking and writing independence. A crucial first step for students to grow into mature, motivated, and inquiring writers is for the teacher to assist each student in the discovery of individual purposes for writing. This is no easy task, given the diverse needs and skill levels of each writer in each class. In the following vignettes, I illustrate this process by describing how and when I first discovered my own purposes for writing.

The Power of the Pen: Why We Write

One of the most difficult experiences for many writers, even in the best situations, is sharing work with peers, especially sharing with an entire class of peers. Some gradually become comfortable over a period of time in a secure setting; some never get to the point of voluntarily agreeing to read a piece of original writing. If we ask other teachers of writing when they felt comfortable reading their writing aloud, most would reply, "Never!" It took me quite a while to get to that point – in fact, I was in university.

Thinking back to undergraduate university days, I remember the process of compiling original poems for a class project we were to share with classmates. I began to lose sleep, dreading the due date, when each student in class was required to choose one or two of their writings to read aloud to the whole class. Up until that point, I had not shown much writing of a personal nature to peers, but knowing that I could pick and choose the pieces made me feel less vulnerable and helped me take the big step of sharing my writing with peers. Yet I was conflicted; wasn't my best writing also that which best showed unmasked feelings and insights? Wasn't this the very reason I so easily took up my pen to write? When it was my turn to read, my words were communicated in a rather shaky voice, but I was relieved to have finally done so. The worst did not happen: no one laughed, a few nodded their heads in understanding, and one even commented on my effective use of descriptive imagery. The professor in that class read one of her own pieces of writing, and this act likely contributed to the feeling of safety within a respectful writing community, because once all had participated in reading, taking the Author's Chair became a regular part of the class to which we all looked forward. Granted, there had been little to no peer response or sharing of writing at school prior to my entrance to university. How much more difficult still might it be for young adolescents to share their work with peers – particularly if they have not experienced sharing their work within a safe community of writers or have not developed the confidence to do so?

The power of the pen still gives me a heady response today, both in its ability to transmit my thoughts and emotions and in its potential influence upon an audience. In fact, one could say that the way I feel while writing is now, nearly always, a motivation for me, just as clearly as it was a discovery of my answer to the question, "Why write?" I write because I can set a mood and share my experiences, knowledge, and even a few embarrassing confessions – and know that they will perhaps be read and reflected upon, and that my words may influence how a reader looks at some aspect of life. In short, perhaps my writing will make a difference to someone.

"Why write?" is a question to which there are infinite answers. Thinking back to my own experiences as a young adolescent, I view writing alone in my room at that time of my life as a saving grace. Amid the confusion of a noisy house and my own insecurities, I lost myself in my writing and reading, imagining a life apart from the conflicts I was experiencing at home and at school. The prized fountain pen from the local "five and dime" store and the notebooks filled with stories and diary entries were my ticket out of my room and my small, disorganized life. With the help of The Beatles, Smokey Robinson and the Miracles, The Supremes, the adventures of Nancy Drew and Trixie Beldon, and my own idealistic adolescent dreams, daily writing provided a safe place to plan my life. To my adolescent psyche, it was a matter of life and death. Maybe I couldn't always express myself in school or at home, but as a writer, the options were limitless and the words and process my own.

In *Dancing with the Pen: The Learner as Writer* (Ministry of Education, Australia, 1992), teachers in New Zealand mention many of the same beliefs about literacy learning and teaching that I have, adding some powerful statements, such as: "Trying to express what we really mean involves the active exploration of ideas" (Ministry of Education, Australia, 1992: 9). The statement reminds teachers that student writing can be inquiry-driven, and that adequate time is needed for students to delve into their ideas, to explore options, and to craft their work. In answer to the question, "Why do we write?" the authors note several purposes, and among them are: to record events, to explain, to predict, to persuade, to request, to amuse, to reflect, to invite response, and to hypothesize (Ministry of Education, Australia, 1992: 9).

Art as an Invitation to Young Adolescents' Personal Expression

As an adolescent, one of my most powerful, inspiring classroom experiences occurred when a high school teacher provided our class with small booklets of famous paintings in our study of religion and asked us what we thought each piece signified. That was in 1968, the year of the Catholic Ecumenical Council under Pope John XXIII, when the Latin Mass was replaced with English, when the nation was in the grip of the Feminist and Civil Rights movements, and when the United States had already overstayed its welcome in Vietnam. Perhaps the time was ripe for "stepping outside the box" in the classroom and elsewhere. I recall being pleasantly surprised, as a private school student back then, at my teacher's request for my opinion because we were not asked very often what we thought – not, that is, without a preconceived notion of a "correct" or expected response, in the traditional information-processing model of teaching. The lesson made an unspoken kind of sense, as the teacher seemed to be in tune with the students and the 1960s youth culture. At a subsequent class reunion, I discovered that the teacher in question was a novice when we sat in her class, empowered by our levels of enthusiasm and participation.

One of the works of art we viewed that day in our booklets was "The Scream," painted in 1895 by Norwegian artist Edvard Munch, depicting an agonized body against a blood red sky (Munch, 1895). (You may view the painting at http://www.edvard-munch.com/gallery/anxiety/scream.htm.) The simplicity of the lines and the terror of a trapped animal in the eyes of the subject are still hauntingly clear in my mind. The entire piece appeared to me as a study in opposites, with life, something most of us take for granted, drowning in all of the complexities of emotions, unfulfilled dreams, prejudice, and judgment – all of which are universal themes. Along with class discussion about the piece, I remember that we were asked to compare elements of the painting with any religious or cultural images we had encountered in our studies and daily life, and to write about these. The assignment opened up a whole new purpose for me as a writer and was a valuable lesson for me later in life on how adolescents can be inspired to write.

Individual Purpose and Response Cultivate Voice

Prior to experiencing the lesson above, school writing mainly encompassed required assignments, such as class notes, essay test responses, and an occasional research paper, which were completed for the teacher and to earn a grade. These forms of writing and responses were not shared with peers; in fact, all stages, including drafting, were usually completed at home. In contrast, my personal writing, which I still own, included keeping a diary, creating poetry, and writing letters to friends. Although I received a great many letters in return from the recipients of my correspondence, I rarely shared the poetry, and never shared the diary; but I was drawn to all of these forms of writing as outlets of expression and the need for connection. The academic writing in contrast rarely invited voice or style, and I felt detached from it; the personal writing allowed meaningful articulation and satisfaction, revealing myself as a developing young adult.

When asked to find similarities between the art we viewed in class and other images studied as well as encountered in life (i.e. television, film, the press), school writing began to meld strongly with personal writing. Suddenly, the horrifying images of live battles in the jungles of Vietnam, the shocking 1968 *Time* magazine photo of a prisoner of war being shot in the head at point-blank range (http:/www.moolf.com/interesting/10-photographs-that-changed-the-world html), and media coverage of the deaths of four Kent State University students gunned down by police in riot gear took on a sense of relevance and connection. Finally, as a writer, I could take a measure of personal control of some of the disparaging events in the world that seemed out of control. Instead of being just an observer and a reporter, I could write about my confusion, revulsion, and terror about the events and images that swirled around me, offer ideas of hope, and, in general, process the experiences and events that affected my life. The teacher who gave us the opportunity to compare, connect, and express ourselves may not have known it, but she instilled new purpose into academic writing, as she invited voice, critical thinking, and self-expression. That was about the time I wrote a poem for our school newspaper and started an advice column. As I continued to grow in knowledge and understanding of world events, I wrote with increased purpose and voice.

Several years following the high school art-centered lesson, I discovered that "The Scream" symbolizes the human species overwhelmed by an attack of existential torment. The painting not only held historical significance; I saw myself reflected in it. Like many adolescents, I regularly felt the disconnection of existing on the fringes of established social groups. Friendly and passive, I shared the characteristics of many adolescents who struggle to fit in. I related directly to the subject in the Munch painting, whose face expressed what I felt in my heart. I recall the continual worry and loss of sleep over upcoming examinations, volatile issues at home, and the fear of a particularly large female bully who traveled with her "posse" and made me a target at school. At home, I had been reinforced not to fight back, to be controlled as well as forgiving. In addition, I was expected to excel not only at English and Latin, but also at calculus, trigonometry, and biology, the last three of which did not come easily to me as a non-analytical, holistic learner. Thus, the opportunity to study a piece of art with which I identified personally was very appealing. To me, *the painting was the poetry that I felt in the art I observed.* Today's young adolescents also connect strongly with art in many forms, including the lyrics and arrangements of favored musical genres as well as literature, film, drama, and poetry, because all of these channel emotions – in particular, hope, fear, loneliness, anger, frustration, and deep joy – which are integral sensations of the maturation process from childhood to adulthood.

Students today are likely to have communicated with friends globally in social networks such as MySpace and Facebook, exchanging images, film, and music clips. In this way, they tend to comprehend the global nature of youth issues more easily than my generation ever did or does. However, the steady diet of communications, music, entertainment news, photos, and movie clips downloaded from the Internet and from friends gives young adults only a partial taste of the arts and mass media. Teachers can gently round out this diet by supplementing it with historically significant sound clips, paintings, classic and contemporary sculpture, music, drama, and film related to content studied in classes. When art is at the center of students' attention, they are invited to be drawn into it and to note the feelings, associations, and ideas that arise within themselves. In other words, their responses to art cultivate their writing voices and purposes for writing. Also, because students are social beings, art-inspired lessons that include components of partner and small-group activities can further enhance response writing, especially when peers become part of a projected audience.

> ***Teachers can profoundly nurture young adolescents' motivation to write when they provide lessons that include invitations to interpret and generate art in its almost endless array of styles and forms, including building upon their experiences as social beings.***

Process Writing: Cyclical in Nature

Many teachers understand that lessons are not only opportunities to explore subject-based materials; they also serve as instruments for learners to interact personally and experientially with art. When students are studying art by means of inferring personal meaning, communicating about it, and possibly creating it, they are learning *through* it in deep, powerful ways. In order for young adolescent writers to discover their individual processes and become successful critical thinkers and writers, they will need to work within classrooms set up as workshops; they must expect to write daily with continual works in progress; and they must be given the ways and means to discover their individual writing processes. Such student discoveries, critical thinking, and writing development necessitate investments of planned time to accommodate the qualitative nature of the teaching and learning.

Writing workshops become additionally potent places when teachers and students work side by side within the classroom writing workshop community, illustrating the recursive, cyclical nature of writing. When writing is recognized as a cyclical process, writers move freely ahead, at times working on a draft or a section longer than originally planned, sometimes rewriting whole sections or starting over in order to try out various organizational and literary crafts. Teachers who work along with students on their own writing may find that sharing all or part of their work and talking about the decisions made in the process support students in their own, varied writing processes, while modeling the importance of reflection and the act of thinking aloud. All of this takes practice.

Donald Murray reminds us in *Write to Learn* (Murray, 2002: 25) that writing, like tuba playing and other processes, is not something that can be taught as much as it is a set of actions and behaviors that must be practiced. Like the apprentice musician, writers must make mistakes in order for the possibilities of good writing to emerge. Writers move three steps forward and two steps back at times in the process of writing, and because they are usually most effective working within a process in which they have already been successful, the individual writer's unique process emerges. This is true in other cases as well when developing a process of writing instruction that attempts to fit each unique learning situation.

Developing a Unique Process

I am reminded of an image of a group of ten young ballerinas practicing in a school gym not far from the house where I grew up. If I close my eyes, I can feel the perspiration running down my back, arms, and forehead, and I can hear the numbers I am counting in my head. But instead of dancing as one, many young ballerinas are like islands unto themselves as they struggle with steps and self-confidence – save for the front three girls dressed in matching pink leotards, mimicking the teacher like robots.

The recital, less than three weeks away, called for some drastic measures. My personal motivation was to not embarrass myself by forgetting the steps. A large, lower level area of our family home, filled with the sounds of Tchaikovsky's "Dance of the Sugar Plum Fairy" on the record player, became my studio and inspiration, so much so that I could close my eyes and imagine the dance in my head. I practiced the steps over and over, interpreting the dance with a certain slant of my head and position of my arms. The dance number did not come together in a week, however.

At each week's class before the recital, I asked my apprehensive fellow dancers to come to my basement "studio," feel the music, and practice, practice, practice! Little by little, our moves came together as unified and complementary rather than individual and isolated, and soon the feeling of success began to well up within us. Some stage fright was present the evening of the recital, but many of us truly enjoyed the dance, as we knew the steps well and so only needed to flow naturally to the music. That night I felt more graceful than ever, as I translated the skills I had learned into my own personal performance. Through this experience, I became convinced that I could not learn only through mimicry; I needed to internalize the learning in a process of practicing form and then adding my own interpretation and passion. From then on, whenever I danced, whether in class or otherwise, once the steps were set, I let my own style and dancing self – or "voice," if you will – come through. In many ways, young adolescent writers are like the dancers in that long-ago class.

> *Getting the form correct is a necessary part of writing, but the real sense of achievement comes when each hears his or her own "music" and capably interprets that sound in his or her own distinctive words.*

How might teachers facilitate students' development of individual writing processes? One way to find out is to try out different approaches, including giving writers permission to set their own pace for early, shorter assignments. Each teacher determines how best to run the writing workshop with varying degrees of structure. Young adolescent writers who understand expectations and have comfortably adjusted to the flow of routines are halfway along in their development into successful writers. It's all about finding a distinctive plan that works for each individual writer. Knowing what motivates student writers assists with development of classroom writing invitations as well as differentiating instruction for individual students who will benefit.

Below is a list of resources suitable for engaging middle school and older students when including the arts and other media in the writing workshop. Perhaps one or more of these as resources can be useful for teachers seeking ways to both motivate and differentiate instruction as needed to support the writing of young adolescent writers.

Strong Lessons with Flexible Templates

In order to illustrate ways to connect use of the arts to process writing lessons, I have created specific lesson plans of varying lengths which teachers might consider adopting or adapting in their own classes. In what follows, I present lesson templates with sample lessons which teachers can apply in their planning for four situations: whole class/large group; small groups; individual work;

Resources for Nurturing Art-Enhanced Lessons

Albers, Peggy (2007) *Finding the Artist Within: Creating and Reading Visual Texts in the English Language Arts Classroom*. Newark, Delaware: International Reading Association.

Bomer, Katherine (2005) *Writing a Life: Teaching Memoir to Sharpen Insight, Shape Meaning –and Triumph Over Tests*. Portsmouth, New Hampshire: Heinemann.

Carroll, Pamela Sissi (2004) *Integrated Literacy in the Middle Grades: Channeling Young Adolescents' Spontaneous Flow of Energy*. Boston, Massachusetts: Pearson Education, Inc.

Chancer, Joni and Rester-Zodrow, Gina (1997) *Moon Journals: Writing, Art, Inquiry*. Portsmouth, New Hampshire: Heinemann.

Close, Elizabeth and Ramsey, Katherine D. (2000) *A Middle Mosaic: A Celebration of Reading, Writing, and Reflective Practice at the Middle Level*. Urbana, Illinois: National Council of Teachers of English.

Crawford, Linda (2004) *Lively Learning: Using the Arts to Teach K–8 Curriculum*. Greenfield, Massachusetts: Northeast Foundation for Children.

Evans, Karen S. (2001) *Literature Discussion Groups in the Intermediate Grades: Dilemmas and Possibilities*. Newark, Delaware: International Reading Association.

Heard, Georgia (1999) *Awakening the Heart: Exploring Poetry in Elementary and Middle School*. Portsmouth, New Hampshire: Heinemann.

Kasten, Wendy C., Kirsto, Janice V., McClure, Amy A. and Garthwait, Abigail. (2005) *Living Literature: Using Children's Literature to Support Reading and Language Arts*. Upper Saddle River, New Jersey: Pearson Education.

Mitchell, Diana and Christenbury, Leila (2000) *Teaching Ideas That Spark Learning*.

Olness, Rebecca (2005) *Using Literature to Enhance Writing Instruction*. Urbana, Illinois: National Council of Teachers of English.

Polette, Keith (2005) *Read & Write It Out Loud: Guided Oral Literacy Strategies*. Boston: Pearson.

Roser, Nancy L. and Martinez, Miriam G. (eds.) (2005) *What a Character! Character Study as a Guide to Literary Meaning Making in Grades K–8*. Newark, Delaware: International Reading Association.

Van Horn, Leigh (2008) *Reading Photographs to Write with Meaning and Purpose, Grades 412*. Newark, Delaware: International Reading Association.

and a combination of whole-class, partner, and individual work. Each template differs slightly from the others, as the templates presented have been created for various class configurations and genres. However, the templates are alike in that each is followed by a sample lesson whose base is art or digital graphic media. The templates are flexible in that they are a starting point; teachers may pick and choose the components that fit their individual circumstances.

Lesson 1: Whole-Class Process Writing – Literary Devices in Narrative Poetry

I begin with a whole-group lesson that invites students to create a narrative poem illustrated by means of graphic art, collage, drawing, or photograph(s). Narration is the act of unfolding a sequence of events, often in chronological order. It is story, whether in prose or poetry; it involves events, characters, and the decisions, actions, and dialog of the characters. It may be fact or fiction, based on history or fact, or wholly imaginary. Whether factual or imaginary, the narrative may start from the beginning of an event or sequence of events and flow to the end, or it can start in the middle of the action, recounting earlier events through flashback, memories, and character dialog (Michigan Department of Education, 2005). Narrative poetry may be characterized as an exception to the story form since it may take on many forms of its own. Figure 4.1 lays out the different possibilities for the narrative genre and may be helpful when considering lesson purposes.

The first flexible lesson template, Lesson Template 1, focused on narrative poetry, is given below, followed by discussion of sample lesson activities and an illustrative, completed template.

Just as we have mentors in our lives such as parents, teachers, and others to support us with knowledge and tasks we have not yet mastered, so too, literature can provide models and supports for young adolescent writers in the way of *mentor texts*. Lynne R. Dorfman and Rose Cappelli describe mentor texts as "pieces

Elements of Prose	Forms of Prose
Setting and mood, characters and their development, problem, universal truth conveyed through basic plot	**Fictional Narratives:** Focus on an imagined event or theme in a form such as a short story, novel, picture book, play, ballad, or fable
Focused body or middle	**Personal Narratives:** Focus on real events in a form such as an article, essay, brochure, or poetry
Creation of dramatic tension and suspense	**Historical or Science Fiction Narratives:** Focus on researched and documented real event (or an imagined science fiction event) in a form such as a short story, novel, or play
Showing rather than telling events and character traits, chronological organization	Chronological biography, realistic or historical fiction, memoir
Resolution as ending or lesson learned	Fable, fairytale
Elements of Poetry	**Forms of Poetry**
Form	Acrostic, couplets, diamond, epic, free verse, haiku, limericks, shape
Story	Speaker, meaning, tone, word choice
Imagery	Metaphor, simile, personification, hyperbole
Music or Resonance	Alliteration, consonance, onomatopoeia, repetition, rhyme, rhythm

Figure 4.1. Elements of Narration in Prose and Poetry (adapted from Michigan's Genre Project, Michigan Department of Education, 2005)

of literature that we can return to again and again as we help our young writers learn to do what they may not yet be able to do on their own" (Dorfman and Cappelli, 2007: 2–3). Selected novels, short stories, poetry, and essays by known authors can be used by teachers to plan dynamic, relevant lessons using excerpts from these by focusing upon specific areas of both form and content.

Shel Silverstein's poem, "Whatif," from the book, *A Light in the Attic* (Silverstein, 1981), serves as a mentor text in demonstrating exemplary adolescent voice, poetic couplets, and absurdity. Students are drawn to the poem, in part, because they connect with the author's personification of nighttime worries as tangible yet conquerable enemies. Young adolescents also enjoy reading the poem aloud, placing emphasis on particular sections of text as they interpret the meaning of the poem and appreciate its humor.

Title of Lesson:

Intended Level(s):

Resources Needed:

Diverse Needs and Accommodations:

Target Content, Craft, and Conventions:

Stage(s) of Writing Supported:

Lesson Goal(s):

Lesson Outcome(s):

Assessment:

State Standards Addressed:

Rationale for Lesson:

Lesson Plan Overview:

Procedure:

    Before Writing

    During Writing

    After Writing

Teacher Reflections on Lesson: What worked well? What needs more thought?

Figure 4.2. Lesson Template 1: Whole-Class Process Writing

In addition, typed texts by former students who have written "Whatif" poems (with permission granted and names removed) may be utilized as mentor texts, as these are especially relevant for young adolescent writers, who can identify with peer voices that convey meaning and craft.

The teacher's own writing can also be the source of mentor texts. During my final years of classroom teaching, I shared my own drafts of classroom writing with students, often asking for some preliminary response with regard to aspects of form and content studied. Along with additional writing samples to critique, students gained some personal glimpses of their teacher as a writer. I have found that young adolescent writers appreciate the opportunity to interact with peer and teacher writers, with questions and comments exchanged freely as the piece of writing is being created and crafted. The active participation by class members, who are also in the process of preparing their own written pieces, acts as an additional motivation to continue a piece of writing through to its completion. This form of sharing and motivation differs greatly from the more polite response to a more formal reading of finished pieces in Author's Chair.

Mentor texts thus provide students with relevant examples for close study, reflection, and in some cases, respectful imitation. Some suggestions for activities using mentor texts of poetry that can be carried out with the whole class prior to presenting a writing invitation or assignment are the following:

- Read the title of the poem and hypothesize what it may be about;
- Read the poem aloud through to the end to get a sense of how it sounds, what form it is, and what the author's intention may be;
- Discuss what is known and highlight the parts that are unknown;
- Hypothesize about what the unknown verses and phrases may mean;
- Discover patterns such as use of imagery, sound, and arrangement, and discuss what the author may be attempting to show through the pattern;
- Note in which person the poem is written;
- Allow students to read the poem silently, prior to reading it aloud, giving sufficient time to note personal or other reactions in notebooks;
- Note changes in tone, focus, voice, narrator, and focal point, and discuss what the author may have in mind;

- Discuss what poetic devices and specific craft the author has used to hold the interest of and clarify meaning for the reader; and
- Do a quickwrite of the meaning of the poem, whether or how it relates to the title, and in which specific ways the author has related to the readers.

Young adolescent writers can greatly profit from our planning of such critical close reading of mentor poetry as they identify personal and other connections, and as they become familiar with the many variations of rhythm, style, and content found in outstanding poetry. You may wish to use the sample empty lesson template provided in Figure 4.2, which includes many important considerations for whole-group lessons, to plan short, before-writing lessons as well as full-length lessons aimed at inviting students to experience, explore, and appreciate narration as well as other writing genres.

A fully planned lesson for study and writing of a short narrative poem is provided in Figure 4.3, complete with a section for curriculum standards, goals, assessment, and step-by-step procedures on how to teach the lesson before, during, and after the writing section of the lesson. As described, the lesson should take about fifty minutes, equal to a typical classroom period.

When working with a whole class of learners during a mini-lesson, prior to the actual writing, it is imperative to engage learners by inviting their active involvement. Along with asking questions about prior knowledge and predictions about the literature to be read, teachers may allow "wait time" following a question so that more students may decide to take part in discussions. All teachers are familiar with the immediate hand-raisers and those who sometimes make sounds while waving wildly; it is prudent to harvest all of the fruit of the growing minds by acknowledging their presence and adding their voices. These efforts by teachers on behalf of those learners who like to think their ideas through or who may be less outgoing than their peers pays off in the long

Lesson 1: Whole-Class Process Writing

Title of Lesson: Exploring Story and Literary Devices within a Narrative Poem

Intended Levels: Upper elementary through middle school

Resources Needed: White board or overhead projector, copies of "Whatif" from *A Light in the Attic* by Shel Silverstein (1981: 90), writing materials.

Diverse Needs and Accommodations: Teacher will wear a microphone and place hearing-impaired and sight-impaired students near front of the room as well as face the class when speaking; thick, black markers will be used when writing on board or overhead transparency. If writing on a computer screen, 14-point font or an enlarged display will be used.

Target Content, Craft, and Conventions: Story elements – beginning, middle, and end; use of element of surprise, dramatic tension, and humor to elevate interest; and exploration of universal childhood fears.

Stages of Writing Supported: Prewriting, drafting, sharing

Lesson Goals: After reading Silverstein's "Whatif" poem, students will:
- Place themselves into the role of speaker of the poem, imagining and noting what worries may keep them awake at night;
- Write a short narrative poem with a beginning, middle, and end and begin to use styles and patterns derived from studying authors, such as dramatic tension, element of surprise, and humor; and
- Illustrate the poem by means of graphic art, collage, drawing, or photograph(s), and affix a copy of the final draft to the art for display.

Lesson Outcome: Students' first drafts will reflect understanding and use of one or more of the literary devices studied in a short narrative poem told with chronological elements.

Assessment: Written self-reflection by student; placement in writing folder for possible inclusion in portfolio; volunteers may share with peers and receive oral feedback.

State (Michigan) Standards Addressed:
W.GN.06.01 Write a cohesive narrative piece such as a personal narrative, adventure, tall tale, folktale, fantasy, or poetry that includes appropriate conventions to the genre, employing elements of characterization for major and minor characters; internal and/or external conflict; and issues of plot, theme, and imagery.
W.PR.06.01 Set a purpose, consider audience, and replicate authors' styles and patterns when writing a narrative or informational piece.
W.PS.06.01 Exhibit personal style and voice to enhance the written message in both narrative (e.g. personification, humor, element of surprise) and informational writing (e.g. emotional appeal, strong opinion, credible support).

Rationale for Lesson: Young adolescents will benefit in their own writing from studying the story elements in a humorous and dramatic mentor text by an author they admire; writers may also benefit from writing and talking about their fears.

Lesson Plan Overview: After reading and studying the narrative elements and literary devices in "Whatif," ask student to brainstorm individually their fears that seem to crop up at night before they sleep or in bad dreams. Using these ideas, students write a short "Whatif" poem which includes a beginning, middle, and end; follows the patterns of the mentor text; and includes one or more of the literary devices studied.

Procedure:

Before Writing
- Invite students to read the "Whatif" poem silently as a class, read the introduction and four more lines aloud, pausing for volunteer readers.
- Ask: "What types of punctuation are present?" and "How might these conventions add to or detract from your enjoyment of the poem?"
- Discuss the visible story elements, such as chronological order, as well as whether students can identify with the writer about having fears that seem larger than life at night.
- Observe the rhyme pattern as well as the elements of humor, dramatic tension, and surprise, and ask for examples of these from the text.
- Ask students to brainstorm ideas on paper of fears that may come at night, and they may add some rhyme if that appeals to them.
- Ask students to share an idea or two with a peer and also decide whether the tone will be humorous or not.

During Writing
- Invite students to draft their own "Whatif" poems within a twenty- to thirty-minute "sacred writing time" (i.e. with no interruptions), employing their brainstormed ideas.
- Caution writers not to get so focused on trying to compose couplets that the content of the poem becomes unclear.
- If possible, the teacher should write along with students.

After Writing
- Invite four or five volunteers to share what they have written in their first drafts.
- Read (the teacher's) own first draft and discuss difficulties as well as what was enjoyable.
- Ask students for positive feedback and what parts of the poems seemed most clear and whether chronological order, patterns, and literary elements were noted in the poetry.
- Instruct students to write a short reflection and response to their work as well as some ideas about how to continue with their writing on the following day.
- Store drafts in writing notebooks.

Teacher Reflections on Lesson: What worked well? What needs more thought?
Example: In general, students enjoyed the lesson. Most students did a good job beginning this writing, but some could have used some concrete examples. The oral reading of the poetry, both that of the mentor text and of volunteer student writers, helped students to visualize and hear the story elements and literary devices as well as to note the end punctuation of lines. Next time, perhaps have one or more short "Whatif" poems ready to show students as examples, following the group share of first drafts. Plan adequate time for continued drafts; those who finish final drafts may begin illustrations for poems. Assist students intent on rhyming not to sacrifice ideas for form; offer to be a scribe if needed and support and praise work accomplished in pieces, as students progress to finish first drafts. Invite students to jot down additional ideas later at home, which may enhance their poetry and bring these to school the next day. Allow two to three periods of 20–30 minutes of workshop time for the project.

Figure 4.3. "Whatif" Poetry Lesson

run, while in the process establishing the practice of inclusion and the importance of listening to others.

Lesson 2: Working with Small Writing Groups – Fable

When working with small groups, it is essential to focus on cooperation, teamwork, and problem-solving, with a clear statement of the goal. In addition, it is necessary to review applicable group norms, roles, responsibilities, and methods of evaluation. Lesson Template 2 is designed for small-group writing and may serve as a helpful planning tool when working with small groups of three to five young adolescent writers. Students relate to themselves and each other much differently in small groups, where the focus is on cooperation and teamwork, than they do as partners in pairs.

> *When students increasingly take on responsibility for development of their work during the writing process, the teacher's role changes from one primarily of leader to that of facilitator and interactive group member.*

Lesson Template 2 for creating small-group process writing circles is presented in Figure 4.4.

Because students become the primary decision-makers with respect to their writing, the writing workshop carried out in small groups of students who create one piece of writing together must be carefully planned, with routines established and the group writing process teacher-facilitated. Small-group writing circles are as strong as, and work as well as, the students within them, so that students need to know, understand, and commit to both group and individual tasks.

Following is a lesson involving fables planned for small-group writing circles consisting of 3-5 students who each have a specific role and are expected to be personally responsible for some duties they have chosen individually while also taking responsibility for group collaboration in planning and creating a group text. Small-group writing circles are often planned by teachers to

Title of Lesson:

Intended Level(s):

Resources Needed:

Diverse Needs/Accommodations:

Target Content, Craft, and Conventions:

Stage(s) of Writing Supported:

Group Norms:

Group Roles:

Group and Individual Responsibilities:

Student Statement(s) of Goal(s):

Lesson Goal(s):

Lesson Outcome(s):

Assessment:

State Standards Addressed:

Rationale for Lesson:

Lesson Plan Overview:

Procedure:

    Before Writing

    During Writing

    After Writing, including Group Evaluation

Teacher Reflections on Lesson: What worked well? What needs more thought?

Figure 4.4. Lesson Template 2: Small-Group Process Writing

enable students to interact with peers at various stages of a writing workshop for support and feedback, while assisting individual students in building their confidence as they work with a limited number of peers. Writing circles are often used as a vehicle for peer response while young adolescents compose individual written pieces; however, they can also be constructed as a unit that composes one piece collaboratively, each student adding an integral writing component. Sylvia Gunnery, in her book, The Writing Circle (Gunnery, 2007: 15–17) offers ways for writing circle members to respond positively to one another's works in progress. These include:

- ✓ Begin with a positive comment;
- ✓ Listen thoughtfully;
- ✓ Ask the writer to read aloud;
- ✓ Use truth and tact;
- ✓ Make responses constructive;
- ✓ Limit what you say; and
- ✓ Resist telling a writer what to write.

These guidelines are helpful for both individual as well as group writing.

When students meet in writing circles as small-group units that produce a piece of writing together, additional careful planning is in order. The template offers a framework adaptable to various teaching situations. Since the sample lesson is one of five, as part of a unit, writing circles must be set up carefully, such as by the following procedures:

1. Select students for each small group when forming the writing circles;
2. Assign roles for each member of each circle;
3. Assist students in preparing for their roles by modeling;
4. Ask the group discussion leader to rotate turns reading mentor texts and developing the fable aloud;
5. Have students note the writing circle dates; and
6. Act as a revolving group member, facilitating collaboration in the writing and group process.

Depending upon the levels of work engagement among individuals within groups, the general level of cooperation within a class, and the level of student experience working in a collaborative group setting, the teacher may take on more or less responsibility for group membership, role assignments, and levels of assistance, or else delegate these aspects of the activity to the students themselves. I found small-group work to be most successful early in a class year or semester when the teacher determines the composition of groups. Until individual students are placed into small groups in various combinations, it is difficult to plan for student and group dynamics. Also, it is a good idea for teachers to suggest or appoint group facilitator roles to assure that these are rotated within the class, sharing the leadership experience. Clarifying and posting expectations for each role within the writing circle aids in keeping students on track. Five sample roles are presented below for illustration.

Sample Writing Circle Roles

Discussion Facilitator: Initiates brainstorming about tasks to be accomplished; invites members to select tasks; persuades all to work on writing and take part in discussions; asks questions; and encourages respect and consensus-building within the group (see model below).

Secretary or Scribe: Records brainstormed ideas for all to see on a white board or poster board, such as concepts for characters, setting, and other parts of the narrative; notes decisions of group; and notes individual tasks and each member's daily writing progress.

Time Keeper: Notes starting and ending times for writing and group discussions, reminding members of time remaining at frequent intervals.

Runner: Provides needed resources, such as paper, pencils, ink, art supplies, and so on, to support the groups' writing.

Reporter: Reports progress of the writing circle to the teacher; reports general progress of the writing circle to the class, when called upon to do so.

Writing circles provide a way for students to engage in critical thinking and reflection as they read, discuss, and plan their writing. Collaboration is at the heart of this approach. Students reshape and add to their understanding as they construct plot, choose descriptive language, and complete each piece that becomes part of the whole. The additional artistic response, which may accompany the fable through technology, art, music, and sound, links the writer to the audience, a critical element in writing narration.

Prior to convening groups, the teacher should present, thoroughly discuss, and show, physically and intellectually, how a consensus-building model works. In my classes, I liked to demonstrate the process by acting it out in a "fish bowl," so named because all actions are transparent and can be openly and plainly analyzed and discussed. I would ask a student to take on the role of facilitator and solicit three volunteers, who would, with me, act out a possible small-group decision.

Consensus-building and collaboration are emergent processes; any and all positive signs of a small group's movement toward the consensus model can be documented, and group members can be recognized for their efforts.

Consensus-building and problem-solving in small groups are complex tasks that are most relevant when topics are based on a larger group goal. Examples include creating an addendum to the class rules about the use of cell phones and other personal digital technology during school; choosing a class motto and song; or designing a plan to build a grade level garden at the entrance to the school building.

Below is the model I developed for building consensus and solving problems within small groups. This model incorporates aspects of several existing models, including the funnel model, which I have used with success in middle school classrooms. The funnel model, upon which my model is loosely based, consists of four basic steps when attempting to reach a group decision: brainstorming (of ideas), narrowing, selecting, and consensus.

These four basic steps are highlighted in the model below. The teacher's role is one of leadership and modeling at the beginning of the group process, morphing into one of facilitator once students become actively involved in their task and roles.

Benefits of consensus-building are many. The main advantage is that those most familiar with the problem (students in the writing circles) are able to take part in solving it. In addition, practicing

---

Consensus-Building Model for Small Groups

1. Appoint a facilitator who understands the role of inclusion, keeping discussion on track, restating ideas via secretary's notes, asking for teacher assistance when needed, and calling for a vote.
2. Appoint a secretary or scribe who understands the role of note-taking verbatim, asking for clarification when needed.
3. Refer often to the steps in an agenda or framework to be used during decision-making, such as this model.
4. Work through the model in the steps below:
    a. Group identifies a broad goal for the group;
    b. Group identifies a problem related to a larger group goal (secretary notes this);
    c. Group analyzes the problem by dividing it into smaller parts and naming these (secretary notes these for all to view);
    d. Group brainstorms ideas, offering alternative suggestions to one or more of the smaller parts of the problem, as the secretary takes notes on all suggestions offered (*brainstorming*);
    e. Each group member voices solutions, opinions, and/or insights with respect;
    f. Each group member listens, resisting the urge to interrupt, writing down ideas privately to bring up when in turn;
    g. Facilitator sums up the main points, merging similar ideas (*narrowing*), and secretary/scribe writes the options for solutions for all to see;
    h. Facilitator reads the options and a vote is taken (*selecting*) and if possible, a group *consensus* is reached;
    i. Group implements the solution (*decision*) to the problem, dividing and assigning the necessary tasks to group members;
    j. Group shows problem and solution to the teacher.

the act of inclusion and listening to all suggested solutions brings about a feeling of unity within the group, especially when the group is successful in implementing the solution chosen. Because all ideas have been heard and duly noted, no member has been left out of the process, which strengthens the relationships among group members. Finally, successful resolution, with or without a teacher's assistance, raises the possibility of future resolution to related issues as they arise in the group's work together. A complete lesson sample, "Composing a Fable," for Lesson Template 2 is presented in Figure 4.5.

Advance organizers have also been included to support small-group brainstorming of ideas and planning of the fable, to clarify individual student roles, and to assist students who have difficulty coming up with even a vague concept when beginning their work. Figure 4.6 assists with brainstorming and general planning while Figure 4.7 provides a sample guiding checklist and scoring guide for the fable lesson.

Teachers can facilitate equitable decision-making among group members by continuous circulation among the groups, reinforcing appropriate, respectful behavior and also being aware of occasions of inadvertent aggressive behavior. One such misbehavior to be alert to is imbalances of participation and power such as one or two students in a small group making the majority of the decisions and completing the majority of the work, while some group members remain uninvolved or are overruled when taking part in decision-making. Just as teachers keep a running record of individual student work to get to know the strengths and concerns of students, teachers can also keep a record for each small group (1) to note progress towards inclusion of all members in what is hoped will be a replica of the consensus-building model and (2) to determine if students are performing their individual tasks in building towards a whole as the group fable takes shape.

Lesson 2: Small-Group Process Writing Circles

Title of Lesson: Composing a Group Fable

Intended Levels: Upper elementary through middle school

Resources Needed: Writing materials; advance organizers for brainstorming ideas and planning the fable as well as a guiding checklist/rubric; class copies of *The Fox and the Grape*, or go to http://www.aesopfables.com to access images and audio of the stories; an overhead projector; access to computer lab; large-size paper.

Diverse Needs and Accommodations: Adult teaching aide can partner with students who need extra help to create the fable, and may invite another friend from the class to join those students.

Target Content, Craft, and Conventions: Elements of a fable, descriptive setting, crafting universal theme as moral, and characterization.

Stages of Writing Supported: Prewriting, drafting

Group Norms: Above all, *collaboration, not domination* is the Golden Rule; state your ideas slowly and clearly; listen carefully to others and keep an open mind; work toward consensus but ask for assistance as needed; take a short time-out when anger arises; give equal sharing time; take responsibility for equal participation and effort.

Group Roles: Discussion director and summarizer, descriptive vocabulary crafter, character developer, plot and moral sketcher, authors (all), and illustrators (all). If there are five group members, you may add an investigator who looks up background information related to the setting and any other needed references.

Group and Individual Responsibilities: Assume individual assigned circle roles daily, and contribute to daily efforts and collaborative planning as a whole. Individuals may work at home if absent or behind schedule; under no circumstances will parents or others complete individual work for a circle member.

Student Statement(s) of Goal(s): Individual circle members set a goal for the day on planning calendar provided. Example: "I will work on creating the setting and introduction of characters after checking with the group on their ideas."

Lesson Goals: After reading and listening to *The Fox and the* Grape, students will:
 ➢ Recognize, use, and plan elements of fable (character, rising action, conflict, resolution, and moral);
 ➢ Collaboratively construct a fable within a small group;
 ➢ Problem-solve using positive means, including teacher in this process when necessary; and
 ➢ Access peers in the editing and revision processes.

Lesson Outcomes: Writing circle members will show evidence of collaboration and planning of the fable; members show evidence of taking an active part in the group in their assigned roles.

Assessment: Each day the circle meets, students and teacher/facilitator will note progress on daily goals, forward progress of fable, active participation in roles and project as a whole. Final evaluation will be by the teacher and audience through positive feedback as each fable is read aloud, dramatized, or otherwise presented by writing circles. Teacher will give the final grade by comparing finished project to a guiding checklist or rubric.

State (Michigan) Standards Addressed:
W.G.N.06.01 Write a cohesive narrative piece that includes appropriate conventions to the genre, employing elements of characterization for major and minor characters, internal and/or external conflict; and issues of plot, theme, and imagery.
W.PR.06.02 Apply a variety of prewriting strategies for narrative writing.
W.PR.06.03 Revise drafts for clarity, coherence, and consistency in content, voice, and genre characteristics with audience and purpose in mind.
W.AT.06.01 Be enthusiastic about writing and learning to write.

Rationale for Lesson: The lesson is planned in the spirit of being with peers, enjoying the fable genre, and building upon cooperation skills in a group.

Lesson Plan Overview: Students will read, listen to, and study two or more fables, including *The Fox and the Grape*, noting the elements of the fable such its short length to present animals as characters, a problem relating to a universal truth, and a solution, stated as a moral. Students will be placed in writing circle groups of 4–5, appoint a facilitator who will have members pull their roles out of a hat, and read one or more other fables from *Aesop's Fables*, noting the components of a fable, then brainstorm ideas for characters, setting, and plot for their own original fable. Each writing workshop will begin with a mini-lesson related to composing an original fable, followed by 20–30 minutes of group work, culminating in a whole class visualization (e.g. Power Point) or handout of a fable with illustrations. Students will fill out planning, cooperation, and work forms daily. Volunteers may present their fables to the whole class at the end of the project.

Procedure:

Before Writing
- Find out what students already know about fables; note qualities and examples on a whiteboard, overhead transparency, or Power Point slides.
- Ask students to give qualities of a "good" descriptive setting and to note qualities listed while listening to the audio.
- Read and listen to the audio of *The Fox and the Grape*.
- Ask students to identify fable components, including the descriptive setting, characters' traits, and the morale.

During Writing
- Place students in small, prearranged writing circles, appoint a facilitator and secretary, and determine other roles.
- Pass out large sheets of paper to each group and ask secretary to write each quality of the fable, as noted on whole-class visual or handout, and then to brainstorm ideas for descriptive setting, plot, characters, etc.
- Circulate around the room to note participation levels, enthusiasm, levels of collaboration, and progress, and to be available to writing circles for questions and group problem-solving.

After Writing
- After 20 minutes, ask students to note their individual progress on daily planning chart, and ask the group for a volunteer to report on progress (without going into the specifics of ideas for the original fable).
- Instruct students to note where they left off in their planning processes, to fold up planning paper and store on shelves or in cabinet for the next day.
- Instruct students to continue thinking about their circle ideas but to reserve actual work for class workshop time the next day.

Teacher Reflections on Lesson: What worked well? What needs more thought?
Example: Most students enjoyed the activities and participated well with others. One group had a member off-task much of the time, however, so perhaps a change in groups may result, or the teacher may sit in on the group in question next time. Students asked about why they were given such a large piece of paper to work with, and so tomorrow the students can be shown how to plan out their "frames" for each page for eventual presentation to the class or printed final draft.

Figure 4.5. Composing a Fable Lesson

1 Title Page	2 Introduction	3 Setting	4 Characters	5 Problem
6 Event 1	7 Event 2	8 Event 3	9 Solution	10 Moral

Figure 4.6. Advance Organizer for Brainstorming Fable Pages

Writing Circle Group Responsibilities
___ Facilitator has been chosen.
___ Secretary has been chosen to fill in brainstormed planning sheets.
___ Roles have been chosen and assumed.
___ Each circle member participates actively in discussion and group tasks.
___ Members consult one another and discuss major ideas, changes, and decisions.
___ Circle members follow set norms:
    ___ Show collaboration, not domination.
    ___ State ideas clearly and slowly.
    ___ Listen carefully to others.
    ___ Keep an open mind.
    ___ Work toward consensus on decisions.
    ___ Ask for assistance as needed.
    ___ Take a short time-out if anger arises.
    ___ Ensure equal "air time."
    ___ Take responsibility for equal participation.

Writing Circle Individual Responsibilities
___ Fill out and consult on daily task plan.
___ Complete daily reflection page.
___ Take part in discussions, group decision-making, problem-solving, and collaboration.
___ Complete daily work as planned; finish at home if necessary on individual basis.
___ Type one or more pages for the final draft of the fable.
___ Illustrate one or more pages for the final draft.
___ Encourage other group members if needed.
___ Access peers in the editing process, and offer to assist others with editing/revision.

Final Checklist for Fable
___ All elements of the fable are present.
___ Characters and setting were described and developed to fit the plot.
___ The problem and solution lead to a universal truth, lesson, or moral.
___ All drafts are in the group folder.
___ Final draft is in its best form:
    ___ Conventions and mechanics are correct.
    ___ The fable has an attractive and correctly spelled title page, acknowledging all authors.
    ___ Illustrations are neat and are appropriate to the plot and characters.
    ___ All circle members have contributed to the composition of the fable.
___ The project was finished on time.
___ A group voice and style has developed and is apparent.
___ Group has filed daily task and reflection forms in the group folder.

A	B	C	D	E
All project responsibilities are complete.	Most project responsibilities are complete.	Some project responsibilities are complete.	Many project responsibilities are incomplete.	Most or all project responsibilities are incomplete.

Figure 4.7. Checklist and Scoring Guide for Fable

Lesson 3: Individual Process Writing – Music-Inspired Descriptive Setting

It is likely that many readers spent the majority of their school days glued to their seats in straight rows and assigned seats, working alone. While I began to experience and enjoy working in small groups as a graduate student, I write best when I work alone and in silence, even if I am in a room with many people. Likewise, young adolescents who write best when they have access to a peer response group must learn to work individually – not only because many careers require it, but also because the successful development of a process to complete tasks, particularly lengthy projects, brings satisfaction and feelings of competence and power. Shorter assignments are also useful in formative assessment of students' individual understanding of grammar, literary craft, and development of voice – all of which are difficult (at best) to teach.

Consider the next lesson template, Lesson Template 3, given in Figure 4.8, designed for working with individual writers. The illustrative lesson designed from this template, shown in Figure 4.9, results in a short piece of descriptive writing, following mini-lessons on first-person character development as well as application of appropriate use of adverbial and adjectival phrases in dialog. Students will be invited, through their imaginations as prompted by instrumental music, to describe the setting into which they write themselves as a main character. I suggest that this piece of writing be one of many placed in individual writing portfolios for later possible selection by students for full development as part of a semester grade.

PROCESS WRITING LINKED TO THE ARTS   167

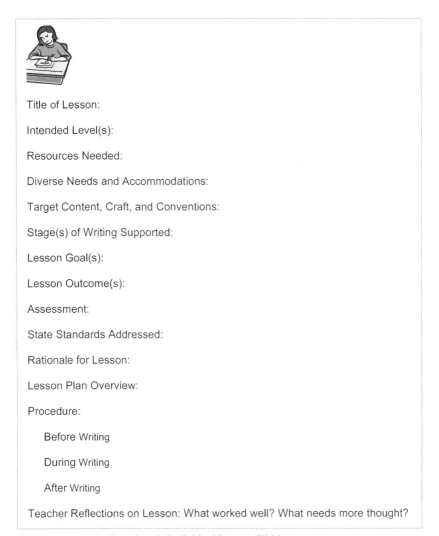

Figure 4.8. Lesson Template 3: Individual Process Writing

Lesson 4: Snowflake Bentley – A Literature, Writing, and Art Workshop

Lessons with a combination of individual, partner, and whole-class components may span 50 minutes or two class periods, depending upon the depth of study and whether the lesson builds upon a new or existing theme. An introductory lesson with many components

Title of Lesson: Writing Me into the Song

Intended Level(s): Upper elementary through middle school

Resources Needed: CD player or CD drive and speakers on a computer; two pieces of instrumental music, such as "Rise" by Herb Alpert, "Theme to Peter Gunn" by Henry Mancini, or other instrumentals by Derek Truck Band, The Eagles, or John Legend.

Diverse Needs and Accommodations: Assist second language learners with dictionary, thesaurus, word choice, and spelling as needed.

Target Content, Craft, and Conventions: Description of setting; first-person development of character; application of crisp, clear dialog; and use of appropriate adverbial and adjectival phrases.

Stages of Writing Supported: Prewriting, drafting

Lesson Goal: To stimulate students' imaginations by providing various music pieces they can literally write themselves into, as a character.

Lesson Outcomes: After listening to the music provided, students will:
- Note details about the place they are imagining as they listen;
- Create the setting they hear in the music by use of strong sensory description;
- Create appropriate characterization of themselves within the setting;
- Compose a descriptive setting after listening to the music provided, including the time, date, and location.

Assessment: Students write just one draft to share with peers, who will attempt to guess which piece of music set the background for the description; students' writing will go into writing folders and may be selected by individuals to take through full process for portfolio grading at semester time.

Rationale for Lesson: The use of music can free students' imaginations to create any setting, time, or place they imagine, so the options are almost endless as to what they create. Adding themselves as a character in the setting and perhaps writing about how and why they are present contributes a creative dimension, inviting students to think imaginatively.

Lesson Plan Overview: Two different pieces of instrumental music from any era are played; students are asked to imagine themselves in a setting of their own creation that they feel matches the music and to insert themselves into the setting, using sensory description to enhance their writing.

Procedure:

Before Writing
- Review sensory description, uses of adjective and adverb phrases, and literary devices such as metaphor, simile, personification, hyperbole, and onomatopoeia.
- Ask for examples of these.
- Instruct students to listen for a place in the musical setting to apply some literary devices.
- Ask students to note sensory description that comes to mind, and to imagine themselves in the setting suggested by the music.
- Note what elements in the music assisted students with imagining a setting.

During Writing
- Using notes taken while listening to music, invite students to create their unique settings and character
- Ask students to include time, place, and emotions in the writing.

After Writing
- Students share drafts of descriptions with peers, who then guess which musical piece inspired the setting.
- Students may volunteer to share their settings with the class in Author's Chair.

Teacher Reflections on Lesson: What worked well? What needs more thought?
The best part of the lesson was the focused listening and studious scribbling of notes while listening, along with the facial expressions of confusion, excitement, and joy. Students were fully engaged, and they seemed to like placing themselves into the setting, often a science fiction-inspired or literary (e.g. Dickens) inspired place and time. Peers also enjoyed the guessing aspect. Many students happily asked if they might finish their descriptive settings for tomorrow's class. Art definitely provided motivation and engagement with the lesson, inviting critical thought and imagination as well as some very well crafted description and characterization.

Figure 4.9. Individual Process Writing – Music

Title of Lesson: *Snowflake Bentley*: A Literature, Writing, and Art Workshop

Intended Level(s): Upper elementary through middle grades

Resources Needed: Picture book, *Snowflake Bentley*, and William Bentley's work in *Snowflakes in Photographs*; overhead transparencies or computer projections of snow crystals if desired; K-W-L organizer (see Procedure 1 below); white or other unlined paper, scissors, cards for vocabulary words, pencils, and lined paper or this handout (see Procedure 3, Written Reflection).

Target Content, Craft, and Conventions: Reading Workshop including K-W-L as a literacy organizer, teacher demonstration, artistic creation and peer talk, written reflection.

Lesson Goals: After taking part in the processes of identifying prior knowledge, what students would like to know, and what they have learned about snowflakes on the basis of discussion about related phenomena, concepts, and vocabulary; filling out an advance organizer; and listening to *Snowflake Bentley*, students will:
- Construct an original snowflake and complete a reflective writing;
- Obtain new comprehension and understanding of a scientific and artistic process;
- Strengthen prediction skills and apply background knowledge while listening to and reading of text; and
- Find pleasure in the process of creating a work of art.

Assessments: Discussion before, during, and after reading; reflective writing.

State (Michigan) Grade Level Content Standards Addressed:
W.AT.06.01 The student will be enthusiastic about writing.
R.WS.06.01 The students will explain and use word structures and prediction to understand words in context.
R.CM.06.01 The student will connect personal knowledge and experiences to themes in text through oral and written responses.
R.CM.06.04 The student will apply significant knowledge from grade level content (i.e. science).

Lesson Plan Overview: Early use of microphotography in the biography, *Snowflake Bentley*, and the creation of snowflakes to understand the uniqueness of snow crystals in their hexagonal shapes when viewed in their complex, magnified state.

Procedure:

1. **Reading Workshop**
   a. **Pre-reading** Review sensory images and this vocabulary (post or hold up on large cards): *etching, negatives, pitch, evaporation, pneumonia, hexagonal, microphotography, molecules, authority*. Ask students to predict meanings for the terms and note these on the board. Share some of the first column of the K-W-L organizer (What do you know?):

K (What do you KNOW?)	W (**WHAT** would you like to know?)	L (What have you LEARNED?)

   b. **During Reading** Direct students to listen carefully and keep the K-W-L organizer handy for notes. Facilitate students' listening with these directions, posted on the board, as the book is read aloud:

   > Jot down sensory images heard while listening, especially as they describe snow on the Notes section of your organizer.
   > Mentally note what you think the vocabulary words mean in the context of the story. See if your predictions and those of the class are correct.
   > Using your K-W-L organizer, circle the statements for which you found evidence in the story as true under the first column, K.

   c. **After Reading** Facilitate whole group discussion and peer talk, completion of column 3, L (What did you learn?):
   Did you notice sensory images? Share some of these.
   Did you like the story? What did you like about it?
   What were some of the positive and negative connotations of snow?
   Were the vocabulary predictions correct? If so, share which ones.
   What statements under the first column, K, were correct as evidenced by information in the story? Discuss these with one peer near you.
   What did you learn? Fill in column three of the K-W-L.

2. **Demonstration and Creation of Snowflakes**
   a. Examine some photographs taken by W. A. Bentley.
   b. Examine some snowflakes made previously from paper.
   c. Demonstrate the steps:
      Cut a piece of white computer paper into a large circle.
      Fold into six sections so it looks like an ice cream cone.
      Randomly cut out shapes, carefully leaving some of the folds intact.
      Open the cone to see what the snowflake looks like.
   Create one or more original snowflakes.
   Show to peers, noting the hexagonal shape.

3. **Written Reflection (may be prepared as a handout)**
   Invite students to respond to two or more of these questions:
      a. Which sensory images did you discuss today? Explain.
      b. Which vocabulary words were new for you today? Explain.
      c. Which parts of the lesson did you enjoy most? Be specific.
      d. How did the book and art project assist with organizing and gaining knowledge?

Figure 4.10. Literature, Writing, and Art Workshop

requires more time because teachers are ascertaining students' background knowledge as well as building upon it. Regardless of whether lessons come at the beginning or in the middle of a unit, those that support a given theme and require students' active involvement are going to be the most engaging – particularly when lessons provide for students' creation of art. Interest accelerates and wisdom expands when literature and writing are both included in one lesson.

Lesson 4 provides places for all of the media of art, literature, and writing within a workshop setting. The illustrative lesson includes a reading workshop, an art demonstration, and a writing component, and it focuses on the history, study, and creation of snowflakes. As a prereading, art, and writing device, a K–W–L advance organizer assists students in determining *what they know* (K), *what they would like to know* (W), and *what they have learned* (L) before, during, and after the lesson. While this lesson is based on an award-winning picture biography, *Snowflake Bentley* (Martin, 1998), additional literature and genres are suggested for reinforcement and extension of the lesson goals. Students will take pleasure in the beautifully written story of the man who first attempted to photograph snowflakes and succeeded, finding each uniquely different. Students will enjoy creating unique art works, talking about them with peers, expanding their vocabulary, and then writing about what they liked best and learned from the workshop lesson. I can almost guarantee that paper snowflakes will begin to show up on teachers' desks as presents, some so tiny and lovely that it's a wonder how the students held the scissors with such dexterity, some large and less attractive visually, but all very different and representative of the young adolescents who made them. As a final note, paper snowflakes taped lightly to winter's dark, morning windows are a great way to display students' creations while adding to the classroom décor.

This lesson may be taught alone but is best integrated into a similar theme that flows across content areas, such as *Survival among Extreme Elements*, because it helps build upon concepts in a deeper social context through its use of literature and extended, hands-on art. Students are asked to predict, call upon prior knowledge, and listen and write critically. Additional resources for a Survival unit are: "To Build a Fire" by Jack London (London, 1986) and *The River* by Gary Paulsen (Paulsen, 1993). This lesson works especially well in northern locales in the middle of winter, when many areas are snow-covered and have minimum sunlight – when snow and extreme weather tend to be viewed as the enemy. Characters in the literature noted above put forth extra effort to endure and survive extreme conditions. Snow poses a hazard and is the "nature" in the conflict of Man vs. Nature, and it is not friendly, pretty, or a means of enjoyment or sport. In direct contrast to those connotations, teachers and students can look at the concept of snow in a positive vein. This lesson has relevance for science, physics, math, and social studies, as well as language arts, depending on individual adaptation and accommodation. Young adolescents will remember the lessons because it included a beloved children's story and because they were invited to create art.

Incorporating Hands-On Art and Other Media into Lessons

Each time I have incorporated art into a middle-grades lesson, such as paper-folding when reading Eleanor Coerr's *Sadako and the Thousand Paper Cranes* (Coerr, 1977), creating two-dimensional "I have a dream" clouds from found objects while viewing *The Ernest Greene Story* (Roman, 1993), listening to Green Day's (2004) "Wake Me Up When September Ends" followed by a free-form sketching, acting out a scene from *Hatchet* (Paulson, 1986) or *Star Girl* (Spinelli, 2000), or building a cardboard and paper garden setting while reading *The Secret Garden* (Burnett, 1911), I have been reminded that students bring much to the classroom that we cannot see and may never know – unless we issue frequent invitations to interpret, converse, and create.

Art, music, film, literature, and drama also give students an outlet to find joy, to make new discoveries and meaning, and to communicate and share talents that may lie dormant, waiting for just the right time to emerge. The time may be now, that is, any time when you are ready to try the suggestions of lesson activities in this chapter or others you might find or develop yourself. Art and other media-focused experiences are powerful, *hands-on and hearts-in motivators* for students who long for authentic expression. Following exposure to the arts, expression of self in writing is the logical next step. At times, when students feel they are having fun and not really working, when the outcome is open-ended and does not have a rubric or grade, they are most apt to freely and creatively produce written works that elicit authentic responses from within themselves as well as from peers. Teachers can craft lessons that allow time for written personal reflection as well as small-group reflective discussion, following students' physical efforts at creating their written texts.

Responding to Literature and the Global Environment

The study of ways to sustain a cleaner, healthier environment for people, plants, and animals has been a special focus in the news and in classrooms throughout the world, and making use of non-fiction and fictional genres of literature often assists in building knowledge and stimulating questions and possible solutions. For example, there has been renewed interest in Rachel Carson's groundbreaking book, *Silent Spring,* which exposed the hazards of the pesticide DDT (Carson, 1962). Published in 1962, Carson movingly questioned humanity's faith in technological progress up to that point, and her book helped set the stage for the environmental movement of the 1960s and 1970s.

Another environmental classic, *The Lorax,* by Dr. Seuss (Geisel, 1971), can serve as an introduction to or review of environmental awareness. In this fable, the little Lorax objects vehemently when his beloved Truffula Trees are chopped down to make Thneeds ("which everyone needs"). Unfortunately, Once-ler, the greedy factory owner and story villain, doesn't quit until the last Truffula falls and the surrounding ecosystem is utterly polluted. Most students enjoy the return of a favorite children's book now and then, especially when they are asked to write a sequel with a partner or to rewrite the story with a different ending and their own illustrations. Through the literature, peer talk, art, and writing invitations, students become personally invested not only in the environmental themes, but also in crafting their writing into works that may suggest some answers to important environmental issues while infusing their own unique experience and style into their written pieces.

Sowing the Seeds of Aesthetic Writing

Invitations to write which are built upon still images, sound recordings, and film or video records of current and historical events as represented in mass media enhance the likelihood that students will become actively involved in their own learning; writers may undergo an aesthetic response, motivating critical conversation and writing.

Any discussion of student response, whether as reader or writer, must include Louise Rosenblatt's socio-educational contributions. Her use of the term *transactional* (Rosenblatt, 1978, 1988) reflects the 20th century shift in thinking with respect to the relationship of humans to the rest of the world. Rosenblatt (1988: 2) says that the newer paradigm reflects a focus on the reciprocal relationship of people to their environment, and that human behaviors can be viewed "as transactions in which the individual, and the social, cultural, and natural elements interfuse." Rosenblatt's discussion is particularly useful when considering what occurs when middle school students respond to social, cultural, and natural elements of the arts. Young adolescents may not fully comprehend their reasons for strong, personal responses to the lyrics in a Taylor Swift song or why a videotape of politicians engaged in negative rhetoric produces feelings of anger in them, yet students know their responses are tangible.

While Louise Rosenblatt's work has focused mainly upon reader response, she also writes about the similarities of reader and writer responses, based on internal, transactional responses along the aesthetic–efferent continuum (Rosenblatt, 1988). *Efferent,* from the Latin *effere*, meaning "to carry away," refers to what the reader acquires or takes away; *aesthetic* is "concerned with literature as art with the 'lived through' experience of the text…" (Enos, 1996: 644). One similarity between reader and writer response is stated this way: "The writer 'composes' a presumably meaningful text; the reader 'composes,' hence, 'writes,' an interpreted meaning" (Rosenblatt, 1988: 2). Psychologist William James wrote about the relationship between words and their referents, emphasizing that words refer to objects as well as carry an internal "coloring of their own" (James, 1890: 18). Linguists view language as a pool of possible symbols, not signs of stationary meanings. Also, the process of making meaning is affected by how the individual feels physically and emotionally. Rosenblatt (1988) states that language activity involves a blend of cognitive, affective, and associational awareness. Language has both public analytic and private experiential components, and the reader's or writer's attention and purpose will largely determine a physical aesthetic or combination [public and private] response (Rosenblatt, 1988).

> ***Writing is an opportunity for young adolescents to draw from their vast store of impressions, experiences, and linguistic knowledge to respond without fear of acceptability of subject, organization, or mechanics, especially during the drafting stage.***

What is Aesthetic Writing?

Students' response can be quite powerful when they are first presented with occasions to study and experience a piece of art that moves them. The transactional process can engender a feeling of freedom within writers, particularly when teachers prompt students to look back at their selected words and phrases to see if the language fits the response that was intended. No matter how unrestrained the writing may be, the stream of memories, ideas, and words is not completely accidental (Rosenblatt, 1988). Words and conveyance of ideas are thus a public expression of a private connection between the art and the writer/observer.

Rosenblatt (1978) described efferent and aesthetic response to reading as transactional literary theory, which describes the two-way connection readers have with text; as noted earlier, the same can be applied to the arts in general. Young adolescent learners can experience, react to, or become transformed by art, and then translate the insights gained from their aesthetic response into writing. In *The Reader, the Text, the Poem*, Rosenblatt (1978: 24) writes: "In aesthetic (reading) the…primary concern is with what happens *during* the actual reading event." I believe the same is true in what I want to call *aesthetic writing,* in which the response is fostered by the writer's concept of himself or herself in reference to the world as well as the writer's internal feelings prior to physically composing text. When I refer to a moving or strong reaction within students who are presented with any form of art, including literature, I mean that an internal cognitive and affective response may take place *while they are engaged with* or *in the study of* art. Thus, I see writing as a transactional experience for many students, when art, particularly art that is highly relevant to them, is part and parcel of the invitation to write. With art as a prompt, students undergo growth and discovery of new ideas and meanings, as well as possible answers to difficult questions. While writing in response to art does not always produce personal connections, I have observed that links often exist between the writer and the art in the form of prior knowledge, interest, or curiosity, which lead to future aesthetic writing. When lessons promote authentic, transformational experiences, students' writing will reveal this.

> ***Educators can look outside the pedagogical box and imagine ways to elicit authentic responses, issue invitations to create original works, and join with students by modeling such efforts.***

Art can elicit connective responses between art and observer from the most angst-ridden adolescent to the most mature adult, and the pay-off with young adolescent writers is huge. Students' reflective writing conveying strong personal voice can unfold in ways that demonstrate insight. In these ways, the writing is transactional, as the meanings flow from the art, literature, music, film, or graphic media to the writer. Since good writing is more than the sum of its grammar and other surface elements, the teacher should aim to stimulate adolescents' potential abilities to tap into the depth of authentic human response – a response that can motivate them to write with passion and wisdom as they grow in the knowledge of their place in the world. Transactional writing – writing that creates a transaction between writer and reader – may then stem from writers' reflections upon personal issues, upon recalling autobiographical events, and upon the motivation to share their experiences and these events in ways that make a difference for their audiences (Whitney, 2008: 162).

Teacher-writers, particularly those who have themselves felt personal satisfaction and joy in their own experiences as writers through professional endeavors such as Summer Invitational Institutes of the National Writing Project (NWP), have related changes in their own lives as teachers and writers (Whitney, 2008: 144). Having taken part in Michigan State University's Red Cedar Writing Project's Invitational Summer Institute toward the end of my classroom teaching career in 2001, I have often wished I had taken part in that cohesive community of writing teachers much earlier. I make note of this NWP professional development here because of the prospective positive effect such experiences can have upon teachers' writing instruction and therefore their students. Part of the institute required each participating teacher to plan and teach a demonstrative writing lesson, many of which involved the arts, including children's literature, news stories, non-fiction texts, and many genres of traditional art. The change that may occur for teachers during the summer institutes becomes activated during the demonstrations as well as during other small-group work such as the reading and discussion about writing research and writing with peers. How much potential for young adolescents exists when their teachers have themselves taken part in NWP summer institutes or other writing seminars designed to specifically enhance writing as a developing, engaging, and satisfying process!

Teachers who are up to the challenge of planning transactional writing invitations that tap into art can expect student motivation and engagement – and hence, writing quality – to soar. Former classroom teacher Mary Bellucci Buckelew, in "The Value of Art in the English Classroom: Imagination, Making the Tacit Visible" (Buckelew, 2003: 50), explains how reading a postcard printed with the art of Matisse, Diego Rivera, and others prompted cognitive connections between students' literary purposes and their conscious emotions. Buckelew discusses the value of teaching students how to find language for expressing how they experience and interpret art. A great part of students' discovery of connections to art lies in both reflective conversation and teacher participation, especially taking part in the writing process of the lessons.

One way to encourage reflective discourse is to model a "think-aloud," an activity in which the writer (in this case the teacher who is discussing a personal composition) looks at the writing, noting aloud some of the decision-making that occurred before and during constructing a piece of writing. For example, the writer may talk briefly about the decision to create a dialog to begin a memoir or a timeline to help focus the sequence of events during the prewriting stage, or may point out the texts deleted from an earlier draft because it did not fit with the chronological flow and narrator's voice in the memoir. Students may also benefit from the writer sharing examples of decisions made as to word choice and rhetorical constructions. Taking time for reflective discourse and then immersing oneself in the classroom writing community illustrates the necessity of critical thought, interaction with peers and the teacher, and role modeling to nurturing young adolescent writing.

Growth through Reflective Writing

Teacher self-reflection in connection to writing lessons is crucial. Suggestions for self-reflection may include a review of approaches, pedagogy, and invitations that have been met with student surprise, interest, and engagement. What parts of these engaging lessons have motivated students to respond with genuine concern and interest? Taking time to reflect and plan must be accompanied by an understanding that most young adolescent learners are wise in the ways of the world. Middle-grades learners have already sat for years in different classrooms and made numerous observations, both positive and negative, and so they have become knowledgeable about teacher intention. They know the difference between *writing from the inside-out* (learner-directed) and *from the outside-in* (teacher-directed writing on demand), even when the prompt is referred to as "an invitation." In addition, not everyone, even the most intrinsically motivated student, is able to continuously respond whenever asked to write. Therefore, middle-grades educators can benefit from this advice: Engage learners by helping them to answer the proverbial question: "Why write?" Thus, part of teacher reflection involves the students' reflections on writing as well.

Once the invitation or assignment has been planned and given, I suggest writing with students, and then talking with them about what goes through the heads of writers as they make decisions about word choice, audience, and options in communicating with clarity and depth of thought.

Reflection throughout the writing process greatly affects students' levels of understanding about their own learning as well as of the ways in which they choose to craft their writing.

When teachers use words like *efferent* (refers to information, facts, solutions, required actions) and *aesthetic* (refers to the feelings, attitudes, and ideas aroused in the reader during association with reflection about literature and the arts), they are able to articulate different motivations for writing in a way that emphasizes their contrasting sources. By using such terms with their students, they model appropriate vocabulary as well as clarity for thinking and talking about what motivates response in writing. The practice of employing appropriate terminology with respect to conversations about written language places a high value on the act of selecting expressions that best suit specific functions and occasions of oral and written communication. Teachers are purveyors of occasions for critical thinking; and students benefit from an awareness of the concrete or abstract ideas that may stimulate human reactions, and of the reality that individuals respond and communicate in varied ways.

In short, teachers must convey the power and wisdom they feel as writers who can choose words to suit mood, audience, and intention; they can explain what is happening within themselves as they write. It is risky for many teachers to ask students what they think and feel, as some students might react with sarcasm or perhaps too much honesty. Still, asking students about their reactions to music, art, or literature and what drives them as they proceed to write in response to it can give direction to the writer and inform the teacher. Some questions to consider asking students during a writing workshop in response to art are the following:

- How did you choose these words and phrases that fit well here?

> What do you do when you are stumped or cannot think of just the right word?
> Does the piece of art, music, or literature appeal to you personally? Why or why not?

Teachers contribute to a writer's sense of power when they invite reflection and discussion, just as my high school English teacher did. In a transfer of power, teachers can treat young adolescents' writing with the respect of an interested reader, implying that all wisdom does not emanate from the teacher. Writing in response to the arts comes with an added benefit, when writers begin to see patterns and similarities of theme in discussions with classmates as well as similarities between characters in literature and those in their own writing. In this way, writing can further empower even the least confident student, who may have previously viewed writing only as a necessary evil upon which he or she would be assessed, once given the freedom to seek varied meaning and connections through art. The importance of teaching students how to write for a test in contrast to writing for authentic audiences is addressed in Chapter 7.

Even with the addition of art and graphic media as referents, some students begin their writing anew each day. Like many adults, a fair number of learners are perfectionists, unwilling to write their thoughts until each idea is clear and fully developed, and until all conventions are correct. Still others may not have a clue about what to write until they are fully into the process, when they may be capable of seeing what adjustments are needed. All adolescent writers, with the support of teachers and the educational system in general, must find ways to both interpret and craft the language in a way that suits their learning style and understanding of the task, and that adds to feelings of self-efficacy which help them to grow into empowered, proficient, prolific writers.

Supporting the Roots of Individual Growth

In this chapter's introductory remarks, I posited that application of the arts, including music, drama, film, literature, and graphic digital media, nurtures motivation in young adolescents to write authentically and critically – particularly when alternative pathways to empowerment are provided for diverse learners. Here are some reminders of ways to establish the routes – or roots – to writing success for all learners:

- Regard the energy spent in planning and accommodation as energy well spent because it takes much more energy to fit students into a standardized system than to plan around individual learners, utilizing what works best for each;
- Build upon each young adolescent writer's strengths;
- Teach lessons that reflect respect for all members of the classroom community;
- Plan with relevance, knowledge, and awareness of students' passions;
- Invite inquiry and incorporate the arts into lessons whenever possible to motivate writing responses across the curriculum;
- Give positive, helpful, continuous feedback;
- Model and provide time for student goal-setting, reflection, and related discussion;
- Share writing on a regular basis;
- Model a think-aloud strategy as part of the writing process when drafting and revising; and
- Use mentor texts as well as unpublished texts as part of mini-lessons on craft and conventions

Concluding Reflections on Chapter 4

Teachers can nurture and motivate growth in student writing by planning lessons that incorporate hands-on, creative activities and processes, including the interaction with, as well as the viewing and making of, art. This includes traditional and contemporary art, music, film, video, graphic art, photography, drama, and literature.

Teachers set the stage for inquiry learning, insight, and aesthetic or efferent responses within writing instruction by presentation of these arts and other media, such as digital graphics, sound clips, and video with which young adolescents may readily connect. As discussed in the preceding chapter, teachers prompt motivation to write by utilization of current, relevant, and, at times, controversial topics portrayed in the mass media as invitations to study, hypothesize, gather information, and problem-solve alternative solutions through discourse and writing. When students consider a musical score, piece of art, or film script from new or different points of view, they may find application to their lives or an increased appreciation of an art genre. Best of all, young adolescents may come to understand that the real sense of achievement comes when they discover voice and purpose in writing. The addition of a process of consensus-building while working with peers in small groups provides for a positive social interaction in the writing process. Finally, self-reflection as a necessary component of growth in writing must be modeled by the teacher, with the knowledge that praise for and acceptance of one's own writing can be difficult.

In Chapter 5, I present an argument for steering clear of conditions for writing that invite literal or textbook, five-paragraph essay responses in favor of planting the seeds of critical thinking. Opportunities for inquiry, personal investment, and choice are discussed, and lessons that support these critical behaviors are presented. In addition, I offer suggestions for assisting students with organizing their thoughts in preparation for various types of required genre-based writing, by means of advance organizers such as anticipation guides, mapping, and classic outlines. Finally, I discuss the benefits of a writer's grammar.

5 Motivating Writing with Choice and Critical Thinking

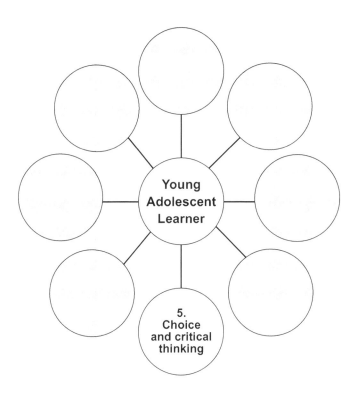

Criticism should not be querulous and wasting, all knife and root puller, but guiding, instructive, inspiring.
– Ralph Waldo Emerson (in Allen and Clark: 1966: 370)

Introductory Remarks to Chapter 5

In the above quotation, Emerson advocates a positive view of criticism as a means of motivating instruction. While writing teachers generally dispense criticism for the purpose of guiding and inspiring students towards improvement, they do not always succeed. However, since young adolescent writers are faced with increasingly difficult literacy tasks that require them to think, solve problems, and write critically, they benefit from teachers' positive criticism, particularly if it involves modeling for students, as Emerson suggests. From this type of criticism, students learn lessons and are then able to apply constructive critiques of their own writing and also those of their peers.

Criticism can be a powerful writing response tool for teachers and students to use when reflective thought and conversation accompany it. The old adage to think before you speak is particularly appropriate here, because teachers can get bogged down in grading papers yet persist, with the best intentions, in providing thorough, written comments that may or may not be taken into account by students. Even quick, focused dialogs with students about specific writing problems don't always take root or effect change in their compositions. In this chapter, I offer my perceptions of the term *criticism* with respect to young adolescent writing. I refer to two Cs, *critical thinking* and *choice*, and I discuss their relationship to motivating young adolescent writers. Lessons illustrative of the inclusion of critical thinking and choice in writing instruction are included.

Criticism and Feedback

At this point, a clarification of terms is in order. Teachers may view *criticism* as correction or negative evaluation, while *feedback* may connote a generally more positive or less evaluative mode of response. At the same time, many educators, professional writers, and academics have used a collection of wide-ranging expressions to convey what they mean by *criticism*. Everyday uses for the word *criticism* represent both a deeper, more analytical response than is implied by *feedback* and a generally negative response.

> ***Young adolescents are not seasoned writers or responders and so need to learn to be open to others' opinions and insights, even if these differ from their own views.***

Feedback as well as critique or criticism per se can serve as motivation for students when delivered with the intention of revealing to them where they are headed as writers – a clear communication of what is being done correctly and what still must be accomplished in order to achieve the desired finished composition. For the current chapter discussion, *criticism* will be used interchangeably with *feedback,* despite the differences in connotations, as my intention here is to encourage all to dispense the types of inspirational guidance, instructional effectiveness, and positive response to which Emerson referred – regardless of how shallow or deep the focal point.

Response to Student Writing within Time Constraints

One of the unfortunate side effects of the standardized, high-stakes testing that is the norm in the United States and many other countries is the additional challenge to squeeze specific literal level content learning into an already crowded school day without excluding meaningful response to writing. Regrettably, this practice of devoting excessive time to test preparation results in further stress for teachers and young adolescent writers alike. In addition, preparation for the test may not equate to preparation for writing. Michelle Tremmel, a former high school teacher during the early years of Michigan's standardized testing and now a university professor, writes:

> The biggest problem I see with at least some curricula's overreliance on formulaic writing as a be-all and end-all is that they teach it as all-purpose and universal...and students not exposed to strategies for generating and arranging ideas organically (rather than fitting them into a template to organize them) are totally at a loss and have to start from scratch with the messy realities of inventing and arranging.... (Tremmel, 2009)

A recent discussion thread about this topic among secondary school teachers on one of the listservs to which I subscribe included Tremmel's comments as well as other proclamations by some self-described "gutsy" and "subversive" educators who found that they need not sacrifice best practice writing pedagogy for test preparation in order for their students to succeed on (writing) tests.

Young adolescent writers must come to understand a range of rhetorical situations and purposes for writing beyond test preparation. They must learn how to craft clear, correct, and creative language within a variety of structures and for a variety of purposes. Along with the basic qualities for each writing genre, writers' motivation and engagement levels rise with teachers' invitations to play or experiment with various versions of a text in order to convey intended meaning. Writers must develop literary crafts such as the use of metaphor and humor, as they become aware that writers possess the power of choice. The necessary time for students' development of both the required concrete writing skills as well as the more abstract writing crafts require teachers' conscientious planning – and administrative support. Being short of time can lead teachers to brief, responsive conversations with writers, at times leaving unintended confusion in their wake. Since managing a thriving, learner-centered classroom is rarely seamless, brevity in response to students' work could be the highly restricted status quo of focusing on conventions and elements of form rather than on students' ideas. At the same time, student writers seek feedback with regard to the more abstract craft elements in their writing; young adolescents want teachers' opinions about whether a chosen phrase fits the topic, whether a transition works to join two related but contrasting details, or whether the writer is on the correct path toward completing an assignment.

> ***While content and form are both important, the teacher's urge to correct errors in form immediately, prior to reading what a student has drafted, defeats the purpose of teacher guidance and inspiration.***

Moreover, teacher response to only surface errors becomes a barrier to motivation for many young adolescent writers. Teachers' written responses, even carefully noted in pencil rather than red pen, can have the same off-putting effect.

How might teachers create ways to strike a balance when responding to the content and form of young adolescents' written work? Being able to give constructive, balanced criticism depends largely upon how a teacher views the teacher-writer relationship, whether writing assessment is viewed as a continuous process using both formal and informal means, such as choosing which writing topics and skills to teach. Both the answer and the challenge for teachers reside in the following three-part sequence of actions:

- Becoming aware of the types of responses given to both the surface errors as well as the deeper qualities of student writing;
- Judging whether the approach being used responds to student writing within varied contexts; and
- Altering response behavior if it turns out to be unproductive.

The myriad factors at play in classroom settings compel teachers to make on-the-spot decisions and to have different goals for feedback depending on need.

Content may be the primary focus for teacher feedback on a first draft essay that is more heavily weighted, as in a semester project, and so would call for a detailed teacher response. In a different kind of case, students may be asked to turn in a first draft intended as an extension of a class lesson to demonstrate correct use of grammar, such as use of tenses or pronouns in a complex chronological account or instructions, requiring a brief response. The teacher might selectively focus feedback on the first draft on the grammar point, saving content-oriented response for the second draft. The justification for a focus on linguistic form before content in this case is to ensure a clear message. A reminder about a reoccurring spelling or rhetorical error may require a brief response while longer feedback may be needed during drafting stages of the writing process, such as a suggestion to add detail to clarify an idea. If extensive revisions to student writing are required, teachers may confer directly rather than writing a long narrative alone, so that the writer may take part in the communication and the teacher may check that writing development is progressing. Every day, hundreds of these decisions are made within the constraints of time and circumstance, and teachers must reserve adequate time to critically consider what works and what does not, adjusting their response to young adolescent writing and planned lessons as needed.

I applaud the teacher education programs, professors, supervising teachers, mentor teachers, and other members of the larger educational community whose work includes specific discussions about and consideration of the teaching of writing as a progressive, reflective process. George Hillocks, Jr., addressed the topic succinctly in his text, *Teaching Writing as Reflective Practice* (Hillocks, 1995). While Hillocks writes to secondary and university teacher audiences, his examinations of students' writing practices and ways to plan lessons appropriate for motivating academic writing are also highly applicable to education in the middle grades. Teachers' thoughtful, initial responses to young adolescents' work may validate students as individuals and as human beings. At the same time, teachers may come to see that the writing and response-to-writing processes function as an intrinsic, satisfying experience for them and the students as well. Writing becomes personally motivating for students when teachers invite them to express themselves for purposes beyond the expected mechanics normally present in a mandated writing curriculum. The writing process, when placed in the hands of reflective teachers, has the potential to elicit critical thinking and satisfaction.

Planning for and responding to student writing takes experience and dedication to learn to do well, particularly when the focus is on students' writing improvement beyond what is required and tested.

A good deal of analytical thinking takes place when both teachers and students have the time and space to do so – often leading to growth in young adolescent writing.

In the Young Adolescent Motivation Model (YAMM), teachers assume continuing facilitative roles as they share the power of literary analysis and criticism with students. *Critical literacy*, a method of thinking rather than a specific teaching strategy, invites insightful thought about substantive issues, with the potential to alter perceptions, prompting action or response.

Once students are cognitively involved and personally invested, they dig more deeply and tend to produce writing that not only meets but also exceeds state and national standards.

Lessons that promote critical thought and that also offer choice drawn from promising practice across the content areas are provided in this chapter, along with texts chosen to inspire teachers to reflect upon and refine their teaching. Still, before harvesting the amazing garden of writing that can be produced by young adolescent learners – that is, before experiencing their success as writers – educators, parents, and others truly interested in their welfare should take a good look at ways to create an aggregate culture, or a system of varied sources that together help to support the roots of garden growth. This type of culture encourages rather than discourages solid growth in the whole learner – intellectually, emotionally, socially, and physically. Teachers, parents, and a supportive community pave the most direct and true path to motivating young adolescent writing. Two very important areas of community support for students' growth as writers are discussed in the next section, "The Two Cs: Critical Thinking and Choice."

The Two Cs: Critical Thinking and Choice

Here I present positive views of critical thinking as a significant process in which students alike can be motivated to actively take part while growing toward and beyond basic writing proficiency. In addition, I offer an argument for the inclusion of choice in middle-grades writing, as it encourages young adolescents to think and to write with engagement and purpose, while posing their own questions and seeking answers that fit into their unique ways of thinking and viewing the world.

Critical Thinking: The First "C"

Enlarging the Learner's Frame of Mind

Facilitating young adolescents' critical thinking about their writing requires consistent planning so that lessons and student experiences build one upon the other, referencing prior knowledge as needed, and growing into a larger framework of information. To further connect the learning process to the writing process necessitates critical thought, including careful planning and then implementation, combined with frequent reflection, whether working toward short-range or long-range goals. Here is an illustration: The teacher talks through the use of bold font or all caps to highlight writers' ideas, reviews the use and misuse of end punctuation and superlatives when attempting to convey the writer's attitude or opinion regarding a topic, and then models examples of these points with the class, enabling students to make applications to their writing. The teacher may use examples such as these to demonstrate the usage:

- Patricia trudged home, head drooping, after the worst school day ever.
  (Correct use of the superlative, *the worst*, shows the writer's strongly negative opinion.)
- NO WAY that pitch was a foul ball!
  (All caps and use of the exclamation point convey writer's strong emotion.)

The teacher might then draw students' attention to an example or two from a novel which the class is reading that demonstrates the usage points, and then students can provide examples of their own. Oftentimes, all it takes is a small reminder or mini-lesson for students to recall past learning that can be accessed and applied in new situations. Young adolescents' understanding and use of prior knowledge are critical thinking in action, representing growth in writing as well as application from one context to another.

It Takes a Village

Support for teachers and young adolescents becomes more and more important as they strive to implement writing and other curriculum that not only meet standards, but also exceed them. In Chapter 2, I discussed the importance of building kinship among writers, even going further than the teacher and students to the larger community beyond the school. Teachers' ongoing efforts to raise motivation and achievement levels in writing are fed and sustained not only by their formal education, professional development, classroom experiences, and common sense; teachers' work also benefits greatly from collaboration and communication with other teachers and with families, administrators, school boards, and other members of the local community such as businesses. In effect, when young adolescents' links to the larger community resemble a type of traditional neighborhood, people in the immediate community are aware of children's lives and seek to protect and nurture them. Of course, nowadays, families have taken on many additional roles, so a firm root system of support among community members does not always develop; but that system is nonetheless a possibility.

Parents' participation in their children's education is a vital element of student success, especially growth in higher order learning such as critical thinking. When parents actively participate in their children's education, discussions about classroom learning and applications to real-world contexts beyond school can result. Thus, the family-teacher partnerships become a vehicle for student success. To reach all parents and families, even those not usually active in schools, teachers may carefully consider ways to invite them into the classroom.

Along with parents, young adolescents' grandparents, aunts, uncles, close family friends, and administrators would be welcome as audience members for student presentations, as work partners for in-class projects, and as visiting experts or speakers on topics related to classroom study. Additionally, teacher newsletters that describe parent and community visits, upcoming events, curriculum units, and past class successes positively affect the larger educational community as not only supports for, but also as partners in, education. And as noted earlier, teachers' attention to responding to voice-mails, e-mails, and parents' requests for face-to-face meetings are a priority. When taken together, the individual sectors, with families at the forefront, build and contribute to the larger, diverse educational community, which in the best case is alive with support for young adolescent writers.

Many students at this age already enjoy a network of online peers and are easily motivated to develop support groups in virtual spaces. But young adolescent writers need much more: they require real relationships with peers and adults.

> ***Young adolescents who interact with real as well as virtual neighbors are better able to understand their place in the community, the region, the state, the country, and the world because they are dynamically occupied with looking beyond their own immediate needs, interests, and knowledge.***

Student success in the future workplace depends upon exposure to a writing curriculum overflowing with opportunities for deep thought and upon creative, determined teachers to facilitate profound learning. No Child Left Behind legislation has resulted in strict adherence to programmed learning for test preparation, leaving many schools with little else in their school day. Not much will change for students unless local and global communities become aware that teachers in the United States have, by and large, been prohibited from not only teaching critical thinking but from being critical thinkers as well. Trust in and support for the teachers who were chosen for their talent and dedication to children are therefore foundational to effective education. Teachers must be encouraged to critically and creatively interpret governmental standards by means of motivating, inquiry-rich writing classrooms. Critical thinking involves freedom of choice within unique contexts, including teacher choice regarding the most appropriate ways to teach lessons and to make use of and create resources, materials, and experiences, based on teachers' and students' learning and communicational styles.

Critical thinking and critical literacy rely upon the freedom and the choice to teach curriculum standards pertaining to individual teaching contexts, teaching styles, and students' individual needs.

Writing teachers have the skills needed for creating an effective teaching-learning process under varying circumstances, and they continually apply and refine their knowledge of teaching writing to new and different applications. In order to stimulate and nurture young adolescents' critical thinking, teachers must have the support of the larger community. Support enables classroom educators to call upon and employ their expertise and experience, and their innovative and critical thinking practices, with young adolescent writers. Advantages to students are many when teachers freely make application of prior knowledge to new contexts and when they take calculated, positive risks through informed pedagogical knowledge. In so doing, teachers model critical thinking for young writers. When teachers bring students into reflective dialog about their own and the students' thought processes with regard to writing, further critical thinking takes place.

Teachers model scholarship and what it means to be educated through engagement with their own work as writers.

The combined efforts of students' families, peers, neighbors, and those who live and work in the community may also foster critical thinking. In the words of Secretary of State Hillary Clinton, "It takes a village" (Clinton, 1996: 7) to raise a child. Young adolescent writers develop the ability to think deeply about and to develop excellence in writing through classroom and community support, which includes the educational community and institutional authorities as well as nurturance by all of the adults involved – in other words, a metaphorical village.

Teacher Behaviors Foster Critical Thinking

Teachers most directly nurture students' abilities to think critically when they devise classroom activities that require a variety of open-ended teaching-learning behaviors with planned introduction, review, practice, and application of specific curricular goals. The goals may include the individual teacher's own goals that match or go beyond state and national standards. The lessons that lead to goal attainment guided by critical thinking will include one or more of the following activities: investigating, contemplating, questioning, challenging, and/or creating (Texas Community College Teachers Association, 2002). Thus, teachers provide experiences that motivate young adolescents to look beyond the traditional classroom walls for answers and ideas, nurturing varied perspectives and original thought.

In the next section, I present an illustrative lesson, written with the expressed goals of reviewing grammatical parts of speech, creating complete and grammatically correct sentences, hypothesizing about why these are complete thoughts, and working in cooperative groups. Each of these goals can be realized as young adolescents are vigorously engaged in utilizing higher level thinking skills and multiple intelligences. I have observed that the more senses are involved in learning, the deeper the learning; and I have found this to be especially true with the addition of visuals and the goal of finding a pattern integrated into a lesson (as is the case with "You Be the Sentence," shown in Figure 5.1 below).

Howard Gardner's seminal text, *Frames of Mind: The Theory of Multiple Intelligences* (Gardner, 1983/2004), draws attention to the concept of the multifaceted nature of recognizing and applying different kinds of "intelligences" or abilities, such as those that include the arts or "emotional intelligence," along with the theory that students of all ages possess one or more of these intelligences. A developmental psychologist, Gardner (2004: xv) based his theory, which can be readily applied to the field of education, on the premise that all human beings have a "set of relatively autonomous intelligences," which center on the spatial, bodily kinesthetic, musical, artistic, interpersonal, and intrapersonal qualities that make us all uniquely human. Gardner (2004: xxiii) expanded the idea of *intelligence* beyond knowledge of traditional, easily testable data, to include the "knowledge of the brain and sensitivity to the diversity of human cultures." Many of these intelligences have been incorporated into the following lesson.

You Be the Sentence: Grammar Review Lesson

How do we plan lessons that facilitate and motivate the application of skills and concepts practiced in class to young adolescents' writing, particularly when the product is analysis or another type of writing requiring abstract thinking? Can this process be evaluated? If so, how? Next, I present an engaging, small-group lesson that reviews sentence structure, requiring students to compose complete thoughts, and to speculate on what makes a sentence a complete thought, resulting in a group hypothesis or theory. The lesson makes use of students' multiple intelligences by including elements of these intelligence types: linguistic, logical, kinesthetic, spatial-visual, and interpersonal. In addition, the lesson sheds light upon students' prior knowledge of basic English grammar while motivating students to think critically and to problem-solve through the formation of hypotheses and applications to new writing contexts. The complete lesson, including the small-group advance organizer, is provided in Figure 5.1.

Title of Lesson: "You Be the Sentence"

Intended Levels: Upper elementary through high school

Resources Needed: Advance organizer with directions; premade activity cards created by writing or printing examples of parts of speech on colored computer paper or color construction paper, a different color for each part of speech; yellow paper for -s and -es; additional blank neutral paper for conjunctions and punctuation; pens or pencils; five to ten plastic bags which can be sealed; large, open spaces for group work on the floor (or large tables); minimum one-half hour of work time; a portable microphone.

Notes:
> Alternatives to colored paper activity cards described may include the use of either multi-color sticky notes ("post-its") or the use of multi-colored markers on white paper.
> Examples: *Grandma* (in pink letters on white paper or on pink paper printed in black, indicating a noun); *may be visiting* (in blue letters or on blue paper, indicating a verb or verb phrase).
> See Appendix D for sample pink (noun) cards and Appendix E for sample blue (verb) cards.

Diverse Needs and Accommodations: Varies; teacher determines.
Suggestions: personal teacher microphone for hearing-impaired students; room aides or parents to work in small groups with learning-disabled or English language learners; adjust workshop steps as needed, depending upon age-appropriateness and context.

Target Content, Craft, and Conventions: Teach or review these sentence elements: subject, predicate, adjectival and adverbial phrases; correct use of conjunctions; correct use of punctuation; and definition of a complete thought (sentence).

Stages of Writing Supported: All – prewriting, drafting, writing, revision, publishing, and reflection.

Group Norms: Varies; teacher determines.
Suggestions: Demonstrate respect for one another; listen actively to learn and understand; participate actively; set aside judgment; and share "air time."

Group Roles: Facilitator or discussion director, writer, deep thinkers (all), editors (all) and runner.

Group Responsibilities: Student Statement's of Goal(s): Varies; set up as appropriate.

Lesson Goals:
1. Students will show knowledge of a complete sentence, specifically noting subject (noun) and predicate (verb) elements of the sentence;
2. Students will recognize basic parts of speech; and
3. Students will work cooperatively and actively in groups.

Lesson Outcomes:
1. Students present color activity cards (varied color paper with each major part of speech represented by a color) in the order of a complete thought, noting in discussion and/or presentation that this requires a pink (noun/subject) and blue (verb/predicate) cards;
2. Students verbally make the connection between colors and parts of speech, as they relate to sentence composition; and
3. Students follow rules and assume roles, as directed, during small group work.

State Standards Matched: Varies.

Rationale for Lesson: Students need to know how to create complete sentences through active involvement in their learning and through understanding parts of speech to support their writing.

Lesson Plan Overview: After a brief review, students meet in small groups to compose complete sentences, using colored activity cards indicating parts of speech; they answer a set of questions that stimulate discussion about the color tiles and their use in composition; they theorize about the necessity of including some of the cards, when taken together, create a complete thought, and they prepare to share theories and sentences with the class. Students hold up the colored activity cards in the order in which the words read to complete the thought; thus *students become the sentence*.

Procedure:

Before Activity

1. Find out what students already know about complete sentences and the parts of speech that compose them via an informal discussion.

2. Demonstrate a complete sentence, using the colored activity cards (e.g. pink contains examples of nouns and noun phrases, blue contains examples of verbs and verb phrases, green for adjectives, gray for adverbs, purple for prepositional phrases, and blank for students to add conjunctions and punctuation). Do not indicate parts of speech at this point; just read the sentence and point to each card as you read.

3. Tell students they will be working in groups of 4 or 5 to play "You Be the Sentence," a game about composing their own unique and sometimes silly sentences. Preselect group members and designate a discussion director, writer, and runner; if students work well together as a rule, you can have them count off to form random groups. Students will have fifteen minutes to complete the entire process, and you will let them know when they have five minutes left.

4. Prior to meeting in small groups:

    a. Designate and post roles for each student within the group so all will be as actively involved as possible;
    b. Post group rules, which may be preset or student-generated, depending on purpose/s and contexts;

> c. Instruct students to take on their role(s) once in groups and to follow group rules;
> d. Direct students to answer the questions provided on the advance organizer and to then work toward completing the final product, which is to compose a complete sentence using the color cards as well as to theorize why the sentence is complete.
>
> 5. Ask one or more students to repeat the directions to you in their own words; ask if there are any questions, and if so, clarify.
>
> 6. Ask runners to pick up a premade kit in large size plastic bags, which contain a variety of colored activity cards, an advance organizer for each group member, blank paper, and pencils.
>
> 7. Direct students to meet in small groups and to begin the activity.
>
> **During Activity**
> Facilitated by the discussion director, students in small groups answer a set of questions that stimulate discussion about the colored cards and their use in composition; they theorize about what they believe each color represents with regard to grammar and how, in certain combinations, complete thoughts may be created; and they prepare to share theories and sentences with the class.
>
> 1. Presentation for understanding: Students hold up the colored cards in the order in which the words need to be read in order to complete the sentence, thus *they become the sentence*. Example sentence, using a card of each color:
>
>   **Oprah Winfrey** (pink) **giggled** (blue) **sweetly** (gray) **and danced** (blue) **mightily** (gray) **around the bend** (purple).
>
>   The nonsensical quality of the sentences engages students and motivates them to think about how and why sentences are constructed.
>
> 2. Alternate presentation: invite students to act out the sentence in parts by demonstrating the sentence meanings (activity cards down), have the rest of the class guess the sentence created by the group, and then line up in order, as above, to *become the sentence*. If there is extra time, students may volunteer to write some new parts of speech for future use of the activity.
>
> **After Activity (includes Group Evaluation)**
> Students write short, individual reflections of their learning and complete item 7 on the advance organizer; teachers reflect upon their teaching and students' learning, noting ideas for future use. Informal evaluation may take place as the teacher observes each group working, presenting, and sharing theories to inform future teaching.
>
> **Teacher Reflections on Lesson:** What worked well? What needs more thought? How might I build today's lesson into future learning?

Figure 5.1. Lesson Plan for Small-Group Process Writing Circles

Students' advance organizer for use in the *You Be the Sentence* lesson includes instructions for both individual and small-group work as well as a student self-assessment, shown in Figure 5.2.

A suggested assessment for the *You Be the Sentence* lesson is built into the last part of the advance organizer, in item 7. The

CHOICE AND CRITICAL THINKING   201

Group members: _____

1. Open the plastic bag containing: colored activity cards, advance organizers, blank activity cards or paper, pencils, and this direction sheet.

2. Select one or more cards of each color (pink, blue, purple, gray, and green), and working with your group, rearrange them to compose a complete thought that will be in the form of a sentence. YOU NEED NOT USE ALL CARDS! (You will use the yellow -s or -es cards in step 3.)

   Optional: Use the blank activity cards provided to print end marks, commas, and other punctuation. You may also use blank activity cards to print the words *and*, *or*, and *but* and to add these conjunctions to your sentence, if you believe one or more of these is needed.

3. After you have what you think is a meaningful, complete thought (i.e. sentence), answer these questions in your small group:

   a. In what part of your sentence is the pink card used?
   b. Now take a yellow -s or -es card and add it meaningfully to a pink card in your sentence. Is there a change in the blue card's meaning? Explain.
   c. What relationships/functions might the other cards have?

4. Develop a theory within your group concerning use and placement of words on color activity cards, based on responses to questions in 3 above. Write your group's theory:
   _____
   _____

5. When directed, share/act out your sentence for the class.

6. When directed, share your theory with the whole class.

7. Answer individually:

   a. What is the relationship in the majority of sentences between the pink and the blue cards?
   _____

   b. What did you learn about complete sentences?
   _____

   c. How might you use this learning in your writing?
   _____

Figure 5.2. Advance Organizer for You Be the Sentence

three questions are meant to aid in student reflection on and understanding of forming complete sentences as well as ways to apply their own and other class members' hypotheses to writing.

Another informal evaluation may take place while the groups are composing their sentences and then presenting them. Using an adapted form of the running record, an observation instrument most often used to assess reading and writing of one student at a time, the teacher could note strengths and areas of concern for groups and particular students. Examples of the running record include informal notes on lined paper, a simple checklist of appropriate behaviors for a given task, or a printed form with space to write students' names, progress on following directions, taking an active part in group work, and level of collaboration. Information gleaned from both the running record and students' responses to questions in their advance organizer informs future course planning while conveying students' individual and group progress. The *You Be the Sentence* lesson ends with student reflection, which assists teachers in determining student understanding of topic (identification and use of parts of speech to form complete thoughts) and the likelihood that students will apply learning to composition.

Growing Beyond the Parts of Speech with Authentic Writing

While I believe that all educators should be teachers of writing, many teachers in content areas other than English do not agree. Consequently, the teaching of writing, viewed mainly as the production of correct grammar and usage, falls to English teachers. Yet, the teaching of mechanistic grammar alone fails to take into consideration that exemplary writing includes an ability to harness imagination, experience, and multiple intelligences in writing. Warriner's (1988) *English Grammar and Composition*, a book by means of which many readers (especially in the United States) have been schooled, has influenced the teaching of composition as a highly organized, rule-oriented series of mechanical steps – which writing most certainly is not. For young adolescent writers, becoming adept at applying grammar in the context of their writing is a process of critical thought and selection. Teaching adolescent writers to write through experiences that include modeling and reflection, set within a writing process approach, is difficult yet doable. That said, what are the best ways to teach grammar in the context of writing?

How and when to teach grammar has been a continuing battleground between those who believe it is best taught within a series of specific practice exercises versus those who believe grammar is best taught in the context of authentic language use or literacy study. The discussion is much more complex than that, but I support the teaching of grammar in the context of writing. Classroom mini-lessons, short reviews that assist students in learning how one piece of information fits within the larger whole, and individualized lessons targeted to the immediate needs of a student during writing conferences are of most benefit to young adolescent novice writers.

> *Students must not only see rules applied, they must also come to appreciate that they have choices in word selection, sentence composition, and other aspects of their writing, choices which are part of the development of style and voice.*

Constance Weaver has written several texts that serve as useful teacher resources, particularly when the topic of how to teach grammar arises. I have found two, *Teaching Grammar in Context* (Weaver, 1996) and the sequel, *Lessons to Share on Teaching Grammar in Context* (Weaver, 1998), especially helpful and thought-provoking. These texts answer many questions while presenting both educational research and practice-based action research by teachers about grammar, which Weaver (1996: 2) defines as "the unconscious command of syntax that enables us to understand and speak the language." In Weaver's view (1996: 145), grammar is taught for the express purposes of editing and revising writing, in order to assist in students' growth as writers. This view fits well with the Young Adolescent Model of Motivation (YAMM), in which student-centered learning includes the facilitation of connections between writing and the application of grammar within a workshop setting.

Formal grammar instruction contrasts significantly with teaching grammar in the context of writing. Rei Noguchi maintains that formal instruction offers little assistance when students organize writing, but may assist writers in developing their style (Noguchi,

1991: 11). It is discouraging to teachers when grammatical rules they have taught and assessed using assigned exercises checked off as correct and seemingly understood when encountered in isolation from writing do not transfer to students' writing process. Many educators continue to be surprised and frustrated that students who are able to identify dependent clauses in a class exercise are unable to use these constructions in their essays.

> *Writing is more than a collection of learned conventions, grammar, and spelling; it also requires knowing when to use, and when not to use, certain kinds of language – and how to do this while writing.*

Given the level of abstract knowledge and decision-making involved in the composing process, teachers need to plan lessons in which students have opportunities to think deeply and write passionately about issues that matter to them, with the inclusion of appropriate lessons about grammar and usage.

One example of an abstract composing process sure to engage students to think deeply is that of preparing for and then writing a persuasive argument on a controversial topic. The persuasive essay, often a requirement on standardized writing exams, begins with a set topic. To plan for in-class assignments that invite authentic writing in this genre, I suggest allowing students to choose from a selection of topics in order to invite interest and promote critical thought. Adolescent writers' engagement levels rise when they have imaginatively come up with a selection of issues about which to write though brainstorming. The issues will vary with life experiences and settings and will require teacher approval. Some suggested topics might include reinstatement of an enforced military service draft, common yet unhealthy adolescent behaviors, the case for becoming a vegetarian, or proper use of cell phones in a public space such as a restaurant or a bus.

Still, providing students with choice will not alone ensure a well-written persuasive argument. First and foremost, to build a good argument, an issue must be studied and understood from more than one point of view. Taking the time to learn about and study both sides of an issue affords the writer a substantive, critical knowledge base. Next, a stand must be taken and explained clearly; then a convincing argument must be made, with the audience in mind, stating and sequencing facts and propositions plainly and logically. These steps in the writer's process are taken in order to lead readers and to try to convince them to arrive at the same conclusion as the writer. Finally, an appropriate assessment of such a complex piece of writing requires intricate, informed, human judgment by teacher and writer, not just a check of surface errors.

In spite of the complexity of scoring student writing, non-educators and educators alike, possibly untrained in the art of writing and thinking, assess primarily surface elements of persuasive writing for standardized tests. Having sat in on early training for the evaluation of Michigan's state standards and the related, continually evolving high-stakes test, the Michigan Educational Assessment Program (http://www.michigan.gov/mde/0,1607,7-140-22709_31168--,00.html), I can verify that no one grading rubric can adequately suffice for scoring student writing, particularly when word length, the appearance of capital letters and end punctuation, and a beginning, middle, and end in the form of a standard five-paragraph essay rank high on the list of meeting writing expectations. Each of the writing skills noted conveys a student's ability to use *form* and apply surface features; yet standard writing rubrics and thus those who use these to score student writing may largely ignore the *content* of the writer's work. Evidence of such attributes as development of a logical argument, appropriate and innovative word selection, and the application of prior knowledge displaying a writer's ability to think critically denote maturity in the content of a text. The writer's proficiencies in the development of form and content both need to be assessed in order to gain an accurate view of the student's abilities to compose. Because standardized tests do not accurately measure critical thinking, the teacher's use of informal, authentic assessments, as discussed in depth in Chapter 7, is a must.

Superficial scoring of complex proficiencies does not result in a true picture of a writer's levels of competence in different components of writing.

The result of writing to fit the criteria of examination rubrics that address only writing form is an extreme amount of standardization of student writing. Do we really want adolescent writers to all sound the same? Many state tests have eliminated the writing portion for middle school students altogether, or have converted the writing assessment to multiple-choice; both of these alternatives are, in my opinion, ill-advised and difficult to justify. Nevertheless, state departments of education and others responsible for scoring standardized writing examinations choose the efficiency of time and money over paying knowledgeable, experienced human beings to assess writing, often instead preferring machine-scored writing.

Over the past several years, teachers' objections to standardized writing examinations maintain that the underlying expectations for the test are inappropriate, too low, or irrelevant to diverse student populations. In addition, many standardized assessment measures lack the data to support students' observable classroom achievement (Kohn, 2006; Krashen, 2008; Writing Study Group of the NCTE Executive Committee, 2004). Stephen Krashen says that every moment spent on testing is one stolen from students, and that teachers, not high-stakes tests, are best able to evaluate students' work (Krashen, 2008: 7). Alfie Kohn notes that students' writing is much more than the sum of its individual parts; young adolescents produce writing that is full of rich thought and complexities that cannot be reflected on a standardized rubric (Kohn, 2006). Evaluating young adolescents' writing "involves complex, informed, human judgment" (Writing Study Group of the NCTE Executive Committee, 2004).

Facilitation of students' progress in writing is severely hampered by the continual demand for concrete accountability in what is necessarily a subjective application of abstract concepts.

As will be discussed in Chapter 7, evaluation of young adolescents' writing must include many informal methods, in addition to the required formal yearly testing, in order for a complete picture of students' progress to emerge. *Progress* is the operative word. Young adolescents are in the process of making continual progress and growth in writing; that progress and growth should be documented in an array of carefully constructed methods, starting with those created by the students' classroom teachers.

Teacher Action Research, Peer Dialog, and Ongoing Inquiry: Critical Practices

Following a lesson, teachers regularly take note of approaches and methods they observe which have been successful along with those that need more thought. The notes may inform teachers' knowledge about students' progress and success in writing as well as a lesson's future potential use. Teachers often instruct, revise, and document their lessons under varied conditions over a period of years. This phenomenon has been termed *teacher reflection* or *action research*. Whether documenting empirical learning in a notebook, sharing it with peers through e-mail and dialog, or writing and publishing for a larger audience:

> **Teachers most often choose the methods that yield the most success, as learned through their classroom experiences.**

Formally or informally, teachers the world over are conducting valuable classroom research (Kruch, 2009). This is an important consideration since classroom teachers do not usually author nor choose to use most commercial classroom writing programs, backed by controlled, out-of-classroom experiences. The flexible, recursive nature of the writing process which supports critical thinking rarely fits with a set of programmed modules, or lessons present in prepackaged writing instruction. The very term "module" implies that there are precise pieces of knowledge which, when presented in a specific order, guarantee writing improvement.

There is, however, no one correct way to teach anything – least of all, writing.

Studies that promote programmed instruction are generally based on data-driven knowledge geared for a specific group and are often conducted primarily by private organizations outside the teaching profession, whose members may lack extensive or recent teaching experience. Although they may be testing experts, many are not actual classroom practitioners; therefore, their results may not resonate within the context of a real classroom, which exemplifies higher level, more subjective and abstract data within individual student populations. In testing studies, "data-driven" research variables are controlled so that the studies can be seen as "objective" or "scientific." However, many teachers consider the notion of controlling variables within a classroom irrelevant to teaching and learning because students are not educated within controlled settings. Each day, the specific combination of students present and the social, emotional, academic, and physical condition of young adolescents may alter the classroom community, sometimes in small, controllable ways, while at other times, the effect may be much greater.

Experienced and knowledgeable teachers capably adjust their teaching and assessments to the changing classroom variables when they select the appropriate materials and teaching approach, and then differentiate instruction for specific individuals. From this perspective, it seems that teachers might use commercial programs already purchased only as resources from which lessons may spring, by means of teacher adaptations as they fit a particular classroom context, rather than adopting them wholesale. When too many variables are controlled, as in commercial, programmed instruction, classroom teachers' informed, human judgment is negated, and the writing curriculum lacks the necessary ways and means to allow suitable planning for young adolescents' individual characteristics in order to enhance their learning and critical thinking.

Classroom research and experiences are authentic indicators for future research, theory, and practice, and they thus connect action research to the classroom, enlightening teachers while motivating student achievement in writing. I am drawn to the perceptive views of Patricia Lambert Stock, a classroom teacher, university professor, organizational leader, keynote speaker, teacher-researcher, and writer who advocates for recognition and validation of teacher research as a viable means of support for chosen pedagogies. In *The Dialogic Curriculum,* Stock (1995: 99) notes that classroom teachers often share their significant classroom discoveries with colleagues and ask them to join in "making sense of them so that we may improve our teaching practice." Students are the beneficiaries of these significant classroom discoveries, and because teachers have invested themselves in learning through their experiences, they are eager to bring their new learning to class – often motivating young adolescent writing in meaningful ways that connect to specific classroom circumstances and student groups. This is also why team teaching can be a powerful force and source of support for teachers, who benefit from continuous reflection and insight from the feedback they exchange with peers. The team process further supports teacher evaluation and revision of classroom materials and methods as needed, passing on insights gained, as the fruits of their labor, to young adolescent writers.

In her Introduction to *The Dialogic Curriculum,* Stock (1995: 3) urges teachers to consider becoming "co-inquirers" with students, particularly as they write about topics of personal consequence. When teachers invite students to pose questions and support student inquiry during the writing process, they set the stage for true critical thinking, taking on responsibility for producing exemplary writing among young adolescent writers. The inquiry-rich classroom places considerable responsibility upon not only teachers but also students, whose writing grows in quality when they are encouraged to think more critically, converse more deeply, and put forward questions rather than merely provide answers. When this happens, teacher and students function on richer and more comparable ground, more easily interacting with other human beings, reinforcing the learner-centered classroom approach.

Choice: The Second "C"

Self-Expression through Choice

In order to fully plan for exciting, unexpected experiences, teachers must create opportunities for writers to engage with *critical pedagogy*, an approach that, according to Joan Wink, mirrors the complexities of the interactions between teaching and learning (Wink, 2000: 30). Lessons that nurture young adolescent motivation through critical pedagogy include elements of choice and critical thinking. Original or adapted plans create experiences for students which are purposeful, at times promote uncertainty, and allow decision-making as well as occasions to reflect, self-correct, evaluate evidence, and develop informed decisions. In all of these ways, opportunities to make choices at school build problem-solving skills transferable to other situations and contribute to young adolescents' development as independent problem-solvers both inside and outside the classroom.

Raising Individual Thinkers and Writers

Young adolescent writing cannot be deemed a successful venture if students merely parrot back exactly what they have been taught. Now more than ever, as students connect with peers globally on the Internet and become influenced by world events and media opinions, young adolescent writers must have opportunities for self-expression that channel individual voice to action.

The recent earthquakes in Haiti, Pakistan, and Japan, and the ongoing wars in Afghanistan and Iraq exemplify not only real life but also occasions for social action projects, including collecting money for the International Red Cross to provide food and shelter for displaced or homeless people and writing letters of thanks to the troops stationed on foreign soil. Closer to home, students may be motivated to write editorials for student and community publications; to write ongoing blogs (a form of Internet journal with frequent entries) conveying their personal, social, political, and world views; or to organize, promote, and run a local food or fund drive to benefit the families of the unemployed. Providing such opportunities for students takes a certain amount of willingness on the part of the teacher to loosen control and allow students to go beyond the basic, literal content-based curriculum. Writing inspired by deep knowledge, thought, and personal action motivates writers. Otherwise, young adolescents feel constrained and separate from the events and the people that affect their lives.

Young adolescent writers long to be motivated and given a chance to discover, problem-solve, engage socially, and propose new ideas or refine old ones. Teachers utilize their own proven pedagogies as well as selected outside sources to awaken writers' craving for choice. Imagine offering young adolescents the occasional option to select a topic of personal significance within a broader, required research project or to nourish their hunger to explore issues and ideas below the surface. Young adolescents possess vast potential for intellectual, social, and emotional growth – in addition to their more obvious physical growth. Adolescence is a time for educators to dig deeply, fostering critical literacy while nurturing the motivation of young adolescent writers.

> *Young adolescent writers are on the threshold of budding possibilities, empowered by teacher and community guidance, inspiration, and real-world challenges.*

Authentic Writing through Expanded Perspectives

As I view them, *critical thinking* and *choice* are not mutually exclusive propositions. In some standard circles, the first term connotes quality and accomplished writing while the other, *choice*, can convey a relinquishment of traditional teacher control. However, the act of making a selection requires more critical thought than merely meeting basic expectations on a particular writing assignment. A wider perspective includes consideration that the simultaneous loosening of traditional power and refinement of educator roles enable young adolescents to become more successful writers. When power is shared in the classroom, responsive teaching becomes the norm because students will be anticipating their active involvement in their own learning. When responsive teaching becomes the norm, the interactive teaching and learning process necessitates reflection and redefinition. Here the concept of *choice* becomes an important aspect of motivating young adolescent writers.

Kelly Gallagher says that before students can produce "fake writing," his term for writing assigned by teachers to fulfill a curriculum standard or to jump through a hoop, they must first become comfortable with the act of writing (Gallagher, 2006: 90–91). In his ninth grade class, Gallagher invites students to develop *writing territories* (Atwell, 1998), to write short, explosive pieces he calls "blasts." Gallagher also does a lot of modeling as he writes and shares his writing with his classes. Some refer to short writing assignments of choice that start students writing, with the goal of getting students' thoughts and pens flowing onto the paper (or fingers to the keyboard), as warm-ups or quickwrites. These choice writings are as important as those that are geared directly toward meeting a standard or teaching a particular genre because they allow students to write fluently and for themselves, to voice a concern, to express an opinion, or to share a humorous story while possessing a measure of control about content from start to finish. Some educators downplay the value of such writing, negatively labeling it "creative," meaning "unstructured," "effusive," or "unfocused." Yet these short writings provide excellent opportunities for building strong teacher-student interaction in a workshop setting, as they lend themselves well to discussion and feedback. Because short choice writings are student-initiated, the writers are invested in making needed revisions and in their completion. Thus, what may start as unstructured or "creative" may result in students' most authentic, self-invested writing.

Short choice writings may also serve as writing experiences for young adolescents that are linked to a larger whole, such as a portfolio or class publication. They may transition writers to another, progressively complex writing task; or they may stand alone. Additional quality and accomplished writing grows out of students' opportunities to express themselves in engaging, original ways, revealing their voices while demonstrating their maturing writing. As short choice writings illustrate, writing comes in all sizes and types, and for various purposes, including providing for students' satisfaction in completion of work well done.

Inviting Writers' Voice

One of the most difficult, abstract literary devices to teach is the development of *voice* in writing. Teachers can talk about it, show examples from mentor texts, and invite students to respond to "hot button" issues about which they care greatly, yet find that many young adolescent writers struggle with finding their own voices as writers. One way for young adolescents to develop a writer's voice is to pen or type a letter to a favorite author, asking about the author's writing process and possibly also giving complimentary feedback on a specific title. Many young adult and children's authors have Web sites and willingly respond to their student readers. Here is a sampling:

- Jacqueline Woodson, children's and young adult author (www/jacquelinewoodson.com);
- Gary Paulson (www.randomhouse.com/features/garypaulsen);
- Lois Duncan (loisduncan.arquettes.com); and on Twitter, (http://twitter.com/duncanauthor);
- Chris Crutcher (www.chriscrutcher.com);
- Chris Van Allsburg (chrisvanallsburg.com);
- Sherman Alexie (www.fallsapart.com);
- Patricia Polacco (patriciapolacco.com);
- Christopher Paul Curtis (www.randomhouse.com/features/christopherpaulcurtis);
- Beverly Cleary (www.beverlycleary.com);
- Judy Blume at (www.judyblume.com).

In addition, Google lists a Young Adults Directory (www.google.com>Arts>Literature>Authors).

Another way to find out about how young adult authors develop voice and create characters and plots is to read a variety of student letters to young adult authors along with the authors' personal responses in *Dear Author: Letters of Hope* (Kaywell, 2007) and to make the book available to class members. In the book, Chris Crutcher addressed a question from a student who asked about how he was able to write the book, *Chinese Handcuffs* (Crutcher, 1989), from the viewpoint of a female narrator when he, the author, is a man. Chris Crutcher's response is a reminder for all authors: that writers compose from what they know. Writing about what one knows well prompts authentic language in writing style and voice. Since Crutcher had worked for eight years as a child and family therapist, he was acquainted with the truth and pain of someone like Jen, the main character, who had gone through sexual abuse (Kaywell, 2007: 59–62). The student writer also inquired as to what the author would tell someone who had experienced abuse like Jen, the main character. Crutcher responded that he would tell them, "You are not alone," that, sadly, one in four girls and one in six boys are victims of family sexual abuse, and that there is help available (Kaywell, 2007: 61–62).

In a letter to author Cherie Bennet, who wrote *Life in the Fat Lane* (Bennet, 1999), a student said that she could relate to so much of the book, such as the "in crowd" and cliques, and to how it feels to obsess over weight. Among the questions to Bennet were whether the book was based on real characters and if one of the characters was actually the author herself (Kaywell, 2007: 38–41). Bennet replied that the main character, Lara, is not based fully on herself although she was overweight, and as a young adult witnessed a lot of what she wrote about. Bennet concluded the response with the hope that readers "will be stronger, braver, and wiser" for having read it (Kaywell, 2007: 41–45). Being able to detect voice in other writers' works through their characters demonstrates to young adolescent writers that development of a writer's voice depends, in great measure, upon the act of conveying the authentic self in a unique, relatable context to readers. Donald M. Murray calls voice the most compelling factor in grabbing and keeping readers' attention and describes voice as "the music of your language, the music of your meaning" (Murray, 1996: 39).

Since I am a writer of narrative poetry, I have shared some of my own writing, as well as some of my favorite poetry (e.g. Robert Frost, Maya Angelou) and music lyrics (e.g. James Taylor, Nora Jones, Joan Baez, and others), with students at various times, including the occasions in which I try to model voice. Young adolescents can be encouraged to comment on what the writer is trying to convey through words or lyrics, even though there may be some student comments or complaints about the texts' irrelevance to their lives. In that case, teachers can invite students to bring in a poem or song of their choosing, along with the lyrics, to share with the class, who can then be prompted to try to explain what the writer was trying to say and the reasons for writing what they did in the way they did. It is recommended that all poetry and music brought in by students for use in class be previewed and preapproved by the teacher. A stock approval might include these requirements: engaging words, lyrics and/or music, relevant theme, appropriate language, approved by parents with written permission, and suitable for public broadcast. Such requirements will prevent students from introducing inappropriate material (such as obscene, racist, or sexist language) into the classroom.

Getting young adolescent writers into an inquiring frame of mind motivates answers to some of their questions, encourages visualization of multiple points of view, and enhances understanding of little known topics. Students may be invited to draft their choice of a poem or paragraph from a child's point of view and give the child a voice. They may not always be able to describe voice, but young adolescents can find their own once they practice creating a voice for others.

Asking young people to reveal themselves in their writing places them in a vulnerable position and thus might make them hesitant or resistant to doing so.

Children this age are painfully aware of how their peers regard them. What if something embarrassing is divulged when writing from the inside-out, so to speak? Will they be judged? Labeled? This is why all writing, particularly with young adolescents, must be done in a safe, respectful writing community. Teachers may not always be able to prevent students from verbally hurting their classmates, but they can surely put a quick stop to any such incidents. There is no recipe for teaching voice or best behavior (that's an entirely different book). However, teachers increase the chances that writers will develop voice when they:

- inject elements of choice into lessons;
- model open-ended critical analyses of written text; and
- encourage young adolescent writers to venture out of their comfort zones and into literacy's gray areas, where black or white, specific answers are rarely the norm.

The use of others' poetry (such as "Finished Landscape," Figure 5.3), or your own poetry or selections may serve as an impetus for students' development of voice, particularly when the three points above are kept front and center. Figure 5.3 presents one of my original poems. If you use your own writing, you may want to wait until after the discussion to disclose the author's name. Although the setting may be familiar to students, the "mother" voice may not be, but I like to include mentor texts with unfamiliar voices, particularly because the understanding requires students to view a familiar event from an unfamiliar point of view. It also elicits questions, such as:

- What was the author feeling and trying to say?
- Which phrases and language convey how the writer felt?
- How does my experience in the setting differ from the writer's?

> **Finished Landscape**
> Mary Anna Kruch (2009)
>
> Sighting, then selecting the fallen, eye-shaped ash or
> The ruby-hued maple leaves
> On a bed of lush, autumn lawn
> Eases the place inside
> Where children-changed-adults now live.
>
> Visions of two lolling, lop-sided rolling
> Peas in a pod
> Bump down the slight hill in front.
> Bright-eyed, noisy whirly-girls raise the dust,
> Ready to replay.
>
> Under the shady, all-encompassing arms of
> Lady Sycamore, once broken but not beaten
> Neither by October storms nor winter winds,
> They climb then leap ungracefully
> Into up-swept heaps of golden brown, acorn orange,
> And burning-bush red,
> Raising pungent puffs of dusty, sappy grit.
>
> They hide-and-seek, snow-angel, and revolve yet again,
> Oblivious to the efforts of Mr. Rake or their mother.
> Foliage, moist still magnificent, remains glued
> To arms, legs, hair, and Mary Janes.
>
> Together, all make a half-hearted effort to tidy
> An already finished landscape,
> Compelling some of the fallen leaves into bags,
> Allowing the rest to compost and fertilize and
> Continue the cycle one more year.

Figure 5.3. "Finished Landscape" Poem

- Would I recognize this author in a different piece of writing? If so, how?
- Can a writer have more than one voice?

Cultivating Choice with Multi-Genre Projects and Learning Circles

Beginning with my earliest years as a teacher, choice has held a prominent place in my pedagogical philosophy because I have always thought students should, to varying degrees, have command over how to grow their own garden, so to speak. Young adolescent writers can complete larger writing tasks and take part in multi-genre units of study, individually or in small groups. In such projects, my philosophy has been to start the year with less choice and work gradually into more student choice as the year unfolds and as students exhibit responsibility for making appropriate choices. Young adolescents need clear direction and boundaries, regardless of the amount of choice given. As noted in earlier chapters, students also rely on teachers to establish routines so that their decision-making is based partially on how the classroom runs, for example, during writing circles. Establishing a comfortable routine in the classroom diverges widely from one which revolves around prepackaged writing programs and teaching guides.

A teacher-established classroom routine which provides familiarity with the daily procedures of the writing community, keeping learners at the center of classroom activity, contrasts with a rigid sequence of scripted lessons that push learning at students, often from a source and a perspective far away from their own.

With teachers such as my colleagues and others I have observed who establish classroom routines inviting critical thinking and choice within teacher-created lessons, rather than setting up classrooms driven solely by prescribed sequenced lessons, students prosper and writing progresses far beyond basic writing skills. Furthermore, learner-centered writing pedagogies support young adolescents' increased levels of responsibility for learning, so they are most apt to take writing through their individual writing processes to complete final drafts. The expectations and routines during a writing workshop become internalized and represent a source of pride in knowledge and achievement of writing processes and skills.

Small-group work refined by teachers over time can invite inquiry-rich, active learning. In the classroom, what I term *learning circles* resembles a combination of Harvey Daniels' *literature circles*, as presented in his book, *Literature Circles: Voice and Choice in the Student-Centered Classroom* (Daniels, 2002) and also Stephanie Harvey and Harvey Daniels' *inquiry circles*, as fully discussed in *Comprehension and Collaboration: Inquiry Circles in Action* (Harvey and Daniels, 2009). *Learning circles* became my designation for small groups of students who gather for a common purpose or goal, assume rotating roles, and take active part in experiences such as question-posing, reading, discussion, and writing, culminating in a project for presentation to the class. Learning circles exist to more fully experience, synthesize, and collaborate in work inspired by written texts, including published novels, poetry, and student writing, and to demonstrate different kinds of individual and group learning and problem-solving in the process.

An element of student choice with adequate teacher direction drives the success of learning circles. Harvey and Daniels (2009: 287–288) stress the necessity of assisting students with organization of their materials and also the importance of modeling this organization. There is no use making elaborate plans for students to work together unless they:

- understand the assignment and can visualize steps to completion;
- are capable of assuming roles such as rotating leadership;
- are clear on how to manage research tasks;
- are able to find a common organization for their collective work;
- are able to create and store illustrations and other supplementary materials; and
- are able to take part equally in the work that results in a culminating project.

It is well to talk through some collaborative strategies with young adolescents prior to beginning learning circles. Individual student journals or notebooks can hold their own notes, research findings, and accompanying mini-lesson notes, and are kept in the classroom; a two-pocket folder stored in the classroom can hold group planning schedules, individual work logs, group-posed questions and responses, and ongoing written components of an assigned project. Teachers may supply 3x5 cards and sticky notes for students to take outside of class when reading, writing, and completing their work; these can be used for taking brief notes and then brought back to class to inform discussion and other learning circle activities. If a class or individual students have access to computers, they might use these for taking notes while researching. Writers can then send their notes to themselves as attachments within a school e-mail account in order to continue their work at home. My experience with technology has led me always to have a back-up plan, as sometimes the technology is unavailable or may not be working correctly. In some schools, students may have their own computer laptop or digital notebook (such as an iPad) and carry these from class to class for use, but this is not (yet) the norm.

Offering Choice over Time

Student choice, even under the most highly planned circumstances, must be offered in stages. For example, at the beginning of the school year, I might form small groups of four or five students each, assign roles for each learning circle and a novel to be read, then model questions to pose and discuss. Finally, I might suggest two different options from which to choose for a writing assignment offering similar content and student experiences. At another time, I might select group members, separating close friends from one another and appointing a group facilitator, and offer sets of novels from which students with varying expected interests and known reading levels may choose. I might ask students to provide a few discussion and response questions related to the reading, then to brainstorm individual answers while reading, and offer three or more final project choices. Much later in the school year, I might let students choose their own group, select the texts and other written resources to read and study, write their own discussion questions on the reading, create a large, grand-scale inquiry question based on interest, and create a plan for a social action project related to the reading and/or their discussion growing out of the reading. Or, more realistically, I might allow one or two groups to operate in this manner if they have demonstrated responsibility along with respect for class members and resources. Some students may be less comfortable with choice and prefer that a teacher provide a more traditional arrangement in which to work. It is my philosophy to meet the student halfway, giving somewhat more structure when needed but also requiring a degree of choice, in order to move the student in stages to greater autonomy and independence as a writer and as a learner.

Some students require more structure and direction than others, yet they rise to the occasion when limited areas of choice are made available to them.

All learning circles, regardless of their purposes and goals, require close monitoring of the groups, and effecting changes when needed. Teachers who make use of learning circles may find that students can be steered toward rich, collaborative peer interaction while taking part in differentiated, progressively sophisticated inquiry and critical thought. All of these active experiences further enhance young adolescent writing.

At times, choice and opportunities for collaboration with peers are not enough to motivate students' engagement and effort; at times, young adolescents may be ready to take on independent multi-genre projects in which a large amount of writing, critical thinking, and joy make for a feeling of being "large and in charge" – and without the support of peers. A *multi-genre writing project* can be described as a compilation of research and work about a given topic, which is then presented in a way that is unique to the writer and may include more than one genre involving reading, writing, art, and/or digital media, thus creating a strong, learner-centered experience.

In the following section, I present two sample multi-genre projects, *Deck the Halls with Chocolate* and *Dream Maker*, units which promote review and application of prior knowledge about various writing genres and which provide opportunities for inquiry and research and for the development of strong voice, style, and self-efficacy – all within a platform of critical and creative writing. Barbara McCombs and Jo Sue Whisler list twelve learner-centered principles in *The Learner-Centered Classroom and School: Strategies for Increasing Student Motivation and Achievement* (McCombs and Whisler, 1997: 4–8), among which are: construction of knowledge; higher-order thinking; motivational influences on learning; intrinsic motivation to learn; social acceptance, esteem, and learning; individual differences; and cognitive filters. The illustrative multi-genre projects have been designed specifically for a learner-centered classroom with these principles in mind.

Multi-Genre Project 1: Deck the Halls with Chocolate

Figure 5.4 contains an overview of *Deck the Halls with Chocolate*, a multi-genre project for individual students that embodies choice and critical thinking within a 3-week research, writing, and art project. Inspired by the young adult novel, *Charlie and the Chocolate Factory* (Dahl, 1964), it is suitable to use during the December holidays, particularly when schools discourage assignments that celebrate faith-based traditions. In Figure 5.5, a sample checklist and scoring guide for the project is provided.

As the overview of *Deck the Halls with Chocolate* conveys in Figure 5.4, students have a choice of writing, research, art, and combinations of these available for selection in the completion of the multi-genre unit. While teachers are free to brainstorm additional selections or revise a checklist and scoring guide for a unit that more appropriately reflects their current classroom study, a sample is made available in Figure 5.5 to show the importance of including areas of both content and form for evaluation and to give readers an idea of how a project such as this might be assessed.

Multi-Genre Unit Title: "Deck the Halls with Chocolate"

Suggested Mini Lessons: Introduce the project, including explanation of project checklist and writing invitations; introduce *Charlie and the Chocolate Factory* (which can be read daily by the teacher for fifteen minutes at the end of class); review the writing process for individual projects; review business letters and e-mail business inquiries; review use of dictionaries, thesaurus, and Web resources to enhance writing; review peer revision process; examine elements of finished project, all of which can be stored and submitted in a two-pocket folder, file folder, or small box labeled with the student's name.

Intended Levels: Grades 4–7

Suggested Time Frame: 2–3 weeks of in-class work, including 20–30 minutes each day, with the remainder completed outside of class, in a media center if available, and at home; 1–2 more days per week; 2 hours for showing video, *Willie Wonka and the Chocolate Factory*.

Resources Needed: Writing notebook, journal, two-pocket folder, lined and unlined paper; thesaurus, dictionaries, class set of *Write Source 2000* or comparable writing handbook; copies of the books, *Charlie and the Chocolate Factory* and *The Great Glass Elevator*; copy of DVD *Charlie and the Chocolate Factory* starring either Gene Wilder or Johnny Depp (The Gene Wilder version follows the novel more closely); collected candy wrappers (students can provide), tag board, glue, color markers, color pencils, stencils; model business letters; encyclopedias or Web access.

Diverse Needs and Accommodations: Parent volunteers or older student volunteers to assist class with organization, early drafting, and early research, as needed; volunteers to assist with peer revision, editing process, and final stages of the project; microphone for teacher's use during mini-lessons for students with hearing difficulties, and stencils for students with fine motor skill needs.

Target Content, Craft, and Conventions: Business letters, personal narrative, descriptive essay, research on growth of cacao beans and chocolate-making, and organization of board game rules.

Stages of Writing Supported: All

Lesson Goals:

1. Engage students in mid-year writing project with elements of varied genres, art, critical thinking, and choice;
2. Serve as a review of writing genres studied previously;
3. Model and practice voice and style in writing;
4. Enhance students' listening skills;
5. Encourage students to read one or both of the Roald Dahl texts;
6. Transition students' efforts and understanding of literacy and language to the second semester; and
7. Offer a unique multi-media unit of active study that addresses the seasonal theme of celebration.

Lesson Outcomes:

1. Young adolescent writers work conscientiously, with purpose, and enjoyment, holding their attention on the work at hand rather than commercial holiday distractions.
2. Young adolescent writing demonstrates overall use of correct qualities for each genre chosen, as students make use of classroom, Web, and volunteer resources.
3. Teacher reads one or both Roald Dahl books, giving appropriate voice to characters, assisted by parent and student volunteers, and writers demonstrate progressively developed voice and style in their chosen writing pieces for the project.
4. Students demonstrate improved listening skills as they work silently on their individual projects and attend to the story read by the teacher; peer revision is conducted in an appropriate, routine manner so that classmates may continue their work.
5. Young adolescent writers who are caught up with daily work are invited to read aloud and do so at various points in the story, and all students are invited to check out a copy of one or both Dahl books to read at the end of class and/or at home.
6. Young adolescents' writing and understanding of various genres shows progressive improvement.

7. Young adolescents' writing process demonstrates deeper inquiry, more active responsibility for accomplishing selected writing for the project, and obvious appreciation for the various elements of the multi-genre unit itself.

Assessment: See *Deck the Halls with Chocolate* Checklist and Scoring Guide in Figure 5.5, which details student choices, required number of selections, suggestions for quality writing content and form, and a scoring guide showing possible points with grade.

State Standards Matched: Varies.

Rationale for Unit: See Goals above.

Teacher Reflections on Unit: What worked well? What parts need revision?

Teacher Roles: Instructor, Facilitator, Co-Inquirer, and Evaluator

Figure 5.4. Overview of Chocolate Multi-Genre Writing Project

---

CHECKLIST

A. Content (Choose and check off three writing invitations to complete; store all drafts, notes, etc., in two-pocket folder labeled "Final Draft.")

__ Business letter to chocolate company (e.g. Hershey or Nestles) to convey enthusiasm for products and to request samples.
__ Research report with a minimum of three citations describing the manufacturing process of chocolate.
__ Descriptive essay on the Life of a Cacao Bean.
__ Short narrative play whose main character gains super powers from consuming chocolate.
__ Ballad (may be set to music) summarizing Charlie's story from *Charlie and the Chocolate Factory*.
__ Original recipe (may bake and bring in) for brownies, cake, candy, or fudge.
__ Poem and collage of objects, language, and art to convey love of or disgust for chocolate.
__ Appropriate rap lyrics describing a run-in with a bully who stole your chocolate or beat up Charlie.
__ E-mail to a character in the book *describing* a respectful offer of help for the family.
__ Summary of two or more news articles about recent consumption of chocolate by teens.
__ Film or book review of *Willie Wonka, Charlie & the Chocolate Factory,* or *The Great Glass Elevator.*

Note: No extra credit until all tasks are completed thoroughly and have passed teacher's inspection!

B. Culminating Project (Choose one.)
__ Original board game, detailing the plot of either *Charlie* book read or the film viewed and set of rules.
__ Crossword puzzle with clues related to the plot of *Charlie and the Chocolate Factory* and answer key.
__ Readers' Theater science fiction script for five or more classmates related to chocolate, set in the future.

C. Form (Read and include as many as possible in your work)
__ All writing tasks, including culminating project, are taken through the entire writing process.
__ All writing tasks, including culminating project, have been edited and revised after meeting with peers.
__ All final drafts have been shown to teacher or parent volunteer, who has conferred with writer.
__ All drafts are dated with the final drafts labeled as such and are stored in classroom file folder.
__ Final drafts have been placed into two-pocket folder with full name and class hour.
__ Board game pieces are placed in plastic bags, labeled with full name and class hour, stored in folder.
__ Writing demonstrates correct elements of chosen genre (class and Web resources have been accessed).
__ Writing demonstrates correct spelling and usage.
__ Writing reflects voice and style.
__ All accompanying art, music, illustrations, and food must be neat and in good taste!
__ Writer's first and last names appears clearly on each chosen task as well as the culminating project.
__ This checklist and scoring guide are included in the writer's two-pocket folder.

SCORING GUIDE (50 points possible)

A	B	C	D	E
All qualities in content and form are in evidence.	Most qualities in content and form are in evidence.	Many qualities in content and form are in evidence; some work is incomplete.	Few qualities in content and form are in evidence; some work is incomplete.	Work is unacceptable; teacher conference is required for resubmission.
50 – 48 points	47 – 45 points	44 – 40 points	39 – 37 points	36 points or less

Figure 5.5. Checklist and Scoring Guide for Chocolate Project

Multi-Genre Project 2: Dream Maker

Dream Maker is a multi-genre project created for individual students and abounding in elements of critical thinking, choice, research, art, and writing. Always a favorite pick-me-up for the mid-winter blues as felt in northern climes, this unit is one in which teachers may want to take an active part along with students, who will delight in knowing something special about their teacher as well as benefit from teacher modeling of the steps to some of the more complex tasks. The project begins with this question:

> In fifteen years, where will you likely be, and in which career will you be engaged?

A short description of that unit, created for use in February, during celebration of Martin Luther King, Jr.'s Birthday and President's Day in the United States, appears in Figure 5.6.

Writing for Understanding in Science

The final lesson presented in this chapter concerns writing to learn, and in this case, writing both to learn and to show understanding of a process, by using a method called "Doodle Writing," with the addition of peer talk and drawing. The lesson, which is presented in Figure 5.7, may be adapted for use with the teaching of virtually any process that can be visualized. The lesson template is very similar to previous templates for whole-group work, with the addition of the 5 E's, a lesson form used widely in the United States for elementary and middle school science lessons. The 5 E's stand for *engage*, *explore*, *explain*, *elaborate*, and *evaluate*. Science is a content area in which students are required to write hypothesis statements, lab reports with scientific theory, and essays explaining their understanding of processes and ideas studied. The Doodle Writing lesson of Figure 5.7, which is intended to assist students in their comprehension of the water cycle, works well at the beginning of a unit and is suggested for grades 4–7. The lesson shown includes an advance organizer in the form of a KWL, along

Title of Lesson: "Dream Maker"

Intended Levels: Grades 5–8.

Resources Needed: Videotape of Dr. Martin Luther King, Jr.'s "I Have a Dream" speech; access to Web or media center with available computers and research materials, including encyclopedias, nonfiction texts, and biographies about women and men who endured hardship to become leaders and work toward their dreams such as Martin Luther King, Jr., Nelson Mandela, Supreme Court Justice Sonia Sotomayor, U. S. President Barak Obama, and others; journals or notebooks; two-pocket folders, pencils, pens, color pencils, color markers; precut cloud shapes (e.g. cut from cardboard or poster board), about 8 x 10 inches in size; scissors, hole punch, string.

Target Content, Craft, and Conventions: Critical thinking through posing questions, brainstorming, and conducting research; reflection and the development of an organized plan through use of a traditional outline form, concept maps, or computer applications that provide advance organizers, such as *Inspiration* or *MindRaider*.

Stages of Writing Supported: All

Prewriting Activity: As a class, view Martin Luther King, Jr.'s "I Have a Dream" speech, read the text of the speech, and study major events in Dr. King's life; together, describe Dr. King's dream and the steps he took toward accomplishing it; discuss the brainstormed ideas about a dream or goal for students that they wish to accomplish in 15 years; and ask students to choose the goal of a future dream.

Smaller Tasks:
- On a precut cloud shape, ask students to create an illustration of who and where each would like to be in 15 years and add a label, such as "Children's Author," "NASA Engineer," "Senator," or "Musician." Using a hole punch and string, hang the dream cloud above each student's desk when complete.
- Have students research and take notes about their chosen career, based on an historical or current figure who made a difference in the world, developing an outline or concept map with specific steps needed to accomplish the dream or goal, using biographies, news articles, encyclopedias, and available digital media.
- Have students convert the outline or concept map to a personal narrative drawing from research, history, and current events for support. This short report will serve as a starting point from which to develop the culminating project.

Culminating Project for Presentation to Audience of Peers and Significant Adults:
After reviewing persuasive advertisements and viewing examples such as promotional materials and commercials (e.g. to join the Marines), invite students to choose from one of these activities:

- Create and script a Power Point, brochure, or television commercial to persuade others to consider becoming an author, astronaut, politician, singer, or other occupation. Include necessary training and experiences needed as well as the benefits, impact on the larger population, and satisfaction that come from following your dream.

Assessment: Students will submit their folders with all smaller tasks and a script of the culminating presentation to the teacher. Ask students to take notes on 3 x 5 cards as peers present culminating projects, including such qualities as: degree to which the student covered the assignment, ability to persuade, eye contact, and interaction with the audience. Students will award neither points nor letter grades to their peers; teachers can make informal notations on the above qualities and then assign a grade after conferring with each student writer.

Reflective Writing and Discussion: Students write what they think is intended by the "Dream Maker" title of this unit and whether they have a clearer picture of what efforts their chosen dreams or vocations require; discuss answers with class.

Teacher Reflections on Lesson: What worked well? What needs more thought? What adaptations might be made for future use of the unit?

Figure 5.6. Brief Description of Dream-Maker Unit

Name: _____ Date: _____

1. **ENGAGE**: You will listen to a description of the water cycle.

2. **EXPLORE**: As you listen to the text read aloud to you, draw what you hear as each step of the process in the first column, DOODLE; take a few notes about each doodle or drawing in the second column, NOTES; and in the third column, TRANSLATION, try to write each step more clearly and fully.

   TERMS: *water vapor, atmosphere, evaporation, liquid,* and *condensation*

DOODLE	NOTES	TRANSLATION

3. Next, **EXPLAIN** the water cycle process to a partner, making sure to use as many of these terms as possible. Revise your Notes or Translation if wanted.

4. Finally, using your doodles, notes, and translation, **ELABORATE** upon all of the above and write out the water cycle as a paragraph with full sentences, correct spelling, and correct punctuation.

5. **EVALUATE**: When finished writing, read your paragraph all the way through to yourself, revising as necessary. How did you do? Compare with a partner, make a fresh drawing with color pencils to illustrate the water cycle, and begin thinking about how the weather may affect the water cycle.

The Water Cycle

_____

Figure 5.7. Advance Organizer for Doodle Writing – The Water Cycle

with teacher directions that correspond to each of the 5 E's noted above. Since the lesson is hands-on and multi-sensory, it engages students while increasing their level of recall, thereby nurturing writers' motivation.

Suggested print and digital resources to supplement the lesson above are:

- *A Drop Around the World* by Barbara Shaw McKinney (McKinney, 1998)

- *The Drop in My Drink: The Story of Water on Our Planet* by Meredith Hooper (Hooper, 1998)
- *The Water Cycle: Evaporation, Condensation, & Erosion* by Rebecca Harmon (Harmon, 2005)
- http://www.*readwritethink*.org/ (a collaboration of the International Reading Association, The National Council of Teachers of English, and Verizon)
- http://people.ehe.ohio-state.edu/edl/ (Digital Resources for Math and Science educators, The Ohio State University)
- http://www.teachersdomain.org/resources 05.sci.ess.watcyc.lp_watercycle/ (Teachers Domain, National Science Digital Library)

In addition to classroom lessons focused upon developing inquiry and guided by teachers, young adolescent writers must develop critical thinking and inquiry independently, and teachers can nurture this type of growth as well. In order to successfully write across many genres, for many purposes, and in multiple contexts, students must develop self-reliant processes of inquiry in addition to what is provided in school. Young adolescent writers exercise the process of inquiry when they take part in critical thinking geared toward making judgments, finding answers, and selecting the most appropriate approach for themselves as learners. For these purposes, writers must become familiar with and employ more than one method or pathway.

While most writers have no trouble making judgments, they benefit from teacher guidance related to effective problem-solving techniques and from the freedom to choose methods that work best for them.

> *As a complex process, writing requires not only capabilities to call forth and incorporate prior knowledge; it also requires independent thought, whereby ideas are noted, identified for possible use, and then chosen if applicable to the topic at hand.*

Students come to school with the ability to recall and gather information through conversation with peers but have no such schema for recalling and developing content in their writing (Hillocks, 1995: 107). George Hillocks says that students must learn to develop writing schemas, or plans, by "learning how to recall content without prompts from conversational partners" (Hillocks, 1995: 107).

Development of writing schemas matters because young adolescent writers will, more often than not, work as individuals, particularly on such compositions as research papers, essays, and other non-fiction genres.

Prewriting Strategies That Support Inquiry

Since the composition of fiction genres requires students to look beyond their own experiences, memories, and opinions, inquiry can also necessitate an unsettling state for students, in which they feel disconcerted about not having an exact answer. Their efforts to arrive at satisfactory solutions in the writing process can be reinforced verbally, through teachers' written recognition and through teachers' habitual provision of time for prewriting activities and behaviors.

Young adolescents' development over time of a *writing schema* – which is a set of personalized skills and procedures that learners gradually evolve, through writing experience, for controlling their own writing process – requires a classroom community in which inquiry learning is the norm. Inquiry learning promotes the freedom to pose questions and look for more than one right answer and by means of more than the same finite set of steps for all. Individuals' writing schemas evolve within this type of less structured, more open environment of inquiry which nurtures each student's exploration of writing and development of a personally effective writing approach.

In support of student inquiry and writing development, teachers can provide a range of prewriting strategies explicitly modeling, ways to begin writing, such as using an advance organizer to state a problem, noting prior attempts by others at finding a solution, and developing a sample plan of where and how to proceed with the writing task at hand. The modeled behaviors then assist students with development of their own individual writing process, which can become increasingly organized into a routine that evolves as their own writing process schema.

Student-posed questions are an additional prewriting strategy that is especially useful prior to independent study, reading, and research. Rather than providing students a set of questions to which they respond prior to reading text or literature, teachers may nurture and develop a writer's sense of inquiry and prediction by inviting students to add questions of their own to which they respond. Student-posed questions complement the assignment by motivating them to read, study, or research with a purpose, poised to select knowledge pertinent to their questions. Students in my classroom profited over time by learning to rely less upon my guided reading and writing questions, and more upon their own questions, over the course of a semester or an academic year. Starting from their own thoughtful questions, students' studying, reading, and dialoging about answers with peers further assisted reflective, critical thought and revealed itself in the richness of their writing.

As in the "5 Es" lesson presented earlier, student-posed questions may occur in the form of a K–W–L advance organizer. The first part of the organizer provides a space for what students already **K**now, and the second part assists students in setting a purpose for reading by formulating statements and questions about **W**hat they would like to know. The third part of the K–W–L organizer provides a space for students to reflect upon and write about what they have **L**earned. Use of information noted on the K–W–L organizer can thus provide support for a writer's description of the water cycle in the lesson template of Figure 5.7 while contributing to the writer's knowledge about himself/herself as a writer. Composition of non-fiction essays, whether as short-answer responses like those required in the "5 Es" or longer essays, pose a particular challenge for many writers. The use of advance organizers designed to address students' reflective thought and development of their writing schemas beneficially nurtures young adolescents' growth in writing.

In addition to student-posed questions, young adolescent writers may benefit from the use of journals when writing in first and second person genres. Students may use individual journals to develop topics, to note a particularly inspiring sentence, or to note topics and questions for future use. The journal may also serve as a place for personal reflection about one's own writing as well as random ideas that may occur to students at home or during class. Ralph Fletcher says that many writers are attracted to language for its own sake – and he includes himself, going on to list examples from his personal journal, *Pyrotechnics on the Page: Playful Craft That Sparks Writing* (Fletcher, 2010: 7). Students may note phrases in journals that seem to roll off their tongues when spoken, like the alliterative, "Sufferin' succotash," muttered by cartoon legend Sylvester the Cat in Looney Tunes; the onomatopoeia of Lady Gaga's lyrics in "Paparazzi"; or a beautiful, poetic line like "Then carry happiness like water in our cupped hands..." from a poem by young adult author, Gary Soto, in "Street Scene on the Fulton Mall" (Soto, 2003: 24). After students have noted playful or appealing examples of writing craft, the samples may lie dormant in journals until writers' inspiration is brought to life through their pens, upon rereading, rediscovery, and reflection on these previous thoughts, resulting in additional insights or new compositions. Teacher and student participation in reflective thought, writing, and dialog about successful pathways to develop content and focus thus stimulates writing growth.

A Challenge to Teach Our Children Well

In Chapter 1, I posed a challenge to educators and the community that essentially asked the question: Why not take all of our energy as educators and adults involved in the education of our youth to nurture, uplift, and support their growth in writing within an inquiry-rich environment? Or, to put this a different way: Why spend so much time, energy, and money attempting to produce standard, predictable, passive learners when our children in fact need to actively take part in all aspects of their education in order to grow into successful writers and prosperous adults?

While much energy is required in the planning and implementation of a learner-centered classroom that honors critical thinking and choice, the efforts will bear plentiful fruits.

I repeat this challenge to, as Crosby, Stills, Nash, and Young, a late 1960s rock band sang, "Teach Your Children Well." This effort is not beyond possibility because the vision of students succeeding by refocusing our sights from testing to nurturing the whole child is within reach. Honoring this vision, I have often proclaimed that teachers are the captains of their own ships; in this case, teachers are the master gardeners, the ones who make the critical decisions about designing the education of their charges. These decisions need not be made by the textbook companies, the authors of commercial writing programs, nor governmental agencies, aroused by the fear of lost federal dollars or incomplete, high-stakes testing data. Rather, they should be in the hands of those most closely and intimately involved with the teaching enterprise, the teachers and learners themselves.

While it takes courage and work to dig in our heels and to produce and disseminate research in support of the writing workshop approach within a learner-centered classroom, teachers and the greater educational community must strive to do so. Why not take the funds spent on programmed learning and instead fund classroom libraries, visits from authors, improved classroom resources such as technology, and professional development and collaborative teaching and curriculum writing for teachers? I encourage all readers to recognize the benefits of writing instruction ripe with opportunities for students' higher level growth, resisting the easy way out of building lessons upon worksheets, programs, and texts designed to push a writing curriculum into the learner at the cost of disengagement, mediocrity, and further failure. My praise goes to parents and community members who recognize and support teaching and learning that challenges students to think critically and that cultivates independent choice.

Concluding Reflections on Chapter 5

Young adolescent writers are motivated by criticism and response that is conferred with the best of intentions from both teachers and peers. Teachers may learn this by practicing and modeling response to writing that is clear, fair, and offers suggestions as well as feedback. Criticism based on reflective thought guides the writer and inspires improvement. As part of the writing workshop, peers respond to one another's papers, offering feedback and suggestions, and they will do so as appropriately as they have observed from their teacher. At times, reteaching and rewriting are in order; young adolescent writers will be most apt to take an active part in the writing process, including the final, revised draft, when such criticism and support is given positively and routinely. Middle-grades writers also benefit from instruction that routinely provides occasions for critical thought and choice, which speaks to higher level learning. While some commercial and test preparation materials may offer lessons that seem to address critical thinking and choice, they are best used as resources from which to choose or adapt individual activities and content to individual classrooms. The most appropriate writing instruction is that which is designed with multiple formats and can be authentically assessed by the teacher. Why rely upon standard materials produced by strangers unacquainted with each unique seedling in our garden? A much better alternative is to discover each student's individual strengths and needs and use learner-centered approaches to tend these.

In Chapter 6, "Learner-Centered Writing in an e-Universe," I explore and suggest the potentials, growing contexts, and opportunities that digital technologies have and will bring to students' writing. Specific issues and potential trouble spots are discussed, and exemplary resources created by teachers and for teachers are presented. Well-tested lessons written to engage and motivate young adolescents are also offered.

6 Learner-Centered Writing in an e-Universe

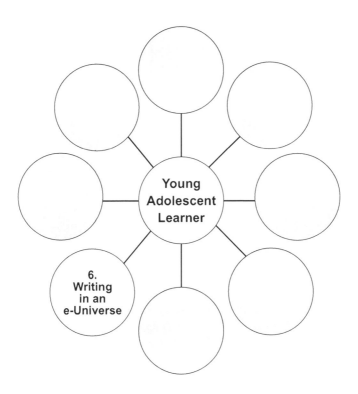

There will always be a frontier where there is an open mind and a willing hand.
– Charles F. Kettering, American electrical engineer and inventor, 1876–1958 (Boyd, 1961: 240)

Introductory Remarks to Chapter 6

Writing instruction for middle-grades students calls for an open mind, appropriate resources, and a vision. Planning instruction is an ongoing process of locating, selecting, and implementing suitable instructional and resource materials that represent best practice for a particular audience of students. An open mindset includes the understanding that no one new or traditional practice is an automatic fit for each setting, age group, and context.

Given the prevalence of electronic learning, especially what has been termed *Web 2.0*, where communication and collaboration are continuous digital mainstays, students are now able to find additional writing resources by themselves. Surpassing the use of mere word-processing, the teaching of writing now empowers students with the potential to personally and actively engage in each stage of the process with a high level of independence, when connected with the Internet. Students are now able to e-mail writing drafts to others for feedback; use a series of Web sites with which to refine details, factual information, and conventions; and post writing on sites in the e-universe, where students may offer feedback to other writers and where even strangers may respond. Young adolescents may create original graphic novels, including both art and text, by using a variety of applications and incorporating artistic tools that exist not only on their own computers but also in a wide array of digital locations.

Much of the writing can be accomplished at school, yet a great deal of students' work may also be prepared outside of school. With additional independence come additional steps for teachers (and parents) to check so as to ensure students' appropriate activity and safety in online contexts. Teachers must also create explicit instruction with clear directions for electronic writing and must also continue to actively monitor students and their work. Understandably, not all teachers welcome the context change, and not all young adolescent writers will take such an active role in their own learning; but the vision and the capability exist for these changes to occur.

In this chapter, I address the issues involved in teaching writing in an electronic age, including discussion of: how young adolescents view their writing, future growth and vision in digital writing instruction, steps that teachers may take to motivate and assist developing writers, the importance of collegial interaction and support for writing teachers, and experts' projected technological trends for schools. Two "teched-up" versions of primarily print-based lessons are offered – not only in recognition of young adolescent writers as users of multi-modal literacies, but also as motivation for an interconnected dialog among peers, both local and global. I acknowledge that the greatest potential and also the greatest risk of Internet use by young adolescents are embodied in the freedom to search for and discover information relative to their learning and research projects. To that end, I offer a flowchart, adaptable to various online projects, to guide students with organization prior to and during research. While I address many suggestions to teachers, I also invite administrators, parents, and other adults who play important roles in young adolescents' lives to consider the importance of utilizing of the vast stores of resources available in our e-universe and to provide ongoing professional development for all teachers, so that the process of motivating student writing becomes a community-based enterprise, both real and virtual. Finally, I argue that digital literacies may peacefully co-exist as choices for writers and teachers of writing alongside print-based versions, from which the most appropriate, authentic, enjoyable, and effective writing may emerge.

Writing Instruction: Necessarily Progressive

Writing instruction has evolved from the practice of isolated skills to a wider, more inclusive process of crafting content and form. Throughout the development of theory and practice in writing, familiar debates over which pedagogies best serve learners continue, including the extent to which technology should be used in the classroom. This debate represents educators' individual preferences, understandings, selections, and frequencies of use with regard to Web technologies.

Regardless of individual teachers' views concerning inclusion of digital resources in the classroom writing workshop, it seems clear that technological resources provide motivation, engagement, and assistance to young adolescent writers – particularly, because these resources require students' active involvement in their writing processes. According to a recent Public Broadcasting Service (PBS) survey, teachers' use of Web resources in their classroom instruction has risen (Prabhu, 2010).

> *At the risk of stunting student growth in writing – or of becoming irrelevant to their students' world – teachers must find their way into the process of jumping the digital divide, if they have not yet done so.*

With experience, teachers can regulate the levels and kinds of Web use with their students as they reimagine and plan for an educational world that stretches beyond, but also includes, the conventional classroom. They can arrange for both virtual discussions online with teachers and peers as well as more traditional, face-to-face interactions (Van Dusen, 2009). Scott Warnock refers to the combination of onsite and online composition as *hybrid writing*, noting more similarities than differences between the two (Warnock, 2009: 7). If writing pedagogy is viewed as a process within a learner-centered teaching model, both traditional as well as online resources may be utilized in developmental, process-based workshops.

> *The heart of the writing workshop model is its sense of forward progression, inviting active engagement and increased responsibilities for the writer over time via both online and offline activities.*

Why and How Young Adolescents Write

According to the National Commission on Writing report by Amanda Lenhart, Sousan Arafeh, Aaron Smith, and Alexandra Rankin Macgill in Writing, Technology, and Teens (2008: i), most writing by adolescents is informal, and they do not view their e-communication such as text messages, instant messages, and e-mails as writing. Young adolescents look upon their social, digital forms of communication as connecting with friends rather than as "real writing." Because the purpose is primarily social, the spelling and grammar conventions students apply in that context are lenient, and acronyms and other sorts of abbreviations are plentiful. Students may also write outside of the classroom off the computer, most often in personal journals. In the same report that studied teens aged 12–17, researchers found their student subjects well-informed on the topic of writing instruction, citing the choice of meaningful topics, more time to write creatively, challenging lessons, detailed teacher response, and writing for authentic audiences as motivators to write well (National Commission on Writing, 2008: iii).

> ***Students' critical understanding of why they write and which classroom practices will encourage them to write more and write well will inform teachers' instructional planning.***

In fact, the topics mentioned by students in the study conducted by the National Commission of Writing align with the Young Adolescent Motivation Model's components. For example *Formative, authentic assessment* and *Process writing* matches students' wish for more detailed teacher response; *Critical thinking* matches students' desire for challenging lessons; *High interest lessons* matches students' preference for writing topics of relevance and interest to their lives, and for more time to write creatively; and *Writing community* matches students' desire to write for and connect with a real audience.

Young adolescents believe that the more frequent use of technology and digital resources has further implications for teachers to consider in planning writing instruction (National Commission on Writing, 2008: iv). Their belief coincides with *Writing in an e-universe* and *Teaching to the whole child* – both components of the YAMM. While some teachers choose to utilize traditional modes of instruction, it is impossible to ignore the potential for differentiating and motivating independent writing experiences via electronic technologies.

A quick review of the Young Adolescent Motivation Model (YAMM), reprinted in Figure 6.1, might serve as a helpful guide for individual teachers when reflecting upon the degree of accomplishment of the century-old shared goal: writing growth for all learners. Writing growth and achievement feed on creativity and vision because solutions to difficult problems require alternate routes along new, open frontiers of thought, as Charles Kettering stated in the chapter's opening quotation. If the status quo of writing instruction has not provided high-yield growth and achievement, then it's time to think outside the box, with fresh imagination, determination, and reflection. The need to rethink content and process when outcomes are not what is wanted or expected is known in all fields, including evolving technological literacies. Why not provide the same for young adolescent students in our schools?

Divergent, uncharted directions and resolutions to problems exist, awaiting discovery through introspection and reflection.

The Young Adolescent Motivation Model (YAMM) supports varied, complex, and useful pathways as it plants the necessary seeds of vision, placing the learner's needs front and center. What nurtures students' motivation to develop into mature writers? The model, based upon personal experience and study, reflects specific, qualitative efforts that nurture young adolescents' motivation to learn to write well. These efforts are: creation of lessons based upon the differentiated needs of the whole learner; planting and growing an interdependent writing community; nourishing young adolescent appetites with high-interest lessons that include the arts; sowing seeds and nurturing the roots to make a strong foundation for

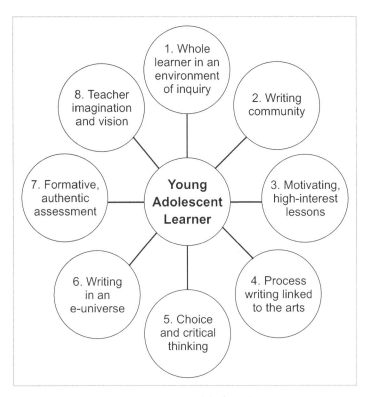

Figure 6.1. Young Adolescent Motivation Model of Writing

process writing through choice and critical thinking; incorporating digital technologies; and determining growth and future instruction based upon a set of formative, authentic assessments.

Moving Forward with Study, Planning, and Differentiated Instruction

Heidi Hayes Jacobs states (Jacobs, 2010: 1) that schools must be focused upon a curriculum that prepares students for the world that will exist for them in the next 5 to 10 years and beyond, including using innovative resources for connecting and sharing. Jacobs (2010: 1) notes that when academic attainment is compared internationally, the United States does not measure up because "our school structures are fundamentally based on an antiquated system established in the late 1800s."

Educational scholars, teachers, and lawmakers must take part in continuous study and ongoing communication research and practice in a current and historical context, taking a close look at whether what is being taught now will benefit students in the long run.

While it is difficult to influence, update, and educate state and national departments of government, the community at large, including the school administration and parents, can offer the support needed for teachers to carry out their jobs. In a best-case scenario, teachers would have that type of regular, progressive support, which enables them to more efficiently plan for writing instruction that is relevant now and in the future.

A living writing curriculum, reflective of students' growing and changing academic needs, must convey clear purposes for writing that nurture increased independence in and responsibility for learning. Some of these purposes include the development of organization, pacing, style, voice, research skills, and correct grammar and usage for personal, academic, and creative writing. Young adolescent writers will become increasingly adept at all of these aspects of writing through using digital tools that advance their individual literacy and knowledge level. While many of these elements of writing may be addressed via both traditional and digital means, it is virtually impossible to instill independence, knowledge, and skill in navigating the Internet unless students have access to and utilize the technology.

Writing instruction at its best facilitates students' increased responsibility for personally engaging communication and collaboration with others during the writing workshop process. Along with face-to-face discourse and teamwork, students' use of appropriate digital resources enables additional powerful, engaging communication and collaboration with peers as well as experts in particular fields of study. Young adolescents already know this;

teachers' continually changing roles necessitate the facilitation of such communication and collaboration in recognition of the specialized and ongoing, global nature of learning.

While the most obvious goal for students concerning their writing is for continued growth and achievement, teachers might restate their objectives on a regular basis, once they have discerned students' current level of knowledge and identified future needs. Some teachers already do so on a daily or weekly basis by taking note of what worked and what parts of an instructional sequence might be adjusted in order to meet goals set for students. Taking into account grade level standards along with the needs of individuals, teachers might also note which skills require immediate, explicit focus and then plan for these to be addressed first.

Far too many classrooms, unfortunately, are moving along at one speed, repeating and reviewing content for some students while barely scratching the surface of the skills needed by others; this can be a frustrating venture for teacher and students alike. When writing is viewed as the recursive and long-term developmental process it is, teachers acknowledge the variance in writing background and skill levels, creating daily plans via continuous observation, useful notations, and informal evaluation to accommodate divergent learner needs. These latter efforts are worthwhile, as the writing instruction becomes purposefully focused upon what is known, what is yet to be mastered, and which practices best fit the learners in a specific class. The discovery and the use of digital technologies that enable students to exercise critical thinking skills can be especially helpful in differentiating and accommodating instruction for young adolescent writers.

Differentiating writing instruction is among the efforts that bring satisfaction for teachers, as they become more knowledgeable about each young adolescent writer's achievements and potential for success.

Teachers and administrators should be wary, however, of computer programs that claim to teach students to write but that are essentially practice-based, "one right answer" exercises that contribute nothing to students' critical thinking and are the equivalent of the traditional workbook. These cannot deliver appropriate, individualized, and focused student and context-specific writing experiences. Still, many will try, and federal funds will be wasted, as literal-level skill practice disguised as computer-based writing lessons are perpetuated, the goal being to raise test scores rather than students' long-range writing achievement. Teachers should recognize these generic, mass-produced materials for what they are: resources from which to choose and adapt for selected students, if and when appropriate.

In his text, *Teaching Writing Online: How & Why,* Scott Warnock suggests (Warnock, 2009: 133) that teachers may profit from pre-instructional reflection on a regular basis, such as prior to each marking period or semester, in order to provide suitable starting input and feedback to each new group of students. Some of the questions for teachers to consider might be:

- Will students be writing comparative and persuasive essays, whose forms coincide with traditional language and form for these genres?
- Will students be concentrating their efforts on a multi-genre project or research paper?
- Might they be responding principally to literature through short, non-graded daily writing assignments culminating in selection of some writing to include in a portfolio?

Warnock (2009: 133) asks teachers to consider not only the amount of formal and informal writing planned for students, but also the ways in which teachers might respond to students' compositions and degree of willingness to explore more complex technologies. Connected to this last consideration are additional relevant matters, such as the availability of technological support, accessible training for teachers, and opportunities for teachers to dialog and collaborate with colleagues. Building upon the knowledge that young adolescents seek challenge, detailed feedback, opportunities for choice of relevant, interesting topics, more rigorous work, and teachers' use of digital tools, teachers can prepare writing instruction with more clarity than ever before.

Current Practices and Future Frontiers

Along with consideration of student goals, the types of writing that students will be doing, modes of response to writing, and the degree of willingness to navigate digital writing frontiers, teachers are bound to reflect upon their current practices. Such reflection determines the value of each current procedure with respect to goals and objectives for students. Which existing routines and approaches support young adolescents in writing for many purposes, across many genres, and with success? Most significantly, which writing practices motivate young adolescents to write authentically – that is, for real functions?

Those writing experiences through which students' efforts fulfill meaningful, natural purposes yield the most motivation and satisfaction. These may include memorable lessons such as composing a sequel to a play following the reading of it aloud with peers beneath a shady maple tree in June, creating a Power Point presentation of photos and journal entries following a family vacation to the Museum of Modern Art in New York City, or using Internet research and face-to-face interviews of long-time residents to craft interactive history lessons about students' hometowns or of the city, town, or neighborhood where the school is located. Working creatively and collaborating with others often yields a sense of contentment during the process of preparing a final written product, regardless of the educational tools employed.

> *In general, memorable writing experiences are those that bring about unexpected, extraordinary insight and understanding from students and teachers as writers.*

Memorable practices may also include successful digital lessons that involve group efforts with peers and that engage writers to compose personal narratives and essays with depth and passion. For example, teachers might invite students to e-mail drafts of their papers to one another for immediate response concerning whether the composition illustrates a focused craft or literary device, such as the development of mood and use of sensory description in a setting. Bringing out-of-class writing experiences into the classroom, such as allowing students to convene peer response groups to read and react to early drafts written at home provides immediate feedback and encourages consideration of suggestions for ongoing improvements and revisions to early drafts. Collaboration inside and outside of class often contributes to a general sense of classroom community, purposeful writing, and the growth of self-esteem, placing teamwork in a highly worthwhile and valuable light.

Writing methods that take up valuable instructional and writing time but that appear not to be improving students' writing, on the other hand, may be adapted or dropped. Perhaps these did not fully engage students nor adequately address student goals, or perhaps they failed to support transference to independent writing. Perhaps one or more of the lessons might be presented in an alternative, higher interest way that challenges writers to take a risk, such as writing metaphorically about newsworthy yet complex issues such as the ecological effects of the 2010 BP oil spill in the Gulf of Mexico, the different kinds of effects of the 2011 Japanese earthquake, or students' opinions about gun control in relation to First Amendment rights in the United States. When writing about controversial and multifaceted events and issues, young adolescents may be aware of some of the facts as well as their parents' views on potentially high-interest topics; however, discussion, study, and in-depth research place topics into ever-widening perspectives about which students can develop personal opinions and are prompted to apply their growing wealth of knowledge and writing schema to their writing process.

Teachers who are pressed for time and inexperienced with technology other than e-mail and electronic grade books may find it difficult to create lessons that can engender the types of engaging discussion and writing to which students may best respond. This is particularly true when the set writing curriculum reflects only traditional print and face-to-face methods to address standards and instructional goals. Teachers in such a position may benefit from consultations with their more media-savvy colleagues who have adopted a set of beliefs about increasingly technological ways to teach writing in the Web 2.0 21st century. Such beliefs may include the use of digital media to access magazines, news reports, Web sites, articles, and experts dedicated to topics of study. Utilizing technology in these ways nurtures critical thought and reflection, providing occasions for exceptional writing. In addition, progressive schools in the United States have increasingly supported teacher collaboration by encouraging the creation of teacher communities for the purpose of study, reflection, and teamwork. Some online teacher communities such as various Nings (specific social networking sites) unite teachers in a specific region or state, or across the country (see below). Other online teacher communities such as the Webheads in Action (*WiA*, or just *Webheads*; http://webheads.info) group offer support for the use of electronic media by teachers of English around the world.

Through reflection, analysis, and synthesis of past and ongoing practices, followed by educational decisions to incorporate potentially valuable adjustments, teachers empower themselves as competent, knowledgeable experts who discern the strengths and needs of individual students and who act on that knowledge to help each individual student learn to the best of his or her ability. Viewing teaching practice through a reflective lens such as this further counters a dependence upon premade, scripted materials.

Once current writing practices have been identified, teachers may then match them to student goals, teacher objectives, writing feedback and evaluation, and appropriate writing resources, including digital ones. In so doing, many curricular standards may be addressed. Identification of standards addressed and met further clarifies and shapes teacher planning and instruction, making way for directing lessons toward student needs.

Accessing Digital Writing Resources

Rather than direct teachers to specific decisions about writing instruction, I next suggest books and online resources for teachers and then present classroom lessons, supportive educational research, and writing invitations in order to explore the range of digital resources available for nurturing students' collaborative and active experiences. In a broad sense, middle-grades teachers and other educators (e.g. school administrators and professors at universities teaching future teachers) are asked to reimagine the potential for teaching writing, given the wide range of possibilities. Fortunately, the current academic writing market is rich with an abundance of useful texts for teachers who seek the ways and means of incorporating digital technology into research, writing, and daily discourse. Among the most helpful, clearly written texts for teachers are:

- *The Digital Writing Workshop* by Troy Hicks (Hicks, 2009);
- *Literature and the Web: Reading and Responding with New Technologies* by Robert Rozema and Allen Webb (Rozema and Webb, 2008);
- *The Socially Networked Classroom: Teaching in the New Media Age* by William Kist (Kist, 2010);
- *The Tech-Savvy English Classroom* by Sara B. Kajder (Kajder, 2003);
- *Adolescents and Digital Literacies: Learning Alongside Our Students* by Sara Kajder (Kajder, 2010); and
- *Teaching Writing Online: How & Why* by Scott Warnock (Warnock, 2009).

The optimum training for teachers is a workshop approach in which participants utilize hands-on experience to explore their instructional options via either professional development or self-study and navigation of the Web. I have been fortunate to know Rob Rozema as a former colleague and to be able to observe his development of digital curriculum for his students, who are preservice teachers. I have also attended several of Troy Hicks' digital workshops held under the auspices of my local National Writing Project affiliate, The Red Cedar Writing Project at Michigan State University. Teachers desiring ongoing training with their educational peers might check the home page of the National Writing Project (www.nwp.org) to find their closest affiliate sites. The National Council of Teachers of English (www.ncte.org) and National Writing Project, among other educational organizations, host *podcasts*, a series of audio or video broadcasts released intermittently via files and computer software (*PCMagazine Encyclopedia*, 2010). Online study groups and visual conferences conducted via the Web using personal computers have also contributed to teacher training and collaboration with peers worldwide. In short, there are a wealth of opportunities for teachers to observe, talk about, and learn the language and pedagogy of digital writing.

Towards a Digital Writing Pedagogy

Since writing instruction is an ongoing process of locating, selecting, and implementing suitable materials that represent best practice for a particular audience of students, use of digital media and lessons is likely to nurture motivation in young adolescent writers. Whether the transition from print to digital use results in a hybrid or a fully digitalized writing program, teachers will benefit from support from the school administration via ongoing professional development, collegial sharing, and sample writing lessons. In addition, teachers might consider matching digital tools to writers and contexts, beginning with one tool at a time;

establishing a Web presence; and broadening the views of writing instruction. A starting point for initiating change within writing instruction is an acknowledgment that writing in online and other non-school contexts is valid writing and an important part of students' literacy context.

Acknowledging Writing outside the School Setting

Web technologies permeate nearly every aspect of life; young adolescents are, for the most part, not only capable of but also comfortable with using digital media in many of the forms of communication in which they participate throughout their day. It therefore makes sense for students to hone their written communication skills within an academic context such as a *message board*, an online forum similar to traditional bulletin boards, where students may participate in multi-genre projects incorporating images and video (Oronson, 2009: 18). For many students, the availability and personal use of blogging becomes a motivation in itself, as it permits not only contact but also collaboration among an extensive audience of peers. A blog can also function very practically as a writer's notebook, and studies by the National Writing Project that were conducted in 2006 support engaged writing practices involving blogging, linked to student literacy improvements (Hicks, 2009). Blogs and other digital tools connect students to writing by connecting them personally not only with peers, but also with the sites and content experts they find helpful in both formal and informal writing. The same National Writing Project study, *Local Site Research Initiative Report: Cohort II, 2004–2005* (National Writing Project, 2006), also shows a strong connection between teachers' experiences as writers and their ability to support students who employ these digital strategies.

> ***Teachers who acknowledge and support young adolescent writing that occurs outside of school as well as in the classroom motivate writers by validating all digital and print forms of their written communication as authentic and useful.***

One of the best ways to demonstrate this validation is when teachers explicitly model their varied kinds of writing both inside and outside of school for their students, while also taking time for students to perform some metacognitive reflection and awareness-raising through class discussion. Some questions that may prompt an appropriate discussion are:

- What are the purposes of your writing?
- Who are your audiences?
- What needs, functions, or purposes do the different kinds of writings address or fulfill?
- What are the similarities and differences between personal writing, writing for class assignments, and writing in online social networks?

A Venn diagram with room for responses to all three types of writing – social, personal, and school writing – may be used to show that while some qualities of the different types of writing are distinctive, some will overlap.

> ***The value of each kind of text is distinct and subjective in terms of the writing and the writer; nevertheless, each type of writing has merit.***

Validation of out-of-class, online social communication does not necessarily equate to acceptance of informal vocabulary, spelling, and grammar for many forms of class writing. This is an important point for young adolescents to internalize: purpose, audience, and focus of writing help determine the writing genre that is appropriate and its required and consistent elements. No one type of writing is necessarily any better or any worse than another; each has unique features, depending on its content and on why and for whom it is composed.

Finding Collegial Support

My own experience exploring Web resources to utilize in class as well as to develop my professional writing can serve as an example of efforts made that have brought many positive returns. My levels of interest and expertise increased gradually with practice and continuous professional development about digital writing tools as well as my ongoing Web presence. In late 2008, I joined the *NCTE Ning* (http://mcte.info/), a social network for English educators, rapidly followed by a foray onto Facebook (with grown-up daughters' blessings). Jim Burke, author and secondary English teacher, created an *English Companion Ning* (http://englishcompanion.ning.com/), followed by Rob Rozema's formation of the *MCTE* (Michigan Council of Teachers of English) *Ning* (http://mcte.info/). All of these Nings bustle with teacher discussions, collaborative planning, calls for ideas and support, and networking. Recently, I became a member of *Classroom 2.0* (http://www.classroom20.com/), a ning created for teachers of all content areas wishing to integrate more online resources, particularly the *open source*, or free tools. Each ning hosts a multitude of special-interest discussion groups that focus on particular areas of interest and need, such as the discussion group, Digital Storytelling (http://www.classroom20.com/group/digitalstorytelling).

Social networks have become a valued, significant part of my professional work and personal life because they enable continuous, critical discourse concerning pedagogical and theoretical issues while offering many positive ways to incorporate technology into my day-to-day life. Additionally, these networks have made possible connections with former students and the helpful support of peers; facilitated my interest in utilizing each site's available tools, such as taking part in discussions, posting messages, downloading photos, and adding links; and provided additional forums and purposes for my writing. The more I take part in digital experiences such as *webinars* (online seminars), research online literary archives, and participate in ning and listserv discussions, the more capable I feel about selecting and suggesting appropriate digital technologies to others. Thus, the e-Universe has enabled me to remain active in the field from my own home – or anywhere I choose to "tune in." The same is true for many teachers currently making use of digital resources and is also possible for those who have just begun. Just as young adolescent writers work and progress within a range of proficiency levels, teachers are digital learners with varied skills who progress more quickly when working and writing in context, for multiple purposes, and motivated by personal success.

Lesson 1: Composing a Class Sonnet with a Wiki

Along with traditional class discussions, another ongoing dialog may be used to compose class poetry. A class *wiki*, a collaborative space with tools for digital conversation, may be utilized for peer discussions and one-on-one conferences with young writers (Rozema and Webb, 2008: 33). Although discussion via wikis does not take place in real time, the benefit is that since the dialog is written and saved, it may be continuously viewed and then also read as a finished session, that is, when a student has added a comment and saved it. The wiki is set up ahead of time on a free source such as www.wikispaces.com, where teachers may click on a link and are then clearly prompted in steps to set up the wiki, including selection of a password that is given to students for their access and participation in the wiki.

This type of writing works well when set up as a whole-class activity and monitored for students' understanding. For example, following an in-class study of sonnets, young adolescents might enjoy the creation of a group poem. Named for the Italian *sonetto*, translated "little song or sound," sonnets may be one of two types, the Italian or the Shakespearean format (Geller, 2001). Most sonnets are characterized by a regular rhyme scheme, usually iambic pentameter, which moves along musically within fourteen lines. Young adolescents may become personally motivated to compose an exceptional poem with the addition of an appropriate literary device, such as hyperbole, to the assignment. I can recall the joy and sense of engagement students exhibited while writing a group poem, each student actively participating, building upon the work of classmates. The digital version of a group poem builds on students' motivation while also making use of a wiki or other digital writing forum established by the teacher for writing collaboration. Unlike the traditional class poem, the digital group sonnet provides young adolescents with accessibility and active involvement in the composition process beyond the classroom.

Following face-to-face lessons reviewing both the sonnet and hyperbole that include examples for students to read, analyze, and discuss, students can write an in-class group sonnet. Figure 6.2 shows what an illustrative group sonnet might look like, with an *a–b–b–a, a–b–b–a, c–d–c–d–c–d* rhyme scheme. While my entire sonnet is presented in Figure 6.2 as a sample, students should also be able to build upon a teacher's first line or idea, such as an ode to a certain food, plant, place, person, animal, etc. Students can concentrate on the musicality of their lines and the addition of exaggeration. The teacher may offer feedback and ask students for their input and evaluation of the group-written poem.

For less structured rhyme, you can start by having students study one of Robert Frost's sonnets, such as "Mowing," whose rhyme is more intermittent. Ask students to consider this rhyme scheme when contributing lines to a sonnet via a class wiki. Invite each student writer to add one line, either beginning another sonnet by composing the first line, or contributing to a sonnet in progress by adding a line or proposing a substitution. Start students off with a title like "Ode to an E-mail Break-Up." Students will likely respond with lines incorporating exaggeration, humor, and other emotions.

The following class day, print a copy of the class poem or poems and display it/them for the class to view all together, or present students' work by means of a projector and wall screen or other available means. Ask for a volunteer to read the poetry aloud, and provide time for students' reflection and feedback, including elements of the sonnet, use of hyperbole, and lesson components found most helpful to them as writers. Knowing that the poetry will be read aloud in class, with time to critique and respond, will further engage and motivate young adolescent writers. Perhaps

Ode to a Pepperoni Pizza
Mary Anna Kruch

Tangy blend of basil with tomatoes

Lapped upon my outstretched tongue;

Sweet peppers, onions danced and sung

Sent aromatic passion to my nose.

Olives and ham were swept up as one

Fragrance heartily draped the air;

Cheese and garlic formed a sumptuous pair

Breath-taking as the setting sun.

Unaware of sighs through lovesick pout

You ignore my enthusiastic call;

Friends find my passion lacking clout

They say I'll take another fall;

Yet, no one yearns as me to sneak you out

As medium, large, or extra small!

Figure 6.2. Illustrative Class Sonnet

a subsequent group composition might include an invitation for students to contribute original art, appropriate music, poetry, or song lyrics with similar themes. Keep in mind that class members have the wiki password; therefore, they also possess the ability to change lines written by others! This can be a drawback, but the process can also set the stage for a critical conversation and clarifications about both sonnets and the use of class wikis.

Matching Resources to Writers

Classroom educators are encouraged to match the most appropriate writing tool to the writer (Kajder, 2003), to recognize that students live in an "environment where they control information flow and access with ease" (Strommen and Lincoln, 1992: 466), and, most importantly, to be aware that the definition of work in the 21st century has changed and will continue to do so in ways that incorporate digital and other technologies. For some teachers more than others, this is a challenge, but not an insurmountable one.

For many teachers of writing over the past twenty years, the issue has shifted from one of fear and suspicion of unknown technologies to increasingly more open-minded inquiry of the most suitable ways to utilize digital tools. The National Council of Teachers of English *Definition of 21st Century Literacies*, adopted in 2008, states that literate persons must have an extensive array of capabilities and proficiencies because technology has "increased the intensity and complexity of literate environments" and also because the term *literacy* implies "a collection of cultural and communicative practices shared among groups" (NCTE Executive Committee, 2008). NCTE promotes individual and group projects and collaborations within academic, global, and social contexts, including ones on building proficiency with digital tools, cross-cultural problem-solving, devising and sharing information for many purposes, performing critical analyses of multimedia texts, and enhancing knowledge and respect for systems of ethics within intricate Web milieus. The full NCTE Position Statement may be accessed at http://www.ncte.org/positions/statements/21stcentdefinition. This does not, of course, negate the necessity and importance of face-to-face teaching and learning environments. In fact, Web contexts that closely mirror successful face-to-face teaching pedagogies have continued to grow in value, particularly among the most hesitant and in experienced users.

Writing may occur using computers rather than by hand, but there is more to writing online than this, as digital writing operates upon very different suppositions and values than writing in tangible space, such as its nature to continually change and reflect change. Transitioning to all or part-time online writing thus requires the recognition that information on the World Wide Web undergoes continual growth and transformation. Whatever ways and means of writing are planned, the central consideration is to strive to complement young adolescents with the most promising means to grow as writers.

Having considered the purposes for writing in their classes, their current and future pedagogical practices, and the available resources for implementing these, teachers willing to consider digital tools may want to become active assessors of Web-based applications, programs, and materials. Just as educators should not assign text materials provided by publishers sight unseen, so must they become active participant-assessors of digital resources in advance of their possible classroom use.

Motivating with Technology, One Tool at a Time

Of course, not all technological resources require accessing the Internet. Still, I must admit to a sense of wonder regarding not only the available technology but also the continual additions of present and future resources. When search engines, educational Web sites, and applications such as Microsoft's *PowerPoint* became readily available for teachers in my school, I was impressed by their utility and growing importance to writers. However, I sensed some dismay and hesitation among a few colleagues at taking the time to explore and learn how they might use these in their instruction.

Seven years later, *PowerPoint* is no longer a novel utility but instead an accepted method of presenting information. Instead of relying only upon a classroom computer and a difficult to sign out LCD projector to show PowerPoint slides and other visuals, many teachers design documents on their computers at home and save these to a *flash drive,* a small, portable memory device functioning for storage of documents and digital media. Also called a *jump drive, thumb drive,* or *USB drive,* the flash drive can then be placed into the USB port of a school computer, enabling interactive instruction when attached to a classroom LCD projector. A growing number of schools are fortunate to have classrooms equipped with this and other relevant technology, but that situation is far from the norm. The most likely scenario might include the existence of one or more computer labs for an entire school's use. Possibly a school has been granted technology funds to purchase some interactive, electronic *whiteboards*, which are equivalent to a traditional white board but instead project information from software on the teacher's computer or from a detached electronic device. A cart with a number of working laptops may be available as well. Yet the laptops or electronic whiteboards may rarely be used by more than a few teachers; some devices and even school computer labs may be available yet remain underused. The reasons for underused technology in a school vary but may include a lack of experience and expertise with accessible technology or Web tools and/or a position of having tried some newer technologies but having found them cumbersome or in need of repairs. As with any devices or resources used to support classroom teaching, digital tools require patience, a can-do attitude to problem-solve, and a willingness to learn on the part of the teacher, with back-up by a school-based computer technician.

Since young adolescents today reside in and interact with people, places, and events worldwide via the Internet, and also because learning is social, teachers, administrators, and the larger community must set a high priority on digital writing processes (Wilmarth, 2010: 21, 4).

At home and at school, my best technology teachers were my children and my students, both of whom were willing teachers; these youngsters expected and were impressed by a willingness on my part to find answers for my own questions, which then translated into a sense of more natural confidence when working alone. I share this fact with teachers who may be hesitant to make the leap to digital writing instruction as well as those who may feel tied to a set curriculum that may not include specific use of available technology. One point is clear: those who have leaped across the digital divide have taken a calculated risk that their new learning will benefit students, and it will most likely do so. A first step is becoming familiar with available resources.

When teachers are familiar with available Web tools, meaning they understand how and why the tools work, they are able to select those that fit teaching contexts and suit individual student needs (Rozema and Webb, 2008: 106).

> *When teachers choose resources with which they have experienced successful Web-based composition and other text-related creations, they bring an informed enthusiasm to the classroom, further fueling motivation for young adolescents.*

Fortunately, more and more university teacher education courses now implement tools such as class Web sites, *wikis* (virtual collaborative writing spaces), *blogs* (online journals where posts may be updated on a regular basis), and class social networks through *Ning*, a service that allows the creation of public and private social networks (Rozema and Webb: 77). When they use digital media themselves, instructors provide modeling as well as time to reflect upon potential classroom utilization. These instructional practices serve as models for preservice and veteran teachers, who may then actively incorporate them into future personal practice.

Some adults either have not managed to cross the "digital divide" of their own free will or feel understandably threatened by the rapidly changing, seemingly endless array of technological advances. To the new or the veteran educator who may panic when faced with an overload of technical information and applications, I suggest implementing one tool at a time, as it is possible to become familiar with it and to see what technological applications represent a good match for a specific class project or function.

The gradual exploration of Web-based tools makes the most sense for individual classroom teachers ready and willing to begin the internal transformation that goes along with the external application of new ideas and resources in the classroom. One way to do so is to take time outside of work to freely engage with and experience potential classroom writing tools and activities on the Internet. It's not easy to let go of free time outside of work, as teachers spend more and more minutes and hours on work-related, non-academic duties; yet the time spent perusing possible Web tools is more than worth it.

Establishing a Web Presence: Teachers Planting Digital Roots

Teachers and other significant adults in the greater learning community who wish to further their Web knowledge might begin with the establishment of what Rozema and Webb (2008: 107) term a "Web presence." This means incorporating Internet activity into lesson preparation, research, and other Web navigation for a variety of purposes. Web activities may include navigating the e-Universe to check out Web sites of personal and professional interest, trying out downloaded applications and programs suggested by peers, developing an approved list of appropriate research sites for students, conducting research on specific topics and units of study, and creating a Web page or perhaps a *blog*. Short for *weblog*, blogs may be used as an academic notebook or as a personal diary, inviting readers to leave comments (Rozema and Webb, 2009: 52).

Collaboration with and support of colleagues near and far can be found in academic social networks such as the Michigan Council of Teachers of English Ning (www.mcte.info); in the National Writing Project affiliate wikis; and by participation in *webinars*, online professional development seminars. In addition, taking part in conversation threads on one or more *listservs,* a collection of e-mail addresses linked to one e-mail address set up in an office or by national and affiliate organizations, results in further Web presence. Conversations by means of discussion groups on social networks created for particular interests may result in valuable face-to-face meetings as well as ongoing dialog with colleagues that one may not otherwise know (Kist, 2010: 34). Such Web presence also offers teachers substantial support and camaraderie in what often feels like a hurried, solo performance on an academic day.

Forming collaborative environments has been and continues to be a practice and a goal in teaching writing in a writing workshop environment. An early attempt to build technology and to support collaborative environments follows.

Lesson 2: Building a Brilliant Biography

An early attempt to build technology into my lessons occurred for me in the late 1990s, upon noting that the state standards called for a variety of student presentations, including by digital means. That humble start resulted in the creation of "Brilliant Biographies." I taught a 2-week unit early in the academic year that included studying the elements of a biography and reading short biographies. For practice, each class wrote a script for *Readers' Theater*, a dramatization of short, written work intended to be read aloud, based on the lives of then-current pop icons like Bart Simpson, Princess Diana, and the rock group, Nine Inch Nails, which we humorously referred to as "Nine Inch Toenails!"

After acting out selected scenes from scripts written as a whole group, I invited students to choose an icon, trend or fad (such as the Rubic's Cube or pet rocks), or a living legend, and to compose original works, their Brilliant Biographies. Beanie Babies, *NSYNC, Hanson, Brittany Spears, hula hoops, and even the Macarena (a short-lived dance craze) all found their way into students' writing. Teachers now might find students writing about the Jonas Brothers, Maroon Five, Twitter, or Michelle Obama. The inclusion of fads or trends as subjects for biography worked well, as writers delighted in bringing them to life through personification, the use of archived dialogs and comments regarding the trend in various news and entertainment media, and in other imaginative ways. I found that the simplicity, familiarity, humor, and presence of the subject's central biggest contribution laid the groundwork for a writing invitation that few students could resist.

We discussed possible presentation options, and many students were intent upon applying digital technology as yet untried. Along with PowerPoint slide presentations, with which writers had previous experience, we agreed on three choices for the biography assignment. Working individually or in pairs, students could select a task from among the following prompts:

- Compose a script, act it out, and film it if a movie camera or other appropriate technology is accessible;
- Compose and produce a digital narrative via computer, incorporating art, text, and sound; or
- Compose a traditional short biography of a chosen icon, accompanied by an illustrative piece of art, photography, music, or video via traditional or digital technology.

Figure 6.3 presents a sample advance organizer to assist students with inclusion of the elements which they were asked to include in their scripts, digital narratives, or traditional compositions. The project was a great success, I suspect because I had given students a lot of leeway to compose and create, and also because the work was filled with self-directed, active engagement, bouts of laughter, and considerable success in terms of the quality of writing produced.

Broadening the View of Writing Instruction

Inspired by Kettering's words as quoted at the beginning of this chapter, I advocate an expansive, critical view of the educational frontier – particularly as it relates to the teaching of writing – composed of vast planes, complex layers, and varied possibilities open to individual teachers' and students' understanding, selection, interpretation, and creation. As they take part in digital writing experiences, young adolescents grow in familiarity with and understanding of the numerous choices within their complex communication systems, affording them increased confidence and proficiency in writing.

> While reading, researching, and composing, take into account why you chose the subject(s) that you did, such as their celebrity status, historical success, or fascinating personal details. Include all of these elements for a full representation of your subject(s):
>
> - Date of birth (or rise to fame if a trend)
> - Place of birth (or origination)
> - Family
>   - ➢
>   - ➢
>   - ➢
>   - ➢
> - Major events of life
>   - ➢
>   - ➢
>   - ➢
>   - ➢
> - Lifetime achievements
>   - ➢
>   - ➢
>   - ➢
>   - ➢
> - Impact on society
>
> - Biggest contribution to fans and devotees

Figure 6.3. Advance Organizer for Biography

Regardless of the resources chosen, teachers need to determine students' knowledge level and then attempt to create lessons that enhance learning and engage writers of all competency levels.

Teachers must be empowered to harness students' knowledge, understandings, and emerging writing competencies in order to guide their writing and literacy, engage their interests, and model critical decision-making in both their virtual online and their real (classroom or other face-to-face) writing communities. Working online, students can be guided to pose and respond in writing to questions ordinarily provided by the teacher. The act of creating and then finding answers to questions such as "Which 20th Century writers present conflict between father and son?" and "What social, cultural, and political lessons may be learned from the United States' involvement in Vietnam and Iraq?" assist young adolescents in acquiring the skills such as close reading, helpful peer response, consideration of multiple viewpoints, and becoming open to suggestions to clarify ideas, add details, and support arguments. Additionally, digital writing provides immediate, context-specific practice for young adolescent writers' progressive growth in reading and writing of expository texts, a frequent focus area of standardized tests. In addition, competency requirements for particular digital literacies like wikis and digital narratives are slowly but surely making their way into state and national standards (Hicks, 2009: 15).

Young adolescents benefit most when teachers willingly integrate both face-to-face and Web technologies into the writing workshop.

As noted earlier, the integration of Web technologies must occur willingly and thoughtfully, so that teachers' efforts enable them to own their evolving instructional practices. Also, just as digital technologies are in a state of continuous change, teachers need to regularly review and adapt instruction in order to match students' differentiated progress in writing.

Incorporating Digital Research

Planning writing lessons that hinge on digital research requires, as has been suggested, increased vision of what it means to teach writing. Along with existing Internet issues, teachers must know how to proceed with digital research when part of a writing unit. Along with a specific research route that teachers might take with their students, an overview of a research project exploring volunteerism and requiring research on the Web is offered.

Internet Issues Affecting Young Adolescent Writers

Adolescents plow through the Internet to get to their favorite social networks like *Facebook.com* and *MySpace.com*, download music via *iTunes*, and access search engines like *Google.com*. They check their e-mail; search for videos on *YouTube*; and visit and bookmark favorite sites, such as *fanfiction.com*, to read and respond to narratives written by other users, inspired by film, television, and literature.

Young adolescents also seek verification of data, and may mistakenly interpret information for fact at Wikipedia.com without checking other sources. Because this popular site is a wiki, users may add their own, undocumented versions of knowledge about a given topic with an account and a password, although the site administrators regularly check for informational accuracy. As a rule of thumb, teachers can remind students that three or more traditional text sources or online sites are needed to verify specific data for use in compositions. Visiting sites and making use of the data and services offered takes place often and easily; however, some students are not as tech-savvy as they believe, especially when they are faced with an assignment that requires them to conduct precise, project-specific research and to cite sources correctly, distinguishing between others' work and their own. The maze of links to Web sites, nings, wikis, and blogs, often interchangeable to the unpracticed eye, may overwhelm and confuse young adolescent writers. Without guidance, many young adolescents may not grasp ideas such as the wide variance in audience related to both publishing and accessing text on the Internet. They may lack the appropriate use of rhetoric for academic writing and may not fully grasp the style of writing for more formal purposes.

Young adolescents who communicate primarily by means of digital devices such as personal cell phones, Blackberries, iPods, and iPads may lack the experience and know-how necessary for additional, more approved or prescribed educational uses of the Web.

As educators' understanding about and application of Web-based writing resources grows, so do the vast frontiers of future digital discoveries.

Along with the fascination and facilitation of using digital tools for teacher-directed writing, specific topics affect young adolescents and their motivation and success as writers in an e-universe. Because choice enhances student motivation and because independent success brings about empowerment and satisfaction, teachers might seek to include opportunities for choice and independence when assigning research projects. I know I wish I had known more and included more opportunities while I was in the classroom. The scenario described next illustrates why.

During my last twelve years as a middle school classroom teacher, I taught sixth grade humanities, meeting with students two hours per day, five days a week for a combination of English language arts and history, geography, and culture of countries in the Western Hemisphere. One of the benchmark projects for sixth grade students was the completion of a promotional trifold pamphlet or short video promoting one of the South American countries, including basic geographical, historical and cultural data, present-day life, and a 5-day itinerary of events and places that would appeal to potential tourists. To pique their interest, students brainstormed and prepared an original Web site or travel shop name and logo. For research preparation, we took a digital video tour of a museum in Chile and visited an art gallery via video stream from Bolivia. I also modeled for students the necessary steps to accessing and applying primary and secondary sources in their work. Digital research for my students was then in its infancy, and I was surprised at the number of color, printed pages of information taken word-for-word from encyclopedia and geographical Web sources brought in by students when I asked to see their research notes.

It became painfully clear that my team-teaching peers and I had neglected to model appropriate ways to select information, take notes, and organize data. The following year, we assigned a similar benchmark research project, this time including prewriting techniques for selecting pertinent data from a variety of print and digital resources, taking notes, and then organizing the data into a useful form such as a concept map or outline. Mini-lessons prior to writing included instruction and review of paraphrase versus original quotation, and ways to correctly cite sources. As expected, students' work improved in its quality and accuracy.

If I were to make the same assignment today, eight years later, I would suggest that teachers become familiar with the concept of *fair use,* a set of guidelines developed over a period of years to balance the rights of copyright owners with those who seek restricted use of print as well as digital information and media. Since writers may consider incorporating a combination of digital excerpts and media into their work, they need know the boundaries as they create new pieces of writing building on those already in existence on the Web. TeacherTube (http://www.teachertube.com/), a free site that shares digital media projects produced by students and teachers, is a good place to view the practice of *mashup,* a process where excerpts or entire digital files of text, graphics, audio, video, and animation already in existence are used to create a new work (wikipedia.org/wiki/Mashup). "The Water Cycle Rap" is an example of how graphics, text, music, and the inclusion of video of a young adolescent performing a rap about the water cycle was assembled to create a new work (http://www.teachertube.com/viewVideo.php?video_id=196231&title=The_Water_Cycle_Rap). Students' and teachers' collaboration on projects like this benefits both teaching and learning processes. I chose this particular example from TeacherTube in order to compare it to the print-based lesson, "5Es Doodle Writing: Water Cycle" in Chapter 5. Both kinds of lessons serve to meet identical teacher goals for both lessons as well as state and national standards, while providing dynamic motivation for young adolescent writers.

With the continuing proliferation of available, highly motivating Web tools, teachers walk a difficult line, attempting to inspire creativity while staying within given boundaries of fair use and copyright law. Renee Hobbs has written a short, helpful article that clarifies fair use guidelines for teachers, entitled "Best Practices Help End Copyright Confusion" (Hobbs, 2009: 12–14).

Illustrative Research Route

While students' use of digital tools and technology have improved over the past ten years, a research project such as the one described above would be assigned and then completed quite differently now than in the past. For one thing, more time would be set aside for topic selection and for explicit instruction regarding expected steps in the research and writing process, and I would conduct frequent, short writing conferences with each student in order to track progress and offer the appropriate, differentiated guidance necessary for each individual learner. Just as writing is an ongoing, progressive, recursive process, so too is the development of research skills. One of the main differences in a research process now, as opposed to just ten years ago, is the overwhelming number of seemingly infinite, changing sources amidst masses of available information online. Therefore, much attention must be given to assisting students in articulating their research questions and goals. How might writers progress in their research step-by-step, and what are the necessary steps or the possible options? Even given that some students may be familiar to a point with how to conduct their own inquiry, each young adolescent needs to first plan a path through the information highway in order to establish a research route that will be most likely to result in individual success.

Educators with regular access to a computer lab might be interested in plotting a digital research route for their students, particularly when some of the work may be conducted at home or outside of class. In *The Digital Writing Workshop* (Hicks, 2009),

Troy Hicks offers some very practical suggestions for students' prewriting and organization in preparation for a digital writing assignment. In order to deal with and make sense of the magnitude of available Internet data, three tools support students' contemplation, organization, and writing: blogging, social book marking, and the use of *RSS* (alternately called *rich site summary* or *real simple syndication*) feeds (Hicks, 2009: 18). Rozema and Webb (2008: 69) define an RSS feeder as "a tool that reinvents the way we gather and sort information." The RSS feeder combines electronic information, along with its updated versions, and then sends these to Web sites, blogs, online newsletters, e-mail addresses, and other digital communication tools, from which the reader may select information (Rozema and Webb, 2008: 69).

Lesson 3 is an overview of a research project exploring volunteerism, and it includes ideas for suggested mini-lessons prior to students' work online, along with a flowchart illustrating a digital research process and employing a variety of digital resources.

Lesson 3: Volunteerism Project

Students' enthusiasm and devotion to an idea or cause is motivated by their background knowledge and their levels of curiosity in connection with learning more about their chosen topic. The topic of volunteerism can serve as an example of relevance to young adolescents. While many young adolescent students may already have taken part in volunteer activities, such as collecting newspapers to recycle, selling cookies, or going door-to-door promoting a summer youth group, they may not have consciously chosen nor reflected upon the experience. In addition, they may not have felt a personal connection to the volunteer activity or personalized the effort in any way. Young adolescents may benefit from looking beyond their own worlds, learning about and relating to others through a study of volunteerism, and accepting an invitation to pursue a cause of choice.

To introduce a project about volunteerism, a teacher might begin with a short discussion of the purposes of volunteerism and why citizens become involved in work without pay, followed by a survey of the class as to who has been a volunteer in the past and what benefits resulted from their efforts. The teacher may raise the question that now students are older and have more choices about why and how they might volunteer in the future, what are some of their options? Perhaps a brainstorming session with responses listed for class members to view would encourage and motivate contributions, such as working for a neighbor running for City Council or a state office, tutoring elementary school students, or serving food at a community center or church function. The teacher might then ask students to think more broadly or globally as to how their time, hard work, and expertise might be harnessed to affect an even larger group of people.

Young adolescents possess potentially untapped abilities for work like taking part in a run in order to raise money to combat childhood leukemia or directing a program to send letters to troops serving in other countries. Taking part in these efforts empowers students to contribute toward causes about which they may not have previously connected or may have experienced a feeling of powerlessness. Students may add larger goals, such as assisting Haitian refugees following the devastating earthquakes, chairing a fact-finding operation in response to needed immigration reform, and actively campaigning for someone running for office with ideas about how to better fund or improve public schools. With ideas posted for all to see, the teacher can then ask students to come up with additional ideas and to place these in either print or electronic notebooks.

The process of inquiry typically begins with framing a topic or a question, so the teacher can next ask students to pose a question or clearly defined cause on which they may focus their research and writing efforts. They can then create a document intended to inform, motivate, and invite others to take part in their volunteer project. The purpose of the document, an essay with the goal of either a public service announcement or a general action plan or proposal, would be to learn more about efforts already in progress, to set one or more goals specifying contributions students might make, and to enlist others to join with them in their chosen volunteer efforts.

Once a topic has been identified and questions posed, the exploration, discovery, selection, organization, and citations of information follow, moving into a first draft, inspired by data relevant to the topic. A flowchart that illustrates the major course of planning a digital research project is shown in Figure 6.4 and includes some of Hicks' (2009) suggestions for digitalizing student writing, including the utilization of blogging, bookmarking,

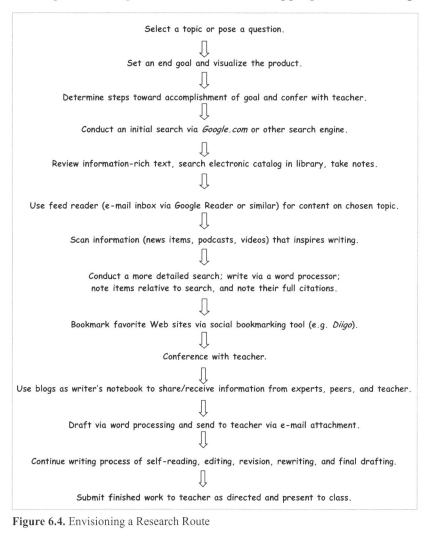

Figure 6.4. Envisioning a Research Route

and RSS feeds. The flowchart may be adapted to various online projects.

A sample checklist is presented in Figure 6.5 to direct students' attention to required components of the essay on volunteerism. Each writer sets up the parameters for the additional public service announcement, general action plan, or proposal for the volunteer cause or organization chosen, in consultation with the teacher; or the teacher may establish these as a rubric or checklist to guide the work.

The checklist may be adapted as needed to support the digital writing project created by the students or chosen by the teacher. Grading through both informal (during the writing process) and formal (after completion of the project) means is suggested, keeping in mind the benefits of frequent teacher and peer feedback during the entire writing workshop. Addition of the volunteerism project to a student portfolio can be accomplished digitally in more than one way, but Hicks (2009: 84–88) recommends the use of an *open source* (free) blog such as *WordPress* (www.wordpress.com) and describes the set-up process in an easy-to-follow format. Young adolescent writers take an active part in the digital portfolio process, which then further engages and motivates them.

All essays should reflect or contain:

__ Framing question
__ Sense of audience: peers, teacher
__ Purpose: Make the case for the value of involvement via volunteerism
__ Engaging introduction
__ Thesis statement: Focus on selected cause or organization
__ Support for thesis
  __ Paragraphs for separate ideas
  __ Correctly cited data
__ Explicit organization
__ Unity through transitional words and phrases, sequence
__ Use of logic and reason
__ Strong conclusion: Given the thesis and support, invite others to join cause or organization
__ Adherence to the rules of Standard English

Please note: There is no prescribed number of paragraphs or pages; compose the best possible writing!

Figure 6.5. Components of Essay on Volunteerism

How the Tech-sperts View Future Writing Instruction

The *2010 Horizon Report: K–12 Edition* (Smith, Johnson, Brown, and Levine, 2010) highlights some of the issues discussed in this chapter. The annual report focuses upon technologies that are expected to shape education over the next five years and lists several critical challenges for K–12 technology. Among the challenges are: insufficient digital literacy training and techniques for teachers, dated teaching materials, disagreement about educational change, unsuccessful attempts to adjust to online and home-based learning, a traditional educational model of learning, and a lack of recognition of out-of-classroom learning as viable and valuable (Smith *et al.*, 2010: 4–6). The need to offer adequate professional development for teachers as well as appropriate teaching materials has been addressed here, and these issues appear to be problems more easily solved than agreeing on which changes to make and how to deal with non-traditional forms of education such as informal, online, and home-based learning. I observe progress by educators in the acknowledgement of young adolescents' writing when they take the time and interest to respond to it, both inside and outside of school, by digital and other means; and that is a good start.

Rachel Smith, Laurence F. Johnson, Malcolm B. Brown, and Alan Levine, authors of *The Horizon Report: K–12 Edition* (Smith *et al.*, 2010), reiterate the importance of an acceptance of students' writing in its totality. They present a detailed, innovative view of the technologies they say will shape and are shaping education. The authors cite the following six technologies as those that will affect education within the next five years:

- *Cloud computing*, a public or private service that involves delivering hosted benefits from specialized data centers over the Internet (*SearchCloudComputing.com*);
- *Collaborative environments*;
- *Game-based learning*;

- *Mobile technologies* (including cellular networks);
- *Augmented reality* (a convergence of virtual and real data to augment what is apparent to the senses; and
- *Flexible displays*, thin display screens printed onto stretchable materials and then affixed to other surfaces. (Smith *et al.*, 2010: 9, 26, 30)

The Digital Youth Project, another large U. S. study on teen use of digital media, funded by the John D. and Catherine T. MacArthur Foundation, found that American adolescents' time online assists them with the development of essential technical and social competencies needed to prepare them for the demands of future study and careers (Chrenka, 2009). Growth and development of relevant curricula must follow, continuing to reinvent education as required. Thus, the argument that young people are wasting time online and making them lazy may no longer hold true. In many cases, students' time online has, instead, increased their overall engagement in reading and writing. Educators' focused use of digital technology has the potential to broaden and apply students' present Web knowledge to additional learning environments, including that of school writing.

Concluding Reflections on Chapter 6

As I have attempted to show, digital literacies can and do complement print-based text versions as choices for writers and teachers of writing. To facilitate the nurturance of young adolescent writers now and in the future, it takes an educational village of support, empowering teachers as the instructional writing experts. This support benefits young adolescents most profoundly when accompanied by a continuous study of and conversation about writing instruction and resources.

When all is said and done, it will be the intention and the attempt to facilitate the growth of knowledge, confidence, and success in writing that young adolescents will remember, once they have taken their places in life beyond the classroom. If educators have celebrated choice and supported the students' quest for independent exploration and discovery with regard to their writing, then the efforts will have been a triumph. Each bit of progress in learning reflects nurturing steps toward motivation of the young adolescent writer. As noted American scientist and inventor Charles F. Kettering believed, "There will always be a frontier where there is an open mind and a willing hand" (Boyd, 1961: 240). Writing teachers and other significant adults in young adolescents' lives must approach the new as well as the older multi-modal tools with an open, ever-widening mind. The process of jumping the digital divide frees teachers to know, to understand, and to select those writing resources deemed most suitable for each writing context while allowing them to differentiate and provide for writers' growth and development.

Chapter 7 presents a discussion of the benefits of using a selection of formative, informal authentic assessments along with more summative, formal evaluations in order to determine what adolescent writers already know, what they need to learn, and their progress level at any given time along the way. Also, in the spirit of continuing to nurture writers throughout the entire writing process, Chapter 7 addresses the planned inclusion of young adolescent writers during the evaluative stages of the writing workshop.

7 Sowing the Seeds of Formative, Authentic Assessment

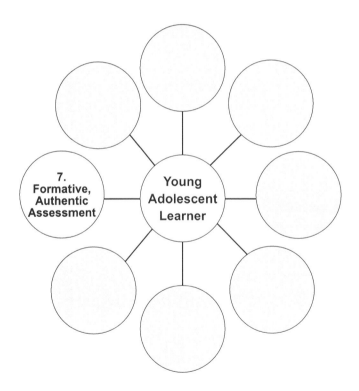

I find the great thing in this world is not so much where we stand, as in what direction we are moving....
 – Oliver Wendell Holmes, American physician, professor, lecturer, and author (Whitaker and Lumpa, 2005: 57)

Introductory Remarks to Chapter 7

Young adolescent writers achieve success and mastery in learning on a continuing, back and forth, ebb-and-flow basis, which requires assessment measures that are ongoing and multifaceted. Concepts and facts attained gradually in earlier years become the foundation for future learning; what is learned on any given day must be linked to past knowledge and future need in order for some forward progression of learning to take place.

Prior to teaching writing lessons at the start of an academic year, teachers must first find out what young adolescent writers *already know* about both the conventions and literary crafts of writing, in order to inform their future planning. The most appropriate way to gauge what writers already know is to utilize a variety of suitable, formative measures.

In this chapter, I argue for the use of a varied set of teacher-selected, formative assessments, along with the more standard, summative writing assessments ("writing on demand"), in order to best measure young adolescent writing. Examples of several formative assessments are given, along with suggestions for including students in the evaluation process at all stages of their writing. Research is provided in support of continuous assessment measures best suited for young adolescents in the learner-centered writing workshop.

Gauging Growth: An Ongoing, Integrated Approach to Assessment

Harvey Daniels and Marilyn Bizar, in *Teaching the Best Practice Way: Methods That Matter K-12*, offer six basic structures that match formative, reflective assessment suitable for all grades and content areas of study: portfolios, conferences, anecdotal records, checklists, performance assessment rubrics, and classroom tests (Daniels and Bizar, 2005: 229). These authors also suggest that the evaluative measures become a regular part of everyday instruction;

provide ongoing assessment that is an integral part of learning; and, most importantly, should be a process by which the teacher can learn more each day about individual students – all criteria which reflect a learner-centered model of writing instruction. But how might teachers plan writing assignments that double as assessments? Are there ways to nurture young adolescents' maturation processes in writing while also assessing it? There are!

Teachers can build upon the knowledge that young adolescents are passionate beings, capable of applying depth and insight to their work as well as transferring skills practiced in mini-lessons to their writing. They can invite students to open up to express themselves authentically, within a writing workshop routine where respect is the rule. Young adolescents can thus be encouraged to stretch themselves as writers without fear of ridicule from classmates, often producing some of their best writing.

Along with a safe writing community, another key to getting students to write their very best is to offer choices and relevant topics that nurture their motivation to write. For example, teachers may ask students to contribute short writings, drawings, and photos about class events for a virtual or digital scrapbook to be given to a classmate recuperating at home following an operation. Or, teachers might invite writers to attempt the correct use of metaphor, a skill practiced in class, to an ungraded, personal memoir. During or after the drafting stages of these particular writing invitations, students' writing progress may be assessed informally by one of several methods such as saving drafts of writing in digital or other portfolios for later grading; asking student volunteers to share writing in Author's Chair followed by a class discussion of the best features of the written works, informing future needed mini-lessons; or meeting with students on an as-needed basis and then noting their progress on a state-of-the class chart. Over a period of time, a young adolescent's process of making his or her writing public shows maturity as well as an acceptance of responsibility for growth in writing, qualities discovered through teachers' use of informal measures.

Belief in and Support of Each Young Adolescent Writer

An educational environment headed by a knowledgeable teacher must nurture risk-taking with respect, insight, and wisdom, in consideration that all young adolescents are budding, capable writers. Expectations of their growth in writing must reflect sound teaching pedagogy guided by sound assessment measures. The National Council of Teachers of English supports approaching writing in a holistic manner that takes into consideration the potential of each learner – and teacher of writing.

> *Everyone has the capacity to write, writing can be taught, and teachers can help students become better writers.*
> (Guidelines from the *NCTE Beliefs about the Teaching of Writing* by the Writing Study Group of the NCTE Executive Committee, 2004)

The above statement presupposes that students have skills and talents in writing *when they arrive in the classroom*; moreover, teachers can build upon these skills and talents to facilitate and motivate further learning. In other words, young adolescent writers grow progressively from the experiences, lessons, practice, and inquiry offered to them over time. This statement is in full text at http://www.ncte.org/positions/statements/writingbeliefs.

> *Students are **not** unfilled plots in a barren garden; they are fully alive, growing in knowledge and confidence as the adults, peers, and experiences in their world nurture them.*

Differentiation, an approach which includes educationally responsive, personalized teaching, first began to appear in educational literature in the 1990s, in reaction to the growing outrage against the impersonal nature of high-stakes testing and the return to past views of students that in effect treat them as educational products (Kruch, 2001; Tomlinson, 1999, 2004). The Back to Basics movement of the 1980s should have shown us that knowing how to read, write, and compute mathematics does not, in and of itself, equal a quality education. Then as now, some people equate educational reform with control and standardization. But, of course, no child is "standard"; therefore, attempts to standardize education have failed and will continue to fail. Learning takes place when students apply prior knowledge to new situations, particularly when the learning takes place under natural, authentic circumstances. No amount of correctly bubbled, multiple-choice responses can demonstrate this application process. Learning under the traditional information-processing model is a highly restricted and unnaturally decontextualized mode of study.

It is highly unlikely that facts memorized and tested in isolation, viewed by traditionalists as the key indicators of learning, will be carried beyond the classroom and applied to authentic situations.

Much more thought should be given to approaching learning as a process with unique characteristics for unique students. Differentiation is the process of creating and providing instruction that addresses the differing needs of students within a given class: "Differentiation, a philosophy of learning, is what *should be* the focus (rather than memorization of facts), as it is based on strong beliefs [about what impacts] not just student learning, but student assessment" (Kruch, 2001: 43; emphasis in original). My strong belief in the value of differentiation emerges from research-based and experienced-based studies as well as the understanding that writers' needs must be accommodated in order for them to reach their individual potentials. This philosophy of learning involves development and customization, learning process rather than product. Differentiated learning makes use of best practice methodology to find out what learners already know in order to build upon their strengths, not drill on their deficits. Most importantly, differentiation of teaching, learning, and assessment raises the likelihood that writers will make long-range, authentic application of their learning – an effective and efficient, achievement-oriented use of time and energy.

As presented in Chapter 1, middle school students' emotional, academic, physical, and social needs differ substantially from those of elementary and older secondary students. Differentiation assumes that each child is unique and brings individual past experiences, knowledge, and interests into the classroom. Examples of differentiation in classroom pedagogy which parallel the Young Adolescent Motivation Model within a learner-centered classroom are:

- Planning connections between the curriculum and students' interests and life experiences;
- Allowing students to choose, with teacher guidance, ways to learn and to demonstrate what has been learned;
- Using or creating classroom areas to serve as learning centers, with activities and materials appropriate to various learning styles, interests, and levels of achievement;
- Structuring class work to require high levels of critical thinking while accepting a wide range of responses;
- Creating projects that allow students to think for themselves;
- Setting and maintaining high expectations for all students;
- Implementing flexible grouping that allows collaboration among students by interest, achievement in a subject area, learning style, or personal choice;
- Providing authentic learning opportunities that reflect real-world connections; and
- Creating a sense of community in which students feel significant and respected.

Best Practice Pedagogy and Assessment

Insight about and understanding of individual students' interests, abilities, and needs provides a foundation for teachers to be creative about motivating students to exhibit what they have already mastered, no matter which assessment measure is used. Teachers must think beyond standards in order to plan for young adolescents' writing now and in the future; they may do so by becoming familiar with research supportive of learner-based views of writing and assessment. The longer that teaching practices hold up under the most careful scrutiny and study, the more support and credence they have; long-term trends can be identified in research or best classroom practices. When pressured by administrators to use standard, evaluative measures, teachers can provide examples of best practice research that demonstrate the value of alternative pedagogical models for writing and its assessment. Along with benefits for students, teachers gain a growing stockpile of instructional and assessment options.

What are "best practices"? In a 2001 Red Cedar Writing Project Summer Institute I attended at Michigan State University, a National Writing Project site, the term *best practices* was in such widespread overuse within educational literature and conversation, and even among some programmed instructional materials' advertisements, that my group and I came to refer to teaching pedagogy based on research and classroom use as *promising practice*, rather than the term which seemed a mere "buzz word," not necessarily based on research or any other evidence of effectiveness, and almost a cliché. As has been discussed, no one methodology or program of instruction is appropriate for every student writer, particularly in today's classroom, where a variety of languages and dialects are spoken in addition to English, in addition to the many further variables that distinguish learners and their interests, abilities, and needs. Today's classroom consists of many learners, including bilingual, English language learners and immigrants, all of whom require specific attention to language when planning for the needs of the entire writing community. Students may have additional physical and academic needs that require teachers to use a range of methods that will be most successful for the class as a whole and each individual middle-grades learner. Veronica E. Valdez and

Rebecca M. Callahan, in the *Handbook of Research on Teaching the English Language Arts* (Valdez and Callahan, 2011: 7–8), note the importance of getting to know the whole child, finding out what each one needs, and then choosing pedagogy that best nurtures the individual learners in a particular class. In the writing class, best practice pedagogies are consequently those that reach out to individual writers to bring out and validate everyone's highest levels of success, that is, those practices that support individual achievement through differentiation, including differentiated assessment measures.

Teachers who go out on a limb by using alternate approaches to discover, validate, and teach to students' individual talents and needs deserve recognition and support. As an aspect of recognizing and supporting teachers who seek to provide differentiated pedagogy, administrators need to keep in mind that no one teacher will necessarily select the same best practice pedagogy for use in the classroom; this may explain why teachers do not always make application of information presented to them in expensive, mandated in-service programs. Teachers will not operate upon what research prescribes unless they have had the opportunity to personally adapt and experience suggested strategies first-hand within their classes. In electing not to apply a particular approach, they may be applying the process of differentiation of the suggested approach to their individual students. Such rational, selective decision-making calls for administrative and public support of teachers, who work to create and select appropriate activities and evaluations before, during, and after and learning occurs.

A pedagogy of differentiation means setting aside scripted, one-size-fits-all methodology while pursuing higher level teaching, placing the focus on students' needs rather than on a generic lesson guide and assessments meant for all.

From time to time, I hear the evaluation of student writing referred to as "nothing personal," but it certainly is personal. Young adolescents in the process of developing writing identities can be daunted by formal, summative marks based on surface elements, or when a score on one exam, often at the end of a marking period or semester, accounts for the majority of the grade. Young adolescents can feel and behave differently based on their changing physical and social-emotional states on any given day. Thus, one exam represents just part of the academic writing picture – a snapshot view that may or may not be representative of a larger portrait of the writer. This is true not only for middle-grades students, but also for students in general. Best practice calls for an acknowledgement of writing as process and product, requiring both formal and informal evaluative measures throughout the writing process.

Reflective Teaching and a Common Paradox

Fortunately, there are as many ways to personalize instruction and its related informal assessment as there are individual students. First and foremost, teachers who wish to go beyond the (traditional) status quo in favor of motivating the best writing from their students may need to step out of their "comfort zones." They must be willing and able to be continual reflective learners, to recognize the differences in students' experience, and to embrace these in order to plant the seeds of authentic, process-driven and integral writing assessment. In addition, teachers benefit from recalling how they were taught in middle school and then decide whether, if they are teaching the same way as they were taught as students, the models of writing used at that time match the circumstances and the students of their present-day classroom. Pedagogical choices by teachers become a part of the rich and fertile soil that makes the student garden grow. Irene Clark and Betty Bamberg, in *Concepts in Composition: Theory and Practice in the Teaching of Writing* (Clark and Bamberg, 2003: xviii), suggest that novice teachers reflect upon how the educational research they have studied influences their own classroom teaching, as each develops his or her own unique writing pedagogy. Teachers' reflective practices about how and why they teach determine, in large part, whether their students will become reflective learners – a learning strategy which is vital for young adolescent motivation and writing growth. For that reason, I suggest that when in doubt about whether students are exhibiting desired qualities such as reflection within their writing, teachers should model those qualities, and then talk to the students about how their use enhances and elevates writing.

Conversations with teachers educated in the theory of process writing and differentiated learning point to their occasional regression back to more traditional approaches paralleling their own elementary and secondary education, at times excluding separate drafting or editing stages of writing and any kind of in-class writing preparation or practice. These teachers, though educated in process writing, thus demonstrate a lack of commitment to the recursive nature of writing and the need for individual writers to follow their own path, or a tendency to cut corners under time pressure. Such a move away from a pedagogically managed writing process negatively affects young adolescent writers, whose writing growth depends upon the unwavering commitment to best practices and ongoing professional growth of those who teach them. In other words, if the teacher regresses, falling back on traditional or short-cut practices, the students also regress. Unfortunately, teachers who revert to outdated or oversimplified methods of writing instruction far from best practice may receive positive feedback from administrators for compliance with the status quo by "teaching to the test." Teachers may thus find themselves reinforced for practices which they themselves recognize as *teaching under pressure*.

Classroom teachers dedicated to test preparation for their students sometimes abandon contemporary process-oriented approaches against their better judgment.

When process writing is abandoned, dusty old workbooks may emerge from closet shelves, along with shiny new, expensive programmed materials, while research journals and stimulation of peer response fall by the wayside. Many teachers cite the reality and pressures of high-stakes tests as rationalization for using writing time to familiarize students with test form and test grammar, such as never starting a sentence with *and*, *but*, or *because* (Buckner, 2002: 213). More often than not, large urban schools whose students have not made adequate yearly progress (AYP) under the No Child Left Behind Act purchase and require teachers to use programmed practice materials with the specific goal of raising test scores on standardized literacy tests. The conflicting values of teaching and testing cultures result in the paradox of contemporary classroom instruction: rewards for mediocre methods aimed at propping up test scores alongside penalties for those willing and able to trust their expertise and their instincts to reach for the sky. Teaching to the test is a problem for writing instruction not only in U. S. schools (Poole, 2011; Roberts, 2009) but also in England and Wales (Sargent, 2011), and other parts of the world where standardized testing drives the curriculum.

Charting Growth

Learning Records

Timothy Shanahan says that assessments used with differentiated learners must reflect the key components of classroom pedagogy, and he calls for frequent observation with an informal measure such as running records and frequent attention to student's learning success (Shanahan, 2008). Although running records were developed and widely written about by Marie M. Clay and the Goodmans in the 1970s as applied to assessment of the reading process (Clay, 1979, 2000; Goodman and Goodman, 1979), I believe that writers' processes may also be observed and noted in a similar way. *Observation records* and *annotated checklists* are two informal assessment methods that chart progress and can provide information about writing to inform future planning. A caution that Mary Shea mentions (Shea, 2006) is the attempt to classify all of students' actions in writing into an inflexible list of skills. In her view (and mine), it is better to keep a more open-ended record of students' progress within general categories and with adequate space in these records for taking note of both strengths as well as concerns. I suggest that teachers create and use an assessment format that matches the range of literacy tasks required on a particular assignment as well as the abilities of the students under consideration. In this way, learners' progress in writing (as well as reading) may be noted and then assessed with what Mary A. Barr and colleagues call a *learning record* (Barr, Craig, Fisette, and Syverson, 1999; Barr and Syverson, 1999). While Barr and colleagues' learning record is based on all of the subjects studied in school, my focus is on the design and use of a record that is beneficial for recording and assessing writing.

The British Primary Language Record (Barrs, Ellis, Hester, and Thomas, 1988) was developed in the late 1980s as an alternative structure for evaluation of learning. Teachers in inner-city London schools participated in its early use, hailing it as a framework for discovering, tracking, and planning for future student progress in writing, oral language, and literacy development. The Primary Language Record drew the attention of teachers in Australia, New Zealand, and the United States who sought ways to make authentic assessment a manageable process (Barr and Syverson, 1999; Barr *et al.*, 1999: vii). Forward-thinking educators revisualized the role of assessment as a usable measure that students and parents alike could interpret in order to gauge students' vital preparation for a more complex future.

Within a few years, The Primary Language Record became known to K–12 teachers in the United States through the work of Mary A. Barr (Barr and Syverson, 1999; Barr *et al.*, 1999), who had been directing the California Literature Project and Center for Language in Learning. The California Learning Record was developed as a result of Barr's partnership with California teachers, extending language learning beyond elementary levels. Presently known as The Learning Record System and described in the handbook, *Assessing Literacy with the Learning Record* (Barr and Syverson, 1999; Barr *et al.*, 1999), the framework includes a year-long process. Part A documents students' prior experience and knowledge early in the school year; Part B documents students' ongoing learning during the second and third quarters of the academic year; and teachers reflect upon students' work over the whole year during the fourth quarter, noting suggestions for future learning in Part C. The Learning Record is multidimensional, encompassing the following collections of evidence of student progress: observation notes; student writing; running records and other informal reading assessments; test scores; information from outside of school; and reading, writing, and math scales. For example, Writing Scale 2, Grades 4–8: Becoming an Experienced Writer, describes several levels of writers from 1-Inexperienced ("…may compose orally with confidence but be reluctant to write or take risks with transcription…"), to 5-Exceptionally Experienced ("…making conscious decisions about appropriate forms and styles of writing…") (Barr and Syverson, 1999: 76).

Mary A. Barr and Margaret A. Syverson have created an assessment guide for teachers of older students, *Assessing Literacy with the Learning Record: A Handbook for Teachers, Grades 6–12* (Barr and Syverson, 1999). The volume contains extended, appropriate collection measures, along with clearly stated scales and student data collection sheets. Barr and Syverson (1999: 2) acknowledge that at each level, teachers need to recognize that evaluation must be suitable to the content area and the individual student, facilitating students' success in meeting standards by means of different paths.

The Writing Record: Authentic, Formative Assessment

What I like most about learning records that have been developed over the past twenty years are their successful collection and presentation of a variety of individual assessment vehicles necessary for a complete, fair, and accurate view of students' progress. Building upon the essential works of Myra Barrs and colleagues (Barrs *et*

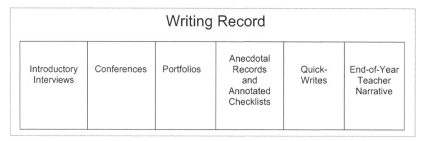

Figure 7.1. Writing Record Components

al., 1988, Barrs, Ellis, Hester, and Thomas, 1993) in the U. K. and Mary Barr and colleagues (Barr and Syverson, 1999; Barr *et al.*, 1999) in the United States, I propose the creation of an assessment framework that specifically applies to young adolescent writing.

The Writing Record components shown in Figure 7.1 include introductory interviews, observation checklists, anecdotal records, portfolios, conferences, quickwrites, and end-of-year teacher narratives. This record represents a collection of information and reporting framework on individual learners and their writing that is geared to young adolescent writers' development and progress. Informal and authentic, many of the Writing Record's components could be planned to take place in everyday classroom lessons within a writing workshop format. Students would assume some of the responsibility and teachers would assume the various facilitative roles required. Created with teacher choice in mind, the Writing Record is easily adapted to mirror the formative assessments selected by the teacher.

__Each situation is different, and teachers should utilize an assessment framework that is both learner-appropriate and manageable.__

Teachers may wish to omit or make substitutions for some of the components of the Writing Record shown in Figure 7.1. Barr's writing scales could be added to the Writing Record and accessed by the teacher when composing the end-of-year narrative with suggestions for continued improvement. Alternative writing scales

FORMATIVE, AUTHENTIC ASSESSMENT

| Introductory Interviews | Conferences Instant and Scheduled | Portfolios | Running Records and Anecdotal Checklists | Quick-Writes | End-of-Year Teacher Narrative |

Introductory Interview for <u>Jonathan G.</u> Date: <u>September 10, 2010</u>

> Jonathan prefers to be called "Jon," is new to the school, and spends a lot of his free time using Play Station 3 and going to Boy Scout meetings – he hopes to be an Eagle Scout when he reaches high school. Jon likes to read graphic novels and draw anime characters for his own future graphic novel.

Anecdotal (Running) Record for <u>Jon G.</u>   Date: <u>October 4, 2010</u>

_____ Scheduled   __X__ Instant / As Needed

> Watching Jon, as he is new to the class. When asked how he was doing on the fable, Jon said he completed his revised draft and did not choose to join peer response group for feedback. I asked if he would read the introduction to me, and he did so willingly and with great voice expression, and I scanned his fable, noting that like many others, this draft is quite polished. Noted he used extra time to draw and doodle. Seems eager to please. Check with parent, guardian, or previous teacher for writing samples.

Writing Workshop Conference Record for <u>Jon G.</u>
  <u>X</u> Scheduled ____ Instant / As Needed

Week of <u>April 5 – 9, 2010</u>

	Writing/Project	Stage?	Notes	Date
LaTia	Dream and How to Get There: Supreme Court Justice	Early draft	Excellent use of book and Web references	04/05
Jon	**Dream: Graphic Novel Writer and Artist**	**Self-revised draft and looks good.**	**Encourage taking part in peer response Confided that he won a writing award**	**04/05**
Miguel	Dream: Pirate	Early draft	Research needed in addition to Johnny Depp films!	04/05
Renee	Valentine Poetry	2 free verse Drafts	Provide varied poetry written by other students as guides	04/06
Vittorio	Dream: Live with Grandpa in Italy	Early draft	Intro needed	04/06
Brandon	Social studies persuasive essay on NAFTA	Drafted and self-read; questions noted	Volunteer worked with him on form only; needs more support for argument	04/07
Jen	Dream: Artist making a living	Floor plan of the shop; early draft	Encourage drafting/getting the thoughts into words	04/07
Emma	Dream: Art Gallery owner	Draft	Add more steps on how to reach this goal/dream	04/09
Lana	Biographical report on Dr. M. L. King	Note-taking and intro	Alternative to Dream writing	04/09

Quick Write Jon G. Date: May 19, 2010
Topic: Response to Colin, a Main Character in The Secret Garden

> No offense, but Colin was a wimp – and worse, all the girls in that story seemed to like to boss and be bossed around. Not appealing! Even though this is a classic novel set in Great Britain in the 19th Century, it's hard to believe boys would act so dumb. (I did like Dickon a lot, though!)
>
> I think I disliked Colin not because of his disability, but because he was weak of spirit. What would happen if Stephen Hawking acted like Colin? I am guessing the story and Colin would interest me more if made into a comedy for the stage.

Figure 7.2. Assessment Samples for Writing Record

could be developed to reflect curricular goals, including state and national standards, written as a descriptive continuum. Figure 7.2 illustrates some of the components of the Writing Record, such as a sample introductory interview, a running record, a writing workshop conference record, and two examples of quickwrites.

Figure 7.3 shows a sample writing scale that I created to reflect the state of Michigan's Grade Level Content Expectations (GLCEs) for sixth grade writers (Michigan Department of Education, 2011b). My Writing Scale for Grade 6 has been inspired by Writing Scale 2, Grades 4–8: Becoming Experienced as a Writer, in *Assessing Literacy with the Learning Record: A Handbook for Teachers, Grades K–6* by Mary A. Barr, Dana A. Craig, and Dolores Fisette, and Margaret A. Syverson (Barr *et al.*,1999: 85). The Michigan Department of Education (2011a, c) has published a complete set of GLCEs for each grade level, representing the areas of reading, writing, speaking, and listening. The Writing Scale in Figure 7.3 reflects the GLCEs for only sixth grade writing (Michigan Department of Education, 2011b), and while the Department noted each of the following skill areas – writing genre, writing process, personal style, grammar and usage, spelling, handwriting, and writing attitude – the Writing Scales include only genre, process, grammar and usage, personal style, and writing attitude.

WRITING SCALE GRADE 6				
1 **Beginning**	**2** **Novice**	**3** **Intermediate**	**4** **Advanced Intermediate**	**5** **Advanced**
Writing shows little confidence or practice: composes mainly in one genre (personal narrative with self as main character); requires much assistance when attempting organization and exploration of problems for expository writing; hesitant to work independently or self-correct; occasionally uses end punctuation; avoids writing and prefers not to share work with peers.	Writing shows some confidence and practice: composes two or more types of narratives, such as folk tale and personal story; begins work independently but requires assistance with vocabulary and spelling; uses humor to develop voice; uses language structures which resemble speech; significant use of end punctuation, commas, and correct use of capital letters; contributes to class discussion.	Writing shows significant confidence and practice: composes in familiar genres modeled on class study; is aware of audience and purpose and makes some selection of language for personal style; spells words with regular patterns well; uses punctuation correctly; easily takes part in small group and partner work.	Writing shows high confidence and some versatility in writing genres and process: exhibits self-motivation and self-corrects; is developing own style but requires help with creating complex narrative and expository work; reflects on writing and chooses clarifying language; spells and punctuates consistently well, and willingly adds detail and length to writing pieces; approaches work with knowledge.	Writing shows high confidence and high versatility in writing genres and process: composes with voice; reflects critically upon drafts and chooses appropriate forms and styles of writing; draws from multiple experiences and readings; correctly uses conventions and a wide variety of grammatical structures; is enthusiastic about writing and learning to write.

Figure 7.3. Writing Scale for Grade 6

The scales are meant to reflect a student's starting point as well as the place on the progressive learning continuum at which a student is working at given times in the school year, such as a specific marking period. These scales can be used to convey the student's progress over the year and can, with the other informal assessment components, inform the teacher's year-end narrative, which in turn transitions the student writer into the next academic year. Imagine the benefit to teachers of young adolescent writers and students alike of documenting and collecting assessment measures that are ongoing and multifaceted, take place year-to-year, and may be shared with writers and their teachers each successive year.

Teachers have much to gain in terms of their own teaching while conducting in-class, authentic assessments. Ginette Delandshere and Anthony Petrosky suggest that teaching must be viewed as a continuous process of inquiry about learners and learning (Delandshere and Petrosky, 1998: 164) in which classroom experiences and interactions alter a teacher's insights and actions by shedding further light on all individuals in the classroom community. As part of routine classroom activities, teachers may select and utilize multiple, varied informal assessment tools which are appropriate to their settings and which involve students in active learning throughout the year. Richard J. Stiggins reminds us that many adults carry negative emotional associations from childhood about testing; it was in fact once widely believed that the road to maximum success on a test was to create maximum anxiety (Stiggins, 2005). Nowadays, the educational establishment and parents realize the many kinds of detrimental effects on students of high levels of anxiety and the need to build their confidence and sense of self-efficacy. One way for teachers to help build students' confidence and sense of self-efficacy is to help them become sure of and comfortable with the assessment measures chosen (Stiggins, 2005: 2). In what follows, I explore the purposes and uses of each informal assessment component within the Writing Record.

Introductory Interviews

Students deserve not only a fresh start each school year, but also recognition for their prior knowledge. Writing texts often include excellent models for students to conduct interviews but rarely note the importance of introductory interviews by teachers with students as a way to establish rapport, give personal, one-on-one attention, and discover what writers feel they already know, as well as areas upon which to focus learning in the coming year. The benefits for teachers as well as students are well worth the initial investment of time. One way to conduct interviews early in the school year is to schedule two or three per day in the early weeks of class during daily silent reading periods of fifteen to twenty minutes, or during another routine activity in which the class is independently engaged. William Zinsser, in *On Writing Well* (Zinsser, 1990), suggests ways teachers may carry out successful interviews with students. I have selected the qualities teachers might include in their introductory interviews of students:

- Take some time to chat and to get to know one another to establish trust;
- Find out some pertinent information before starting;
- Make a list of possible questions to use as a guide;
- Ask questions about items of interest and importance;
- Remember that the student's words and thoughts are more important that those of the teacher;
- Refrain from using a tape recorder; and
- Ask if there is anything the student wishes the teacher had asked, ask it, and then conclude.

If learning records or writing records were created the year before for students, particularly if they contained portfolios and teachers' end-of-year narratives, these informal assessments can provide additional information about writers' strengths, progress, and areas of potential development.

Conferences

Ordinarily, like a call home from the teacher, a conference can send a negative message to a student that something is wrong. However, when using the writing conference as one of several informal assessment measures, frequent, one-on-one conferences are of great benefit to students. For practicality, these one-on-one conferences can be of two types: a short, instant conference or a more scheduled, routine conference.

The *instant conference* can be employed to answer questions, to briefly check in with students on how they are doing, or to suggest supplemental resources. Teachers are not able to meet with students as often and as regularly as they would like, so this type of short meeting may be the norm in many classes. The difference between the instant conference and dashing around the room attempting to solve all students' writing problems on cue is the addition of short notes taken by the teacher. I suggest keeping a clipboard handy, stocked with multiple copies of class lists and space after each student's name to take notes. These notes may later become part of an observation checklist report and end-of-year narrative (explained below), in which teachers can then look back at notes taken during the short conferences; these may over time fall into a recognizable pattern, providing information about students' progress.

During the *scheduled conference*, which may take place while the class is involved in an independent assignment, the student writer's requests for assistance can be met and ideas can be shared, as teachers take a close look at a student's writing process and progress while assessing how well the student is learning. Information can flow both ways, from teacher to student and from student to teacher, for a variety of purposes. The more often a teacher and a student communicate, the more knowledge and insight can be gained by both parties. Notes can be taken on topics discussed or progress being made on a particular piece of writing, and questions asked and answered. While teachers may not always be available to answer all questions as they arise, students can write down their questions and wait for their turn for an individual conference, either as part of a posted list or as part of a routine, expected rotation. One-on-one conferences work best when the routine is established, followed by the teacher, and made known early in the academic year. Students' active participation and proactive measures to continue writing through to the end of a draft are major benchmarks of independent writing. To confer with a teacher is not to become dependent; instead, it can be seen as an opportunity to share information, talk through some ideas, get some feedback, note students' progress, and support students' writing through to completion.

The most difficult parts of the conference are managing class time and then keeping calm when the schedule does not go as planned, such as when time runs out before meeting with writers as intended. One way to resolve the situation is to empower students with the facilitative power to teach their classmates a mastered craft or skill. For example, when an assignment has been made with the expectation of correct punctuation of dialog as previously practiced, many of student writers' questions will concern the new learning; a teacher may ask the student with whom he or she has just conferred to then teach the skill to a small group of peers in need of the information. When students teach others, they learn most deeply. In addition, students may begin to use many of the same strategies with their classmates that the teacher has modeled for them day after day in conferences. Writers see how the conferencing process works and then make applications to other contexts, also a sign of powerful learning.

Aside from those described above, the most common type of conference, the traditional parent-teacher conference, is not a component of the Writing Record in that it is not considered an informal assessment. Often scheduled twice a year and used principally as a vehicle to convey summative information, these meetings could instead become a teacher-parent-student conference. When used in conjunction with a leaner-centered classroom, these conferences can involve the information and insight gleaned from the previously administered informal assessments as well as summative measures, and they should focus on the student's progress.

Annotated Observation Checklists and Anecdotal Records

Students reason abstractly much of the time, but their thoughts are not always aligned with the content of their classes, and their reasoning processes are rarely documented. Since writing improvement is a process which takes place over time, the use of an annotated checklist is one way to document writing behaviors. During preparation of a persuasive essay, students access prior knowledge to choose a side of an issue, state a thesis, outline a plan for supportive information, and search for data from multiple sources to support the thesis, in addition to other kinds of writing-related activities. The many steps prior to the actual essay draft

FORMATIVE, AUTHENTIC ASSESSMENT 301

reveal important information to the teacher, and the annotated observation checklist and anecdotal record enable teachers to note this information about writers' observable behaviors, such as students' participation in class discussion prior to writing, note-taking during discussions, incorporation of prior knowledge, and exploration of resources that yield more global or broader applications. The annotated observation checklist also alerts the teacher to individuals who may need more one-on-one support, such as talking through steps and the information needed to write the essay. Knowing writers' capabilities enhances the possibility that they will succeed at producing a good composition. A sample annotated observation checklist for a paper requiring students to take a side following a class debate is presented in Figure 7.4. Annotated Observation Checklist for Debate Paper. Besides the checklist for observable behaviors, a section is provided on the

Name: _____ Date: _____

Observable Behaviors	O	NO	NA
Takes notes during the debate.			
Participates in class discussions following the debate.			
Summarizes major concepts and interprets them.			
Incorporates prior knowledge of topic with new information.			
Clearly chooses a viewpoint or side.			
Substantiates viewpoint with supportive data.			
Explores additional resources for broader application.			
Questions opposing viewpoint when discrepancies are found.			
Persuades those undecided to consider writer's viewpoint.			
(Add a behavior)			

Anecdotal Record and Additional Notes:

Legend: *O* = Observed; *NO* = Not Observed; *NA* = Not Applicable

Figure 7.4. Annotated Observation Checklist for Debate Paper

Week of 04/02/10 - 04/08/10				
	Writing/Project	*Stage?*	*Notes*	*Date*
LaTia	Dream and How to Get There: Supreme Court Justice	Early draft	Excellent use of book and Web references	04/02
Maggie	Dream: Singer on Broadway	Map of details to include	Very specific; stuck on prewriting stage	04/02
Miguel	Dream: Pirate	Early draft	Research needed in addition to Johnny Depp films	04/02
Renee	Valentine Poetry	2 free verse drafts	Provide varied poetry written by other students as guides	04/02
Vittorio	Dream: Live with Grandpa in Italy	Early draft	Intro needed	04/03
Brandon	Social studies persuasive essay on NAFTA	Drafted and self-read; questions noted	Volunteer worked with him on form only; needs more support for argument	04/03
Jen	Dream: Artist making a living	Floor plan of the shop; early draft	Encourage drafting/getting the thoughts into words	04/04
Emma	Dream: Art Gallery owner	Draft	Add more steps on how to reach this goal/dream	04/04
Lana	Biographical report on Dr. M. L. King	Note-taking and intro	Alternative to Dream writing	04/08

Figure 7.5. Writing Workshop Conference Record

document for additional notes. Descriptions of unique observations become potentially useful anecdotes that provide the teacher with additional insights about writers' processes.

Figure 7.5 illustrates a record-keeping template that may be used to document routine checks on individual writers working on various pieces of writing during the writing workshop.

Portfolios

One of the most efficient, ongoing displays of young adolescent writers' progress is the writing portfolio, the central component of the Writing Record. The writing portfolio contains not only drafts of multiple varieties and pieces of students' work, but also their reflections about their writing. The quality of the writing and the writer's insights convey the steady progress made as well as the limitations for which future lessons must be planned. The portfolio therefore assists teachers in taking stock of students' improvement over time. In order to establish a clear sense of what writers know, I suggest that portfolios be kept all year and that they contain many required writing assignments over multiple content areas or topics for various purposes, as well as some pieces of writing selected by students. Students should include all drafts of their writing, with peer respondents' and their own comments and reflections attached. Teachers and students should take part in a one-on-one conference at least once per marking period, focusing upon strengths and continuing progress, and ending with general goal-setting by teacher and student. Teachers may want writers to include an end-of-unit, end-of-semester, or whole-year self-assessment in the portfolios, highlighting skills and concepts mastered as well as information about their own writing processes and areas that might be improved.

Quickwrites

The quickwrite, a strategy that is designed to give students the opportunity to reflect upon their learning by means of a short, often just 5-minute writing task, can be used at the beginning, middle, or end of a lesson. Quickwrites provide students with an opportunity to preview or to pause momentarily during research, study, or discussion to record their thoughts and feelings in written form. While there are many ways to make use of quickwrites, I prefer to ask students to write at the beginning of class about a skill or craft they recently learned that "works" for their writing, problems they encountered in their writing, or what they liked or didn't like about a class. Donald Graves' and Penny Kittle's book, *My Quick Writes* (Graves and Kittle, 2005), offers about fifty of the authors' favorite quickwrite invitations. These run the gamut from modifying a short story into a poem to retelling a personal narrative. Young adolescent writers don't like to do busy work; if there is room for choice and self-expression and an audience available, writers will gladly and openly share their thoughts. Quickwrites are an excellent way to begin a class, too, because they serve as a warm-up activity for fingers and minds that long to *move*, having spent much of their class day inactive, listening (or not) to one voice doing much of the talking – and it is not *theirs*! As an evaluative device, these short writings can tell the teacher quite a bit about individual students' writing fluency as well as impart critical information about writers' impressions of their own writing and about class concepts that may need more clarification.

A sample quickwrite can be seen above in Figure 7.2 and another in Figure 7.6, illustrating two different purposes. The first quickwrite is written in response to the main character of *The Secret Garden* (Burnett, 1911), and the second is a response to the question, "What kinds of writing do you consider to be your best?" Notice that the purposes of these writings differ. The first purpose is to give young adolescents a chance to honestly say what they felt about one of the main characters in a book that many boys this age are not fond of but many girls like. The purpose of the second quickwrite is for the teacher to discover what the writer thinks about his or her own work. Since these quickwrites are informal and will not be given a letter grade, there is no need for revision.

Topic: **"What kinds of writing do you consider to be your best?"**

Lana D.   Best Writing

Not sure what you mean. I like to write pet stories and fables and on my blog don't like to write essys about stuff I hate to think about like wars and the earth getting hotter every year and how much junk my uncle and aunt don't even think about recyling. I guess my best writing is when I have **time** to think and you let us use computers. Is this what you mean? Or if it's not what you mean then maybe you mean which exact story or poem I think is best hands down that's my whatif poem. By the way thanks for letting me use my laptop for this.

Your fave student. Lana D. ☺

Figure 7.6. Sample Quickwrite

End-of-Year Teacher Narrative

The purposes of the end-of-year narrative, which may be any length, are: to document and share each student's writing process and progress during the year towards accomplishing specific goals or standards; to convey insights gained about the writer's use of strategic actions, such as self-regulation and independent use of resources; to give a summary of each component of the Writing Record; and to plan for future instruction. Narratives can be shared with students, their parents, and school faculty, and comments should be written in clear language that can be understood by all. A short glossary may be included to explain some specific educational terms, if these must be used. Unlike a progress report or report of grades, this narrative may be shared in conferences with parents and students, making room for celebration of progress as well as sharing some ways that students and parents can support writing growth over the summer holidays.

Sharing both information and power requires facilitative roles for the teacher, parent, and student, resulting in young adolescents taking over more responsibility for their own continued growth.

Sharing the power, celebrating the progress, and treating the reporting process with respect for all elevates the incentive to write well. In this way, the end-of-year narrative plays a part in nurturing motivation for young adolescent writers. Figure 7.7 shows a sample end-of-year teacher narrative.

The narrative is a place to overview major areas of writing growth, documented by examples of specific skills mastered, goals set and accomplished, and suggestions for areas of focus for ongoing writing improvement in the following academic year. It is also a place to thank students for their voluminous efforts, to say goodbye, and to wish them the best in their future progress and enjoyment of writing.

> End-of-Year Teacher Narrative for: <u>Melissa R.</u> Date: <u>June 15, 2010</u>
>
> Melissa has shown tremendous growth in writing this year, entering grade 6 with the ability to compose mainly personal narratives, and finishing the year with success in composing essays, reports, blog posts, friendly and business letters, reviews, and letters to the editor. Writing craft has developed substantially, as Melissa has attentively developed style and voice in her writing, feeling more comfortable using dialog, metaphor, and hyperbole (exaggeration). In addition, Melissa's use of conventions has improved in that she has shown success in using correct punctuation, spelling, and usage on a regular basis. One of the strategies Melissa uses is to circle words, phrases, or punctuation that she suspects may be incorrect or more clearly written, followed by her independent use of resources such as spell-check, a dictionary, thesaurus, or her writing notebook with notes and examples from grammar and other lessons. She then makes needed changes.
>
> One of Melissa's greatest accomplishments this year has been her ability to work constructively with her peers, particularly in whole group situations. Melissa needs quiet and structure while composing and revising drafts during the writing workshop, and she has successfully developed a cueing system with peers (finger to lips and eyebrows raised) to indicate that she must not be interrupted. As a peer respondent to classmates' work, Melissa has developed a level of comfort in offering three comments of feedback that we call "P.Q.S," which is praise, question, and a suggestion. As a student who often resisted sharing her work with others and was not open at first to peer response, Melissa now is able to both accept and give such response. This took a lot of effort on Melissa's part, and we should all be very proud of her.
>
> Melissa chose three pieces of writing for her portfolio, and one of these is entitled, "Mom is My Role Model." If you have not read this wonderful tribute, I hope you do. She was going to give it to her mom for Mother's Day, but then was not happy with all parts of it, so she elected to give it to her on her birthday in early June. The writing shows maturity in her conveyance of thoughts, use of examples, and her choice of words. Melissa, our perfectionist, is learning to see the positives in her own work, as can be seen in a sentence from her reflection of the writing: "I tried to show the grace and patience of my mother without actually saying it literally, and I think I may have accomplished this with the examples I used." Melissa has become quite proficient in creating anecdotes from real life, and this tribute shows it.
>
> This has been a year in which Melissa has grown by leaps and bounds as a writer and member of our classroom community, and Melissa and I both feel that she is more than ready for the challenges of seventh grade. She has decided to continue to blog over the summer, attempting more poetry and anecdotal writing and adding possible journal entries. She has also decided to share some of her work with her new teacher next year. I have truly enjoyed watching Melissa grow!

Figure 7.7. Sample End-of-Year Teacher Narrative

The Power of Insight and Daily Writing Time

The Writing Record and its individual components facilitate conditions for teachers to develop insights about individual students through their reflective understanding of how each writer applies various strategies, from keeping on topic to revision. Such insights demonstrate the value of teachers' focused inquiry, which will result in sensitivity about how young adolescents see the world while providing clarity for the teacher as to how individual student writers develop both concrete and abstract skills in their work.

When teachers observe, take note of, and think about how new knowledge is reflected in students' writing, deep wisdom can be gained. Teachers can become further enlightened about critical writing skills, such as what literary devices have been mastered and how to best plan future lessons, by holding two-way conversations with young adolescent writers. An extra benefit is the growing rapport and trust that develops between teacher and student. Pedagogy that nurtures students' critical thinking during the writing process, thoroughly reviewed in Chapter 5, is also relevant to our discussion of formative assessment of young adolescent writers. This is because teachers' understanding of their students' progress in writing is dependent upon students' maturation in the process of close reading as well as their ability to recognize the elements of good writing. The Young Adolescent Motivation Model has the highest chance for success when writers may grow and thrive in a classroom community far removed from the usual, garden-variety educational experience – a classroom where the young adolescent writer is placed at the core of lesson planning and where, through various types of formative assessment, the strong roots of perennial progress are cultivated. Perhaps one of the most positive benefits of teachers' concerted efforts is the ongoing validation of students' growth as writers, resulting in a personal nurturance of spirit for both teacher and students. This is also the heart and soul of formative assessment – a gathering of information and insight about students as they learn, day by day.

The education community has known for years that students learn to write by writing. None of the many valuable types of information that can be collected on student writers' progress in writing and knowledge can be determined unless students are given the *time* necessary to make authentic, contextual application of newly learned or recently reviewed content or skills. Application of the student writer's developing knowledge may materialize in many ways, in an evolving personal voice or style as well as in the ability to make lexical and grammatical decisions. An example of evolving writing ability would include the decision to create a compound sentence versus using a semicolon to set off independent thoughts. The essential ingredient for improvement is to give writers the space to grow by writing every day, which takes both planning and time. Theodore R. Smith, who conducted educational research projects for the California Department of Education, related some time ago that, although much research has been conducted which points to the necessity of students spending time writing each day in order to become better writers, "findings are in conflict with widespread practice in schools" (Smith, 1982: 3). Smith's findings in the 1980s would no doubt apply in today's schools as well. Yet teachers who schedule adequate writing time into their daily plans are likely to profit from the practice along with their students, as they become adept at "reading" the individuals in class by getting to know them personally. In this way, teachers more easily recognize whether or not students are truly learning writing craft and skills by becoming familiar with individual writers' developing work, taking part in informal oral and written response, listening to peer respondents, and taking an active part in writing circles. This information, which results from the "close reading," or assessment, of students' knowledge base about writing, helps to motivate and frame future lessons and one-on-one conferences, while at the same time nurturing young adolescents as developing writers.

Writing Development through Revision

Focusing Revision

In Chapter 7, "Using Assessment to Drive Better Student Writing," of Kelly Gallagher's book, *Teaching Adolescent Writers* (Gallagher, 2006), classroom teachers can find specific strategies addressing both writing craft and editing. In Gallagher's secondary classroom, clear routines are established with respect to students' active roles in the revision process, beginning with first drafts. He, like most teachers, understands that there is a wide range of student abilities, yet each can advance; the goal for the class is that everyone improves (Gallagher, 2006: 142). Students can, and do, make forward progress, as weak writers transition into average writers, average writers grow into strong ones, and strong writers become excellent ones. Gallagher (2006) has the correct take on what actually helps students write: rather than focus on what students cannot do, he provides helpful response by pointing out an area of concern about each of two areas, content and editing. A piece of writing may contain twenty surface errors, but students who receive papers with all of these pointed out will, by and large, ignore them, looking instead at the final grade. However, when just a couple of areas of concern are pointed out in a first draft, especially when the onus is on students to find out how to correct them, the focus becomes improvement.

Young adolescent learners are most motivated to improve their writing when they are obliged to reflect upon and apply alternative routes to solving their problems in a piece of writing.

In Gallagher's classes, students are directed to elicit help from a peer when they find they are stumped, or failing that, from the members of a small group; when a small group cannot find out how to make a correction, the group asks for a conference with the teacher. Students in the above vignette who need the teacher place their names on the board and continue with other work on their writing, meeting with the teacher as their turn comes up. I find Gallagher's approach to teaching writing refreshing; there is no rush to complete workbook pages, no papers covered in corrective red pen, no wasted time. Gallagher (2006: 148) notes that writing will improve when teachers "provide the student with meaningful feedback *before* a paper is finished." This approach works in part because it is an appropriate routine; I believe whatever practices the teacher develops that result in students' improvement, engagement, and growing motivation to write are valuable. Teachers can find delight and even satisfaction in a working system they have developed after much trial and error and some risk-taking. Continuing the garden metaphors running through this book, finding an approach that really works is like turning over a new leaf!

Engaging Peer Response

In the spirit of starting small and thinking big, students can be taught how to conduct efficient and appropriate peer response on early drafts by means of a simple method, such as PQS (Praise – Question – Suggestion). Like Gallagher's method above, this one resists correcting each error and instead focuses upon specific comments of praise, clarifying questions, and meaningful suggestions. The feedback is specific yet sparse in the beginning of the writing process; as the composition develops, more attention can be given to close correction of conventions and grammar usage. For many writers, when the latter becomes a focus too early in the writing process, the meaning to be conveyed may get lost, and the writer may become sidetracked, attempting to regain the thought process.

Peer response works best with preselected partners and when modeled very clearly prior to meeting with peer respondents. This can be accomplished with two volunteer students and a short script (supplied by the teacher) illustrating appropriate conversation. Below is a sample of what PQS peer response may look like, following the writing of a first draft of a persuasive essay about adults' versus children's use or misuse of the Internet.

> *Praise*: The reader got right into the essay with your use of a question as an opening sentence: "Why is it always the kids who are accused of misusing the Internet?"
> *Question*: Where is your conclusion? I feel like the essay just stopped without wrapping things up. Here is an example of what I mean: "That adult spent six hours playing online poker."

Suggestion: Instead of bringing in so many examples to support your thesis statement, perhaps focus on two or three, as this may make the argument stronger: For example, instead of bringing in a lot of unproductive adult habits, you could focus on one of those and then bring to light a positive use of time and effort by a teen.

An important step following peer response partners with a process like PQS is to ask students what worked and what didn't, as far as being able to respond to a peer and also being able to take some peer suggestions for improvement. It is important to reinforce the notion that the writer makes the final decisions as to which suggestions he or she takes into the revision process for the next draft. Once students understand and can demonstrate the process, teachers may want to move on to the use of *writing circles,* peer response groups of three to four writers.

Creating Student Involvement and Knowledge of Writing Process and Progress

Students' involvement in the revision process is critical. Jane Hansen's book, *When Learners Evaluate* (Hansen, 1998)*,* offers many vignettes for teachers' consideration, when the goal is for students to be more reflectively responsible for their own work. Along with setting goals for themselves, students must be able to look back at their writing and value the progress they have made in their work. The more students are aware of their abilities and what they are trying to accomplish, the more direction they will be able to take for themselves. For example, when writers reflect upon and discuss what they did when they wrote a paper, they become more articulate about their efforts, while enabling teachers to learn more about them (Hansen, 1998: 27). Students can look at their writing and that of their peers and then recognize clarity and organization of thought, correctness of form, unique style and voice – and on that basis, select models of good writing for themselves. Young adolescent writers can also look closely at what their favorite authors do as writers to draw their readers in and then reflect upon ways the writing craft those authors use can be effectively replicated by them.

Another way for students to become more fully aware of the progress in their work is for teachers to share information and insights collected from observations, annotated checklists, quickwrites, and other informal measures, highlighting the efforts ventured in the creation of writing. The idea of process writing is concentrating on just that: taking risks while in the process of development – with description and dialog, hyperbole or alliteration, or perhaps beginning with a question rather than a statement. Young adolescent writers are often additionally motivated by the knowledge of exactly what they are doing well.

Considering the Purposes and Approaches of Assessment

Assessment Must Not Contradict Best Practice

The main purpose of assessment is to improve teaching and learning, and to note students' forward progress in writing. Regardless of what tests are called, they must validly measure what they claim to measure; for example, a writing assessment requires an expression of ideas through the production of written text (International Reading Association / National Council of Teachers of English, Joint Task Force on Assessment, 1994: 40). However, many summative, standardized tests do not measure expression of ideas, a subjective ability, because the scorers (often machines) search for a finite set of "correct" or accepted responses. The discussion about assessment thus far has focused generally upon continuous, or *formative*, determinations of progress in writing, as distinguished from more formal, *summative* assessments, generally viewed as end-point indicators of achievement.

> *If a score becomes the sole indicator of the quality of written text, and if it is dispensed with no follow-up reflection and necessary adjustments to teaching and learning on the part*

of both teachers and students, the measure is irrelevant or inappropriate and should therefore not be utilized.

If a number or a grade is the most frequent feedback that a student receives, there is no opportunity for learning, especially if the grade or number lacks written narrative response and the writer is not allowed to take the piece of writing to another, revised draft. If this is the case, what is the purpose of assigning a number or a letter grade? And why does this practice continue? Letter grades alone, without extended feedback regarding the positive and negative features of a composition, fail to consider the expertise and mastery of teachers while reducing writers to a numeric or letter grade. It is a sad state of affairs when educators are judged in terms of their grading practices, rather than, or more than, their complete store of successful instructional practices. Thus, the brilliant practitioners who view writing as a lifelong endeavor and who do not direct their lessons solely to the goal of their students making high scores on standardized tests may be judged harshly by school administrators and those outside the field of education, such as politicians and the general public, who read negative headlines and blindly accept that teachers are to blame for students' poor performance on standardized tests. Surely, teachers want and need more than a sorting device in the assessments they use. Most choose the teaching vocation because they are passionate about learning, enjoy the satisfaction of nurturing students, and are dedicated to their fields of expertise. This being the case, clearly the heavy emphasis on testing does not sit well with many teachers.

The National Council of Teachers of English voted upon and approved a resolution at the annual business meeting in San Antonio, Texas, in November of 2008 (National Council of Teachers of English, 2008a), which can be viewed in its complete form at http://www.ncte.org/positions/statements/scriptedcurricula. The action of the resolution strongly opposes the use or adoption of scripted or programmed materials and considers the mandate to use such materials as censorship of teachers and students. This resolution was prompted by many factors, one of which is the growing pressure on classroom teachers to replace the study of authentic literature and writing experiences with test-preparation programs. The resolution states:

RESOLVED, that the National Council of Teachers of English

- Continue to conduct research that documents the effects of scripted programs and high-stakes testing on teacher retention and job performance;
- Oppose policies that require educators to utilize scripted programs and materials;
- Oppose attempts by state legislatures, other elected or appointed officials, or school administrators to dictate scripted programs, materials, and methods; and
- Label such mandates as censorship.

Resolution on Scripted Curricula from The NCTE Position Statement of the NCTE Executive Committee (NCTE, 2008a)

Traditional Assessments Are a Limiting Yardstick

A traditional pedagogy of writing will not necessarily encourage writers' growth or best learning behaviors, even when students make commendable scores on standardized examinations reflecting prestructured, predetermined topics for compositions. This is because the outcomes fail to communicate students' progress or achievement in higher level areas of writing craft, style, and voice. These higher level, qualitative and subjective skills take time to observe and are not so easily measured, particularly by standardized tests. The traditional process of teaching and assessing writing tends to produce more literal and artificial work, such as the structured, 5-paragraph essay for an audience of one (the teacher), with drafting and revision completed mainly at home. Perhaps some new and veteran teachers approach the teaching of writing this way by justifying it as future test preparation: students must be set on the narrow track of writing on demand in order to "make the grade" on standardized tests. When writing occurs in the classroom with this orientation, generally the teaching focus is, first, on efficiency under time pressure and, second, on the correctness of the language, the length and formality of the words, and the complexity of the sentence structures. This type of teaching sets unnatural constraints on the writing process and is actually a form of censorship – of ideas, intellectual growth, and individuality – as noted in the NCTE resolution above.

Like plants tied to and growing up a yardstick, writers who replicate the content and form fed to them in traditional classes will only be able to grow in one set direction. Their writing may be correct, though still constrained, as healthy branches of creativity and individuality that go in their own direction are cut off to make a straight branch. This strong support and direction may work for some student writers, but for many, it will not. Like plants in our classroom gardens, young adolescent writers thrive when they are allowed the freedom to twist, to spread out, and to reach in whatever directions they naturally grow, with their ever-strengthening branches being nourished by encouragement towards creating a rich canopy of knowledge and skills. This is the way young adolescent writers grow and flourish. Educators can nurture the process by allowing the unique development and maturation of beautiful, living specimens within writers and throughout their writing life.

The following variables affect all assessment measures, and in particular, standardized tests:

- The learner's health and level of alertness;
- Whether the learner ate a balanced meal and had a healthy night's sleep prior to testing;
- The learner's level of fear with regard to testing;
- The self-concept of the learner;
- Noise and room distractions;
- The learner's level of comfort with regard to room temperature;

- ➢ The learner's recognition of the form in which the questions or tasks appear;
- ➢ The organizational ability of the learner;
- ➢ The learner's understanding of what he or she is being asked to do; and
- ➢ The learner's long-term and short-term memory.

A student who correctly identifies a grammatical structure, for example, as a dependent or independent clause may or may not know when to use a dependent or independent clause while in the process of writing. Application of knowledge, such as identifying a type of clause, can be transferred to new contexts when teachers weave those skills into mini-lessons prior to a writing assignment. Students who respond to a standardized essay prompt when writing on demand may fulfill rubric requirements but are also reinforced to respond in passive, traditional ways. This practice, coupled with a student's disinterest in or ignorance of an assigned topic for writing-on-demand tests, precludes knowledge-based, passionate, high-level writing. Similarly, when required to respond by a short answer or an essay to a text following its reading in a standardized test, young adolescent writers must make a connection from the text to their lives in order to earn a high score on a standard rubric. Yet, a good many writers may not connect to the text, which may or may not be part of their experience, culture, background, or interest.

Machine-Scoring Cannot Capture Complex, Intellectual Thinking

Assessments administered within a traditional approach such as the one described above do not reflect the intricate intellectual and social nature of language and written expression. Unfortunately, the growing trend is for states to develop and implement end-of-semester assessments whose content coincides with standardized end-of-year tests. Year-end tests in large school districts are often scored by machine, preset to point out spelling and grammatical errors and to recognize multisyllabic words but reflecting none of the abstract thinking that accompanies a writer's style, voice, passion, and knowledge of topic. When young adolescent writers are caught up in the whirlwind of preparation for this type of test, a strong message is sent: the educational establishment values a standard performance, and the numbers game is more important than the development of students as writers over time – a period of many semesters or years. Yet actual writing has higher, non-standard goals, as set by the students' own interest and desire to communicate, than any writing test. On the other hand, students who are expected to reason at an abstract level before, during, or after writing are apt to draw on long-term memory to pull up and reconfigure critical, deep knowledge for unique, exceptional essay responses.

Unfortunately, since traditional scoring methods cannot detect the more abstract, complex, and subjective components of exceptional responses such as writer's style, voice, passion, unique interpretation of symbolism and theme, and deep knowledge of topic, the growing use of machines rather than people to score writing exacerbates the problem of determining writing quality (Bennett, 2006; National Council of Teachers of English, 2006). Neither computers nor machines can comprehend student writing in the meaningful ways living beings can. As stated by the National Council of Teachers of English (2006): "Best assessment practice is direct assessment by human readers." Moreover, writing competencies must be measured by scoring more than one piece of writing; assessment must respect diversity of language, assessing "writing on the basis of effectiveness for readers, acknowledging that as purposes vary, criteria will as well" (National Council of Teachers of English, 2006). Finally, assessment must allow young adolescent writers to demonstrate their knowledge and craft of writing rather than highlight the deficits, as standardized assessments do.

Is Error-Free, Objective Accountability a Realistic Goal?

The public demands for high-stakes, standardized testing stem, in great measure, from a fear that children in their country may fall behind other nations' mathematics, science, and literacy achievements, resulting in a citizenry that lacks future preparedness. The growing literature and calls for teacher accountability and student success transmit a strong call to action. However, obtaining error-free, objective accountability for a great variety of subjective, constantly changing learners is unrealistic as well as counterproductive if the goal is to develop every individual to his or her fullest potential. In addition to the aforementioned variables that come into play for students during testing, it is well to remember that as for most complex skills, for writing, there is no discrete set of knowledge and behaviors which can be memorized and applied to all writing tasks. That is, students' proficiency in writing cannot be memorized and then word for word, rule by rule, applied in a given set of circumstances. Rather, writing proficiency hinges on the forward movement of the writers' ability to build upon developing writing knowledge and skill by choice in order to apply appropriate aspects of craft and form in each context. The teachers who are most familiar with their students' capabilities and areas of concern best measure writing proficiency on a regular basis as integral to instruction – and are thus the most qualified to do so.

One Writing Test or Many?

The National Council of Teachers of English opposes the sole reliance on standardized tests as a means of determining student learning. They support using a variety of informal assessment measures so as to ensure an authentic, accurate, and full picture of students' learning (National Council of Teachers of English, 2008b). In addition, NCTE's (2004) *Framing Statement on Assessment* notes that those who use the information gathered during assessment should understand what the data says about learning, with teachers and schools having the right to choose site-specific assessment tools from a set of alternatives and/or to create their own.

One of the first steps in providing authentic assessments for young adolescent writers, along with having an appropriate assessment framework (such as the Writing Record provided in this chapter), is to be aware of the negative consequences of external, programmed evaluation measures. In addition to providing little, if any, usable data, standard measures equate learning with a finite set of step-by-step lessons based on associative, ordered skills – which, of course, it is not. While some writing program packages advertise themselves as essential for mastering skills, teachers might better use their time and energy to themselves read about and study successful approaches to teaching and assessing writing, and then adapt or create lessons and evaluative measures that are appropriate to their specific student population and needs.

Authentic Assessments Help Make the Garden Grow

Jean Piaget and Barbel Inhelder referred to the process of filtering, modifying, and then fusing new knowledge into what is already known as assimilation (Piaget and Inhelder, 1969/2000: 6). Assimilation is necessarily related to accommodation (the alteration made to concepts in one's mind by the process of assimilation): you can't have one without the other. In order for accommodation to take place, writers must reflect upon what they have learned. Thus, these two cognitive processes, integral to young adolescents' internal stimuli to write, must be taken into account if teachers are to nurture students' motivation to write. As teachers work with and observe their students assimilating and then accommodating new information into their own organization of ideas, they are able to gain significant insight into how students make connections and solve problems – while at the same time conducting informal, authentic assessment of student learning.

Consider a young adolescent writer who has been working on a descriptive, historical narrative, attempting to add more detail and substance to both the setting and the characters that are being portrayed in the narrative. The writer recalls a list of 40 common prepositions from an earlier lesson, along with some ways these might be used alone and in phrases to enhance and clarify details; she checks her notebook, where she has written some ideas about how prepositions may be utilized to define characters and settings. The writer then makes a transfer of this previous knowledge to current writing, creating appropriate phrases in order to enhance the narrative flow, showcasing specifically *how* a character walks into the stillness of a room, *when* lamps are lit to greet visitors, *where* the character has journeyed, and *to what extent* the character feels comfort and acceptance in a room full of strangers. In other words, the writer has successfully assimilated prior knowledge into a new context.

Teachers and other significant adults can assist young adolescent writers with the assimilation process by asking them about their choice of a phrase or whether a text they are writing seems to be working so far and why, noting circumstances where learning has taken place. Teachers may suggest that a student writer read a portion of the developing a piece of writing to a peer for quick feedback, taking some time to discuss whether the choice of language or literary device such as the use of dialog appears to be effective. These interactions with adults and peers mark students' forward progress in applying literary craft to writing while offering fertile fields for documentation of assimilated learning.

In elementary and middle-grades classrooms, it is common for teachers to make use of running records to note progress in the skills and concepts for reading comprehension. Likewise, teachers in the writing workshop can record continuous notes relative to students' progress in the creation of finished pieces of writing. Teachers may then access their notes when planning for writers' development and advancement. The knowledge of students' progress is necessary not only for assessment, but also for setting realistic goals for students when planning contiguous writing workshop lessons. Informal student conferences, interactions with teacher and peers, running records, and writers' portfolios have taken the place of red marks and the teacher as both audience and judge. The example above illustrates types of assessment that can fit well with and also motivate young adolescents at work within a writing workshop.

When evaluations of learning are representative of students' continuous improvement and include many forms of data with regard to developing competencies, a more accurate picture of progress emerges than one based on exclusive use of a standardized, summative measure. Formative, authentic assessment of writing, the focus of this chapter, tends to engage and motivate young adolescent writers whose needs are known and taken into account. In order to concentrate efforts on more authentic assessment – the kind that informs teachers, students, and parents about young adolescents' progress in writing – first, a plan must be made to eliminate the concerns about testing over which educators have some control.

Managing Writing on Demand

Teachers have more power over writing assessment than they may think or have been led to believe. Some of the power resides in placing assessment into clear perspective for students – that is, taking the role of standardized testing in stride and approaching upcoming assessments with confidence and knowledge, preparing students for what can be expected, and taking charge of the related classroom variables that may be controlled (see list below). When opportunities arise while in communication with parents about how they can help, they can be asked to assist by providing healthy meals, setting appropriate bedtimes, and keeping stress to a minimum at home. Teachers may also consider becoming more involved in their school's curriculum planning in order to take part in and become aware of decisions that may affect assessment. But first, the "dark" mystery of testing must be dispelled for young adolescents.

Unravel the Mystery for Students

Young adolescents are not immune to the stress of writing on demand. Teachers can provide students with the ways and means to approach this type of writing in concrete ways that empower students and solve the mystery of what they believe is the unknown. Teachers foster students' confidence in their writing abilities in these ways:

- Become familiar with test formats, items, vocabulary, and requirements which are often available online at testing sites;
- Plan practice with sample texts and short writing assignments that resemble those on upcoming examinations;
- With students, write sample test questions and practice oral and written responses;
- Determine what students already know and are able to apply to writing in new contexts; and
- With students, list the skills and concepts they may encounter on tests; ask students to note those skills and concepts upon which they feel they have made progress as well as those that need more practice.
- Plan future lessons based on writing skills and crafts in need of practice.

Become Involved in Decision-Making

At school, administrators seek out teachers willing to serve on committees which meet to plan professional development in writing and to make decisions about writing assessment. After careful thought, study, and reflection on what the staff presently knows, the committee may then seek out sources of information and training that address teachers' writing goals. Too often, teachers are given in-service professional development with little regard to letting them take time to reflect first and then talk with their peers about what they are already doing that works – and to take time to look at most recent standards and benchmarks. Some administrators don't understand that teachers need time to connect with colleagues and to talk about their efforts before being bombarded with what feels to the teachers like "random" or unnecessary input from "outside experts." Taking an active part in decision-making processes strengthens teachers' contributions to the determination of appropriate and fair assessment of young students' writing.

The most troublesome aspect of standardized testing is the potential for misrepresentation of its scores – by local school districts, states, and the Department of Education – which have responded to the general public's demand for excellence in education, including a system of accountability. It is well to keep this in mind as teachers seek out and pursue alternative, formative, authentic assessment choices, such as those presented here. Young adolescent writers who are assessed fairly, openly, and clearly, and who are secure in the knowledge that they have some control within the assessment process in writing, are most motivated to succeed. For these students, the sky's the limit!

Concluding Reflections on Chapter 7

In this chapter, I presented an argument in support of continuous and varied informal assessment, in addition to writing on demand. The argument sustains a learner-centered approach, evident in the Young Adolescent Motivation Model of Writing (YAMM), while also recognizing the need to prepare students for standardized tests. When we as teachers, along with the larger educational community, fully understand and commit to this approach, young adolescents will excel – and each one of us, having contributed to nurturing their writing growth, will be a winner.

In the next and final chapter, Chapter 8: Maxim-izing Motivation via Teacher Imagination, I revisit some of the main ideas, or *maxims*, that appear throughout the first seven chapters of the book. Following each maxim, I invite teachers to engage their imaginations, step outside the box, and consider how an idea such as that presented in each maxim might grow to fruition in their own unique teaching contexts. The discussion of selected maxims in Chapter 8 is also a way to celebrate teachers' continuous efforts and vision.

8 Maxim-izing Motivation via Teacher Imagination

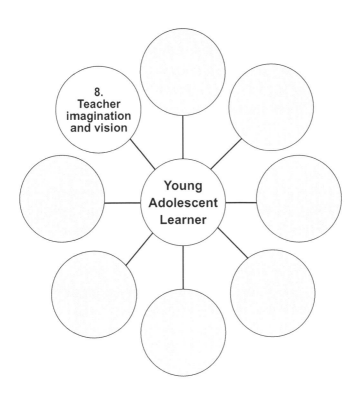

An idea is salvation by imagination.
– Frank Lloyd Wright, *Collected Writings, Volume 2* (Wright and Pfeiffer, 1995: 84)

Introductory Remarks to Chapter 8

The final chapter concerns itself with maxims and teachers' vision and power. I begin with a personal anecdote about maxims, defined by *Dictionary.com* as broad expressions of principle, "the truth and reasonableness of which are self-evident." The majority of the maxims discussed here are self-evident mainly to those whose vocation places them face-to-face with learner. To illustrate, I again share an anecdotal narrative.

My high school journalism teacher, whom I will call Mr. Cook, inspired me to integrate our senior class theme – "Some men see things as they are and say why? I dream things that never were and say why not?" (Kennedy, 1968) – into the high school yearbook's introduction both visually and textually. He also encouraged me to write and publish original poetry and an advice column in our school newspaper, and he was partially responsible for my choice to minor in Journalism at university. The decision to pursue a career in journalism, should I not secure a teaching position, was based on my belief that I am writer. That realization, then as now, is significant. As a recent college graduate working in a private school in the late 1960s, Mr. Cook may not have possessed teaching credentials, but he certainly knew the power of words accompanied by action. By day a high school teacher, by night a university instructor and yearbook editor, he offered the continuous hands-on knowledge of a working journalist. At the time, newspaper and yearbook layout pages were done manually, using t-squares and rulers, guided by the experience and insight of the faculty advisor rather than a digital program. The process required a specific, complex set of skills that could only be learned through practice. My classmates and I were apprentices during class and for many afternoons and evenings after school. Our teacher showed us, rather than told us, how to create large, collaborative writing projects as well as how to interpret events and processes. He rarely spoke in broad principles, and so I was surprised to read what he had penned in the back of my high school yearbook. Here is the last line: "The student gives meaning to the teacher's existence."

At that time, I thought the message referred to my efforts to visualize Robert F. Kennedy's famous statement, to move outside of my comfort zone by sharing my viewpoints, and to learn from and continue on, regardless of success or failure. I view both the Kennedy quotation and my former teacher's yearbook message as maxims, since they express broad statements of personal belief. Mr. Cook likely wrote similar messages to other conscientious students who set and accomplished goals, inspired by their teacher's display of professionalism, world knowledge, and vision.

Much later, I understood that Mr. Cook wrote as he taught: with the conviction that he had chosen the right career, realizing that the substantive rewards of teaching lay in working in concert with, and believing in, students. Schools are fortunate when they are able to employ educators who live to lead and to nurture the growth of others. Such educators operate from a set of general truths, which they have discovered over time to apply in their classrooms, and the truths become apparent through actions rather than as merely a set of written mottos or maxims. The great majority of educators exemplify those whose main purpose is to lead – by interaction with and instruction of their students – and the leadership is generated by each teacher's individual set of personal beliefs, including his or her philosophy of teaching. These professionals demonstrate, often implicitly, that the powers of imagination and vision in teaching are boundless!

In a spirit of acknowledgment of classroom teachers' passion and vision, I present a collection of selected maxims, previously highlighted throughout book, each followed by a specific reflection, invitation, or example offered for readers' consideration. The discussion of the maxims is intended to provide more food for thought and practical classroom applications to supplement the material in the other chapters. The power of learning rests on the visions of teachers. The combination of imagination and interpretation, knowledge of content, and the educator's choice of pedagogy based on personal philosophy most directly affect young adolescent writers. When teachers collaborate with parents, students' motivation to write and to learn increases considerably.

Following the maxims and reflections, I share an excerpt of a poem written by a classroom teacher, Michael Gordon, who validates teachers as writers, rebels, and, in so many words, gardeners on a mission.

Maxims from the Introduction: How I Came to Tend My Garden

Effective teachers teach the learner, not just the content.

When you consider your reasons for becoming a teacher, do you see yourself as an integral part of students' lives? You likely have already discovered that your vocation extends far beyond content and test preparation and that no matter the teaching level, your presence ranks high on the list of what can influence and inspire learners of any age.

Although I prepared to teach secondary (grades 7–12) students, I saw the immediate benefits of applying hands-on, inquiry-based, learner-centered approaches, methods employed most by elementary educators. While many educators plan instruction with a focus on discovery, teachers of younger students most often understand the underlying motivation inherent in lively discovery and physical interaction with the environment. Had I not allowed myself to view education through the lens of young adolescents as learners, I would have missed acres of delightful growth – in my students as well as in myself as an evolving educator.

> ***When students work diligently for the satisfaction of learning, teacher and students feel successful; when they compose for the joy of writing, all triumph!***

Students' level and range of interests expand when you write along with them, whether it be with young adolescents on a given class assignment or on your own work-related writing. Teachers can model authentic purposes for writing, its complex processes, and the satisfaction and joy that accompany planning, progressing in, and completing work. Showing while telling is powerful teaching – especially the expression of the joy of interweaving a personal interest, a vivid memory, or a special cause into your own work, giving voice and originality to a written work. Before you know it, students will be so engaged in their writing that they will hesitate when asked to stop at the end of class. This is one of the indications that writing is becoming intrinsically motivating.

Maxims from Chapter 1: Nurturing the Whole Learner in an Inquiry-Rich Environment

One of the best ways to proceed in the motivation of young adolescents' writing is to discover what key experiences, interests, knowledge, talents, and needs each brings as a whole person to the writing process – and what each can contribute to the community of learners.

Young adolescents yearn to be recognized for what they bring to the classroom in terms of knowledge and personality, as well as positive peer perception. They wish to be accepted and included by their peers, and teachers can assist with this. To facilitate the process, you can create opportunities for your students to reveal interests and talents in situations most likely to provide high levels of success and low risks of failure. One way for teachers and students to get to know one another's preferred pastimes and key talents is to plan a Student of the Week celebration in each first period class, for example. Our sixth grade teaching team found this very helpful in promoting a sense of class community and enhanced motivation to engage in learning. On a rotating basis, each young adolescent was honored for a week via a personal bulletin board, set up by the student and, if desired, his or her parents. Photos, ribbons, essays, awards, and other artifacts could be displayed, along with the student's birthday and a timeline. Students' positive self-images and feelings of empowerment bolster their rates of learning while earning the respect of their peers. Teachers can also make use of one-on-one conferences with writers, along with positive e-mails, notes, and phone calls to parents, to deliver good news about students' efforts. Parents appreciate such teacher endeavors and grow into supportive academic partners. In addition, as students become more accepting of one another and their capabilities are known, they become better able to interact with one another during long-term, interdependent projects, such as a writers' workshop – and sustain themselves during their independent work as well.

Teachers tune into young adolescents' worlds by offering choice, facilitating the writing and performance of original compositions, and by taking an interest in inquiry learning.

Tuning into students translates as a recognition and respect of our young adolescent charges as intelligent, talented, worthy people who crave the same basic needs as all human beings, including affection and belonging, self-actualization, and esteem (Maslow, 1970). When you invite students to become actively involved, allow them some decision-making power, and promote enjoyment and understanding of authentic emotions, you address their basic needs while enhancing their motivation to learn. Why not invite a student or two, whom you know would like to volunteer but may be shy or reticent, to read the main parts in a short play? *Scope* magazine, published by Scholastic Inc., from September through June, generally includes a short play based on popular culture, along with related class and individual literacy activities. Young adolescents can experiment with voice, tone, and mood of the literary characters as they read the short plays aloud – the equivalent of a Readers' Theater. Writers can follow up with an alternate ending or an idea for a sequel to the play. A pack of 15 shared student *Scope* magazines with a teaching guide is reasonably affordable, brings contemporary texts to the class on a frequent basis, and motivates teachers and students alike. Teachers understand the importance of maintaining an environment where all can participate and speak without fear of inappropriate peer behavior. Maintaining a positive classroom climate is essential to nurturing young adolescents' motivation to learn. The Readers' Theater activity addresses the needs for safety, belonging and esteem, components that also enhance students' enjoyment of class.

Even in each adolescent learner's short life, a great and complex canvas exists.

Teachers learn as much and as deeply about young adolescents as they care to share in writing, in discussion, through one-on-one interactions, and through the opportunities they create for students' self-expression, problem-solving, and inquiry. Reading a book aloud during the first or last fifteen minutes of class, such as Laurie Halse Anderson's *Speak* (Anderson, 1999), Clare Vanderpool's *Moon Over Manifest* (Vanderpool, 2010), Chris Crutcher's *Angry Management: Three Novellas* (Crutcher, 2009) or *Athletic Shorts: Six Short Stories* (Crutcher, 1991), or Richard Peck's *Remembering the Good Times* (Peck, 1986), may engage students in reflection and discussion about the depth of its young adolescent characters and their efforts to reveal themselves, despite serious physical and emotional traumas, as stronger, deeper, and more capable human beings. These texts contain authentic dialog to which students will be able to relate, but you may want to discuss with them alternate language that includes regionally acceptable terms. Young adolescents will get the message, and parents will thank you. Young adolescents bring their own stories and a number of skills to the classroom; some students will identify with characters or experiences described in specific stories, while others may be more sheltered or less experienced, or may have experienced lives very different from those of the characters they read about. Nonetheless, oral reading of and response to literature assists students as they gain additional knowledge, texture, and a depth of understanding about the world. Best of all, they are being nurtured with the teacher's gifts of time and attention.

Students sometimes seek self-confidence and peer acceptance in clumsy ways; fulfillment of these needs matters more than an "A" grade or first place in the lunch line.

You can provide some carefully constructed small-group and partner work to give students time to get to know peers on an academic level. When students are asked to complete a task together, to group problem-solve, or to create a common piece of writing, their feelings of self-efficacy grow. An example might be to write a rebus story, a short narrative substituting words for pictures (or the other way around), with a partner following the reading of a picture book. An example of a picture book that may inspire students to write a rebus story is Gloria Whelan's *Friend on Freedom River* (Whelan, 2004), an 1850 historic fictional account of young adolescents who demonstrate doing what is right rather than doing nothing, a theme that has relevance for today's young teens.

Writers might create a rebus conveying a situation in their lives in which making a correct choice shows civility, integrity, or tolerance – such as when a peer is being bullied, an occasion to cheat on a test arises, or a racist remark is made in the school lunchroom. Another way to use rebus is to invite students to visualize and reflect upon people and events in their lives and then create a dramatic retelling of a selected day away from school during a holiday. Examples are spending time with a quirky relative, being stuck in the car with an angry parent in rush-hour traffic, or learning gracefully to lose a game of soccer to one's younger sibling. The assignment works well following a week or more of vacation, promoting increased dialog with peers as well opportunities to reflect upon the multitude of future choices to be made as one grows into adulthood – as well as seeking the humor in situations which are out of one's control. The assignment supports cognitive awareness in decision-making and acts as a helpful transition to the variety of demands of school – thereby enhancing students' sense of self-worth.

Maxims from Chapter 2: Cultivating a Writing Community

Students are encouraged to engage in social learning activities that have authentic meaning for them as individuals and that promote analysis and synthesis of information in context.

One way to facilitate students' feelings of investment about their work is to plan a social action research project, one in which they choose from a brainstormed set of initiatives or projects and show a willingness to participate. Issues of social justice can invite analysis and synthesis, making use of students' prior knowledge as well as directing them to research questions and problems about which they care deeply. An excellent resource is *Reading, Writing, and Rising Up: Teaching about Social Justice and the Power of the Written Word* (Christensen, 2000). A growing number of students are becoming involved in community projects such as Habitat for Humanity and tutoring younger students in reading within their home school districts. Some students may wish to become involved in the preservation of historic parks and landmarks; other students question regional and state politics and how they might influence a vote directly affecting their lives; still other others may wish to organize an initiative giving students more of a voice in school policy, such as a requirement to wear uniforms or the decision process in setting required textbooks or readings. Students who have not yet been published in an adult arena might benefit from the research and writing of a letter to the editor of a school, local, or online publication on the topics of racism, gender bias, or other civil rights issues. The middle grades are an appropriate time to plan lessons addressing critical literacy topics such as how to distinguish fact from opinion, fair use, and plagiarism, which require critical analysis and synthesis. Young adolescents engaged with challenging activities like these are often motivated to reason more critically and learn to expect that great writing requires insight and effort.

When teachers talk with students about their own efforts and struggles as writers, young adolescents can recognize the value of patience and persistence as they struggle to craft their writing into finished products.

Teachers are writers of many genres who compose for varied purposes, many required and some undertaken by choice. In addition to writing with students during assignments, you may try sharing a personal first draft for students to view as you describe your approach to the assignment, beginning with why you chose the opening sentence you did to introduce the topic. You may ask students if they feel the introduction was effective and why. You may then inform them about what sections of the draft you feel work well so far, given the assignment. You might further share decisions made with regard to word selection and sequence, modeling appropriate, content-specific language of literary craft and form with your responses, and invite student discussion about their choices and struggles, encouraging them to be specific. In addition, you might want to discuss the kinds of writing that are expected of you as a teacher, including narrative evaluations and writing on demand for graduate studies or professional development. Discussions with students about their writing may include the necessity of practicing patience while taking the time needed to create outstanding writing, the availability and use of class and online resources, and the benefit of working with peers during the writing process.

Maxims from Chapter 3: Engaging Young Writers with Relevant, High-Interest Lessons

Teachers who model acceptance and high expectations communicate an understanding that each class member's writing growth holds equal importance and will be fairly nurtured.

In order for students to write with compassion, knowledge, viewpoint, and voice, opposing opinions about relevant, controversial topics need be heard and expressed. You must be clear that grades on assigned writing are not influenced by students' opinions about a topic but rather by the overall quality of the composition. Students who regard themselves as being treated justly will express fairness and a sense of equality in their oral and written language as they achieve style, voice, and increased critical thinking skills. All students, not only the poorest or the most gifted writers, deserve and need our attention. In my book, no learner fits the category of "average."

Young adolescents of all abilities and stages of language and writing development can benefit from collaborating with peers to help solve problems requiring the exploration of Web sources.

It is my opinion that English language learners, students with exceptional abilities, and students with special needs all benefit from participation in independent and small-group digital activities. The interaction with adults and peers deepens cognitive, social, and academic skills, contributing to authentic life experiences. With very little effort, you can set up student discussion forums for writers to share written response to their reading and study, to debate the most efficient ways to navigate Web resources for a research paper, and to review the correct way to cite references. A plethora of materials are promoted as self-study writing programs, focusing mainly on conventions and form. While beneficial to students learning the language, you will need to supplement these programs, if used, with authentic opportunities to read, explore, dialog with peers, and write beyond the sentence or standard paragraph. One way to motivate engagement is to begin by inquiring about what students need or want to know, prior to specific, in-depth lessons. Another way to expand and intensify writing is by student use of downloadable books onto devices like Kindles and personal phones, since a broad range of sentence structures may be attained more through reading than through direct instruction.

Young adolescents' goal-setting depends, to a great extent, upon their levels of reasoning as well as how they view themselves as learners.

Not all students have had practice reasoning at an abstract level, even if they have moved beyond the level of concrete thought and expression. Setting long-term goals requires knowing what has been learned and what has not, along with some of the steps to attainment of the goals. You can supply writers with opportunities to exercise their imaginations and to make applications to a broad spectrum of topics through the use of mentor texts spanning different genres and reading levels. You can reinforce the study of literary craft using mentor texts and then ask guided questions about: theme; what additional decisions literary characters might have made; what writers may have done, had they been in the characters' places; and whether themes and character decisions would hold true in other settings. When asked to set goals for themselves as developing writers, students who view themselves as capable learners will go beyond what is required, pushing their efforts and critical literacy to ever-higher levels. Students who do not view themselves as capable learners will require additional time, learning experiences, knowledge, and confidence-building activities, carefully monitored by the teacher.

Besides their social relationships with peers, students find meaning, comfort, and solace in music, literature, and the life stories of others portrayed in film and television.

There is a reason why young adolescents can often be found attached to earphones, glued to their computer screens, and texting on their cell phones. Beyond entertainment, tweens find solace and comfort, even understanding and acceptance, from connections to other human beings and their humanity via music, literature, art, and the lives and opinions of peers. Just as you connect with a film or novel because you empathize and identify with issues and how characters go about dealing with the ordinary and the exceptional events of life, young people seek valued peer opinions and artistic connections in order to grasp life's challenges. You might try to read everything by an author whose work you have enjoyed, seek music by our favorite artists, and lean toward film genres and digital experiences that especially interest and fulfill you; so too do young adolescents. Finding yourself in a song and hearing the artist sing your life is powerful self-actualization. You can make use of the arts in your lessons for the purpose of engaging students actively in response, communication, and creative composition. There is no need to rely on only textbooks and published materials when so many other resources are at our fingertips.

More attention to treatment of gender in classrooms enlightens teachers and students, motivates reflection, and encourages equal and appropriate treatment of all.

As teachers and role models, you can set aside traditional stereotypes in favor of honoring diverse roles for all types of people; you can also learn from current research topics, approaches, and behaviors that best encourage high levels of writing success for both genders. But it is important to recognize that many students will not fit the mold. You can go out on a limb and ask a peer to sit in class and note the percentage of males and females who are called upon, the quality of responses, and the approximate time spent with each. Following the reading of the peer teacher's notes or a videotape of the lesson, you can reflect upon positive ways to continue equal and appropriate behaviors – and consider additional ways to engage and respond to students, should some inequity be discovered. It's a good guess that students will follow your lead when treating peers of both genders with respect, understanding, and fairness.

338 TEND YOUR GARDEN

Maxims from Chapter 4: Growing with Process Writing Linked to the Arts

Teachers can profoundly nurture young adolescents' motivation to write when they provide lessons that include invitations to interpret and generate art in its almost endless array of styles and forms, including building upon their experiences as social beings.

Whenever possible, you can include open-ended tasks and inquiry, particularly when study includes literature, art, music, and drama. One idea for consideration is to encourage writers to interpret a short piece of self-chosen text, such as a favorite quotation from a speech, film, or book. Using digital text, photographs, fonts, clip

> *Some men see things as they are and say WHY? I dream things that never were and say WHY NOT?*
> – Robert F. Kennedy, *Remarks at the University of Kansas* (Kennedy, 1968)

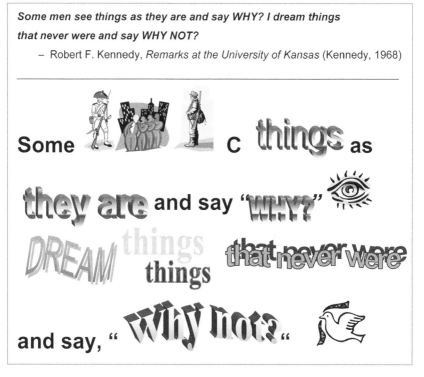

Figure 8.1. Robert F. Kennedy Quotation in Graphic Form

art, color, sound, and other text forms, ask students to interpret the quote and to be ready to share the interpretation with a partner and possibly the class. Figure 8.1 illustrates what Robert F. Kennedy's famous quotation might look like in the form of a digital text and rebus story, applying some basic visual forms.

Robin Williams' *The Non-Designer's Design Book: Design and Typographic Principles for the Visual Novice*, third edition (Williams, 2008), is an excellent resource for information and study. Williams also suggests *Veer.com*, *Before & After* magazine (*BAMagazine.com*), *Layers Magazine* (*LayersMagazine.com*), and *InDesign* PDF *Magazine* (*InDesignMag.com*). Other ways to add art as motivation include hand-drawn designs or digital graphics for a previously written short story, comic strip, or political cartoon of a recent news event, and/or choosing music and film clips to enhance a persuasive essay. The act of conveying meaning in more than one modality deepens comprehension, increases critical literacy, and adds to the enjoyment of a project.

Getting the form correct is a necessary part of writing, but the real sense of achievement comes when each hears his or her own "music" and capably interprets that sound in his or her own distinctive words.

Young adolescent writers' voice and style are developed progressively, day by day, through close attention to each student's growth and maturity as literate beings. In addition to dispensing positive reinforcement when conventions and form become increasingly correct, we can also take note of small improvements and guide students to develop their topics and ideas as a comprehensive whole – attending to revision near the end of the writing process. When the bulk of improvement comes about naturally and is initiated mainly through students' efforts, they become intrinsically motivated to continue developing as writers. You can plant the seeds of success by gradually giving students more choice and opportunities to express themselves, as they become ready to do so. Some young adolescent writers require additional scaffolding through a longer period of teacher guidance or more frequent one-on-one conferences; others require freedom to push in new directions independently, taking more calculated risks with craft and language as they develop a strong voice in their writing.

Consensus-building and collaboration are emergent processes; any and all positive signs of a small group's movement toward the classroom model need to be documented, and group members need to be recognized for their efforts.

Since many young adolescents struggle to be accepted by peers as part of their social growth, our recognition of their choice to behave authentically in complex group tasks when working with peers deserves validation. Success builds upon success, especially when falling in with an accepted classroom process is considered "cool." Resist the inclination to respond only to negative behaviors. Accentuate the positive whenever possible! One of the best ways to recognize appropriate behavior is to ask a student with whom you have recently conferred in order to reteach a skill to share the instruction within a peer response group. You might also redirect the student to teach others the skill as the need arises. Teaching others deepens and expands the writer's own understanding as it builds confidence and self-reliance. Finally, validate collaboration with others through invitations to suggest resources and specific applications within future units you are planning. For example, what digital tools, Internet sites, and which favorite fiction and non-fiction texts might motivate classmates in the study of discoveries leading to new medical treatments for heart disease? What types of writing other than research reports might be suggested to check understanding of new medical treatments? You could create a unit in which young adolescent writers could choose to write an article for the school paper, to design a digital presentation to share with elementary students, or to write a traditional paper to demonstrate their writing skills, knowledge of writing genre, and application of the data about new medical treatments. In the long run, you will have students' respect while classmates will want to imitate their positive behaviors, supplemented most likely by added engagement, interest, and motivation to write. Thus, your efforts can create a win-win situation!

Writing is an opportunity for young adolescents to draw from their vast stores of impressions, experiences, and linguistic knowledge to respond without fear of acceptability of subject, organization, or mechanics, especially during the drafting stage*.*

One way to establish credibility for staged drafting is to ask students to turn in an early draft of a piece of writing and then you respond to one or more of their ideas, word choices, emerging voice, style, or original viewpoints. Responding to an early draft is most effective if you address suggestions to the entire work with reference to content, rather than form or conventions, which will be addressed in responding to a later draft. You can begin a class year with a folder for each student to use for ongoing drafts of their writing, and allow some student choice when it comes to selecting pieces of writing to include in a graded portfolio. You can give special recognition to writers' inclusion of original insights, use of authentic language in composing dialog, and application of themes previously studied in class. These practices place the emphasis on *what* students have to say, and not merely on *how they say it*.

Reflection throughout the writing process greatly affects students' understanding about their own learning as well as their understanding of the ways in which they choose to craft their writing.

Peer response and teacher suggestions are offered to writers, who make the final choice about how their compositions appear in final draft form. You can facilitate writers' continuous improvement in content and form by planning mini-lessons that focus on revision strategies concerning narrative elements and literary devices. For example, to model the crafting of a mood and tone foreshadowing danger, obtain paper copies of the text (Poe, 1984: 121–124) along with a recording by Basil Rathbone of Edgar Allan Poe's *Tell Tale Heart* (Poe, 1965). Talk with students about what they think brings fear to a narrative. Ask students to circle words and phrases that Poe used to bring feelings of fear and imminent danger; invite them to look closely at Poe's choices regarding the dialog, description, and order of events. How does word placement in sentences make a difference to the story's tone? Has Poe used simile and metaphor? How about onomatopoeia or personification? Invite students to find these in the text. Writers might remember how they have employed these literary devices and choices before in their own work and then choose one past piece of writing that exemplifies these literary crafts. Invite students to rework one or more sections of a selected paper and to note, in the margins, ideas for future consideration of word choice and appropriate literary devices. Share some of these in class discussion to further emphasize the importance of reflection and continuous improvements when crafting writing.

Maxims from Chapter 5: Motivating Writing with Choice and Critical Thinking

Young adolescents are not seasoned writers or responders and so need to learn to be open to others' opinions and insights, even if these differ from their own views.

While young adolescents are opinionated and may be used to blocking out, talking over, or ignoring conflicting viewpoints, learning to be more open-minded and to listen to others assists them as developing writers. This goes for more than seeing both sides of an argument in order to create an exceptional persuasive essay; the behaviors also apply to helpful criticism of work in progress. Young adolescents may hear suggestions to stating main ideas or adding details as a negative response to them as people, since their ideas are in question; they can become quite invested in what they consider their best pieces. Talking with writers about the benefits of helpful criticism gently reminds them that they are not supposed to have mastered all there is to learn about exemplary writing. Young adolescent writers can be reminded to think about the suggestions as just that – propositions about what is possible, again reminding writers that they do make the final decisions after weighing criticism intended as constructive. The word "constructive" connotes a building up and a creation of a whole from many parts, so perhaps the term "constructive criticism" might be compared to the ongoing process of creating – in this case, creating a whole with the details of written language. Finally, teachers and volunteers must model positive response to further reinforce civility, equity, and tolerance.

Teachers most often choose the methods that yield the most success, as learned through their classroom experiences.

Most educators can sometimes not relate to professional development that is either touted as the latest best practice method by a hired consultant or an organization such as a state Department of Education. Due to high-stakes testing, professional development most often revolves around raising test scores. Occasionally, teachers are invited to attend a conference of their choice, but with district funds for teacher professional development decreasing, administrators select what they feel their districts need most. Frequently, best practices are already in use in most classrooms, including those practices that lead to student achievement on tests; however, districts tend to place all their funds into whole-day development programs that repeat or review past input, sometimes without benefit of checking current pedagogy in use. Although well-intentioned, this type of instruction can be disheartening, resulting in teachers feeling disrespected for non-recognition of their successful work with students. Frequently, teachers believe that the day might have been better spent working with peers on programs and units of great potential already in progress. Regardless of the topic or type of input offered, teachers will choose instruction and assessment based on what they have found assists students' success in learning, and what works for them as teachers and individuals.

Asking young people to reveal themselves in their writing places them in a vulnerable position and thus might make them hesitant or resistant to doing so.

The most exemplary writing is that which surpasses correct form, expresses a writer's intention, reaches out to the audience through voice and characterization, and affects readers' knowledge, insights, and experiences. Facilitating writing that progresses toward this level of excellence necessitates conscious planning of writing experiences that both challenge and satisfy writers. When you consider and can identify what you enjoy most about reading your students' compositions, you may help to make them less reluctant to write from the heart and so move toward eliciting these exemplary qualities in your young writers. Also, young adolescent writers will require the feeling of being personally invested in their topic and writing purpose in order to reveal themselves fully. Signs that students are becoming personally invested include: increased active participation in partner and group work, such as accepting leadership roles; heightened interest in critical literacy assignments such as research and critical oral or written response; and an amplified tendency to write and share first person narratives that place them in vulnerable positions. Building classroom community, offering choice within assignments, and providing multiple opportunities to share writing in a respectful, safe environment all support students' personal investment in the writing process.

Some students require more structure and direction than others, yet they rise to the occasion when limited areas of choice are made available to them.

Most students, even those who work best on their own and at an individual pace, need clarity of directions and set boundaries. Facilitation of young adolescent writers as active, motivated learners within a set of classroom expectations for assigned work and behavior can, at times, prove a complex balancing act. Students who learn best with more structure may find that templates and advance organizers greatly assist their understanding of and response to longer assignments and projects. Students who are less confident, are easily distracted, or find it difficult to begin might find work more palatable if given concrete directions with a little choice. For example, you might try offering two topics as options, rather than asking students to come up with their own. Also, taking a few minutes to talk with writers who hesitate to engage can facilitate focus, assist with prewriting, and increase overall opportunities for success.

Maxims from Chapter 6: Learner-Centered Writing in an e-Universe

As educators' understanding about and application of Web-based writing resources grows, so do the vast frontiers of future digital discoveries.

The most efficient avenue for teachers to gain understanding of and to implement digital resources is to make time for students to apply the resources to an authentic purpose, such as a compiled list of appropriate search engines, topic-related sites, and online experts for student access. Teachers' research on digital resources as part of lesson preparation is growth in their Web-based knowledge and competencies, and the process may yield the enjoyable sense of discovery that many students experience. From conducting such research yourself, you may be able to recognize and set the necessary boundaries for work in digital domains by students, who are nurtured and empowered by the guidance. In addition, resources such as Google Docs, a free online word processor and presentation system that enables writers to work on their files from any computer, may be used on a regular basis in the classroom. Much other free and low-cost technology that is readily available can motivate students to take control of their learning in powerful, satisfying ways.

Educational scholars, teachers, and lawmakers must take part in continuous study and ongoing communication about research and practice in both a current and historical context, taking a close look at whether what is being taught at any given point in time will benefit students in the long run.

The great majority of educators were shut out of the process when the National Governors' Association, along with private business and educational companies created the Common Core State Standards (CCSS), released simultaneously to the public, mass media, and teachers in July of 2010. Some major educational organizations such as the International Reading Association and the National Council of Teachers of English, along with some secondary and university institutions, were invited to send representatives to meetings in the later stages of the process, in order to review the standards and then make suggestions for revisions. Some recommendations from these educational groups, though not many, were integrated into the final document. Although few educators were called, many were ready to participate in all stages of the study, communication, and writing processes creating these standards. It is no wonder that many teachers, the ones destined to implement the CCSS, reacted with frustration and a sense of having been disrespected, when they were made public. The CCSS are written in quite general terms in comparison with individual state standards, upon which many more educators pre-K through university collaborated and with which they have become familiar, although it was the state departments of education that had the final say on how the standards were worded.

Having taken part in some stages of writing and response to individually developed state standards and benchmarks, including Michigan's Grade Level Content Expectations (GLCEs), I better understand how the system of writing, revising, and "rolling out" (presenting) the vast curriculum documents works. Although I think that educators and educational leaders should have fully authored the GLCEs, I recognize that they have value in guiding the curriculum planning and assessment process. I strongly recommend that when given the opportunity to meet and work with other teachers, university scholars, and lawmakers in order to collaborate, no matter to what degree, interested teachers should do so.

At a time when teachers' unions must unite to support both teachers' welfare and more direct involvement in the construction of curriculum and assessment that they will be expected to implement in their teaching, many unions are being attacked as hindering educational reform. I urge every teacher to become knowledgeable about all issues that affect students' writing and learning overall. Our actions as professional individuals and groups who are actively involved in bringing about positive change and in exercising our expertise – including our knowledge of historical reform, educational research, and pedagogy – honor students in terms of their future academic, social, and emotional growth.

Maxims from Chapter 7: Sowing the Seeds of Formative, Authentic Assessment

Classroom teachers dedicated to test preparation for their students sometimes abandon contemporary process-oriented approaches against their better judgment.

If the situation arises, attempt to integrate some of the tasks required for tests into your reading and writing workshops, and then provide time for students to talk with one another and to discuss why particular responses might be more desirable than others. Help students to become familiar with the writing test rubric for an upcoming examination so that they are aware of required writing qualities and components, and then set it aside. Recall, with students, how some of the qualities listed on the rubric have already been or are being addressed within class assignments. Talk about what literary crafts and writing skills you have already practiced, and ask students what they feel most confident about and what they feel needs improvement. Plan lessons around those skills and crafts that need practice, incorporating high-interest texts and active learning experiences. When the tasks required for the exam are less mysterious and more familiar, students approach the test situation with more confidence and less stress. When the application of writing tasks to those texts is united with assignments that inspire and empower students, they have every reason to succeed on formal assessments that require writing-on-demand, such as high-stakes tests.

Young adolescent learners are most motivated to improve their writing when they are obliged to reflect upon and to apply alternative routes to solving their problems with a piece of writing.

You can best nurture students' development of writing schemas, or individual writing processes and plans, by allowing them time to process and discuss their ideas about writing on a regular basis. For instance, you can remember to allow "wait-time" during whole-class instruction, small-group work involving the teacher, and one-on-one conferences between teacher and student; you can require students to write and reflect daily during a quiet or "sacred" writing time, for optimum focus; you can ask students to clarify oral and written responses with audience in mind rather than providing a ready answer; and you can observe how your students go about solving problems involving word choice, organization, sequence, and staying on topic. When writers appear stalled, you can ask them what has worked in the past in similar situations or suggest possible routes to remedy the problem once they have given it some thought. Even allowing a writer to set the composition aside and to pick it up later may be beneficial. It is also helpful for student writers to observe teachers modeling the necessary reflection of individual writing schemas. Above all, establishing routines within the classroom community demonstrates that reflection and alternative problem-solving methods are worth the writer's time and efforts.

Each situation is different, and teachers should utilize an assessment framework that is both learner-appropriate and manageable.

Every formative writing assessment, when used in harmony with a varied set of other measures, has the potential to "work" for some teachers and writers. Yet a similar framework may be totally wrong for others. An assessment structure "works" when its assorted components yield a full picture of students' writing abilities and needs, reflect the teacher's philosophical and pedagogical views, and mesh adequately with the ongoing writing workshop routines. Teachers tend their gardens well by not only knowing that contexts and learners differ, but also by growing in understanding and knowledge, right along with their young adolescent charges.

Concluding Reflections: The Garden Lives and Grows

As an ending to this book, I present excerpts from a poem by teacher Michael Gordon, who spent twenty years as a business development and national accounts manager prior to becoming certified to teach middle and elementary students. With the continuing debate about educational reform, in the context of teachers' determination to teach writing as they see fit and the seemingly never-ending governmental demands, these words hold special meaning. Spring in my home state of Michigan is just around the corner, and with it the promise of new growth and anticipation of a million buds ready to burst into bloom, as we all tend our gardens.

Tidal Basin
by Michael Gordon

It is
cherry blossom
time…

…We
are writers,
poets,
teachers
on a mission. We
are mountain
rebels and
sneak the spring
into their senate and congressional offices –
a small handful of petals at a time –
concealed beneath the soles
of our shoes, and past the limestone,
past the marble, past the bronze, past security…

…we
walk spring petals in unnoticed; and,
with each
breath we speak, exhale pink-white aromas we
have breathed in
deeply, understanding,
believing; and, in exhaling,
shower legislators and their aides, with
the passion
of
spring
of
cherry blossoms of
children blooming back on the trees that are
each of our classrooms

each with the potential to bring forth
a thousand springs to come.
We are gentle revolutionaries, and they
behind these walls are –
Are poets at heart
many of them.
I see it,
I hope it,
I believe it, and
I know,
at the very least,
we
are, spring's emissaries; its quietest, most
persistent of revolutionaries.

– Michael Gordon (2010)
Used with the permission of the author.

Thank you to all middle-grades teachers called to nurture the motivation of young adolescent writers. Special thanks to Michael Gordon, who in his poem likens student writers to cherry blooms on trees bright with the potential to "bring forth a thousand springs to come." May the reflections, invitations, and poetry in this, the final chapter, celebrate teachers, confirm their worthy efforts, and motivate them and all of you readers of this book to continue nurturing the growth of young adolescent writers through their, and your, vision and power.

References

Albers, Peggy (2007) *Finding the Artist Within: Creating and Reading Visual Texts in the English Language Arts Classroom*. Newark, Delaware: International Reading Association.
Alcott, Louisa May (1955) *Little Women*. New York: Nelson Doubleday, Inc.
Alexie, Sherman (2007) *The Absolutely True Diary of a Part-Time Indian*. New York: Little, Brown, and Company.
Allen, Bay Wilson and Clark, Harry Hayden (1966) *Literary Criticism, Pope to Croce*. Detroit, Michigan: Wayne State University Press.
Allen, Janet (1995) *It's Never Too Late: Leading Adolescents to Lifelong Literacy*. Portsmouth, New Hampshire: Heinemann.
Alschuler, Alfred S., Tabor, Diane and McIntyre, James (1970) *Teaching Achievement Motivation*. Middletown, Connecticut: Education Ventures, Inc.
Anderman, Eric M. and Maehr, Martin L. (1994) Motivation and schooling in the middle grades. *Review of Educational Research*, 64(2): 287–309.
Anderson, Laurie Halse (1999) *Speak*. New York: Penguin Books for Young Readers.
Atwell, Nancie (1998) *In the Middle* (2nd edition). Portsmouth, New Hampshire: Heinemann.
Barr, Mary A. and Syverson, Margaret A. (1999) *Assessing Literacy with the Learning Record: A Handbook for Teachers, Grades 6–12*. Portsmouth, New Hampshire: Heinemann.
Barr, Mary A., Craig, Dana A., Fisette, Dolores and Syverson, Margaret A. (1999) *Assessing Literacy with The Learning Record: A Handbook for Teachers, Grades K–6*. Portsmouth, New Hampshire: Heinemann.

Barrs, Myra, Ellis, Sue, Hester, Hilary and Thomas, Anne (1988) *The Primary Language Record Handbook*. London: Centre for Literacy in Education.

Bartlett, Lora (2004) Expanding teacher work roles: A resource for retention or recipe for overwork? *Journal of Education Policy* 19(5): 565–582.

Bennet, Cherie (1999) *Life in the Fat Lane*. New York: Laurel Leaf Books.

Bennett, Randy Elliott (2006) *Technology and Writing Assessment: Lessons Learned from the U. S. National Assessment of Educational Progress* (Revised from keynote presentation at the Annual Conference of the International Association for Educational Assessment, Singapore, May 2006). Princeton, New Jersey: Educational Testing Service.

Bentley, William A. (2000) *Snowflakes in Photographs*. Minneola, New York: Dover Publications.

Berryman, Julia C., Smythe, Pamela K., Lamont, Alexandra and Joiner, Richard (2002) *Developmental Psychology and You* (2nd edition). Malden, Massachusetts: BPS Blackwell.

Blume, Judy (1973/2003a) *Deenie*. New York: Delacorte Press.

Blume, Judy (2002/2003b) *Double Fudge*. New York: Macmillan Children's Books.

Blume, Judy (1979/2003c) *Tales of a Fourth Grade Nothing*. New York: Macmillan Children's Books.

Bobek, Becky L. (2002) Teacher resiliency: A key to career longevity. *The Clearing House* 75(4): 202–205. Retrieved on 22 March 2011 from Education Periodicals database (Document ID: 119553592).

Bomer, Katherine (2005) *Writing a Life: Teaching Memoir to Sharpen Insight, Shape Meaning–and Triumph Over Tests*. Portsmouth, New Hampshire: Heinemann.

Boyd, Thomas A. (ed.) (1961) *Prophet of Progress: Selections from the Speeches of Charles F. Kettering*. New York: Dutton.

Brophy, Jere (2010) *Motivating Students to Learn* (3rd edition). New York: Routledge.

Buckelew, Mary Bellucci (2003) The value of art in the English classroom: Imagination, making the tacit visible. *English Journal* 92(5): 49–55.

Buckner, Aimee (2002) Teaching in a world focused on testing. *Language Arts* 79(3): 212–215. Retrieved on 1 June 2009 from http://www.iaea2006.seab.gov.sg/conference/download/papers/KeynoteTechnology%20and%20writing%20assessment%20%20Lessons%20learned%20from%20 the%20US%20National%20Assessment%20of%20Educational%20Progress.pdf.

Burke (2010) *English Companion Ning*. Retrieved on 7 December 2010 from englishcompanion.ning.com/.

Burnett, Frances Hodgson (1911) *The Secret Garden*. New York: Frederick A. Stokes Co.

BusinessDictionary.com (2011) Definition of Skype. Web-Finance Inc. Retrieved on 25 March 2011 from www.businesdictionary.com/definition/Skype.html.

Byrk, Anthony S. and Schneider, Barbara (2003)Trust in schools: A core resource for school reform. *Educational Leadership* 60(6): 40–45. Retrieved on 21 August 2010 at https://peoplebox.aea11.k12.ia.us//LN000289Trust in Schools.pdf.

Calkins, Lucy McCormick (1994) *The Art of Teaching Writing* (2nd edition). Concord, Ontario, Canada: Irwin Publishing.

Carbo, Marie, Dunn, Rita and Dunn, Kenneth (1986) *Learning to Read Through Their Individual Learning Styles*. Englewood Cliffs, New Jersey: Prentice-Hall.

Carroll, Pamela Sissi (2004) *Integrated Literacy in the Middle Grades: Channeling Young Adolescents' Spontaneous Flow of Energy*. Boston, Massachusetts: Pearson Education, Inc.

Carson, Rachel (1962) *Silent Spring*. New York: Houghton-Mifflin.

Chancer, Joni and Rester-Zodrow, Gina (1997) *Moon Journals: Writing, Art, Inquiry*. Portsmouth, New Hampshire: Heinemann.

Chickering, Arthur W. and Gamson, F. Zelda (1987) Seven principles of good practice in undergraduate education. *AAHE Bulletin* 39(7): 3–7.

Chrenka, Lynn (April 28, 2009) Surprising findings from a study of U. S. teens and their use of digital media. *L and L on Line, Newsletter of the Online Teaching Committee* 4: 1. Big Rapids, Michigan: Ferris State University, Department of Languages and Literature. Retrieved on 27 September 2010 from http://www.google.com/search?hl=en&q=Chrenka,+Lynn+(April+28,+2009)+Surprising+findings+from+a+study+of+U.+S.+teens+and+their+use+of+digital+media.

Christensen, Linda (2000) *Reading, Writing, and Rising Up: Teaching About Social Justice and the Power of the Written Word*. Milwaukee, Wisconsin: Rethinking Schools Limited.

Clark, Irene and Bamberg, Betty (2003) *Concepts in Composition: Theory and Practice in the Teaching of Writing*. Mahwah, New Jersey: Lawrence Erlbaum Associates.

Clay, Marie M. (1979) *Reading the Pattering of Complex Behaviors.* Portsmouth, New Hampshire: Heinemann.

Clay, Marie M. (2000) *Running Records for Classroom Teachers.* Portsmouth, New Hampshire: Heinemann.

Clinton, Hillary (1996) *It Takes a Village: And Other Lessons Children Teach Us.* New York: Simon & Schuster.

Close, Elizabeth and Ramsey, Katherine D. (2000) *A Middle Mosaic: A Celebration of Reading, Writing, and Reflective Practice at the Middle Level.* Urbana, Illinois: National Council of Teachers of English.

Coerr, Eleanor (1977) *Sadako and the Thousand Paper Cranes.* New York: G. P. Putnam's Sons.

Crawford, Linda (2004) *Lively Learning: Using the Arts to Teach K–8 Curriculum.* Greenfield, Massachusetts: Northeast Foundation for Children.

Crutcher, Chris (1989) *Chinese Handcuffs.* New York: HarperCollins.

Crutcher, Chris (1991) *Athletic Shorts: Six Short Stories.* New York: HarperCollins.

Crutcher, Chris (1993) *Staying Fat for Sarah Byrnes.* New York: HarperCollins.

Crutcher, Chris (1995) *Ironman.* New York: HarperCollins.

Crutcher, Chris (2001) *Whale Talk.* New York: HarperCollins.

Crutcher, Chris (2009) *Angry Management: Three Novellas.* New York: Greenwillow Books.

Csikszentmihalyi, Mihaly (1990) *Flow: The Psychology of Optimal Experience.* New York: HarperCollins.

Curtis, Christopher Paul (1995) *Watsons Go to Birmingham – 1963.* New York: Delacorte Press.

Curtis, Christopher Paul (1999) *Bud, Not Buddy.* New York: Delacorte Press.

Curtis, Christopher Paul (2004) *Bucking the Sarge.* New York: Random House.

Dahl, Roald (1964) *Charlie and the Chocolate Factory.* New York: Alfred A. Knopf, Inc.

Daniels, Harvey (2002) *Literature Circles: Voice and Choice in the Student-Centered Classroom.* York, Maine: Stenhouse Publishers.

Daniels, Harvey and Bizar, Marilyn (2005) *Teaching the Best Practice Way: Methods That Matter, K–12.* Portland, Maine: Stenhouse.

Darling-Hammond, Linda (2006) *Powerful Teacher Education: Lessons from Exemplary Programs.* San Francisco: Jossey-Bass.

Da Vinci, Leonardo (2002) *Treatise on Painting*. Amherst, New York: Prometheus Books. Originally published in 1892, London and New York: G. Bell.

Delandshere, Ginette and Petrosky, Anthony (1998) Assessment of complex performances: Limitations of key measurement assumptions. *Educational Researcher* 27(2): 14–24.

Dewey, John (1916/1944) *Democracy and Education: An Introduction to the Philosophy of Education*. New York: The Free Press, Simon & Schuster, Inc.

Dewey, John (1938) *Experience and Education*. New York: Collier Books.

DiCamillo, Kate (2001a) *Because of Winn Dixie*. Cambridge, Massachusetts: Candlewick Press.

DiCamillo, Kate (2001b) *The Tiger Rising*. Cambridge, Massachusetts: Candlewick Press.

Digital Resources for Math and Science Educator (2011) The Ohio State University. Retrieved on 24 January, 2011 from http://people.ehe.ohio-state.edu/ed/.

Dorfman, Lynne R. and Cappelli, Rose (2007) *Teaching Writing Through Children's Literature, K–6*. Portland, Maine: Stenhouse Publishers.

Dörnyei, Zoltan (2001) *Motivational Strategies in the Language Classroom*. Cambridge, U. K.: Cambridge University Press.

Dörnyei, Zoltan (2005) *The Psychology of the Language Learner: Individual Differences in Second Language Acquisition*. Mahwah, New Jersey: Lawrence Erlbaum Associates, Inc.

Dunn, Rita (2007) *What If? Promising Practices for Improving Schools*. Lanham, Maryland: Rowman & Littlefield Education.

Dunn, Rita and Dunn, Kenneth (1975) *Manual: Learning Style Inventory*. Lawrence, Kansas: Price Systems.

Eccles, Jacquelynne S. and Wigfield, Allan (2002) Motivational beliefs, values, and goals. *Annual Review of Psychology* 53: 109–132.

Edwards, M. Craig and Briers, Gary E. (2001) Selected variables related to expected longevity in teaching of entry-phrase agriculture teachers. *Journal of Career and Technical Education* 18(1). Retrieved on 20 August 2010 at scholar.lib.vt.edu/ejournals/JCTE/v18n1/pdf/Edwards.pdf.

Eichorn, Donald H. (1966) *The Middle School*. New York: The Center for Applied Research in Education, Inc.

Elkind, David (2001) The *Hurried Child: Growing Up Too Fast Too Soon*. Cambridge, Massachusetts: Perseus Book Group.

Emig, Janet (1971) *The Composing Processes of Twelfth Graders*. Urbana, Illinois: National Council of Teachers of English

Enos, Theresa (1996) *Encyclopedia of Rhetoric and Composition: Communication from Ancient Times to the Information Age*. New York: Routledge.

Ericsson, K. Anders and Simon, Herbert A. (1993) *Protocol Analysis – Revised Edition: Verbal Reports as Data*. Cambridge, Massachusetts: MIT Press.

Evans, Karen S. (2001) *Literature Discussion Groups in the Intermediate Grades: Dilemmas and Possibilities*. Newark, Delaware: International Reading Association.

Fine, Carla (2001) *Strong Smart & Bold: Empowering Girls for Life*. New York: HarperCollins Publishers.

Fletcher, Ralph (1993) *What a Writer Needs*. Portsmouth, New Hampshire: Heinemann.

Fletcher, Ralph (2006) *Boy Writers: Reclaiming Their Voices*. Portland, Maine: Stenhouse Publishers.

Fletcher, Ralph (2010) *Pyrotechnics on the Page: Playful Craft That Sparks Writing*. Portland, Maine: Stenhouse Publishers.

Fletcher, Ralph and Portalupi, JoAnn (2001) *Writing Workshop: The Essential Guide*. Portsmouth, New Hampshire: Heinemann.

Gage, Nathaniel L. (1963) *Handbook of Research on Teaching*. Chicago: Rand McNally.

Gallagher, Kelly (2006) *Teaching Adolescent Writers*. Portland, Maine: Stenhouse Publishers.

Gardner, Howard (1983/2004) *Frames of Mind: The Theory of Multiple Intelligences* New York: Perseus Books Group.

Gay, Geneva (2010) *Culturally Responsive Teaching*. New York: Teachers College Press.

Geisel, Theodore (Dr. Seuss) (1971) The *Lorax*. New York: Random House.

Geller, Conrad (2001) *Poetic Forms: The Sonnet*. Retrieved on 9 December 2009 from http://www.writing-world.com/poetry/sonnet.shtml.

Goodlad, John (1984) *A Place Called School*. New York: McGraw-Hill Book Company.

Goodlad, John (1990) *Teachers for Our Nation's Schools*. San Francisco: Jossey-Bass Publishers.

Goodman, Kenneth and Goodman, Yetta (1979) Learning to read is natural. In Lauren B. Resnick and Phyllis A. Weaver (eds.) *Theory and Practice of Early Reading* 1: 137–154. Hillsdale, New Jersey: Erlbaum.

Graves, Donald H. (1983/1994) *Writing: Teachers & Children at Work.* Portsmouth, New Hampshire: Heinemann.

Graves, Donald H. and Kittle, Penny (2005) *My Quick Writes.* Portsmouth, New Hampshire: Heinemann.

Green Day (2004) Wake me up when September comes. *American Idiot.* Burbank, California: Reprise Records.

Gunnery, Sylvia (2007) *The Writing Circle.* Markham, Ontario: Pembroke Publishers, Ltd.

Gurian, Michael and Ballew, Arlette C. (2003) *The Boys and Girls Learn Differently Action Guide for Teachers.* San Francisco: Jossey-Bass.

Hall, Maureen P. and Waxler, Robert P. (2010) Engaging future teachers to reflect on how reading and writing can change lives, *Writing & Pedagogy* 2(1): 91–100.

Hansen, Jane (1998) *When Learners Evaluate.* Portsmouth, New Hampshire: Heinemann.

Harmon, Rebecca (2005) *The Water Cycle: Evaporation, Condensation & Erosion (Earth's Processes)* Chicago, Illinois: Heinemann–Raintree.

Harvey, Stephanie and Daniels, Harvey (2009) *Comprehension and Collaboration: Inquiry Circles in Action.* Portsmouth, New Hampshire: Heinemann.

Haskell, Robert (2000) Transfer of Learning: Cognition, Instruction, and Reasoning. San Diego: Academic Press.

Heard, Georgia (1999) *Awakening the Heart: Exploring Poetry in Elementary and Middle School.* Portsmouth, New Hampshire: Heinemann.

Hicks, Troy (2009) *The Digital Writing Workshop.* Portsmouth, New Hampshire: Heinemann.

Hillocks, George, Jr. (1995) *Teaching Writing as Reflective Practice.* New York: Teachers College Press.

Hirsch, E. D., Jr. (1987) *Cultural Literacy: What Every American Needs to Know.* New York: Random House.

Hobbs, Renee (2009) Best Practices Help End Copyright Confusion, *The Council Chronicle* March 2009: 12–14. Retrieved on 22 September 2010 from http://www.ncte.org/library/NCTEFiles/Resources/Magazine/CC0183_Best%20Practice.pdf.

Hooper, Meredith (1998) *The Drop in My Drink: The Story of Water on Our Planet.* New York: Penguin Group.

Houston, Gloria (2004) *How Writing Works.* Boston: Allyn & Bacon.

Inness, Sherrie A. (1998) *Delinquents and Debutantes: Twentieth-Century American Girls' Cultures.* New York: New York University Press.

International Reading Association / National Council of Teachers of English Joint Task Force on Assessment (1994) *Standards of the Assessment of Reading and Writing*. Newark, Delaware: International Reading Association, and Urbana, Illinois: National Council of Teachers of English.

Jacobs, Heidi Hayes (ed.) (2010) *Curriculum 21: Essential Education for a Changing World*. Alexandria, Virginia: Association for Supervision and Curriculum Development.

James, William (1890) *The Principles of Psychology* (2 Vols.). New York: Henry Holt. Retrieved on 13 July 2011 from http://books.google.com/books/about/The_principles_of_psychology.html?d=HRwuAAAAIAAJ.

Kajder, Sara B. (2003) *The Tech-Savvy English Classroom*. Portland, Maine: Stenhouse.

Kajder, Sara B. (2010) *Adolescents and Digital Literacies: Learning Alongside Our Students*. Urbana, Illinois: National Council of Teachers of English.

Kasten, Wendy C., Kirsto, Janice V., McClure, Amy A. and Garthwait, Abigail (2005) *Living Literature: Using Children's Literature to Support Reading and Language Arts*. Upper Saddle River, New Jersey: Pearson Education.

Kaywell, Joan F. (2007) *Dear Author: Letters of Hope Top Young Adult Authors Respond to Kids' Toughest Issues*. New York: Penguin Young Readers Group.

Kennedy, Robert F. (1968) Remarks at the University of Kansas, March 18, 1968.

Kist, William (2010) *The Socially Networked Classroom: Teaching in the New Media Age*. Thousand Oaks, California: Corwin.

Kohn, Alfie (2006) The trouble with rubrics. *English Journal* 95(4): 12–15.

Kozol, Jonathan (1972) *Free Schools*. Boston: Houghton Mifflin Co.

Krashen, Stephen (2008) A fundamental principle: No unnecessary testing (NUT). *The Colorado Communicator* 32(1): 7.

Kruch, Mary Anna (Spring, 2001) Slaying the MEAP monster. *Language Arts Journal of Michigan* 18–22. Mount Pleasant, Michigan: Michigan Council of Teachers of English.

Kruch, Mary Anna (2007) The human face of war. *English Language Arts Vignette Project*. Lansing, Michigan: Michigan Department of Education.

Kruch, Mary Anna (September, 2009) Teaching tips: Apples for your teaching eye. *The Michigan English Teacher (EMET)*. Retrieved on 10 October 2009 at http://mienglishteacher.ning.com/page/publications.

Lain, Sheryl (2007) Reaffirming the writing workshop for young adolescents. *Voices from the Middle* 14(3): 20–28.

Laneuville, Eric (Director) and Roman, Lawrence (Writer) (1993) *The Ernest Green Story*. Glendale, California: Buena Vista International/Walt Disney Television.

Lantolf, James P. (2000) *Sociocultural Theory and Secondary Language Learning*. Oxford: Oxford University Press.

Larcom, Lucy (1879) "Plant a Tree." New York: Houghton-Mifflin. Retrieved on 13 July 2011 from http://www.marinrose.org/poemmarch.html.

Lee, Carol D. and Smagorinsky, Peter (2000) *Vygotskian Perspectives on Literacy Research: Constructing Meaning through Collaborative Inquiry*. Cambridge, U. K.: Cambridge University Press.

Lee, Dorris M. and Allen, R. V. (1963) *Learning to Read through Experience* (2nd edition). New York: Meredith Publishing Company.

Lenhart, Amanda, Arafeh, Sousan, Smith, Aaron and Macgill, Alexandra Rankin (April 2008) *Writing, Technology, and Teens*. College Board National Commission on Writing. Washington, D. C.: PEW Internet & American Life Project. Retrieved on 9 December 2009 from http://www.pewinternet.org/.

London, Jack (1915) *The Call of the Wild*. New York: Grosset & Dunlap.

London, Jack (1986) To build a fire. *To Build a Fire and Other Stories*. New York: Bantam Classics.

Manzo, Kathleen Kennedy (2008) Motivating students in the middle years. *Education Week* (March 19, 2008) Retrieved on 19 March 2008 from http://www.cdwcck.org/wc/articles/2008/03/19/28middle_cp.h27.html.

Martin, Jacqueline Briggs (1998) *Snowflake Bentley* (illus. Mary Azarian). New York: Houghton Mifflin Books for Children.

Maslow, Abraham Harold (1970) *Motivation and Personality* (2nd edition). New York: Harper & Row.

McClelland, David, Atkinson, John, Clark, Russell A. and Lowell, Edgar L. (1976) *The Achievement Motive*. New York: Irvington Publishers.

McClelland, David C. (1972) *What is the effect of achievement motivation training in the schools?* Teachers College Record *74(2) 129–146 Retrieved on 30 March 2008 from http://www.tcrecord.org ID Number: 1537.

McCombs, Barbara L. and Whisler, Jo Sue (1997) *The Learner-Centered Classroom and School: Strategies for Increasing Student Motivation and Achievement*. San Francisco: Jossey-Bass Publishers.

McCracken, Robert A. (1971) Initiating sustained silent reading, *Journal of Reading* 14(8): 521–524, 582–583. International Reading Association. Retrieved on 7 December 2010 from http://www.jstor.org/40009700.

McKinney, Barbara Shaw (1998) *A Drop Around the World*. Nevada City, California: Dawn Publications.

McLeod, Gregory (2003) Learning theory and instructional design. *Learning Matters* 35(4): 282–288. Durham, North Carolina: Durham Technical Community College. Retrieved on 13 May 2008 from http://courses.durhamtech.edu/tlc/www/html/Resources/Learning_Matters.htm.

Mendler, Allen N. (2000) *Motivating Students Who Don't Care: Successful Techniques for Educators*. Bloomington, Indiana: Solution Tree.

Michigan Council of Teachers of English Ning (2011) Retrieved on 21 March 2011 from www.mcte.info.

Michigan Department of Education (2005) *Michigan's Genre Project*. Retrieved on 1 September 2009 from www.michigan.gov/documents/mde/Genre_Project_197249_7.pdf.

Michigan Department of Education (2011a) K–12 Curriculum and Standards Web page. Retrieved on 17 April 2011 from http://www.michigan.gov/mde/0,1607,7-140-28753–,00/html.

Michigan Department of Education (2011b) *Sixth Grade English Language Arts Grade Level Content Expectations*. Retrieved on 17 April 2011 from 6th_ELA-Intro_Ltrweb_135114_7[1]. pdf.

Michigan Department of Education (2011c) *Grade Level Content Expectations* Retrieved on 17 April 2011 from http://www.michigan.gov/documents/ELS_06_87359_7.pdf.

Ministry of Education, Australia (1992) *Dancing with the Pen: The Learner as Writer*. Wellington, New Zealand: Learning Media, Ltd.

Mitchell, Diana and Christenbury, Leila (2000) *Both Art and Craft: Teaching Ideas That Spark Learning*. Urbana, Illinois: National Council of Teachers of English

Morrison, Gary R., Ross, Steven M. and Kemp, Jerrold E. (2001) *Designing Effective Instruction* (3rd edition). New York: John Wiley and Sons

Muller, Chandra (2001) The role of caring in the teacher-student relationship for at-risk students. *Sociological Inquiry* 71: 241–255.

Munch, Edvard (1895) "The Scream." Retrieved on 30 August 2010 from http://www.edvard-munch.com/gallery/anxiety/scream.htm.

Murray, Donald M. (1984) *Write to Learn*. Fort Worth, Texas: Holt, Rinehart, & Winston.

Murray, Donald M. (1996) *Crafting a Life in Essay, Story, Poem*. Portsmouth, New Hampshire: Boynton/Cook Publishers.

Murray, Donald M. (2002) *Write to Learn* (7th edition). Belmont, California: Wadsworth Publishing.

National Commission on Writing (2008) *Writing, Technology, and Teens*. Retrieved on 12 December 2009 from http://www.pewinternet.org.

National Council of Teachers of English Executive Committee Writing Study Group (November, 2004) *NCTE Beliefs about the Teaching of Writing*. Retrieved on 20 December 2008 from http://www.ncte.org/positions/statements/writingbeliefs.

National Council of Teachers of English (2004) *Framing Statements on Assessment: Revised Report of the Assessment and Testing Study Group of the NCTE Executive Committee*. Retrieved on 14 December 2009 from http://ncte.org/print.asp?id=11887andnode=1381.

National Council of Teachers of English (2006) *Writing Assessment: A Position Statement*. Conference on College Composition and Communication (CCCC) Position Paper. Retrieved on 1 June 2009 from http://www.ncte.org/cccc/resources/positions/writingassessment.

National Council of Teachers of English (2008a) *Resolution on Scripted Curricula*. From The NCTE Position Statement of the NCTE Executive Committee. Retrieved on 20 December 2009 from http://www.ncte.org/positions/statements/scriptedcurricula.

National Council of Teachers of English (2008b) NCTE *Guideline: 2008 NCTE Legislative Platform*. Retrieved on 18 May 2011 from http://www.ncte.org/positions/statements/2008legisplatform. Urbana, Illinois: National Council of Teachers of English.

National Council of Teachers of English Executive Committee (September, 2008) *Writing Now: A Policy Brief*. Urbana, Illinois: National Council of Teachers of English.

National Writing Project (2006) *Local Site Research Initiative Report: Cohort II, 2004–2005*. Berkeley: National Writing Project, University of California. Retrieved on 22 April 2010 from www.nwp.org/cs/public/download/nwp_file/10381/LSRI_III.pdf?x-r=pcfile_d.

Nettles, Diane H. (2006) *Comprehensive Literacy Instruction in Today's Classrooms: The Whole, the Heart, and the Parts*. Boston, Massachusetts: Allyn & Bacon.

Noguchi, Rei (1991) *Grammar and the Teaching of Writing: Limits and Possibilities*. Urbana, Illinois: National Council of Teachers of English.

Null, Kathleen (1998) *How to Write a Poem*. Huntington Beach, California: Teacher Created Materials, Inc.

Oronson, Deb (2009) Online writing instruction: no longer a novelty. *The Council Chronicle* 19(2): 18–21.

Palmer, Parker (1998) The *Courage to Teach: Exploring the Inner Landscape of a Teacher's Life*. San Francisco: Jossey-Bass, Publishers.

Pantel, Christian (1997) *Educational Theory: A Framework for Comparing Web-Based Learning Environments*. Chapter 2, Education theory 11–39. Unpublished Masters Thesis: Simon Fraser University.

Paulsen, Gary (1986) *Hatchet*. New York: Simon & Schuster.

Paulsen, Gary (1993) *The River*. New York: Yearling.

PC Magazine Encyclopedia (2010) Definition of podcast. The Computer Language Company Inc. Retrieved on 15 April 2010 from http://pcmag.com/encyclopedia_term/02542,t=podcast&I=49433.

Peck, Richard (1986) *Remembering the Good Times*. New York: Laurel Leaf.

Peale, Norman Vincent (1982) *Positive Imaging*. Pawling, New York: Foundation for Christian Living.

Piaget, Jean (2007) *The Child's Conception of the World: A 20th-Century Classic of Child Psychology* (trans. Joan Tomlinson and Andrew Tomlinson). New York: Rowman and Littlefield.

Piaget, Jean and Inhelder, Barbara (1969/2000) *The Psychology of the Child*. New York: Basic Books – Perseus.

Pipher, Mary (1995) *Reviving Ophelia: Saving the Selves of Adolescent Girls* New York: Ballantine Books.

Poe, Edgar Allan (1843/1984) "The Telltale Heart." *Complete Stories and Poems of Edgar Allan Poe*: 121–124. New York: Doubleday. Originally published in *The Pioneer* January 1843 (ed. James Russell Lowell.), Cambridge, Massachusetts.

Poe, Edgar Allen (1965) *Edgar Allan Poe*, Volume 3: *Basil Rathbone Reads The Telltale Heart, The Fall of the House of Usher, The Bells, The Haunted Palace*. New York: Caedmon Records, Book Printing, & Publishing.

Polette, Keith (2005) *Read & Write It Out Loud! Guided Oral Literacy Strategies*. Boston: Pearson.

Poole, John (2011) True to ourselves: Effective writing practice in a No Child Left Behind world. *Writing & Pedagogy* 3(1): 131–140.

Postman, Neil and Weingartner, Charles (1969) *Teaching as a Subversive Activity*. New York: Dell Publishing Co., Inc.

Prabhu, Maya T. (2010) Teachers' digital media use on the rise, *eSchool News*. Retrieved on 19 January 2010 from *www.eschoolnews.com/2010/.../survey-teachers-digital-media-use-is-increasing*.

Ray, Katie Wood (2002) *What You Know by Heart: How to Develop Curriculum for Your Writing Workshop*. Portsmouth, New Hampshire: Heinemann.

ReadWriteThink.Org (2011) International Reading Association, National Council of Teachers of English, and Verizon. Retrieved on 24 January, 2011 from http://www.*readwritethink*.org/.

Roberts, Candace (2009) Professional development and high-stakes testing: Disparate influences on student writing performance. *Writing & Pedagogy* 1(1): 63–88.

Romano, Louis G. and Georgiady, Nicholas P. (1994) *Building an Effective Middle School*. Dubuque, Iowa: Wm. C. Brown Communications, Inc.

Rose, Mike (2009) 21st century skills: Education's new cliché. *Truthdig*. Retrieved on 8 March 2010 at www.truthdig.com/.../21st_century_skills_educations_new_cliche_20091208/.

Rosenblatt, Louise M. (1978) *The Reader, the Text, the Poem: The Transactional Theory of the Literary Work*. Carbondale, Illinois: Southern Illinois University Press.

Rosenblatt, Louise M. (1988) *Writing and Reading: The Transactional Theory*. National Center for the Study of Writing and Literacy Technical Report. Washington, D. C.: U. S. Department of Education.

Roser, Nancy L. and Martinez, Miriam G. (eds.) (2005) *What a Character! Character Study as a Guide to Literary Meaning Making in Grades K–8*. Newark, Delaware: International Reading Association.

Routman, Regie (2000) *Conversations: Strategies for Teaching, Learning, and Evaluating*. Portsmouth, New Hampshire: Heinemann.

Rozema, Robert and Webb, Allen (2008) *Literature and the Web: Reading and Responding with New Technologies*. Portsmouth, New Hampshire: Heinemann.

Sargent, Sandie (2011) A view of education reform from across the pond. *Writing & Pedagogy* 3(1): 141–151.

Satir, Virginia (1972) *Peoplemaking*. Palo Alto, California: Science & Behavior Books.

Scope Magazine. St. Jefferson City, Missouri: Scholastic Inc.

SearchCloudComputing.com (2010) Cloud computing. Retrieved on 21 April 2010 from http://searchcloudcomputing.techtarget.com/sDefinition/0,,sid201_gci1287881,00.html.

Shanahan, Timothy (2008, February 22) Making a difference means making it different. *Literacy Learning: Timothy Shanahan's Weblog*. Retrieved on 4 March 2008 from http://www.shanahanonliteracy.com/2008/02/making-difference-means-making-it.html.

Shea, Mary (2006) Where's *the Glitch? How to Use Running Records with Older Readers, Grades 5–8*. Portsmouth, New Hampshire: Heinemann.

Silberman, Charles E. (ed.) (1973) *The Open Classroom Reader*. New York: Vintage Books.

Silverstein, Shel (1981) "Whatif." *A Light in the Attic*. New York: HarperCollins Publishers.

Sipe, Rebecca Bowers and Rosewarne, Tracy (2006) *Purposeful Writing: Genre Study in the Secondary Writing Workshop*. Portsmouth, New Hampshire: Heinemann.

Skinner, B. F. (2002) *Beyond Freedom and Dignity*. Cambridge, Massachusetts: Hackett Publishing Co.

Smith, Michael W. and Wilhelm, Jeffrey D. (2006) *Going with the Flow: How to Engage Boys (and Girls) in Their Literacy Learning*. Portsmouth, New Hampshire: Heinemann.

Smith, Rachel, Johnson, Laurence F., Brown, Malcolm B. and Levine, Alan (2010) *2010 Horizon Report: K–12 Edition*. Retrieved on 21 September2010 from www.nmc.org/pdf/2010-Horizon-Report-K12pdf.

Smith, Theodore R. (1982) *Handbook for Planning an Effective Writing Program: Kindergarten through Grade Twelve*. Sacramento: California State Department of Education.

Soifer, Avian (1995) *Law and the Company We Keep*. Boston: Harvard University Press.

Soto, Gary (2003) "Street Scene on the Fulton Mall." In *One Kind of Faith*. San Francisco, California: Chronicle Books.

Spinelli, Jerry (2000) Star *Girl*. New York: Alfred A. Knopf.

Sprenger, Marilee (2008) *Differentiation through Learning Styles and Memory* (2nd edition). Thousand Oaks, California: Corwin Press.

Stiggins, Richard J. (2005) *Student-Involved Assessment for Learning*. Upper Saddle River, New Jersey: Pearson.

Stock, Patricia L. (ed.) (1983) *Forum: Essays on Theory and Practice in the Teaching of Writing*. Portsmouth, New Hampshire: Boynton/Cook.

Stock, Patricia L. (1995) *The Dialogic Curriculum*. Portsmouth, New Hampshire: Heinemann.

Stevenson, Robert Louis (1926) *Kidnapped* (illus. Frances Brundage). Akron, Ohio: The Saalfield Publishing Co.

Strommen, Erik F. and Lincoln, Bruce (1992) Constructivism, technology, and the future of classroom learning. *Education and Urban Society* 24(4): 466–476. New York: Children's Television Workshop.

Sullivan, Susan and Glanz, Jeffrey (2006) *Building Effective Learning Communities*. Thousand Oaks, California: Corwin Press.

Teachers Domain (2011) National Science Digital Library. Retrieved on 24 January, 2011 from http://www.teachersdomain.org/resources 05.sci.ess.watercyc.Ip_watercycle/.

Texas Community College Teachers Association (2002) *Teaching and Assessing for Critical Thinking and Deep Learning*. Participant packet for Teleconference on 22 February 2002.

Tinzmann, Margaret B., Jones, Beau F., Fennimore, Todd F., Bakker, J., Pierce, Jean and Fine, Carol (1990) What is the collaborative classroom? Oak Brook, Illinois: North Central Regional Educational Laboratory. Retrieved on 20 July 2010 from http://www.arp.sprnet.org/admin/supt/collab2.htm.

Tomlinson, Carol Ann (1999) *The Differentiated Classroom: Responding to the Needs of All Learners*. Alexandria, Virginia: Association for the Supervision of Curriculum Development.

Tomlinson, Carol Ann (2004) *How to Differentiate Instruction in Mixed Ability Classrooms* (2nd edition). Alexandria, Virginia: Association for the Supervision of Curriculum Development.

Tremmel, Michelle (2009) Digital response to "Should best practice guide our instruction or MEAP preparation?" RCWPMSU@list.msu.edu (17 October 2009). Retrieved on 18 October 2009 from https://mail.google.com/mail/?ui=2#all/12455d4e166657cf.

Valdez, Veronica E. and Callahan, Rebecca M. (2011) Who is learning language in today's school? In Diane Lapp and Douglas Fisher (eds.) *Handbook of Research on* Teaching *the English Language Arts* (3rd edition) 3–9. New York: Routledge.

Vanderpool, Clare (2010) *Moon Over Manifest*. New York: Delacorte Press.

Van Dusen, Christine (2009) Beyond virtual schools. *eSchoolNews*, Nov/Dec 2009: 22. Bethesda, Maryland: eSchool Media.

Van Horn, Leigh (2008) R*eading Photographs to Write with Meaning and Purpose, Grades 4–12*. Newark, Delaware: International Reading Association.

Vygotsky, Lev S. (1978) *Mind in Society: The Development of Higher Psychological Processes* (eds. Michael Cole, Vera John-Steiner, Sylvia Scribner and Ellen Souberman). Cambridge, Massachusetts: Harvard University Press.

Warnock, Scott (2009) *Teaching Writing Online: How & Why*. Urbana, Illinois: National Council of Teachers of English.

Warriner, John E. (1988) English *Grammar and Composition*. New York: Harcourt Brace Jovanovich.

Weaver, Constance (1996) *Teaching Grammar in Context*. Portsmouth, New Hampshire: Heinemann.

Weaver, Constance (ed.) (1998) *Lessons to Share on Teaching Grammar in Context*. Portsmouth, New Hampshire: Heinemann.

Webb, Patricia Kimberley (1980) Piaget: Implications for teaching. *Theory into Practice* 19(2): 93–97.

Webheads in Action.org (2011) Retrieved on 15 April 2011 from http://webheadsinaction.org/.

Weiner, Bernard (1985) *Human Motivation* (2nd edition). New York: Springer Publishing.

Whelan, Gloria (2004) *Friend on Freedom River*. Chelsea, Michigan: Sleeping Bear Press.

Whitaker, Todd and Lumpa, Dale (2005) *Great Quotes for Great Educators*. Larchmont, New York: Eye on Education.

Whitney, Anne (2008) Teacher transformation in the National Writing Project. *Research in the Teaching of English* 42(2): 144–187.

Williams, Robin (2008) The Non-Designer's Design Book: Design and Typographic Principles for the Visual Novice (3rd edition). Berkeley, California: Peachpit Press.

Wilmarth, Stephen (2010) Five socio-technology trends that change everything in learning and teaching. In Heidi Hayes Jacobs (ed.) *Curriculum 21: Essential Education for a Changing World*: 80–96. Alexandria, Virginia: Association of Supervision and Curriculum Development.

Wink, Joan (2000) *Critical Pedagogy: Notes from the Real World*. Boston: Allyn & Bacon.

Wright, Frank Lloyd and Pfeiffer, Bruce Brooks (1995) *Collected Writings* (Vol. 2). New York: Rizzoli Publishing.

Writing Study Group of the NCTE Executive Committee (November 2004) NCTE Beliefs about the Teaching of Writing. Retrieved on 19 October 2009 from http://www.ncte.org/positions/statements/writingbeliefs.

Yagelski, Robert P. (2009) A thousand writers writing: Seeking change through the radical practice of writing as a way of being, *English Education* 42(1): 6–28.

Zehr, Mary Ann (2007) Interactivity seen as key. *Education Weekly's Digital Directions* 1(29). Retrieved on 1 April 2008 from http://www.edweek.org/dd/articles/2007/09/12/02ell.h01.html?qs=writing+technology.

Zemelman, Steven and Daniels, Harvey (1998) A *Community of Writers: Teaching Writing in the Junior and Senior High School.* Portsmouth, New Hampshire: Heinemann.

Zinsser, William (1990) *On Writing Well* (4th edition). New York: HarperCollins.

Appendix A

Books with Strong, Positive, Global Characters

Young Adult

Abdel-Fattah, Randa (2008) *Does My Head Look Big in This?* New York: Scholastic Paperbacks (Reprint edition).
Alexie, Sherman (2009) *The Absolutely True Diary of a Part-Time Indian.* New York: Little, Brown Books for Young Readers (Reprint edition).
Anderson, Laurie Halse (1999) *Speak.* New York: Penguin Group.
Anderson, Laurie Halse (2009) *Winter Girls.* New York: Viking.
Lockhart, E. (2008) *Disreputable History of Frankie Landau Banks.* New York: Hyperion Books for Children. (Also writes under the name of Emily Jenkins)
Borton de Trevino, Elizabeth (1965) *I, Juan de Pareja.* New York: Square Fish (MacMillan).
Choi, Sook Nyul (1991) *Year of Impossible Goodbyes.* New York: Houghton Mifflin.
Cole, Sheila (1991, 2005) *The Dragon in the Cliff: A Novel Based on the Life of Mary Anning.* Lincoln, Nebraska: iUniverse, Inc.
Collins, Suzanne (2008) *Hunger Games.* New York: Scholastic Press.
Crew, Linda (1991) *Children of the River.* New York: Laurel Leaf.
Crutcher, Chris (1989) *Athletic Shorts.* New York: HarperCollins Children's Books.
Crutcher, Chris (2001) *Whale Talk.* New York: Laurel-Leaf.
Curtis, Christopher Paul (2004) *Bucking the Sarge.* New York: Wendy Lamb Books.

Curtis, Christopher Paul (1999) *Bud, Not Buddy.* New York: Delacourte Press.
Draper, Sharon M. (2006) *Copper Sun.* New York: Atheneum Books for Young Readers.
Estes, Eleanor (1944, 1972) *The Hundred Dresses* (illus., Louis Slobodkin). Orlando, Florida: Harcourt Inc.
Fritz, Jean (1982) *Homesick: My Own Story.* New York: Puffin Books.
Garrique, Sheila (1994) *The Eternal Spring of Mr. Ito.* Madison, Wisconsin: Demco Media.
Gaskins, Pearl Fuyo (1999) *What Are You? Voices of Mixed Race Young People.* New York: Henry Holt & Co.
Hodge, Merle (1994) *For the Life of Laetitia.* New York: Farrar, Straus and Giroux.
Jimenez, Francisco (1977) *The Circuit: Stories from the Life of a Migrant Child.* New York: Houghton Mifflin.
Kephart, Beth (2009) *Nothing But Ghosts.* New York: HarperCollins Children's Books.
Konigsburg, E. L. (2004) *The Outcasts of 19 Schuyler Place.* New York: Antheum Books for Young Readers.
Laird, Elizabeth (1991) *Kiss the Dust.* New York: Puffin Books.
Buss, Fran Leeper [with the assistance of Daily Cubias] (1991) *Journey of the Sparrows* New York: Puffin Books.
Myers, Walter Dean (2001) *Monster.* New York: Amistad.
Pfeffer, Susan Beth (2006) *Life as We Knew It.* Orlando, Florida: Harcourt, Inc.
Rinaldi, Ann (1992) A *Break from Charity.* Orlando, Florida: Harcourt, Inc.
Ryan, Pam Munoz (2000) *Esperanza Rising.* New York: Scholastic Inc.
Schmidt, Gary D. (2004) *Lizzie Bright and the Buckminster Boy.* New York: Laurel-Leaf.
Soto, Gary (1990) *Baseball in April.* San Diego, California: Harcourt, Inc.
Stead, Rebecca (2009) *When You Reach Me.* New York: Wendy Lamb Books.
Stockett, Kathlyn (2009) *The Help.* New York: Amy Finhorn Books (Penguin).
Voight, Cynthia (1982) *Dicey's Song.* New York: Antheum Books for Young Readers.
Voight, Cynthia (1981) *Homecoming.* New York: Aladdin Paperbacks.

Woodson, Jacqueline (2000) *Miracle's Boys.* New York: G. P. Putnam's Sons.
Yolen, Jane (1988) *The Devil's Arithmetic.* New York: Viking.
Zusak, Markus (2005) *The Book Thief.* New York: Random House Children's Books.

Children's Literature and Picture Books

Coerr, Eleanor (1993) *Sadako.* Illus. by Ed Young. New York: Putnam.
Hopkinson, Deborah (1993) *Sweet Clara and the Freedom Quilt.* Illus. James Ransome. New York: Alfred Knopf.
Polacco, Patricia (2000) *The Butterfly.* New York: Philomel.
Woodson, Jacqueline (2001) *The Other Side.* Illus. by E. B. White. New York: Putnam.
Yolen, Jane (1998) *The Ballad of the Pirate Queens.* Illus. by David Shannon. San Diego: Harcourt Brace.
Yolen, Jane (2002) *Hippolyta and the Curse of the Amazons.* New York: HarperCollins.
Yolen, Jane (1992) *Letting Swift River Go.* Illus. Barbara Cooney. Boston: Little Brown.

Appendix B
Suggested Resources for "War" Theme

Middle School and Young Adult

Peace and Social Justice

http://www.education.wisc.edu/ccbc/books/detailListBooks.asp?id BookLists=77.

Lang, Jonny (2003) Dying to live on *Long Time* Coming. Santa Monica, California: A&M Records.

Green Day (2004) Wake me up when September ends on *American Idiot*. Burbank, California: Reprise Records.

Survival

http://www.education.wisc.edu/ccbc/books/detailListBooks.asp?id BookLists=94.

Vietnam War

Buffalo Springfield (1972) For what it's worth on *Retrospective: Best of Buffalo Springfield*. New York: Atlantic Records (vinyl) or (1990) New York: Elektra/Wea (CD).

Sierre Leone's Civil War

Ishmael Beah (2008) *A Long Way Gone: Memoirs of a Boy Soldier*. Logan, Iowa: Perfection Learning.

Bosnian Conflict

Filipovic, Zlata, and Pribichevich-Zoric, Christina (2006) Zlata's *Diary: A Child's Life in Wartime Sarajevo*. New York: Penguin Group.

Holocaust and WWII

Foreman, Michael (2006) *War Game: Village Green to No-Man's-Land*. London, United Kingdom: Anova Books.
Hughes, Dean (2003) *Soldier's Boy*. New York: Simon Pulse.
Bruchac, Joseph (2006) *Code Talker: A Novel About the Navajo Marines of World War Two*. New York: Speak (Penguin's Young Readers Group).
http://www.education.wisc.edu/ccbc/books/detailListBooks.asp?idBookLists=274.
http://www.hclib.org/teens/booklistaction.cfm?list_num=117.

The Spanish-American War

Conroy, Robert (1968) *The Battle of Manila Bay – The Spanish American War in the Philippines*. New York: MacMillan Company. (This book is for young adults).

Elementary

Peace and Social Justice

http://www.education.wisc.edu/ccbc/books/detailListBooks.asp?idBookLists=77.

Survival

http://www.education.wisc.edu/ccbc/books/detailListBooks.asp?idBookLists=94.

WW1

Granfield, Linda (2005) *Where Poppies Grow*. Markham, Ontario (Canada) Fitzhenry and Whiteside.

Holocaust and WWII

Giff, Patricia Reilly (1999) *Lily's Crossing*. New York: Random House Children's Books.

Zusak, Markus (2007) *The Book Thief*. New York: Random House Children's Books.

http://www.education.wisc.edu/ccbc/books/detailListBooks.asp?idBookLists=274.

http://www.monroe.lib.in.us/childrens/wwiibib.html.

The Spanish-American War

Collins, Mary (1998) *The Spanish-American War: Cornerstones of Freedom*. New York: Children's Press. (Reading level: Ages 9–12)

Gay, Kathryn and Martin K. Gay (1995) *Spanish American War (America at War Series)*. Minneapolis, Minnesota: Twenty First Century Books. (Reading level: Ages 9–12)

McNeese, Tim (2001) *Remember the Maine: Spanish-American War Begins (First Battles)*. Greensboro, North Carolina: Morgan Reynolds Publishing.

Appendix C

Gray (ADVERB) Activity Cards "You Be the Sentence" Lesson, Chapter 5

rapidly	very	basically
sweetly	hardly	mightily
remarkably	merely	hungrily
sloppily	dazedly	erroneously
automatically	beautifully	carefully
divisively	eagerly	frighteningly
anonymously	hurriedly	incredibly
jokingly	kinesthetically	insanely
laboriously	markedly	noisily
optimistically	prettily	rudely

Appendix D

Pink (SUBJECT) Activity Cards "You Be the Sentence" Lesson, Chapter 5

Dora the Explorer	Castle	*Alice in Wonderland*
ice cream	Donald Duck	Lady Gaga
Eminem	macaroni	Justin Timberlake
Big Ben	*American Idol*	elephant
headband	Robert Patin	iPad
Harry Potter	Mama	porch
laptop	magician	triangle
hula hoop	bracelet	Captain Hook
The Prime Minister	The President	*New Moon*
Shel Silverstein	toad	jump rope

Appendix E

Blue Activity Cards for "You Be the Sentence" Lesson, Chapter 5

forget	remind	persuade
misunderstand	hear	yap
die	ingratiate	feel
bounce	tip-toe	swim
drift	sigh	contemplate
dance	stand	swing
steal	smell	taste
stray	wave	drown
hope	prevent	wish
pray	dream	skip
migrate	laugh	trace

Appendix F

Green Activity Cards "You Be the Sentence" Lesson, Chapter 5

yellow	sweet	mighty
incredible	fruity	awesome
rude	greedy	disgusting
soulful	loud	regretful
delusional	speedy	sour
bright	fluffy	gigantic
ravenous	absent	drooling
idiotic	cheerful	large
unbelievable	serene	kind
woeful	magical	obnoxious
scrumptious	buttery	scared
hopeful	tiny	belated

Appendix G
Pink (PHRASES) Activity Cards "You Be the Sentence" Lesson, Chapter 5

around the bend	with a black eye	about here
after midnight	along the shore	against the wind
by The Beatles	down by the riverside	during intermission
of lettuce	into the dark	up his nose
down Memory Lane	under my thumb	over the rainbow
among the lions	on the left side	between the eyes
in heaven	In the mashed potatoes	under the chair
in a fit	of anger	aboard *Titanic*
beyond my reach	off the wall	inside the house
if I grow horns	while I sing	when I'm 64

Author Index

Albers, Peggy 147
Alcott, Louisa May 129
Alexie, Sherman 33, 213
Allen, Bay Wilson 185
Allen, Janet 25
Allen, R. V. 20
Alpert, Herb 168
Alschuler, Alfred S. 92
Anderman, Eric M. 88
Anderson, Laurie Halse 331
Angelou, Maya 215
Arafeh, Sousan 241
Atkinson, John 3, 91
Atwell, Nancie xvi, 20, 68, 79, 212

Baez, Joan 215
Bakker, J. 67
Ballew, Arlette C. 122–23
Bamberg, Betty 287
Barr, Mary A. 290–92, 295
Barrs, Myra 290, 291, 292
Bartlett, Lora 102
Bennet, Cherie 214
Bennett, Randy Elliot 317
Bentley, William A. 167–72
Berryman, Julia C. 55
Bizar, Marilyn 280
Blume, Judy 32, 213
Bobek, Becky L. 103
Bomer, Katherine 147
Boyd, Thomas A. 237, 277
Briers, Gary E. 102
Brophy, Jere 88, 89
Brown, Malcolm B. 275
Buckelew, Mary Bellucci 179
Buckner, Aimee 289

Burke, Jim 14, 254
Burnett, Frances Hodgson 173, 304
Byrk, Anthony 106–107

Calkins, Lucy McCormick 20
Callahan, Rebecca M. 286
Cappelli, Rose 148–49
Carbo, Marie 3, 12
Carol, Pamela Sissi 147
Carson, Rachel 174
Chancer, Joni 147
Chickering, Arthur W. 36–37
Chrenka, Lynn 276
Christenbury, Leila 147
Christensen, Linda 333
Clark, Harry Hayden 185
Clark, Irene 287
Clark, Russell A. 3, 91
Clay, Marie M. 289
Cleary, Beverly 213
Clinton, Hillary 196
Clinton, William J. 51
Close, Elizabeth 147
Coerr, Eleanor 173
Craig, Dana A. 290, 295
Crawford, Linda 147
Crosby, Stills, Nash, and Young 233
Crutcher, Chris 32, 213, 214, 331
Csikszentmihalyi, Mihaly 126
Curtis, Christopher Paul 33, 213

Dahl, Roald 222–23
Daniels, Harvey 17–18, 27, 218–19, 280
Darling-Hammond, Linda 68

DaVinci, Leonardo 135
DeCharms, Richard 91, 93
Delandshere, Ginette 296–97
Derek Truck Band 168
Dewey, John 3, 19, 20, 44, 45
DiCamillo, Kate 32
Dorfman, Lynne R. 148–49
Dörnyei, Zoltan 97–98
Dunn, Kenneth 3, 13
Dunn, Rita 3, 13
Duncan, Lois 213

Eccles, Jacquelynne S. 87, 91
Edwards, M. Craig 102
Eichorn, Donald H. 14
Elkind, David 23, 46
Ellis, Sue 290, 292
Emerson, Ralph Waldo 185–87
Emig, Janet 3, 20
Enos, Theresa 176
Ericcson, K. Anders 28
Evans, Karen S. 147

Fennimore, Todd F. 67
Fine, Carla 121
Fine, Carol 67
Fisette, Dolores 290, 295
Fletcher, Ralph 20, 76, 124, 232
Foreman, Michael 63–64, 375
Frost, Robert 215, 256

Gage, Nathaniel L. 36
Gallagher, Kelly 212, 308–10
Gamson, F. Zelda 36–37
Gardner, Howard 197
Garthwait, Abigail 147
Gay, Geneva 97, 376
Geisel, Theodore (Dr. Seuss) 174
Geller, Conrad 255
Georgiady, Nicholas P. 3, 14, 31, 35, 38, 50
Glanz, Jeffrey 55

Goodlad, John 21
Goodman, Kenneth 289
Goodman, Yetta 289
Gordon, Michael xxv, 328, 349–51
Graves, Donald H. 20, 303
Green Day 173, 374
Gunnery, Sylvia 157
Gurian, Michael 122–23

Hall, Maureen P. 57
Hansen, Jane 311
Harmon, Rebecca 229
Harvey, Stephanie 219
Haskell, Robert 125–26
Heard, Georgia 147
Hester, Hilary 290, 292
Hicks, Troy 42, 250–52, 266, 270–71, 273–74
Hillocks, George, Jr. 190, 230
Hirsch, E. D., Jr. 21
Hobbs, Rene 270
Hooper, Meredith 229
Houston, Gloria 95
Holmes, Oliver Wendell 279
Hunt, Lyman C., Jr. 13

Inhelder, Barbara 111, 319
Inness, Sherrie A. 121
International Reading Association 147, 229, 312, 346

Jacobs, Heidi Hayes 243
James, William 176
Johnson, Laurence F. 275
Joiner, Richard 55
Jones, Beau F. 67
Jones, Nora 215

Kajder, Sara B. 250, 258,
Kasten, Wendy C. 147
Kaywell, Joan F. 214
Kemp, Jerrold E. 54

Kennedy, Robert F. 326, 327, 338–39
Kettering, Charles F. 237, 242, 264, 277
King, Martin Luther, Jr. 225
Kirsto, Janice V. 147
Kist, William 250, 262
Kittle, Penny 303
Kohn, Alfie 206
Kozol, Jonathan 23
Krashen, Stephen 206
Kruch, Mary Anna 62, 66, 207, 217, 257, 282, 283

Lady Gaga 232
Lain, Sheryl 76–77
Lamont, Alexandra 55
Lang, Jonny 63–64, 374
Lantolf, James P. 56
Larcom, Lucy 1
Lee, Carol D. 55
Lee, Doris M. 20
Legend, John 168
Lenhart, Amanda 241
Levine, Alan 275
Lincoln, Bruce 258
London, Jack 173
Lowell, Edgar L. 3, 91
Lumpa, Dale 279

Macgill, Alexandra Rankin 241
McClelland, David 3, 7, 84, 91–94, 134
McClure, Amy A. 147
McCombs, Barbara L. 26, 222
McCrachen, Robert A. 13
McIntyre, James 92
McKinney, Barbara Shaw 228
McLeod, Gregory 54
Maehr, Martin L. 88
Mancini, Henry 168
Manzo, Kathleen Kennedy 80

Martin, Jacqueline Briggs 172
Martinez, Miriam G. 147
Maslow, Abraham Harold 330
Mendler, Allen N. 15
Meyer, Stephanie 119
Michigan Council of Teachers of English xx, 254, 262
Michigan Department of Education 63, 66, 148, 149, 295
Ministry of Education, Australia 139
Mitchell, Diana 147
Morrison, Gary R. 54
Muller, Chandra 107
Munch, Edvard 140
Murray, Donald M. 78, 144, 215

National Commission on Writing 241–242
National Council of Teachers of English xv–xvii, xx, 14, 136, 137, 147, 229,
251, 258, 282, 312–314, 317, 318, 346
National Council of Teachers of English Executive Committee Writing Study Group 282, 314
National Writing Project xvii, xx, 76, 178, 251, 252, 262, 285
Nettles, Diane 45
Noguchi, Rei 203
Null, Kathleen 70

Olness, Rebecca 147
Oronson, Deb 252

Palmer, Parker 26, 106
Pantel, Christian 54, 56
Paulson, Gary 173, 213
Peale, Norman Vincent 85
Peck, Richard 331
Petrosky, Anthony 297

Pfeiffer, Bruce Brooks 325
Piaget, Jean 111–12, 319
Pierce, Jean 67
Pipher, Mary 120–121
Poe, Edgar Allan 342
Polacco, Patricia 213, 373
Polette, Keith 147
Poole, John 289
Portalupi, JoAnn 20
Postman, Neil 49
Prabhu, Maya T. 240
Public Broadcasting Service (PBS)

Ramsey, Katherine D. 147
Ray, Katie Wood 20
Resnick, Lauren B. 289
Rester-Zodrow, Gina 147
Richmond, Kia Jane xxv, xviii
Roberts, Candace 289
Roman, Lawrence 173
Romano, Louis G. xxv, 3, 14, 31, 35, 38, 50
Rose, Mike 52
Rosenblatt, Louise M. 3, 175–77
Roser, Nancy L. 147
Rosewarne, Tracy 58
Ross, Steven M. 54
Routman, Regie 57–58
Rozema, Robert xxv, 250, 251, 254–55, 261–62, 271

Sargent, Sandie 289
Satir, Virginia 83
Schneider, Barbara 107
Seuss, Dr. (Geisel, Theodore) 174
Shanahan, Timothy 289
Shea, Mary 289
Silberman, Charles E. 23
Silverstein, Shel 149, 153
Sipe, Rebecca Bowers 58
Skinner, B. F. 54
Smagorinsky, Peter 55

Smith, Aaron 241
Smith, Michael W. 125–26
Smith, Rachel 275–276
Smith, Theodore R. 308
Smythe, Pamela K. 55
Soto, Gary 232
Spinelli, Jerry 173
Sprenger, Marilee 13
Stevenson, Robert Louis 129
Stiggins, Richard J. 297
Stock, Patricia Lambert 20, 209
Strommen, Eric F. 258
Sullivan, Susan 55
Swift, Taylor 176
Syverson, Margaret A. 290–292, 295

Tabor, Diane 92
Taylor, James 215
Texas Community College Teachers Association 196
Tchaikovsky, Pyotr Ilyich 145
The Eagles 168
Thomas, Anne 290, 292
Tinzmann, Margaret B. 67
Tomlinson, Carol Ann 282
Tremmel, Michelle xxv, 187–88

Valdez, Veronica E. 285–286
Van Allsburg, Chris 213
Vanderpool, Clare 331
Van Dusen, Christine 240
Van Horn, Leigh 147
Vygotsky, Lev S. 3, 55

Warnock, Scott 240, 246, 250
Warriner, John E. 202
Waxler, Robert P. 57
Weaver, Constance 203
Weaver, Phyllis A. 289
Webb, Allen 250, 255, 261–62, 271
Webb, Patricia Kimberley 112

Webheads in Action (WIA) 249
Weiner, Bernard 88
Weingartner, Charles 23
Whelen, Gloria 332
Whisler, Jo Sue 26, 222
Whitney, Anne 178
Whitaker, Todd 279
Wigfield, Allan 87, 91
Wilhelm, Jeffrey D. 28, 125, 126
Williams, Robin 339
Wilmarth, Stephen 260

Wink, Joan 210
Wright, Frank Lloyd 325
Woodson, Jacqueline 213
Writing Study Group of the NCTE 206

Yagelski, Robert P. 16

Zehr, Mary Ann 99
Zemelman, Steven 17–18, 27
Zinsser, William 298

Subject Index

abstract level reasoning 12, 126, 181, 188, 197, 204, 206, 208, 213, 301, 307, 317, 336
academic needs 244, 285
academic writing 141, 142, 190, 250, 267, 287
accountability 79, 206, 318, 323
achievement motivation 7, 84, 88, 91–93, 134
action plan 272, 274
action research 203, 207, 209, 333
active learning 37, 218, 297, 348
administrative support 8, 18, 22, 23, 43,102, 107, 188, 193, 194, 239, 244, 245, 250, 251, 260, 285–86, 288, 313, 314, 322–23, 343
advance organizers 7, 42, 76, 133, 161, 162, 164, 170, 172, 184, 198, 200–02, 225–26, 231–32, 264–65, 345,
aesthetic writing 175, 177–78
apathy 15
assessing and building background knowledge 74, 86, 96, 105, 111, 170, 172, 271
at-risk students 15, 29, 335
attitude 16, 24, 36, 38, 48, 102, 181, 192, 260, 295
augmented reality 276
authentic (formative) assessment xix, 3, 4, 8, 39, 42, 73, 129, 166, 242–43, 277, 280, 291–92, 307, 312, 318, 321, 323, 347, 349
    see also informal assessment
authentic conversation 13, 46, 57, 80
authentic purposes for writing 8, 329

authentic writing 3, 5, 202, 204, 237
Author's Chair 58, 60, 75, 138, 151, 169, 281
autonomy 92, 197, 221

balanced approach 45
behaviorism 54, 87, 89
best practice in writing xiii, xiv, xxii, 5, 17, 56, 124, 188, 238, 251, 270, 280, 283, 284–88, 312, 343
blog 8, 210, 252, 261, 262, 267, 271, 273, 274, 304, 306
bookmark 267, 273
brain research 12, 123
brainstorming 43, 114, 153–54, 158–65, 204, 220, 222, 226, 268, 272, 333

career planning 89, 102, 166, 225–226, 276
checklist 42, 129–30, 161–63, 165, 202, 222–24, 274, 280, 289, 292–93, 299–301, 213
choice for students 22–24, 26, 28, 36, 38–41, 55, 60, 62, 69, 72, 76, 107, 118, 124, 126–27, 133, 136, 180–181, 188, 203, 211–12, 215, 221–25, 239, 264, 270, 272, 276, 318, 320, 332, 334, 339–45, 348
choice for teachers xix, xxiii, 3, 6, 7, 23, 33, 35, 37, 28, 41, 55, 75, 80, 88, 93–94, 122, 149, 168, 184, 186, 191–92, 195, 204, 210, 213, 216–23, 233–34, 239, 241, 243, 247, 264, 268, 276–77, 281, 284, 287, 292, 306, 320, 323, 327, 330, 334, 344

Classroom 2.0 254
classroom experience xxiii, 4,140, 193, 207, 297, 343
classroom norms 6, 38, 63, 66–67, 73, 80, 98–99, 126–27, 155, 162, 165, 198
cloud computing 275
cognitive apprenticeship 57
cognitive characteristics of young adolescents 35, 54–56, 87, 112, 176, 332, 335
cognitive processes 35, 54–57, 87, 112, 176–77, 179, 191, 222, 319, 332, 335
collaboration xviii, 38, 57, 62, 66–67, 104, 107, 109, 157, 159, 162–63, 165, 193, 202, 219, 221, 238, 244–45, 248–49, 251–52, 256, 258, 262, 269, 284, 340
collaborative environments 263, 275
collaborative learning 57
common core state standards 346
commercial writing programs 207–08, 233–34
  see also programmed, packaged, or prescriptive writing programs
community of professional peers and professional development xiii, xviii, 5, 8, 12, 13, 23, 85, 178, 186, 193, 233, 239, 251, 254, 262, 322–33, 327, 334, 343, 347
community of writers 17, 25, 36, 49, 53, 57, 66, 138
community support 18, 43, 192–93, 195–96, 260
competition 32, 35
consensus 158–62, 165, 184, 340
constructivist theory of learning xiv, 54–56
control 10, 15, 38, 58, 78, 88, 90, 93–94, 120, 123, 125, 141, 211–12, 230, 258, 283, 321–23, 346

controversial topics 7, 33, 36, 46, 184, 204, 248, 335
conventions 60, 62–63, 68, 75, 87, 101, 105, 127, 130, 150, 153–54, 156, 62–63, 165, 167–68, 170, 182–83, 188, 198, 204, 223, 226, 238, 241, 280, 296, 306, 310, 335, 341
  see also grammar
cooperative groups 197
copyright law 269–70
creative writing 222, 244
critical literacy 191, 195, 211, 333, 336, 339, 344
critical thinking xix, 4, 7, 37, 39, 41, 55, 62, 94, 136, 142, 144, 159, 181, 184, 186, 191–96, 205, 207–10, 218, 221–23, 225–26, 229, 233–34, 241, 243, 245–46, 284, 307, 335, 342
critical writing 178, 307
criticism 38, 42, 121, 185–87, 189, 191, 234, 342–43
culture 95, 97–99, 113, 121, 126, 191, 197, 268, 289, 316
curricular goals 196, 295
curriculum-centered writing instruction 20
curriculum standards 17, 42–43, 62, 152, 195

decision-making 38, 79, 88, 93, 160–61, 165, 179, 204, 210, 218, 266, 287, 322–23, 330, 332
deep knowledge 30, 62, 95, 97, 106–07, 132, 211, 317
developmental changes in adolescents 34, 37, 40, 79, 111, 121
differentiation 13, 282–84, 286
digital devices 268
digital divide 240, 261, 277
digital media 103, 121, 136, 183, 221, 226, 249, 252, 259, 261, 269, 276

SUBJECT INDEX 389

digital portfolio 274
digital research 266–268, 270–71, 273
digital resources and tools 8, 228–29, 240–41, 244, 250, 259, 269, 271, 345–46
digital storytelling 254
digital strategies 252
discussion groups 103, 147, 254, 262
diverse needs 30, 136–37, 150, 153, 156, 162, 167, 168, 198, 223
diversity xviii, 28, 37, 55, 97, 98, 197, 317

efferent response 176–77, 181, 184
emotional development 8, 14, 15, 20, 30, 33, 37–38, 49, 62, 79, 86, 88, 101, 121 122, 125, 138, 140, 142, 176, 179, 191, 208, 211, 284, 287, 330–31, 347
end-of–the-year teacher narrative 292–93, 305–06

fading 56–57
fair use 269–70, 333
feedback xxiii, 25, 42, 53, 56, 58, 60, 65, 75, 78, 87, 92, 94, 101, 110, 126–27, 130–31, 133, 153–154, 156, 162, 183, 187–90, 209, 212–13, 234, 238, 246, 248–49, 256, 274, 293, 299, 306, 309–10, 313, 320
five Es 231
flexible block schedule 6, 61
flexible displays 276
formative assessment
    see authentic (formative) assessment, Informal assessment

game-based learning 275
GLCEs (Grade level content expectations) for Michigan 62–63, 170, 295, 347

global community xvi, 46, 62, 64, 67, 117, 137, 143, 174, 195, 210, 239, 245, 258, 272, 371
goal-setting for students 39, 52, 92–94, 96, 110–116, 118–119, 128, 131, 133, 156, 159–60, 162, 221, 248–49, 270, 272, 311, 317, 336
goal-setting for teachers xv, 3, 5, 18, 25, 35, 45, 55, 64–66, 87, 91, 92–93, 101, 125, 128–29, 150, 152–53, 155–56, 162, 167–68, 170, 172, 189, 192, 196–99, 223, 245, 247, 249, 269, 295, 305, 320, 222
grades 42, 55, 77–78, 86–87, 103, 115, 141, 162, 166, 174, 224, 226, 246, 248, 281, 287, 304–05, 309, 313–14, 332, 335, 341
    see also scores
grammar xv, 23, 44–45, 71, 77, 99, 122, 130, 166, 178, 184, 190,197, 224, 200, 202–04, 241, 244, 253, 289, 295, 306, 310
    see also conventions

high-stakes tests 90, 187, 233, 282, 289, 312
    see also standardized tests
home-based education 5
home schooling 275, 333
Horizon Report, The 275
humanistic xxi, 12, 34, 52, 178, 181, 190, 205–09, 317, 330–31, 336
hybrid writing 8, 240, 251

inclusion xviii, 42, 84, 98, 133, 155, 160–61, 186, 192, 204, 240, 264, 277, 341
independence in writing xxii, 54, 92, 137, 221, 238, 242, 248, 299
independent thinking and decision-making 37, 38, 54, 238, 244, 268

390 TEND YOUR GARDEN

informal assessment 147, 280, 291, 297
   see also authentic assessment
information-processing model 54, 89–90, 283
inquiry-based learning xiv, xv, xviii, 4, 6–7, 18, 22, 24, 28, 35, 39–40, 43–44, 49, 52, 55, 58, 126, 136–37, 139, 147, 183–84, 195, 207–09, 218–24, 229–31, 233, 258, 270, 273, 282, 297, 306, 328–31, 338
intellectual attributes of young adolescent students 14–15, 20–21, 30, 35, 37, 39, 44, 49, 55, 79, 102, 121, 191, 211, 315–16
   see also cognitive processes
internet 103–105, 114, 117, 119–20, 143, 210, 238–39, 244, 247, 259–60, 262, 266–67, 271, 275, 310, 340
   see also Web 2.0

journals 48, 77, 103, 219, 226, 232, 241, 261, 288
   see also writing notebooks

knowledge transfer 7, 9, 54, 125–126, 204, 210, 248, 281, 316, 346
K-W-L organizer 170–72, 231

learner-centered writing instruction xxii, 3, 5–8, 15, 20, 24, 26, 28, 43–45, 49, 52, 68, 80, 84–85, 87, 90, 94, 163,188, 191, 209, 218, 222, 233–35, 239–40, 280–81, 297, 310, 321–23, 328, 345, 348
learning circles 16, 217–19, 221
learning environments 57, 258, 276
learning record 289–91, 295, 298
learning styles 12–13, 59, 77, 84, 103, 124, 182, 284

Listserv 188, 254, 262
literal level content 187, 246
literacy xiv, 21, 29, 44, 46, 48–49, 64, 66, 98, 139, 186, 203, 216, 223, 244, 252, 258, 265, 275, 290, 318, 330
literary craft 33, 130, 144, 166, 188, 280, 320, 334, 336, 342, 348
literary device 33, 62–63, 130, 148, 153–54, 169, 213, 248, 255, 307, 320, 342

mashup 269
maxim xviii, xix, 4, 9, 69, 326–28
mentor texts 4, 34, 128, 148–51, 153–54, 157, 183, 213, 217, 236
message board 252
meta-cognitive reflection 28, 55, 253
mini-lessons 4, 28, 33, 41–42, 45, 61, 65, 68–69, 87, 105, 107, 112–13, 127, 129, 152, 163, 184, 193, 203, 219, 223, 269, 271, 281, 316, 341
mobile technologies 276
modeling 27–28, 55, 67, 79, 98, 106, 126, 144, 157, 160, 178, 180, 186, 202, 212, 219, 225, 230, 234, 261, 334, 375
monitoring class progress 68, 80, 221, 238, 255, 336
motivation, definition of 87–88
motivation, six keys to 94–107
motivation training model 91–93
multigenre writing projects 217–18, 221–25, 246, 252
multiple intelligences 197–98, 202

N-achievement factor 91–92
networking 143, 249, 253–54
Ning, definition of 261
No Child Left Behind (NCLB) 195, 289

online education 8, 103–04, 238–40, 246, 251–54, 258–259, 261, 262, 266–67, 270–71, 274–76, 333, 346

peer dialog 13, 28, 64, 80, 86, 117, 126, 179, 207, 230, 257, 262, 310–11
personal writing 30, 141, 253
physical attributes of young adolescents 15, 20, 30, 31–37, 86, 111, 120, 122–23, 126, 176, 208, 211, 285, 287, 331
popular culture xix, 95, 110, 113, 118–19, 132, 140, 330
portfolio 8, 60, 75–76, 86, 125, 153, 166, 168, 246, 274, 280–81, 292–93, 298, 302–03, 306, 321, 341
Praise, Question, Suggestion (PQS) 73, 310–311
prewriting techniques 59, 68, 71, 76, 98, 128–29, 179, 230–31, 269, 271, 345
prior knowledge 36, 84, 137, 152, 170, 173, 178, 192–93, 195, 198, 205, 222, 229, 283, 297, 300–01, 320, 333
privacy 58, 96
problem-solving skills 34, 49, 103, 110, 155, 159, 163, 165, 219, 229, 331, 349
process writing xix, 6, 26, 28, 39, 41, 49, 58–59, 143, 148, 155, 162, 166, 229, 241, 288, 312
professional development 5, 8, 13, 23, 178, 193, 233, 239, 251, 254, 262, 275, 322, 343–44
professional writing 253
programmed, packaged, or prescriptive writing programs 2, 5, 37, 207, 218

Quickwrite 118, 152, 212, 292, 295, 303–04, 312

Reader's Theater 263, 331
reflective teaching 28, 77, 105, 174, 180, 190–91, 196, 287–88, 306
reflective writing 61, 170, 178–80, 186, 226, 233
relevance 110, 113, 118, 127, 133, 141, 183, 241, 271, 332
responsibility by student 5, 22, 37, 56, 58, 79–80, 93–94, 105, 113, 155, 158, 162, 165, 209, 218, 221, 244, 281, 292, 305
rigor 46, 80, 85, 247
risk-taking (positive) 23, 53, 78, 195, 248, 261, 282, 310, 312, 340
roles for teachers 5–8, 10–11, 27–30, 39, 47, 49, 52, 65, 78, 80, 90, 95, 101–03, 119, 155, 160, 191, 245, 305

roles for students 41, 67, 80, 106, 120–23, 153, 157–58, 160–65, 198–200, 219–20, 309, 344
RSS (*rich site summary* or *real simple syndication*) feed 271, 274
rubric 8, 42, 127, 129, 162–63, 174, 205–06, 274, 280, 316, 348
running record 68, 161, 201–02, 289, 291, 293, 295, 320–21

scaffolding 14, 56–58, 98, 340
scholarship 196
scores 44, 48, 55, 92, 205, 246, 287, 289, 291, 312–14, 316–17, 323, 343
self-efficacy 8, 26, 36, 65, 85–86, 110, 112, 182, 222, 297, 332
self-evaluation (self-assessment) 110, 311–12
sensory description 11, 33–34, 64, 75, 125, 128–30, 168–69, 248
social constructivism 55
social-emotional attributes of young adolescents 6, 15, 20–21, 29–30,

37–38, 55–56, 79, 88–89, 97, 119, 121, 123, 142–143, 172, 184, 208, 211, 222, 241, 253, 258, 260, 262, 266, 276, 284, 287, 333, 336, 338, 340
standardized tests 2, 9, 48, 49, 125, 187, 205–08, 266, 313, 315, 318, 323
state-of-the-class chart 68, 99, 100
stepping outside the box 23, 140, 242, 324
stereotypes 33, 122, 337
Sustained Silent Reading (SSR) 13

talent 22, 34, 40, 95, 174, 195, 282, 286, 329–30
teacher as writer 247, 328
test-driven writing model 3, 6, 8, 44, 46, 48–49, 61, 90, 182, 187, 195, 206, 283, 288, 289, 313–17, 343, 347
transescent 14
tween 336

volunteers 41, 65–68, 70–71, 73, 100–01, 153–54, 159, 163, 169, 200, 223–24, 256

Web 2.0 238, 249
  see also internet
Web presence 252, 254, 262
Webinars 254, 262
white boards 260
Wiki 8, 255–57, 261–62, 266–67
Wordpress 274
writing centers 13
writing circles 155–60, 162–63, 200, 218, 308, 311
writing community xviii, 4, 6, 26, 28, 39, 41, 52–54, 56, 58–59, 66–67, 78–80, 97, 132, 138, 180, 216, 218, 241–42, 285, 333
writing conference 42, 58, 67, 74–75, 87, 100–05, 124–25, 133, 203, 224, 251, 255, 270, 273, 280, 292–95, 298–303, 305, 308–09, 321, 330, 340
writing invitations 69, 133, 146, 151, 175, 179, 223–24, 250, 263, 281
writing notebooks 47, 70–72, 99, 139, 151, 154, 219, 226, 273
writing on demand 8, 77, 180, 280, 314, 316, 321–22, 334, 348
writing process xiv, 5, 7, 22, 27–28, 30, 53, 58–61, 64, 68, 70, 78, 80, 87–88, 105, 127, 130, 144, 146, 155, 179, 183, 190–92, 202, 204, 207, 209, 213, 223–24, 230, 270
writing record 68, 291–92, 295, 297–98, 300, 302, 305–06, 319
writing schema 230–32, 348–49
writing style 127, 214, 222–24, 244, 267, 291, 295–96, 306
writing voice 27, 33, 53, 59, 62–64, 66, 75, 78, 104, 123, 127–30, 141–43, 45, 149, 151, 154, 160–66, 178, 180, 184, 203, 213–14, 308
writing workshop 6–8, 16, 33, 42, 58, 63, 65–66, 68–69, 73–74, 78–79, 129–30, 132, 136, 144, 146, 155–56, 163, 181, 218, 233, 240, 244, 263, 266, 274, 277, 281, 292, 294–95, 302, 306, 320–21, 347, 349

Young Adolescent Motivation Model (YAMM) xviii, 2–4, 6, 18, 26–28, 35–37, 39–43, 56, 61, 86, 94, 191, 203, 242